The 200 SuperFoods That Will Save Your Life

The 200 SuperFoods That Will Save Your Life

Deborah A. Klein, M.S., RD

New York   Chicago   San Francisco   Lisbon   London   Madrid   Mexico City
Milan   New Delhi   San Juan   Seoul   Singapore   Sydney   Toronto

The **McGraw·Hill** Companies

Library of Congress Cataloging-in-Publication Data

1 2 3 4 5 6 7 8 9 10   WFR/WFR   0 9

ISBN   978-0-07-162575-3
MHID   0-07-162575-5

Interior design by Village Bookworks, Inc.

Livitician™ and Livit™ are trademarks of Deborah A. Klein.

McGraw-Hill books are available at special quantity discounts to use as premiums and sales promotions or for use in corporate training programs. To contact a representative, please visit the Contact Us pages at www.mhprofessional.com.

Contents

1

Carbohydrates: Fruits 1

2

Carbohydrates: Starchy Vegetables 64

3

Carbohydrates: "True" Vegetables 100

4

Carbohydrates: Grains 162

5

Carbohydrates: Dairy and Dairy Substitutes 192

6

Proteins 204

7

Fats 245

8

Sweeteners and Desserts 270

9
Dietary "Free" Foods: Herbs and Medicinals 277

10
Beverages 309

11
Sample Livits and Meal Plan Helper 311

12
Grocery Shopping 334

13
Livit Snacks 348

Appendix
Actions That Will Save Your Life 351

Acknowledgments

I wish to thank my two boys, Hayden and Eitan, for letting me sleep through the night most of the time and for all the joy and laughter they add to my life; my mother, for always being excited to hear what I have to say about nutrition and applying it right away in her own life; my brother, Dr. Dan Rudé, for providing his chiropractic expertise with regard to wellness; Kim Stakal, a superb organic chef, for providing her expertise in recipe consulting; The Livitician Network staff, for all their assistance in teaching my Livit philosophy to the thousands of patients who walk through the door and for helping the first Livitician book become a reality; and last and most important, my patients, who continue to fuel my passion to spread the word with tips for achieving optimal health. Thank you!

Introduction

Two out of every three Americans want to live to be 100 years old, and they expect science to help them achieve that goal, according to a 2001 survey on attitudes toward aging and longevity conducted for the Alliance for Aging Research. Survey respondents believed that personal actions—such as keeping a positive outlook, exercising regularly, eating nutritious foods, and keeping stress to a minimum—were important to remaining healthy as they aged.

"[The survey] results indicate that Americans believe staying healthy in old age is not just a matter of fate, but something they themselves can affect," said Daniel Perry, executive director of the Alliance, according to an article about the survey on SeniorJournal.com. "Most Americans want to hit the century mark, but don't view living longer as an end in itself. They want to live with health and vitality and benefit from the many scientific breakthroughs now on the horizon."

Those expectations aren't unfounded. The Centers for Disease Control and Prevention (CDC) noted in its report, *The State of Aging and Health in America 2007*, that the three lifestyle factors of poor nutrition, inactivity, and smoking were the root causes of more than a third of all deaths in the United States, and that these factors underlie the development of some of the nation's most prevalent chronic diseases, including heart disease, cancer, stroke, and diabetes. The CDC also found that people who were 65 years of age or older were more likely than any other group to eat five or more servings of fruits and vegetables each day.

The 200 SuperFoods That Will Save Your Life is designed to be a one-stop nutritional wellness resource, providing expert, professional guidance on choosing—and enjoying—nutritious foods as part of a proactive approach that can add years to your life. The plan is realistic, emphasizing—and encouraging you to make—small incremental changes that are effective and contribute to long-term health. None of the foods I've included are esoteric—they're all easy to find and easy to include in your meals or snacks.

This book is a Livit—instead of a diet—that will allow you to improve your health without feeling deprived. How does a Livit differ from a diet? A diet includes a long list of what not to eat (often excluding whole categories of foods, as in the no-fat and no-carbohydrate fads of the past 20 years) and restricts your daily caloric intake to below your resting metabolic rate. When you eat less than your body needs for survival, your metabolism goes into a hibernation mode that increases fat storage, causes water loss, and breaks down muscle and organ tissue. This is not a good long-term strategy for health—or even for achieving or maintaining a healthy weight!

A Livit is a way of life that you can follow *for* life. You do not need to deprive yourself calorically or be self-denying in your food choices to begin eating more life-sustaining foods.

The foods in this book are organized into categories to emphasize balanced eating and what that really means—balancing carbohydrates, proteins, and fat sources. Balancing these three vital classes of nutrients sustains your energy throughout the day and helps stabilize glucose (sugar) levels, which contributes to preventing and controlling heart disease, diabetes, and obesity. The specific amounts of carbohydrate, protein, and fat per serving are stated for each food, based on the seventeenth edition of *Bowes & Church's Food Values of Portions Commonly Used* (1998).

We begin with the carbohydrate food sources (fruit, starchy vegetables, "true" vegetables, grains, and most dairy) because they provide our bodies' primary *fuel*—glucose. Our brain, muscles, and organs all require glucose to function, and carbohydrates are the best place to get it.

Although many popular weight-loss diets are based on cutting carbohydrates, this macronutrient is essential for optimal metabolism and health. When the body does not get enough carbohydrates from food, it has to convert protein into glucose, which is a very inefficient process. This requires a lot of water, which can lead to dehydration if you don't drink extra to compensate. It also releases excess nitrogen, which the liver and kidneys must work overtime to process and excrete. A diet that's too low in carbohydrates can contribute to fatigue and put stress on the liver and kidneys.

The bottom line is this: *Eliminating food groups is not a healthy choice.* Carbohydrates are essential. Choose high-fiber carbohydrates, which are more nutrient-dense and more slowly absorbed than the more refined, "white," low-fiber versions. Whole grains and other high-fiber carbs tend to include some protein too.

Vegetables are listed under carbohydrates, but their essential role in healthy eating is to provide vitamins, minerals, and fiber. They are not a very efficient source of carbohydrate fuel and need to be balanced with fruits or starches that will provide more energy.

The next chapter focuses on protein foods, which are the *sustainers*—they provide the materials to rebuild muscles and organs, sustaining us in the long run.

Because they are absorbed more slowly than carbohydrate foods, they help provide sustained energy throughout the day. For example, fruit takes about an hour to digest, whereas cheese or nuts, with their higher fat and protein content, take three to four hours to digest. For sustained energy, have cheese or nuts along with your fruit or other carbs. The fruit will keep you from being hungry again in an hour, while the protein foods will stretch your energy out over the next three to four hours—definitely a more efficient use of your eating time!

A good rule of thumb regarding protein foods is to choose predominantly vegetarian protein sources. A number of studies have shown a strong correlation between vegetarian and semi-vegetarian diets and a reduced risk of diabetes, cancer, heart disease, Alzheimer's disease, dementia, age-related ocular macular degeneration, colonic diverticula, and gallstones. Aim to limit meat consumption so that animal protein plays a central role in, at most, one meal a day. If you eat a turkey sandwich at lunch, try to have a vegetable protein source at dinner. (Although fish is an animal protein, many types of fish are low in saturated fat and are such a great source of omega-3 fatty acids that I do not count them against the meat total for the day.)

Fats are our *satisfier*. The third macronutrient in our balancing act, fat is the most slowly digested, keeping us satisfied longer and slowing the absorption of the glucose in carbohydrate foods. Dietary fat is essential for hormonal balance, insulation of our skin and nerves, and healthy skin and hair. These dietary fats must include essential fatty acids, which help lower cholesterol, increase high-density lipoproteins (HDL) or "good" cholesterol, and lower triglycerides.

This book provides not only the nutritional content and special health benefits of each food, but also ways to incorporate the foods into a healthier approach to eating—from grocery lists to meal plans. Learn easy ways to increase your overall health through food choices—increase metabolism and immunity, understand the benefits of fiber, discover what to watch for on food labels, learn alternatives for coping with food intolerance and food allergies, and find out which foods have anti-inflammatory properties that may be the key to preventing disease.

The 200 SuperFoods That Will Save Your Life demonstrates the power you have to be proactive and to make specific food choices that will help you live younger, longer. Read on to unlock the secrets to increasing your energy, helping prevent disease, and attaining optimal health—one bite at a time!

The 200 SuperFoods That Will Save Your Life

Carbohydrates: Fruits

Eating more fruit is an easy strategy for increasing your antioxidant intake and decreasing oxidative stress, which could reduce your risk of cancer. Although fruits are packed with vitamins, minerals, fiber, and water, their reputation has suffered lately because most fruits contain a fair proportion of carbohydrate—and that carbohydrate is mostly sugar. Not long ago at a health fair at the Beverly Hills farmer's market, I overheard the promoters of a popular "cookie diet" cautioning customers not to eat any fruit! Here's a diet where you lose weight by eating *cookies* for breakfast and lunch, along with a healthful dinner, and the warning is "Make sure you do not eat any fruit. It has too much sugar."

Things have really gotten out of hand when fruit is a forbidden food! Fruit is one of the two main dietary sources (along with vegetables) of antioxidants that boost your immune system and help prevent disease. It's also a significant source of fiber, which is key to losing fat, helps us feel fuller longer, and slows the rate at which sugar is absorbed. The sugar and other carbohydrates in fruit make it a great fuel source, keeping us energized throughout the day.

All fruits are healthy for us, but the best ones are those with the most fiber. A good rule of thumb is to stick with the "S or S" fruits, the ones with edible skins or seeds, such as apples, peaches, pears, blueberries, strawberries, blackberries, and grapes. Eating the skin and seeds amps up your fiber intake, and the skin and the seeds contain most of the antioxidants, vitamins, and minerals. That's why it's much better to eat whole fruit, rather than relying on juices.

$\cdot$ $\cdot$ $\cdot$ $\cdot$ $\cdot$

1 Açai Berry

Benefits

The açai (ah-sigh-EE) palm tree grows in Central and South America, with a range that extends from Belize south to Brazil and Peru. The palm produces a small, deep-purple fruit that is one of the primary foodstuffs for native people living in the Amazon region of Brazil where it is harvested. Açai "berry"—actually a drupe—tastes like a mixture of berries and chocolate, and is packed full of antioxidants, amino acids, and essential fatty acids. It has ten times the anthocyanins of red wine. It also has a protein profile similar to egg whites.

At least one study has shown that chemical compounds extracted from the açai berry slow the proliferation of leukemia cells in laboratory cultures, and others have shown that it has a powerful effect against common oxygen free radicals. The açai fruit not only shows potential in cancer prevention, but also reduces inflammation, which has been implicated in heart and lung disease, allergies, and auto-immune disorders.

For a fruit, açai contains a relatively high proportion of fatty acids, including oleic, palmitic, and linoleic (an unsaturated omega-6 fatty acid), as well as aspartic and glutamic amino acids, which contribute to building proteins.

> **NUTRITIONAL COMPOSITION** One ounce of freeze-dried pulp provides 152 calories, 14 g carbohydrate, 2.5 g protein, 9 g fat, 13 g dietary fiber, 286 IU vitamin A, 74 mg calcium, 17 mg phosphorus, and 1.3 mg iron.

Bringing It Home

Like other drupes, açai berries contain a large seed surrounded by the edible pulp, juice, and skin. Açai is available whole or in juices, smoothies, and frozen puree. However, it is most commonly found as a reconstituted freeze-dried pulp, both at health food stores and online from several vendors. In any processed form, make sure açai is the primary ingredient.

Açai Boost

This recipe is an Americanized version of a popular Brazilian snack, açaí na tigela *("açaí in the bowl"), a mix of fruit puree served over granola.*

8 ounces frozen açai puree
8 whole frozen strawberries
¼ cup yogurt
¼ cup unsweetened soy milk
½ teaspoon vanilla extract
½ cup low-fat granola
½ cup fresh berries or seasonal fruit

Carbohydrates:
Fruits
. . . . .
3

• Put the açai, strawberries, yogurt, soy milk, and vanilla into a blender jar, and puree for 1 minute, until smooth. Pour the mixture into a bowl and chill. Sprinkle granola and fresh fruit over the top before serving.

YIELD 2 servings

NUTRITION ANALYSIS PER SERVING 229 calories, 36.1 g carbohydrate, 7.4 g protein, 8.5 g fat, 6.2 g dietary fiber

ABOUT THE LIVIT RECIPES

For all the Livit Recipes, use organic produce whenever possible. A 2001 study showed a genuine difference in the nutrient content of organic and conventional crops. The foods grown organically had more vitamin C, iron, magnesium, and phosphorus and significantly fewer nitrates than produce grown conventionally. The study also found some evidence that the organic foods contained more nutritionally significant minerals and lower amounts of some heavy metals, but these results were too small to be conclusive. So where it's possible, go organic.

However, if the price or availability of organic produce is a problem, don't stress. Conventionally grown fruits and vegetables provide many, if not most, of the benefits of their organic counterparts. The road to health is paved with vegetation—what's important is eating plenty of fruits and vegetables, not holding out for organic-only. One way to save money while getting fresh, high-quality produce is to shop at your local farmer's market. Even if the produce isn't organic, it will be straight from the farm and won't have lost nutrients or flavor in transit.

2 Apples

Benefits

The old adage holds true: "An apple a day keeps the doctor away." Doctors in ancient Greece praised the healing properties of apples. Galen, the famous second-century Greek physician, wrote that apples "restore countless invalids to health" and described the healing properties of different types of apples for several illnesses.

What the ancients didn't know is what substance in apples makes them so good at protecting health. We now know that it's a flavonoid called quercetin and that apples are one of the best dietary sources for it. In laboratory studies, quercetin reduces allergic reactions and inflammation, and it has demonstrated some potential to limit the growth of tumors. It may also reduce symptoms in chronic prostatitis and interstitial cystitis. A study in 2007 found that cyclists given quercetin during a regimen involving three hours of bicycling per day developed fewer respiratory tract infections than a control group that did not get the supplement.

Apples have long been appreciated for their keeping qualities—stored in a cool and dry cellar or barn, they provided crisp, fresh flavor throughout the winter even in the days before refrigeration. Today, properly refrigerated, they will keep for months. Apples are also a good source of pectin, a soluble dietary fiber that helps lower cholesterol and is useful for relieving both constipation and diarrhea. Apples' high fiber content means that they slow the absorption of glucose—good for controlling blood sugar. And they contain alpha hydroxy acids, so you can even use apples as an exfoliating masque for your skin.

Unsweetened organic applesauce makes a great snack by itself and can replace oil and fats in baked goods. I use applesauce in place of the oil in my oat bran muffins, making them much more moist and tasty—and lower in fat and calories—than muffins made with oil. The trick also works for baking brownies, producing a chocolate treat that's fluffy, moist, and cake-like.

NUTRITIONAL COMPOSITION One medium size (about 4-inch diameter) apple with the skin provides 81 calories, 21 g carbohydrate, 0.3 g protein, 0.5 g fat, 3.7 g dietary fiber, 73 IU vitamin A, 8 mg vitamin C, 10 mg calcium, and 159 mg potassium.

Bringing It Home

The best place to get apples in season is your local farmer's market. If you're in the western half of the United States, you can find great, locally grown organic apples. It's harder to get truly organic local apples in the eastern United States, because the climate that supports the apple trees also encourages insect pests and diseases that are hard to control with entirely organic methods. You may need to choose semi-organic apples to encourage local growers.

Soothing Applesauce

- 6 large apples, peeled, cored, and sliced thick (quarters or eighths)
- 1 cup water
- 1 teaspoon cinnamon
- ⅛ teaspoon nutmeg

- Combine the apples, water, cinnamon, and nutmeg in a heavy pot. Cover, and cook over low to medium heat until the apples are tender. Remove from heat.
- Mash the mixture using a potato masher or fork, or blend it, using short bursts, until you are satisfied with the texture. Be careful when blending; applesauce holds heat. Serve warm.
- NOTE Try a mixture of sweet and tart apples, or one of the varieties that combine both tastes, such as Ida Red, Cortland, or Macintosh.
- VARIATION For a balanced snack, serve with ¼ cup of ricotta cheese.

YIELD 5 cups

NUTRITION ANALYSIS PER SERVING 73 calories, 19 g carbohydrate, 0.4 g protein, 0.3 g fat, 3.5 g dietary fiber

Carbohydrates:
Fruits
• • • • •
5

Scrumptious Fudge Brownies

- ⅔ cup unsweetened organic applesauce (prepared, or use the recipe above)
- 1 cup sugar
- ¼ cup water
- 12 ounces semi-sweet chocolate chips
- 2 teaspoons vanilla extract
- 1 whole egg
- ½ cup + 1 tablespoon egg whites OR liquid egg substitute
- 1½ cups flour
- ½ teaspoon salt
- ½ teaspoon baking soda
- Safflower oil

- Preheat oven to 325°F.
- Combine applesauce, sugar, and water in a small saucepan. Heat until the mixture just begins to boil, then remove from heat. Add the chocolate chips and vanilla, and stir until the chocolate has melted. Pour the mixture into a large bowl.
- In a small bowl, stir the egg and egg whites together slightly, then slowly beat them into the chocolate mixture.
- In a separate bowl, combine the flour, salt, and baking soda. Gradually stir the dry ingredients into the chocolate batter.
- Lightly grease a 13″ × 9″ × 2″ baking pan with safflower oil. Spread the batter into the pan. Bake for 50 minutes. Cool and cut into squares.
- VARIATION Use half all-purpose flour and half whole wheat pastry flour for more fiber and nutrients.

YIELD 24 brownies

NUTRITION ANALYSIS PER SERVING 139 calories, 23.8 g carbohydrate, 2.8 g protein, 4.6 g fat, 1.5 g dietary fiber

3 Apricots

Benefits

The apricot has been cultivated for at least 5,000 years. Both fresh and dried, this fruit provides plenty of vitamin A, potassium, beta-carotene, and iron. In addition, a fresh apricot provides 17 percent of the recommended daily allowance of vitamin C. Dried apricots, high in dietary fiber, provide nearly a gram of fiber in just three halves. Fiber is essential for intestinal health, but most Americans consume less than 10 grams per day. Include apricots in your diet as a delicious way to add to your fiber intake.

> **NUTRITIONAL COMPOSITION (RAW APRICOTS)** Three medium raw apricots provide 51 calories, 11.8 grams carbohydrate, 1.5 g protein, 0.4 g fat, 2.5 g dietary fiber, 2769 IU vitamin A, 11 mg vitamin C, 15 mg calcium, 314 mg potassium, and 20 mg phosphorus.

> **NUTRITIONAL COMPOSITION (DRIED APRICOTS)** Three dried apricot halves provide 24 calories, 6.6 g carbohydrate, 0.4 g protein, 0 g fat, and 0.9 g dietary fiber.

Bringing It Home

Choose organic raw apricots and unsulfured dried apricots. Commercially grown dried apricots may be treated with sulfur dioxide gas during processing to keep their color bright or with sulfites to extend shelf life. An estimated one out of every 100 people (and perhaps as many as five percent of people with asthma) are sensitive to sulfites and may have an adverse reaction to them. As with all produce, buy locally and at farmer's markets whenever possible.

Add sliced apricots—either fresh or dried—to hot or cold cereal, or add chopped apricots to the batter the next time you make whole grain pancakes. Give a Middle Eastern flavor to chicken or vegetable stews with the addition of dried, diced apricots. Add fresh apricots to green salads when they are in season, or add chopped apricots to rice or bean salads. Pack a plastic zipper bag of apricots and almonds in your briefcase or gym bag for a handy snack.

Livit Recipe

Apricot Bock Salad

See Safe Handling of Poultry on page 211.

  3 whole skinless, boneless organic chicken breasts (6 breast halves), cut into bite-sized cubes
  ½ cup organic orange juice
  1 stalk organic celery, finely diced
  2 tablespoons finely chopped white onion
  3 large organic raw apricots, pitted and finely diced

1 tablespoon reduced-fat mayonnaise
    Lemon pepper
    Sea salt

- Preheat oven to 375°F.
- Place the chicken in a casserole dish and pour orange juice over the chicken. Bake for 1 hour.
- When the chicken is cooked thoroughly (white, with no pink) remove it from the oven and let it cool slightly.
- In a large serving bowl, toss the cooked chicken with the celery, onion, and apricots, then add in just enough mayonnaise to bind the ingredients. Season to taste with lemon pepper and a dash of sea salt. Serve immediately.

Carbohydrates:
Fruits
· · · · ·
7

YIELD 4 servings

NUTRITION ANALYSIS PER SERVING 230 calories, 7.3 g carbohydrate, 41.6 g protein, 2.9 g fat, 0.9 g dietary fiber

4 Bananas

Benefits

Bananas grow in more than 100 countries and are a major food crop throughout the tropical world, where they are cultivated in many sizes and colors, including red, yellow, purple, and green. Only 10 to 15 percent of the bananas grown are for export. In the United States, the vast majority of supermarket bananas are the Cavendish variety, a sweet, seedless, yellow "dessert" banana—one eaten without cooking. Plantains, which have become more readily available in recent years, are banana varieties intended for cooking, and they tend to be less sweet and more starchy.

Because our fruit-stand bananas are so sweet, they've gotten a bad reputation among the low-carb crowd. But they are an incredibly rich source of potassium, vital for regulating blood pressure and a factor in preventing heart disease, stroke, and muscle cramps. One medium banana provides more potassium by weight than practically any other fruit.

Most of us can afford the 15 grams of carbohydrate found in half a banana in exchange for its nutrient benefits, given that Americans typically get only about half the recommended daily intake of potassium.

NUTRITIONAL COMPOSITION One medium raw banana provides 105 calories, 26.7 g carbohydrate, 1.2 g protein, 0.5 g fat, 2.7 g dietary fiber, 92 IU vitamin A, 10 mg vitamin C, 22 mcg folic acid, 451 mg potassium, 7 mg calcium, 23 mg phosphorus, and 33 mg magnesium.

Bringing It Home

Since virtually all bananas are imported, this is one food you probably won't find at your local farmer's market, unless you're lucky enough to live in Hawaii. The history of banana exports has been fraught with exploitation, so try to choose fair trade bananas, whose growers are more fairly compensated. Store bananas in a well-ventilated area, but don't refrigerate them. If your bananas are too green when you buy them, put them in a brown paper bag, which traps the ethylene gas that fruits exhale and quickens the ripening process. Peel ripe bananas, break them into four or five pieces, and store them in the freezer. Add one to a smoothie for a little extra potassium and fiber. Use overripe bananas for baking.

Livit Recipe

Banana Bran Muffin Energy Snack

Canola oil spray
¾ cup unbleached organic all-purpose flour
¼ cup whole wheat pastry flour
½ cup oat bran
¼ cup sugar
1 teaspoon baking soda
2 egg whites, slightly beaten
¼ cup mashed, very ripe banana
½ cup organic nonfat milk
1 tablespoon canola oil

- Preheat oven to 400°F.
- Spray a 6-cup muffin tin with canola oil spray.
- In a medium mixing bowl, combine flours, oat bran, sugar, and baking soda.
- In a small bowl, combine egg whites, banana, milk, and oil. Add the liquid mixture to the dry ingredients, stirring just enough to blend.
- Spoon the batter into the cups of the muffin tin, filling each about two-thirds full to leave room for expansion as the muffins bake. Bake for 18 minutes. Serve warm.
- NOTE Make your own canola oil spray by putting canola oil in a spray bottle. The store-bought sprays add an unpleasant propellant smell to your cooking, and they cost too much!
- VARIATION Add ½ cup blueberries or chopped fresh apricots.

YIELD 6 servings

NUTRITION ANALYSIS PER SERVING 175 calories, 32 g carbohydrate, 5 g protein, 3 g fat, 1.7 g dietary fiber

THE BENEFITS OF BERRIES

A diet rich in berries improves levels of HDL cholesterol, improves blood pressure, and helps reverse age-related cognitive decline. Berries—blackberries, blueberries, cranberries, strawberries, and others—are rich in polyphenols, including flavonols and anthocyanins, which are powerful antioxidants. It's believed that the berry polyphenols promote proper function in aging neurons.

5 Blackberries

Benefits

Blackberries may extend your life! The pigments that give them their color are strong antioxidants, and they retain that power when eaten. They're also rich in anthocyanins, and there is laboratory evidence that anthocyanins may be effective against cancer, diabetes, inflammation, bacterial infections, and neurological diseases. Every 100 grams of blackberries provides 317 mg of anthocyanins.

> **NUTRITIONAL COMPOSITION** One-half cup of raw blackberries provides 37 calories, 9.2 g carbohydrate, 0.5 g protein, 0.3 g fat, 3.8 g dietary fiber, 119 IU vitamin A, 15 mg vitamin C, 24 mcg folic acid, 141 mg potassium, 23 mg calcium, 15 mg phosphorus, and 14 mg magnesium.

Bringing It Home

Since blackberries are made up of lots of tiny seed-bearing drupelets, they have a lot of surface area where pesticides can hide! So for the nubby berries, please buy organic and, if possible, locally grown; blackberries grow all over the United States. Select plump, richly colored fruit. Shop with your nose—if you can't smell them, or if the stem caps (hulls) are still attached, they were picked too early. At the other end of the spectrum, if the containers appear stained with juice, the berries may have been sitting around too long. Mold on berries spreads quickly, so remove any moldy berries as soon as you get them home. Refrigerate your berries immediately (you can store them in a colander, allowing the cold air to circulate around them), but don't wash them until you're ready to use them. Berries are at their fullest flavor at room temperature, so take them out of the refrigerator an hour or two before eating—perfect timing if you want to pack them as your morning snack on your way out of the house!

Livit Recipe

Energizer Shake

This shake is great both for breakfast and as a snack.

> 6 ounces organic tofu (soft or "silken," packed in water), rinsed and drained OR ¼ cup nonfat dry milk powder OR ¼ cup powdered egg whites
> 6 ounces organic plain low-fat yogurt
> 1 small banana
> ½ cup strawberries
> 1 cup frozen blackberries
> ½ cup other fruit of your choice (frozen peaches, mixed berries, cherries)
> 4 cups organic unsweetened soy milk

- Put the tofu, yogurt, banana, strawberries, blackberries, fruit, and soy milk in a blender jar. (For a thinner shake, replace part of the soy milk with water.) Puree until smooth. Serve.
- NOTE You can make this shake the night before and store it in the refrigerator in your blender jar. The next morning, just blend it again for a quick and easy energizer.
- VARIATION For added fiber and omega-3 essential fatty acids, stir in a tablespoon of ground flaxseed to each serving just before drinking. Don't add the flaxseed if you're going to store your shake for later; it can develop a rancid taste.

YIELD 4 servings

NUTRITION ANALYSIS PER SERVING 239 calories, 31 g carbohydrate, 16 g protein, 6 g fat, 4.4 g dietary fiber

6 Blueberries

Benefits

The health benefits of blueberries have made them one of the hottest topics in anti-aging research. A potent mix of flavonoids, tannins, and anthocyanins make blueberries one of the top antioxidant foods, ranking first among 40 antioxidant-rich fruits and vegetables. A number of studies have shown that blueberries appear to slow down and even reverse age-related neurological degeneration.

Blueberries also have potential as cancer fighters. Lab results show that blueberries appear to slow down the rate of cell mutation and the growth of cancer cells; speed up cell turnover, which gives cancer cells less time to develop; reduce inflammatory agents that have been implicated in the onset of cancer; and slow down the growth of new blood vessels that nourish tumors. Researchers at Ohio State University are in the process of extending this research into human trials. At Rutgers University in New Jersey, researchers have identified a compound in blueberries that promotes urinary tract health and reduces the risk of infection. It appears to work by preventing bacteria from sticking to the cells that line the urinary tract walls.

NUTRITIONAL COMPOSITION One cup of raw blueberries provides 81 calories, 20.5 g carbohydrate, 1 g protein, 0.6 g fat, 3.9 g dietary fiber, 145 IU vitamin A, 19 mg vitamin C, 9 mcg folic acid, 129 mg potassium, 9 mg calcium, 15 mg phosphorus, and 7 mg magnesium.

Bringing It Home

Smaller "wild" blueberries have more anthocyanin-containing skin for their volume, and more blueberry flavor, but a shorter growing season than the larger domesticated types. Fresh blueberries from the farmer's market are an unforgettable treat, so find them fresh when you can. This is one fruit that's so good for you that the frozen version should be a staple in your freezer, too.

Carefully sort through fresh berries before storing, and discard any that are mushy or moldy. (Don't confuse the fuzzy white of mold with the waxy white "blush" that is natural to some strains of blueberry.) Pick off any stems and leaves, but wait to wash the berries until you are ready to use them.

Livit Recipe

Blueberry Boost Muffins

2¼ cups oat bran cereal OR quick-cooking oats, uncooked
 1 tablespoon baking powder
 ¾ cup skim milk
 2 eggs, slightly beaten OR 4 egg whites OR 6 tablespoons pre-packaged liquid egg whites
 ⅓ cup honey
 2 tablespoons unsweetened applesauce
 1 cup frozen organic blueberries, thawed and well drained

- Preheat oven to 425°F.
- Line a medium muffin tin with 12 paper baking cups.
- Combine the oat bran cereal and baking powder in a medium mixing bowl, making sure that the powder is well distributed.
- In a small bowl, combine the milk, eggs, honey, and applesauce. Add the blueberries to this mixture.
- Pour the milk mixture into the dry ingredients, stirring just until the oats are moistened and the blueberries distributed. Fill the prepared muffin cups about three-quarters full. Bake for 15 to 17 minutes, or until golden brown. Serve warm.

YIELD 12 muffins

NUTRITION ANALYSIS PER SERVING 109.3 calories, 20.2 g carbohydrate, 4.2 g protein, 2.1 g fat, 2.5 g dietary fiber

 7 Blueberries (Dried)

Benefits

Also see SuperFood 6, Blueberries.

Blueberries rank first among 40 antioxidant-rich fruits and vegetables, with a potent mix of flavonoids, tannins, and anthocyanins. Dried blueberries provide many of the benefits of fresh ones, with the addition of more fiber. They are a terrific portable snack!

> **NUTRITIONAL COMPOSITION** One-third cup of dried blueberries provides 140 calories, 33 g carbohydrate, 1 g protein, 0 g fat, 4 g dietary fiber, and 6 mg vitamin C.

Bringing It Home

Choose dried blueberries that have no sugar or oil added and that are unsulfured. This rule of thumb applies to most other dried fruits as well. Add dried blueberries to a fruit salad or to a mixed green salad. Dried blueberries are a great on-the-go snack, especially with some nuts or cheese for more sustained energy.

Livit Recipe

Dried Blueberry and Arugula Salad

Salad

- 6 cups fresh arugula, trimmed and torn into bite-sized pieces
- 1 medium red onion, diced
- 1 medium cucumber, diced
- ¼ cup chopped walnuts
- ¼ cup dried blueberries

Dressing

- ¼ cup balsamic vinegar
- ¼ cup extra-virgin olive oil
- ¼ cup blueberry juice
  Salt and pepper

- *To prepare the salad:* In a large serving bowl, combine the arugula, onion, cucumber, walnuts, and dried blueberries.
- *To prepare the dressing:* In a small bowl, whisk together the vinegar, olive oil, and blueberry juice. Add salt and pepper to taste.
- Add the dressing to the salad, and toss lightly together.

YIELD 6 servings

NUTRITION ANALYSIS PER SERVING 169 calories, 15.4 g carbohydrate, 2 g protein, 12.6 g fat, 2.1 g dietary fiber

8 Boysenberries

Benefits

Boysenberries are the result of crosses between raspberries, blackberries, and logan-berries and are named for Rudolph Boysen, a California horticulturist who experimented with a number of berry hybrids in the 1920s. Although Boysen gave up on commercializing his results, Walter Knott later popularized the unique fruit at his theme park, Knott's Berry Farm. A dark reddish-purple berry full of anthocyanins and other antioxidants, the boysenberry is reputed to have more than twice the antioxidant power of blueberries. Boysenberries contain ellagic acid, which binds to some carcinogens, including nitrosamines and polycyclic aromatic hydrocarbons, and thus they may help prevent some cancers.

NUTRITIONAL COMPOSITION One cup of frozen, unsweetened boysenberries provides 66 calories, 16 g carbohydrate, 1.5 g protein, 0.3 g fat, 5.1 g dietary fiber, 88 IU vitamin A, 4 mg vitamin C, 84 mcg folic acid, 183 mg potassium, 36 mg calcium, 36 mg phosphorus, and 21 mg magnesium.

Bringing It Home

Boysenberries are delicate and do not travel well. They're best eaten within three days of picking, and their fresh season is short, primarily the month of July. Keep them in an airtight container in the refrigerator. They can last seven to ten days—that is, if you don't eat them before then!

Livit Recipe

Soothing Berry Parfait

Berry layer

½ cup boysenberries
½ cup raspberries
1 teaspoon lemon juice
1 tablespoon agave nectar OR sugar

Ricotta layer

6 ounces low-fat ricotta cheese
½ tablespoon agave nectar OR sugar
⅛ teaspoon almond extract
¼ teaspoon vanilla extract
¾ tablespoon Amaretto

• *To prepare the berry layer:* Combine the berries with the lemon juice and agave nectar in a small bowl. Let this mixture stand at room temperature for 30 minutes to allow a syrup to develop.

- *To prepare the ricotta layer:* Put the ricotta cheese in a medium bowl and add agave nectar, the almond and vanilla extracts, and the Amaretto. Mix thoroughly. For a finer texture, use a blender.
- Put one fourth of the ricotta mixture into each of two glasses (such as a martini glass or an old-fashioned champagne coupe). Layer one fourth of the berry mixture into each glass, then repeat the layers. Serve immediately.

YIELD 2 parfaits

NUTRITION ANALYSIS PER SERVING 210 calories, 25 g carbohydrate, 10 g protein, 7 g fat, 3.9 g dietary fiber

UNDERSTANDING ORAC

The importance of antioxidants in improving health and longevity and in preventing and controlling disease has led scientists to develop research tools for measuring and understanding antioxidant activity. One of the most important of these is the oxygen radical absorption capacity (ORAC) method, developed at the National Institute on Aging, one of the U.S. National Institutes of Health. ORAC is a laboratory test that measures the effectiveness of a food (or other substance) in "protecting" a specific molecule from oxygen degradation by a free radical known as peroxyl. The test provides a way to compare the antioxidant activity of various foods, but it is not certain how closely a food's ORAC score correlates with its health benefit. The United States Department of Agriculture (USDA) has published a list of the ORAC scores of 277 foods. As of the date of publication, the list is available online at http://www.ars.usda.gov/SP2User Files/Place/12354500/Data/ORAC/ORAC07.pdf.

9 Cantaloupe

Benefits

Both the "true" cantaloupe (the European variety, *Cucumis melo cantalupensis,* which has a smooth or warty skin) and the North American cantaloupe (*Cucumis melo reticulatus,* with its "netted" or reticulated rind) are orange-fleshed melons of the muskmelon species, which also includes honeydews and more exotic melons. What gives cantaloupe a special place among the SuperFoods is its high beta-carotene content, indicated by its rich orange color. It's also a good source of vitamin A. One cup of cantaloupe cubes is just 56 calories, but it provides 103.2 percent of the recommended daily value for vitamin A. Since beta-carotene can be converted into vitamin A in the body, when you eat cantaloupe, it's like getting a double helping! Vitamin A appears to reduce the risk of cataracts, and it's a good source of lutein, which some studies have suggested may have a role in preventing age-related macular degeneration, a major cause of blindness in the elderly.

NUTRITIONAL COMPOSITION One cup of raw cantaloupe provides 56 calories, 13.4 g carbohydrate, 1.4 g protein, 0.4 g fat, 1.3 g dietary fiber, 5158 IU vitamin A, 68 mg vitamin C, 27 mcg folic acid, 494 mg potassium, 18 mg calcium, 27 mg phosphorus, and 18 mg magnesium.

VITAMIN A AND LUNG HEALTH

A series of experiments conducted by researchers at Kansas State University and the Medical School of the University of Missouri at Kansas City have demonstrated some interesting connections between cigarette smoke, vitamin A depletion, and emphysema, at least in rats. Their research found that rats exposed to cigarette smoke showed significantly lower levels of vitamin A in their lungs, liver, and blood; and those rats with the lowest lung concentrations of vitamin A had the most severe emphysema.

So if you smoke, or if you're exposed to second-hand smoke at home or at work, Vitamin A may be especially important to keep you breathing easy.

Bringing It Home

Most of the cantaloupes sold in the United States are grown in California, where the season runs from June to October, but cantaloupes are available in the United States nearly year-round, thanks to growers in the southeastern United States and in Central and South America. It is easiest to find ripe melons when they are in season, because melons that spend more time in transit are likely picked before they are fully ripe. Ripeness increases both their sweetness and their nutritional value. Try to find a melon that is heavy for its size and sounds hollow when tapped. If a cantaloupe seems too firm and unripe, leaving it at room temperature for a few days may help improve its texture and juiciness. Avoid melons that are soft, mushy, or sound like they are full of water, because those are probably overripe. Store ripe cantaloupe in the refrigerator. Whole melons will keep about three days in the refrigerator. Cut melon, properly refrigerated, will retain most of its nutrient value for several days.

Because cantaloupes have sometimes been implicated in outbreaks of salmonella, a form of food poisoning, the U.S. Food and Drug Administration (FDA) recommends washing the outside of a cantaloupe, using a clean vegetable brush and cool water, before you cut into it. The FDA also advises washing your hands in warm soapy water both before and after handling cantaloupe.

Simple Cold Cantaloupe Soup

1 medium cantaloupe, cut into chunks
4 medium peaches, peeled and cut into chunks
1 tablespoon lemon juice
1 tablespoon agave juice
4 tablespoons 2% fat Greek-style yogurt, as garnish

- Place the cantaloupe and peach chunks into a blender jar, and puree until smooth. Add lemon juice and agave juice to taste, and blend well. Pour into bowls.
- Top each bowl with a tablespoon of yogurt. Serve cold.

YIELD 4 servings

NUTRITION ANALYSIS PER SERVING 110 calories, 26.7 g carbohydrate, 2.5 g protein, 0.6 g fat, 3.3 g dietary fiber

10 Cherries

Benefits

Cherries are a colorful fruit whose pigmentation packs an antioxidant punch. In particular, sour or tart cherries have been found to contain high levels of anthocyanins that work to neutralize free radicals and reduce inflammation. Cherries are a good source of beta-carotene, vitamin C, potassium, magnesium, iron, fiber, and folate.

At least two species of tart cherry (Balaton and Montmorency) have been shown to contain melatonin, which may help regulate sleep patterns and help with jet lag. In one study, cherries reduced total weight, body fat (especially the important "belly" fat), inflammation, and cholesterol—all linked to increased risk for heart disease.

NUTRITIONAL COMPOSITION Ten raw sweet cherries provide 49 calories, 11.3 g carbohydrate, 0.8 g protein, 0.7 g fat, 1.6 g dietary fiber, 146 IU vitamin A, 5 mg vitamin C, 3 mcg folic acid, 152 mg potassium, 10 mg calcium, 13 mg phosphorus, and 7 mg magnesium.

Bringing It Home

Buy fresh cherries with the stems still attached. Make sure that they are clean, dry, and bright (not dull) in color. As with so many fruits, ripe cherries are heavy for their size. Store them in the coldest part of the refrigerator. Cherries are especially sensitive to heat, and they can decay quickly at room temperature. Don't wash your cherries until you're ready to use them.

Cherries can be frozen if you aren't going to use them right away. For best results, wash the cherries, drain them until they are dry, spread them out in a single layer on a cookie sheet or tray, and then put them in the freezer. Once they're frozen solid, you can bag them and keep them in the freezer for 12 months—until next cherry season! Frozen cherries, your own or commercially frozen, make a quick treat that will satisfy your sweet tooth.

Livit Recipe

Cherry Couscous Salad

See Add Zest! on page 34.

Couscous

   1 teaspoon olive oil
   ¼ cup minced yellow onion
1½ cups fat-free low-sodium chicken broth OR vegetable broth
   1 cup whole wheat couscous (about 5 ounces)

Dressing

   1 tablespoon cherry juice concentrate
   2 lemons, juice only (about 1½ teaspoons) (reserve zest for assembly)
1½ teaspoons Dijon mustard
   2 tablespoons canola oil

Assembly

   ½ cup chopped dried tart cherries
   3 tablespoons chopped pistachios
   2 tablespoons chopped fresh basil
   2 tablespoons chopped fresh mint
   1 tablespoon fresh lemon zest
   ¼ teaspoon salt
   ¼ teaspoon ground black pepper

- *To prepare the couscous:* In a 1-quart saucepan, heat the olive oil over medium high heat. Add onion and sauté for about 3 minutes or until softened. Add the broth and bring to a boil. Add couscous, stir, cover, and remove from heat. Let stand, covered, for 5 minutes. Transfer to a medium bowl to cool.

- *To prepare the dressing:* In a small bowl, whisk together the cherry juice concentrate, lemon juice, and mustard. Whisk the oil into the juices until the dressing is emulsified. Set aside.

- *To assemble the dish:* In a separate bowl, mix the cherries, pistachios, basil, and mint together. Add the fruit mixture, the dressing, and the lemon zest, salt, and pepper to the couscous and mix well. Serve immediately.

YIELD 4 servings

NUTRITION ANALYSIS PER SERVING 142 calories, 21 g carbohydrate, 3 g protein, 6 g fat, 3 g dietary fiber

FULLY RIPENED FRUIT

To maximize antioxidant benefits from fruit, choose fruit that is fully ripened. Research conducted at the University of Innsbruck in Austria suggests that as fruits fully ripen, almost to the point of spoilage, their antioxidant levels increase.

11 Cocoa Beans

Benefits

You can really taste the difference between a Livit and a diet here, because despite cocoa's association with candy, it really is good for you! Cocoa may help control blood pressure, reduce insulin resistance, and provide other benefits to cardiovascular health. The trick to getting the benefits is to limit the fats and sugar associated with chocolate. Stick to cocoa powder, which lacks the cocoa butter but contains all that good chocolate taste.

NUTRITIONAL COMPOSITION One tablespoon of unsweetened cocoa provides 20 calories, 3 g carbohydrate, 1 g protein, 0.5 g fat, 1 g dietary fiber, 4 IU vitamin A, 202 mg potassium, 97 mg calcium, 89 mg phosphorus, 25 mg magnesium, and 0.35 mg iron.

Bringing It Home

For maximum antioxidant value, select unsweetened cocoa powder that hasn't been treated with alkali.

Livit Recipe

Cocoa Treat

Treat yourself to this soothing, nearly calorie-free drink.

> 1 tablespoon unsweetened cocoa powder
> 1 cup water, heated
> 1 teaspoon cinnamon
>   Agave nectar

· In a mug, combine unsweetened cocoa powder and hot water. Add a teaspoon of cinnamon and agave nectar to taste. Serve hot.

YIELD 1 serving

NUTRITION ANALYSIS PER SERVING 38 calories, 9.8 g carbohydrate, 1.1 g protein, 0.8 g fat, 3 g dietary fiber

12 Cranberries

Benefits

Anyone who has eaten a fresh cranberry knows that these native North American fruits have a unique taste. They also have some unique nutritional benefits. Cranberry procyanidins appear to inhibit the stickiness of bacteria, giving the tart red fruit—and its more popular juice—the ability to help prevent urinary tract infections. That same anti-adhesion property gives cranberries a role in preventing tooth decay, and possibly even the bacterial infection implicated in many stomach ulcers. Cranberries have one of the highest ORAC levels among the 277 foods tested by the USDA. They also provide vitamin C.

Cranberries are relatively low in sugar and carbohydrate—another thing anyone who has tasted them fresh might have guessed. That means that cranberries and cranberry juice can bring the benefits of fruit to those who must limit carbohydrate and sugar.

> **NUTRITIONAL COMPOSITION** One cup of whole raw cranberries provides 47 calories, 12 g carbohydrate, 0.4 g protein, 0.2 g fat, 4 g dietary fiber, 44 IU vitamin A, 13 mg vitamin C, 2 mcg folic acid, 67 mg potassium, 7 mg calcium, 9 mg phosphorus, 5 mg magnesium, 0.19 mg iron, 0.12 mg zinc, and 0.15 mg manganese.

OXALATES

Oxalates are a family of substances that bind with metals and minerals such as calcium, magnesium, and iron to form crystals in the body—sometimes in the form of kidney stones. Although oxalates are present in many foods, including most berries and nuts, cranberries are among the few with a very high concentration (rhubarb is another). Healthy people usually have no problem eating these foods in moderation, but cranberries and other foods high in oxalates can cause problems for those with kidney disease, gout, or rheumatoid arthritis.

Bringing It Home

Because cranberries grow mainly in relatively cold climates where the growing season is short, they are available fresh only for a few months each year, in the autumn. Their role in traditional Thanksgiving and Christmas meals dates to the time before refrigeration when this was the only time of year to get them—and when they provided a late-season berry in regions that would have limited fresh produce until spring. Their timing may explain their wide acceptance (for they are a popular holiday food in Europe, as well as in the United States and Canada) in spite of their extremely tart taste. For a treat that's less astringent, use fresh cranberries in combination with sweeter fruits such as oranges, apples, pineapple, or pears. If desired, add a little fruit juice, agave nectar, honey, or maple syrup to chopped fresh cranberries.

Since they are only available fresh for a short time each year, cranberries have long been available canned, frozen, and dried, as well as in juices, where they are often mixed with sweeter fruits for a more palatable taste. Try to choose cranberry drinks without added sugar. You can also dilute unsweetened 100 percent cranberry juice with sparkling water for a refreshing beverage with a little less bite.

Livit Recipe

Quick Fresh Cranberry Citrus Relish

Cranberry citrus relish is a traditional North American cranberry recipe, and a common accompaniment to the Thanksgiving turkey. This relish is also great on a roast turkey sandwich!

> 12 ounces fresh cranberries, rinsed and drained OR frozen cranberries, thawed and drained
> 1 orange, peeled, seeded, and cut into 8 sections
> ¾ cup raw granulated sugar

- Put the cranberries and orange sections into a food processor or blender jar. Chop coarsely, but don't puree. Transfer the relish to a glass or ceramic bowl (metal can discolor the relish).
- Sprinkle sugar over the top and toss gently to mix. Cover the bowl and refrigerate until serving. The sugar and the stand time will allow the relish to macerate slightly, becoming juicier. (If you chop it too fine, you could end up with a relish that's mushy.) Serve chilled.
- VARIATION If you are serving this relish as a side dish, you may want to garnish it with a few bright curls of orange zest (see Add Zest! on page 34).

YIELD 3 cups

NUTRITION ANALYSIS PER SERVING 67 calories, 17.2 g carbohydrate, 0.2 g protein, 0 g fat, 1.6 g dietary fiber

13 Cranberries (Dried)

Benefits

Also see SuperFood 12, Cranberries.

Cranberry procyanidins appear to inhibit the stickiness of bacteria. This anti-adhesion property helps in the prevention of infections such as those implicated in stomach ulcers and the urinary tract. It also gives cranberries a role in preventing tooth decay. Cranberries provide vitamin C and have one of the highest ORAC levels among the 277 foods tested by the USDA.

Dried cranberries provide many of the same benefits as fresh ones, and at least one study suggests they could even be as effective as cranberry juice in preventing urinary tract infections!

NUTRITIONAL COMPOSITION One-third cup of sweetened dried cranberries provides 120 calories, 29 g carbohydrate, 0.03 g protein, 0.5 g fat, and 2 g dietary fiber.

Bringing It Home

Because cranberries grow mainly in relatively cold climates where the growing season is short, they are available fresh only for a few months each year, in the autumn. Since they are only available fresh for a short time each year, cranberries have long been available in other forms, such as dried.

Dried cranberries are so tart that it may be impossible to find unsweetened ones—and hard to enjoy them if you find them! Do choose dried cranberries that are unsulfured. Add them to salads, or brighten up wild or brown rice with dried cranberries and slivered almonds or pine nuts.

Livit Recipe

Chicken with Dried Cranberries

See Safe Handling of Poultry on page 211.

    4 skinless chicken breast halves, thighs, or drumsticks
    ¾ cup orange juice
    1 teaspoon paprika
    1 teaspoon garlic powder
    1 teaspoon onion powder
    ½ teaspoon lemon pepper
    ¼ cup dried cranberries

- Preheat oven to 350°F.
- Rinse each piece of chicken well and pat dry with a paper towel. Place the chicken in a 9″ × 13″ glass casserole dish. Pour ½ cup of the orange juice over the chicken.
- In a small prep bowl, mix together the paprika, garlic powder, onion powder, and lemon pepper. Sprinkle about three quarters of the seasoning mixture evenly over the chicken pieces. Sprinkle the cranberries over the top.
- Cook the chicken for 45 minutes to an hour, until it is cooked through. Turn the chicken pieces, and sprinkle with the remaining seasoning mixture. Add the remaining ¼ cup of orange juice to the pan. Return the chicken to the oven, and cook for another 15 minutes.
- NOTE This dish freezes well. Wrap individual chicken pieces in foil to freeze. To use, thaw them overnight in the refrigerator and reheat.

YIELD 4 servings

NUTRITION ANALYSIS PER SERVING 174 calories, 11 g carbohydrate, 27.6 g protein, 1.7 g fat, 0.5 g dietary fiber

14 Dates

Benefits

Archaeologists have found evidence that date palm trees were being cultivated in eastern Arabia as long as 8,000 years ago. Such a long agricultural history has allowed many varieties of dates to be developed, in three main types: soft, semi-dry, and dry. All three types are relatively low in water content. However, dates that have been allowed to ripen and dry on the tree lose most of the vitamin C that is present in fresh dates that are harvested before drying. Although dates are grown throughout the Middle East and are a major export of Iraq, they are also grown in California and Arizona—primarily the medjool, which is a soft date, and the deglet noor, a semi-dry.

Dates are very sweet, with one 24-gram medjool date providing 66 calories and almost 16 grams of sugar. The smaller deglet noor, at 7 grams, is still more than half sugar by weight.

A 2008 summary of research on dates showed that they are a significant source of ten minerals, including selenium, copper, potassium, and magnesium—and that 100 grams of dates would provide over 15 percent of the recommended daily allowance for them. The review also found that dates are a good source of antioxidants, primarily carotenoids and phenolics. In addition to the four minerals listed above, dates contain boron, calcium, cobalt, fluoride, iron, phosphorus, sodium, and zinc, as well as 23 types of amino acids, which is unusual for a fruit. Unfortunately, many of the dates' proteins are in the seeds, not the flesh, so it may take new and creative uses of the seeds for dates to realize their role as an ideal food.

> **NUTRITIONAL COMPOSITION** Five dried dates with pits removed provide 114 calories, 30 g carbohydrate, 1 g protein, 0 g fat, 3 g dietary fiber, 21 IU vitamin A, 0.9 mg niacin, 5 mcg folic acid, 1 mg sodium, 270 mg potassium, 13 mg calcium, 16 mg phosphorus, and 14 mg magnesium.

Bringing It Home

Choose dates that have not been treated with sulfur dioxide. Rinse them well and pat dry before consuming or using them in a recipe. They can be stored either at room temperature or in the refrigerator for longer life.

Livit Recipe

Lean Date Squares

2 cups dates, chopped and pitted	1 teaspoon cinnamon
1 cup orange juice	1 teaspoon baking powder
1 teaspoon orange zest	¼ teaspoon baking soda
2 cups old-fashioned rolled oats	½ teaspoon salt
½ cup whole wheat flour	½ cup honey
½ cup wheat germ	½ cup safflower oil OR other light oil

- In a saucepan, combine the dates with the orange juice and zest. Bring to a simmer over medium heat and cook, stirring occasionally, until the dates are very soft. Remove from heat and set aside to cool.

- Preheat oven to 350°F.

- In a large bowl, combine oats, flour, wheat germ, cinnamon, baking powder, baking soda, and salt.

- In a smaller bowl, combine the honey and oil. Strain the liquid from the cooked date mixture into the honey and oil, making sure to get as much liquid from the dates as possible. Combine thoroughly.

- In a separate bowl, mash the dates until smooth.

- Add the liquids to the dry ingredients, mixing thoroughly. Press two thirds of the oat and honey dough into a 9″ × 9″ cake pan. Spread the mashed date filling over it. Gently pat the remaining oat and honey mixture evenly on top. Bake for 30 to 35 minutes, until lightly browned.

- NOTE Use prepared orange zest or see Add Zest! on page 34.

YIELD 24 bars

NUTRITION ANALYSIS PER SERVING 150 calories, 25.6 g carbohydrate, 2.2 g protein, 5.4 g fat, 2.5 g dietary fiber

15 Figs

Benefits

Figs have been part of the human diet for at least 10,000 years and are now grown throughout the Mediterranean, as well as in California, Oregon, Texas, and Washington State. Figs are a good source of fiber and are high in protein, for a fruit. They are also among the best plant sources of calcium. A fig supplies 16 percent of the recommended daily intake for iron, 18 percent for magnesium, and 14 percent for potassium, which benefits your heart and other organs by keeping your blood pressure and hydration in balance. Fig leaves have been found to have some potential in controlling diabetes.

NUTRITIONAL COMPOSITION (RAW FIG) One medium raw fig provides 37 calories, 9.6 g carbohydrate, 0.38 g protein, 0.15 g fat, 1.6 g dietary fiber, 71 IU vitamin A, 1 mg vitamin C, 3 mcg folic acid, 116 mg potassium, 18 mg calcium, 9 mg magnesium, 7 mg phosphorus, and 0.18 mg iron.

NUTRITIONAL COMPOSITION (DRIED FIG) One dried fig provides 21 calories, 5.47 g carbohydrate, 0.28 g protein, 0.08 g fat, and 0.8 g dietary fiber.

Bringing It Home

Fresh figs, though a marvelous treat, are among the most perishable of fruits. Don't plan to store them for more than a day or two, and they should be kept in the refrigerator during that time. Buy figs that are smooth and firm and that have a sweet (not sour) smell. Dried figs will keep for several months if stored in the refrigerator or in a cool, dark place. Wrap them tightly to keep them from drying out.

Livit Recipe

Figgy Rice Dressing

3 sweet potatoes
4 cups water
8 ounces wild rice (about 1¼ cups), rinsed
1 teaspoon salt, if desired
1 tablespoon safflower oil OR non-hydrogenated margarine
5 cloves garlic, minced
16 ounces (1 pint) fresh black mission figs, chopped into ½-inch pieces
Salt and freshly ground black pepper

- Since the sweet potatoes and rice both take about an hour to cook, you will want to prepare those two ingredients and get them started, then prepare the rest of the ingredients.
- Rinse the sweet potatoes, stab the skins several times with a fork, and wrap each separately in foil. Bake for 45 minutes to an hour, until tender.
- In a heavy saucepan with a tightly fitting lid, bring 4 cups of water to a boil, with salt added if desired. When the water has come to a boil, add the wild rice. Bring the water back to a boil, stir, and then reduce heat until the rice is just simmering. Cover, and cook for 50 minutes to an hour, until the kernels begin to open. When the rice is done, drain off any extra water and set the rice aside.
- Preheat oven to 375°F.
- Once the sweet potatoes are tender, unwrap them and let them cool until they are just cool enough to handle. Peel and chop into ½-inch chunks. Set aside.
- Lightly oil a frying pan, using a paper towel to distribute about a tablespoon of oil on the inside of the pan, so the surface is just shiny. Add the garlic and cook over medium heat, stirring often, until it is browned and crispy. Remove from heat.
- In a large bowl, toss the chunks of sweet potato, rice, garlic, and figs together gently. Add salt and pepper to taste.

• NOTES This recipe can be prepared partially in advance by cooking the rice and sweet potatoes ahead, then either keeping them warm or reheating them in the oven at a later time. To maintain the unique textures of the garlic and the figs, wait until just before serving to crisp the garlic, and then add the crisped garlic and the figs. For a balanced meal, serve with a protein source such as chicken, turkey, stir-fried tofu, or fish and some steamed vegetables.

YIELD 6 servings

NUTRITION ANALYSIS PER SERVING 301.7 calories, 63 g carbohydrate, 7.5 g protein, 2.6 g fat, 6.9 g dietary fiber

16 Goji Berries

Benefits

Goji berries have gotten a lot of attention lately in the West, but they are a traditional food in Asia. The name "goji" is probably based on the Mandarin Chinese name for the plant, "gouqi." Before the recent attention, the goji berry was known as the wolfberry. Goji berries are orangey-red, and one-half to one inch long.

Because of its long history of cultivation in Asia, traditional medicine has assigned many healing properties to the goji berry—it has been used to improve eyesight, circulation, sexual function, and fertility, and to promote long life. Most of these claims have not yet been tested scientifically, let alone proven. But what we do know about goji berries is that they are a good source of antioxidants and zeaxanthin, a carotenoid compound that is found, like lutein, in the retina of the eye, and which may have a role in preventing age-related macular degeneration.

NUTRITIONAL COMPOSITION One-third cup of goji berries provides 150 calories, 32 g carbohydrate, 5 g protein, 0 g fat, 1 g dietary fiber, 800 IU vitamin A, 6 mg vitamin C, 190 mg sodium, and 0.8 mg iron.

GOJI BERRIES

It appears that goji berries may interact with some medications, including warfarin (a blood thinner) and some diabetes and blood pressure medicines. Goji berries may also cause problems for people with some types of pollen allergies.

Bringing It Home

In the United States, goji berries are usually available dried and are increasingly available in products such as trail mix. The dried berries look like red raisins. Organic dried berries are available, and those are the best choice.

Goji extracts, powders, and juices are also popular, but they are often over-priced. Read the labels carefully on these, because some "goji berry" drinks contain only a small amount of goji juice mixed with other juices, and thus they may not justify the high price that is sometimes charged.

Both the berries and the leaves can be brewed into a tea. Most of the teas available in the United States mix goji berries with green tea and other herbs, so the goji acts more as a flavoring element. For the maximum goji effect, choose a tea that lists goji first among its ingredients.

Dried goji berries have a sweet and tart taste. Mix some into your morning oatmeal with cinnamon and a squirt of agave nectar, and add a tablespoon of shelled hemp seeds or low-fat plain yogurt for a balanced breakfast. Try a goji berry trail mix with a quarter cup of soy nuts or almonds for a snack that balances carbohydrate with protein. Fill a snack-size plastic zipper bag with a ¼-cup serving for a balanced on-the-go snack.

Livit Recipes

Goji Berry Trail Mix

1 cup dried goji berries
½ cup raw chocolate nibs
1 cup raw pecans
1 cup raw walnuts
1 cup peanuts

- Combine the berries, chocolate nibs, pecans, walnuts, and peanuts. Stir them together so that the ingredients are well distributed.

- Store the mixture in an air-tight glass container. If you choose a container that can hold 5 to 5½ cups, you can mix your ingredients right in the jar by closing the lid and shaking!

- NOTE The peanuts provide a legume, balancing the other nuts for a more complete protein.

YIELD 18 servings (¼ cup each), or about 4½ cups

NUTRITION ANALYSIS PER SERVING 165.5 calories, 4.2 g carbohydrate, 4.4 g protein, 13.4 g fat, 2 g dietary fiber

Goji Berry Energy Bar

The basis for this energy bar is the Goji Berry Trail Mix ingredients.

  1 cup raw pecans
  1 cup raw walnuts
  1 cup peanuts
  1 cup dried goji berries
  ½ cup raw chocolate nibs
  2 tablespoons agave nectar OR honey
     Extra-virgin olive oil

- Crush the pecans, walnuts, and peanuts by hand or in a food processor. Transfer to a large bowl. Add goji berries and chocolate nibs and mix well. Add agave nectar and stir well with a wooden spoon.
- Lightly oil a shallow baking pan or tray with olive oil. Using a rubber spatula, press the mixture into the pan. Refrigerate for one hour to set, then cut into squares.

YIELD 18 squares

NUTRITION ANALYSIS PER SERVING 165.5 calories, 4.2 g carbohydrate, 4.4 g protein, 13.4 g fat, 2 g dietary fiber

17 Grapefruit

Benefits

It may surprise many people, but grapefruit really can help with weight loss! In a small test involving 100 obese people, those who ate half a fresh grapefruit each day lost more weight than the control group that did not. It appears that the effect is partly due to grapefruit's ability to lower glucose levels. Eating grapefruit also appeared to help patients with metabolic syndrome, reducing their insulin resistance. Although these studies were small and more research needs to be done to determine why and how grapefruit works, the results could be significant for the treatment and prevention of type 2 diabetes.

Grapefruit is rich in flavonoids that are helpful in lowering the risk of cancer and cardiovascular disease. It is a good source of pectin (a soluble fiber that helps lower cholesterol) and vitamin C. Because it is not very sweet, it is a good fruit for those who wish to limit carbohydrate. Grapefruit seeds have also been shown to have an antibacterial effect.

As is often the case, the more brightly colored fruit tends to have more antioxidants and other life-saving compounds. That means that pink- and red-fleshed varieties of grapefruit pack more nutrient punch than white grapefruit, including the antioxidant lycopene, which may help prevent age-related blindness.

NUTRITIONAL COMPOSITION One-half medium pink or red grapefruit provides 39 calories, 9.9 g carbohydrate, 0.8 g protein, 0.1 g fat, 1.4 g dietary fiber, 153 IU vitamin A, 42 mg vitamin C, 13 mcg folic acid, 171 mg potassium, 15 mg calcium, 10 mg phosphorus, and 10 mg magnesium.

GRAPEFRUIT AND MEDICATIONS

Grapefruit is known to interact with many medications. There are several drugs that are "potentiated" by taking them with grapefruit or grapefruit juice, meaning their effect is made stronger, and others whose effectiveness is reduced when taken with grapefruit. The categories of medications that may interact with grapefruit include antihistamines, antibiotics, benzodiazepines, calcium-channel blockers, cholesterol-lowering drugs, and immune system suppressants. If you are taking any of these medications, check with your doctor or pharmacist to see if you should avoid grapefruit.

Bringing It Home

Ironically, a grapefruit that looks the most perfect from the outside may not be the best one inside. Uneven color or marks on the skin don't tell us much about the fruit inside, and a perfect-looking skin is often one that is too thick for the best grapefruit taste. But do avoid grapefruit skins that are overly rough or wrinkled. With citrus fruit, the guideline that you should choose a fruit heavy for its size goes double for grapefruit. You want a juicy fruit, and lightweight grapefruit are often dry inside.

Grapefruit are grown in California, Texas, Florida, and Arizona, and although they are available nearly year-round, they are best in winter and early spring. They will keep in the refrigerator for two to three weeks, but they are juicier at room temperature, so you may want to keep them out if you'll be eating them within a few days or set them out for an hour before eating them.

Livit Recipe

Hot Grapefruit Breakfast

1 large pink grapefruit
1 teaspoon non-hydrogenated margarine
1 teaspoon agave nectar OR brown sugar
1 teaspoon cinnamon
2 fresh cherries with pits removed

- Preheat oven to 350°F.
- Cut the grapefruit in half around the middle (not end to end). With a grapefruit knife or short paring knife, cut between the flesh and the shell around the circumference, then cut between the sections. Try not to pierce the skin. Place the grapefruit halves

on a baking sheet. Dot each grapefruit half with ½ teaspoon of margarine. Squirt agave nectar or sprinkle brown sugar over the tops. Sprinkle lightly with cinnamon.

- Bake for 5 minutes, then broil until the top is bubbly. Remove the grapefruit from the oven and place each half in an individual bowl. Garnish with a fresh cherry in the center.
- NOTE For a balanced breakfast, add a half cup of low-fat cottage cheese or a soft-boiled egg on the side.

YIELD 2 servings

NUTRITION ANALYSIS PER SERVING 68.6 calories, 15.2 g carbohydrate, 0.7 g protein, 1.3 g fat, 2.1 g dietary fiber

18 Grapes

Benefits

Grapes and their juice are a source of resveratrol, a polyphenol antioxidant that is thought to be one of the health-promoting elements in red wine. Resveratrol appears to be involved in reducing the risk or slowing the development of cancer, heart disease, degenerative nerve disease, viral infections, and Alzheimer's disease. It also shows potential in treating bronchial asthma and helping to prevent type 2 diabetes. Resveratrol is most highly concentrated in the skin of grapes.

Grapes also contain antioxidant anthocyanins and catechins, and some varieties also provide ellagic acid, myricetin, quercetin, kaempferol, and other phytochemicals and phenolics. They are a moderately good source of vitamin C and potassium, and they contain small amounts of a wide variety of minerals.

> NUTRITIONAL COMPOSITION One cup of raw grapes provides 58 calories, 15.8 g carbohydrate, 0.6 g protein, 0.3 g fat, 0.9 g dietary fiber, 92 IU vitamin A, 4 mg vitamin C, 4 mcg folic acid, 2 mg sodium, 176 mg potassium, 13 mg calcium, 9 mg phosphorus, and 5 mg magnesium.

Bringing It Home

Grapes should be plump, slightly firm, and unwrinkled. Don't buy grapes that are leaking juice or that fall off the stem. Choose organic grapes.

Grapes should always be kept in the refrigerator. Grapes, like other berries, should not be washed until you're ready to use them. Instead, wrap them in a paper towel and put them in a plastic bag. If you wash more grapes than you can eat, dry them thoroughly and store the leftovers in a plastic zipper bag.

Freeze some grapes for a great snack that will satisfy your sweet tooth and refresh your palate!

Livit Recipe

Grape Chicken Salad

2 cups diced or shredded cooked chicken
½ cup organic seedless grapes, sliced in half
2 stalks celery, sliced or chopped
¼ cup chopped walnuts
¼ cup reduced-fat mayonnaise
  Salt

• In a large bowl, combine the chicken, grapes, celery, and walnuts. Toss gently to distribute the ingredients. Stir in the mayonnaise, and add salt to taste.

YIELD 4 servings

NUTRITION ANALYSIS PER SERVING 270.5 calories, 6.3 g carbohydrate, 24.6 g protein, 17 g fat, 1 g dietary fiber

19 Grape Juice

Benefits

Grape juice is a significant source of resveratrol, a polyphenol antioxidant that is thought to be one of the health-promoting elements in red wine. Resveratrol appears to be involved in reducing the risk or slowing the development of cancer, heart disease, degenerative nerve disease, viral infections, and Alzheimer's disease. It also shows potential in treating bronchial asthma and helping prevent type 2 diabetes. Resveratrol is most highly concentrated in grape skins, which is why red wine has greater potential health benefits than white wine, for which the grape skins are less a part of the wine-making process.

Grapes and their juice also contain antioxidant anthocyanins and catechins, and some types also provide ellagic acid, myricetin, quercetin, kaempferol, and other phytochemicals and phenolics. They are a moderately good source of vitamin C and potassium, and they contain small amounts of a wide variety of minerals.

NUTRITIONAL COMPOSITION One-half cup of grape juice provides 77 calories, 19 g carbohydrate, 0 g protein, 0 g fat, 0.3 g dietary fiber, 4 mg sodium, and 10 mg calcium.

DARK PURPLE GRAPE JUICE

Dark purple grape juice may inhibit the absorption of iron, according to a study published in 2002. It appears that some of the same phenolics that help improve health also bind to iron, preventing it from being absorbed. If further research bears out this finding, people at risk for iron-deficiency anemia may wish to avoid the purple varieties, and stick to white grape juice.

Bringing It Home

Choose organic grape juice. There is some evidence that organic, unsweetened grape juice provides more health benefits than conventional types.

For a larger beverage serving with less sugar, mix one-half cup of grape juice with water or sparkling water.

Livit Recipe

Grape Shake

½ cup organic purple grape juice
½ cup 1% milk
¼ cup low-fat vanilla yogurt
3 tablespoons pasteurized liquid egg whites
Nutmeg, as garnish
1 cinnamon stick, as garnish

- Combine grape juice, milk, yogurt, and egg whites in a blender jar. Blend several seconds until smooth and frothy. Serve immediately, garnished with a dash of nutmeg and a cinnamon stick.

YIELD 1 serving

NUTRITION ANALYSIS PER SERVING 232.2 calories, 35.2 g carbohydrate, 21.4 g protein, 2 g fat, 0 g dietary fiber

20 Honeydew Melon

Benefits

Honeydew melon, like cantaloupe, is a variety of muskmelon. Honeydews are in the *Inodorus* group, named for the sweet smell of these melons. Typically, honeydews have a pale green flesh, though some newer hybrid types have orange flesh and these may have more carotenes. Honeydews are a good of vitamin C, potassium, copper, and B vitamins (including thiamine, niacin, B_6, and pantothenic acid). The water and potassium present in honeydews help maintain healthy blood pressure and hydration.

> NUTRITIONAL COMPOSITION One cup of cubed raw honeydew melon provides 60 calories, 15.6 g carbohydrate, 0.8 g protein, 0.2 g fat, 1 g dietary fiber, 68 IU vitamin A, 42 mg vitamin C, 10 mcg folic acid, 461 mg potassium, 17 mg sodium, 10 mg calcium, 17 mg phosphorus, and 12 mg magnesium.

Bringing It Home

Honeydew melons should have a smooth, green rind that seems slightly waxy. You can test for ripeness by pressing the ends—if they have some give, the melon is probably ripe. A honeydew will continue to ripen at room temperature. Store it in the refrigerator when it is ripe enough. Cut melon will keep three or four days in the refrigerator if it is tightly covered.

Livit Recipe

Melon Snack

½ cup low-fat cottage cheese
1 cup honeydew melon cubes

- Put cottage cheese in a small bowl. Top with cubes of honeydew melon.
- VARIATION For a vegan option, have a cup of honeydew mixed with a ½ cup of plain soy yogurt.

YIELD 1 serving

NUTRITION ANALYSIS PER SERVING 142.6 calories, 18.5 g carbohydrate, 14.9 g protein, 1.4 g fat, 1.4 g dietary fiber

21 Kiwifruit

Benefits

Before being popularized by New Zealand growers in the 1950s, the kiwifruit was known as the Chinese gooseberry. It is rich in potassium (with almost as much potassium as a banana) and vitamin C (with more of this vitamin than an orange). A good source of beta-carotene, vitamins A and E, the kiwifruit also provides magnesium, copper, phosphorus, carotenoids, and polyphenols. Kiwifruit may be a natural blood thinner: One study found that eating two or three kiwifruit per day had about the same effect as aspirin therapy for reducing the risk of clots and lowering the amount of fat in the blood.

NUTRITIONAL COMPOSITION One medium raw kiwifruit provides 46 calories, 11.3 g carbohydrate, 0.8 g protein, 0.3 g fat, 2.6 g dietary fiber, 133 IU vitamin A, 74 mg vitamin C, 29 mcg folic acid, 252 mg potassium, 4 mg sodium, 20 mg calcium, 30 mg phosphorus, and 23 mg magnesium.

KIWIFRUIT

Kiwifruit is one of the few foods with high enough levels of oxalates that over-consumption can cause problems for those with kidney disease, gout, or rheumatoid arthritis. It also contains an enzyme called actinidin, which dissolves proteins and can cause allergic reactions in people with allergies to latex, papaya, or pineapple. This same enzyme means that kiwis don't work well in either dairy or gelatin dishes, as it will begin to dissolve the proteins. However, this property does make the fruit a natural meat tenderizer—great in marinades.

Bringing It Home

Most kiwis are imported, so you won't find them at your local farmer's market. Kiwis should not be overly soft or have bruises or damp spots. Ripe kiwifruit will yield slightly to pressure and seem smooth (under the furry skin).

Livit Recipe

Kiwi Zest Marinade

Kiwi's natural meat-tenderizing enzyme makes this sauce a great marinade for meat. It can also add zest to steamed vegetables or salad.

    3 kiwifruit (about ½ pound), peeled and cut into chunks
    2 tablespoons apple cider vinegar
    2 tablespoons apple juice
    1 tablespoon extra-virgin olive oil
    1 tablespoon water
    1 teaspoon agave nectar
    1 small clove garlic
    ½ teaspoon salt
    ¼ teaspoon freshly ground black pepper
    ¼ teaspoon hot pepper sauce, optional

- Put kiwi, vinegar, apple juice, oil, water, agave nectar, garlic, salt, pepper, and hot pepper sauce, if using, into a blender jar and process until smooth. Serve.
- NOTE Refrigerate dressing in an airtight container for up to five days. Stir well before using.

YIELD 1 cup

NUTRITION ANALYSIS PER SERVING 18 calories, 2.7 g carbohydrate, 0.2 g protein, 0.9 g fat, 0.5 g dietary fiber

22 Lemons

Benefits

Christopher Columbus brought lemon seeds to Hispaniola in 1493, introducing lemons to the Americas. Later Spanish immigrants cultivated lemon orchards in Florida, Arizona, and California, where most of the lemons in the United States are grown today.

Rich in vitamin C, lemons were among the foods used to combat scurvy among sailors. Lemons also contain vitamin A, as well as calcium, magnesium, phosphorus, and potassium.

> **NUTRITIONAL COMPOSITION** One medium raw lemon provides 17 calories, 5.4 g carbohydrate, 0.6 g protein, 0.2 g fat, 1.6 g dietary fiber, 17 IU vitamin A, 31 mg vitamin C, 6 mcg folic acid, 80 mg potassium, 15 mg calcium, 9 mg phosphorus, and 5 mg magnesium.

Bringing It Home

Fresh lemons are now available year-round. As with other citrus fruit, a good lemon is a thin-skinned one—thick-skinned lemons are often dry inside. Choose lemons that feel heavy in your hand and whose peels have a fine-grained texture.

Lemons will keep at room temperature for about a week if kept away from light. They keep about four weeks in the refrigerator.

One lemon yields about 1½ fluid ounces of lemon juice, though you get more juice from a lemon at room temperature than from one that's just come from the refrigerator.

Make lemon ice cubes by freezing fresh-squeezed lemon juice in ice cube trays, and pop one in a glass of water or iced tea for a splash of flavor.

ADD ZEST!

The colorful peel of citrus fruit—lemons, limes, and oranges—is called "zest" and is used to add color, flavor, and vitamin C to your cooking.

To zest a piece of citrus fruit, begin by washing it well. Then use a sharp paring knife or a special "zester" tool to cut the peel away from the fruit. Be careful not to dig too deep, because you don't want any of the bitter, spongy white pith. It's much easier to zest a whole lemon, lime, or orange before it's been cut into smaller pieces.

You now have zest!

Use zest as a garnish after foods are cooked, because vitamin C doesn't stand up well to the heat of cooking. One tablespoon of zest provides 13 percent of the recommended daily value for vitamin C.

No-Need-for-Sugar Sweet Lemonade

See Add Zest! on page 34.

    4 organic apples (red delicious, golden delicious), peeled, cored, and chunked
    ¼ lemon, peeled and seeded (reserve some lemon zest, optional)

- Put the apple chunks and lemon into a blender jar. Add lemon zest, if using, and process until liquefied. The result will not be as clear as conventional apple juice or lemonade, but it will contain more good fruit fiber and nutrition!
- NOTE If you have a juicer that can handle fruit with the peel on, wash the apples and lemons well before putting them into the juicer.
- VARIATION For a very tart lemonade, use the lemon with its peel. A milder tartness can be achieved by adding some reserved lemon zest.

YIELD 1 serving

NUTRITION ANALYSIS PER SERVING 331 calories, 87.1 g carbohydrate, 1.4 g protein, 2.1 g fat, 16.2 g dietary fiber

Carbohydrates:
Fruits
· · · · ·
35

23 Limes

Benefits

Limes are sweeter than lemons and they also contain more citric acid, a compound essential to the metabolic process that burns carbohydrates, proteins, and fats to turn them into water and carbon dioxide and release energy in the body. Like lemons, limes are an excellent source of vitamin C. It's limes that were issued to English sailors to prevent scurvy in the 19th century. They also contain calcium, potassium, and vitamin A.

There are two main types of limes—Key limes and Persian limes. Key limes are smaller, darker in color, and thinner skinned. The typical supermarket lime is a Persian lime.

NUTRITIONAL COMPOSITION One medium raw lime provides 20 calories, 7.1 g carbohydrate, 0.5 g protein, 0.1 g fat, 1.9 g dietary fiber, 7 IU vitamin A, 19 mg vitamin C, 5 mcg folic acid, 0.15 mg pantothenic acid, 68 mg potassium, 1 mg sodium, 22 mg calcium, 12 mg phosphorus, 4 mg magnesium, and 0.4 mg iron.

Bringing It Home

Limes are available year-round but are easier to find and will probably have traveled less in the spring and summer. Choose limes that are a deep green color, shiny-skinned, and that feel heavy in the hand. A lime with a few yellow spots is acceptable, but as they get riper and more yellow, their flavor declines somewhat.

Limes will keep at room temperature for about a week, if kept out of sunlight. In the refrigerator, they will last for about two weeks.

You can use limes or lime juice as a variation in nearly any recipe that calls for lemons or lemon juice. For example, try making the lemon juice ice cubes above with lime juice instead, or try lime zest for a colorful garnish.

Livit Recipe

Red Pepper Soup with a Dash of Lime

See Add Zest! on page 34.

1 teaspoon extra-virgin olive oil
1 large onion, chopped
4 organic red bell peppers, seeded and chopped
3 cloves garlic, minced
1 small red chili pepper, seeded and sliced
3 tablespoons tomato puree
3 cups low-sodium vegetable broth
1 lime, juice and zest only
  Black pepper
  Shreds of lime zest, as garnish

- Heat olive oil in a 2-quart saucepan. Put the onion and bell peppers into the sauce pan and cook for about 5 minutes at low to medium heat. Add the garlic, chili pepper, and tomato puree to the saucepan. Stir in 1½ cups of the vegetable broth and bring the mixture to a boil. Reduce heat, cover, and let simmer for 10 minutes.
- Allow the soup to cool enough to handle safely, then puree in a food processor or blender. Return the blended soup to the pan and add the remaining 1½ cups of broth, along with the lime juice, black pepper, and most of the zest (reserve a few curls for garnish). Bring the soup to a boil, then remove from heat. Pour into bowls, garnish each serving with a few curls of lime zest, and serve immediately.

YIELD 4 servings

NUTRITION ANALYSIS PER SERVING 92.2 calories, 18.6 g carbohydrate, 2.3 g protein, 1.5 g fat, 5.1 g dietary fiber

24 Lychees

Benefits

Lychee fruit is an excellent source of vitamin C and potassium, as well as a good source of copper and phosphorus. In traditional Chinese medicine, lychees are used as a pain reliever, as an aid to digestion, and to promote health and long life. They were also used as a treatment for coughs, a sore throat, and swollen glands.

Recently, two Chinese studies have suggested that lychee has potential as a cancer-fighting agent. Research at Zhejiang Gongshang University in Hangzhou,

China, found that polyphenols from lychee fruit pulp appeared to slow the growth and proliferation of cancer cells. It appeared to be especially effective against human breast cancer. A second study, at Sichuan University in Chengdu, China, also showed lychee polyphenols to inhibit the growth of liver cancer cells. Although the research has not established that the lychee flavonoids work the same way inside the human body, the implications are hopeful.

NUTRITIONAL COMPOSITION Ten medium raw lychees provide 66 calories, 16.5 g carbohydrate, 0.8 g protein, 0.4 g fat, 1.3 g dietary fiber, 72 mg vitamin C, 14 mcg folic acid, 171 mg potassium, 5 mg calcium, 31 mg phosphorus, and 10 mg magnesium.

LYCHEE FRUIT

Lychee fruit contains a form of profilin that can cause severe anaphylactic reactions in people who are sensitive to it. As of 2007, only six cases of lychee allergy had been reported, but as more people eat lychee, more reactions may come to light. It is also possible that more exposure to the lychee profilin may cause people to become sensitized, but this has not been established. The risk for allergic reaction appears to be greatest in those who already react to other plant profilins or pollens, or to latex.

Bringing It Home

Fresh lychees were once impossible to find but are now available in Asian groceries and, increasingly, in mainstream produce sections. You can also purchase them online from some specialty growers. The main sources within the United States are in Florida, where the season runs from May through July. Lychees are also imported from Asia, Australia, Mexico, and Israel during the rest of the year.

Lychees have a rough, red outer layer that turns brown when refrigerated. Some imports are subjected to a treatment of cold for two weeks in order to kill insect parasites; opinions differ on whether this harms the lychees' taste. If you can find red lychees, you'll know that they haven't been refrigerated and that they probably haven't traveled as far. Likewise, lychees sold in bunches, with their leaves and stems still attached, are likely to have a fresher taste. Avoid lychees that are leaky or that have broken skins.

The lychee has an edible flesh that is translucent white. The hard seed of the lychee is not edible, although it is sometimes used as a component in traditional Chinese medicine. The term "lychee nut" is an old name for dried lychee fruit, which is available when fresh lychees are not. Canned lychees are also available.

Lychees do not ripen after they are picked, so make sure that the lychees you purchase are ripe. They will last a few days in the refrigerator. If you are going to keep them longer, freeze lychees with the skin on.

Livit Recipe

Lychee Immune Boost Salad

   2 heads romaine lettuce, torn into bite-sized pieces
   ½ cup fresh or canned lychees, drained
   1 orange, peeled and cut into 1-inch pieces
   2 thin slices red onion, separated into rings
   2 tablespoons low-sodium vegetable broth
   1 tablespoon apple cider vinegar
   1 tablespoon orange juice
   1 teaspoon extra-virgin olive oil

- In a large bowl, combine the lettuce, lychees, orange, and onion.
- In a small bowl, whisk together the broth, vinegar, juice, and oil. Pour this dressing over the lettuce mixture, tossing gently to coat.
- VARIATION Use another of the green leaf lettuces for a slightly different taste.

YIELD 4 servings

NUTRITION ANALYSIS PER SERVING 48.5 calories, 8.5 g carbohydrate, 0.5 g protein, 1.2 g fat, 1.4 g dietary fiber

25 Nectarines

Benefits

Nectarines are a type of peach and, like the peach, have the golden-yellow, orange, and reddish coloration that is typical of fruits and vegetables containing lutein. As one of the pigments found in the retina of the eye, lutein may help prevent macular degeneration. Nectarines are also a good source of carotenes, vitamin A, vitamin C, potassium, and niacin, as well as fiber.

NUTRITIONAL COMPOSITION One medium raw nectarine provides 67 calories, 16 g carbohydrate, 1.3 g protein, 0.6 g fat, 2.2 g dietary fiber, 1001 IU vitamin A, 7 mg vitamin C, 1.3 mg niacin, 5 mcg folic acid, 288 mg potassium, 7 mg calcium, 22 mg phosphorus, 11 mg magnesium, and 0.2 mg iron.

Bringing It Home

Nectarines do not ripen much after picking and do not keep well for more than two or three days, so choose nectarines that are soft enough to eat—not hard, and not mushy. They can range in color from golden yellow to mostly red, but they should not have any green spots. Refrigerated, ripe nectarines may keep for three to five days.

Livit Recipe

Spiced Nonfat Nectarine Muffins

  3 nectarines, pitted, peeled, and cut into ½-inch cubes
  1 lemon, juice only (about 2 teaspoons)
  2 teaspoons cane sugar OR raw sugar
1¼ teaspoons ground cinnamon
1½ cups all-purpose flour
  ½ cup organic light brown sugar
  2 teaspoons baking powder
  ¼ teaspoon salt
  ½ cup unsweetened applesauce
  ¼ cup nonfat milk
  3 tablespoons pasteurized liquid egg whites OR 2 egg whites

Carbohydrates:
Fruits
· · · · ·
39

- Preheat oven to 400°F.
- Line a muffin tin with 12 paper baking cups.
- In a small bowl, toss the nectarine cubes with the lemon juice to keep them from turning brown. Set aside.
- In a prep bowl, mix the sugar with ¼ teaspoon of the cinnamon. Set aside.
- In a large bowl, combine the flour, brown sugar, baking powder, salt, and the remaining 1 teaspoon of cinnamon. Break up any stubborn lumps of brown sugar with a fork.
- In a separate bowl, whisk together the applesauce, milk, and egg whites.
- Stir the applesauce mixture into the dry ingredients and mix just until moistened. (Traditional instructions say to stir muffins no more than 50 strokes.) Fold in the diced nectarines.
- Spoon the batter into muffin cups, and sprinkle each muffin with a bit of the prepared cinnamon sugar.
- Bake for 20 to 25 minutes, or until a wooden pick inserted in the center comes out clean. Cool for about 3 minutes in the pan, then gently remove them from the pan to continue cooling. Serve warm.

YIELD 12 muffins

NUTRITION ANALYSIS PER SERVING 119 calories, 26.9 g carbohydrate, 2.8 g protein, 0.3 g fat, 2.8 g dietary fiber

26 Oranges

Benefits

The first oranges to be widely cultivated were bitter. Sweet oranges, which origi-nated in India, were brought to Europe in the 15th century by the Portuguese. Peo-ple were so grateful for this new sweet fruit that sweet oranges are named for Portu-gal in many languages.

Oranges and their juice are almost everybody's favorite source of vitamin C, a vitamin whose many benefits have been known for so long that we sometimes overlook them. Primary among them are that vitamin C is a powerful antioxidant, helps the body absorb iron, and is important to wound healing and heart health. Oranges also provide significant potassium and are a good source of calcium and magnesium (three minerals good for regulating blood pressure), as well as phosphorus, vitamin A, folates, and fiber. Oranges are a good source of citric acid, which plays a vital role in cell metabolism. Its citrus limonoids are being studied for their antiviral, antifungal, antibacterial, anti-malarial, and cancer-fighting properties.

NUTRITIONAL COMPOSITION One raw navel orange provides 60 calories, 15.2 g carbohydrate, 1.3 g protein, 0.1 g fat, 3.1 g dietary fiber, 240 IU vitamin A, 75 mg vitamin C, 44 mcg folic acid, 1 mg sodium, 233 mg potassium, 52 mg calcium, 25 mg phosphorus, 13 mg magnesium, and 0.16 mg iron.

Bringing It Home

As we endeavor to limit our use of artificial chemicals in growing food, we need to learn to distinguish between cosmetic blemishes on fruit that indicate poor quality and those that are a natural part of fruit's growing process. Oranges are a great case in point: An orange with green areas or small amounts of brown on its peel may be just as good as one that is solid orange all over. Soft spots and mold are a different story—avoid fruit that shows those signs.

Buying organic oranges whenever possible will help you learn to differentiate between superficial beauty and good quality. As with all citrus fruit, look for oranges that have smooth, thin skin and that are heavy for their size. A vivid color and thick skin, especially with navel oranges, can indicate a dry fruit that lacks juice and flavor. Small oranges are often juicier than big ones.

Livit Recipe

Citrus Frappé

This is a refreshing and balanced snack.

½ cup part-skim ricotta cheese
2 teaspoons nonfat dry milk
1 tablespoon agave nectar OR honey

1 teaspoon orange zest
1 cup fresh strawberries, sliced OR partially
   thawed loose-pack frozen strawberries, sliced

• Combine the ricotta cheese, dry milk, agave nectar, and orange zest in a small bowl. Stir briskly until very smooth. Top with the sliced strawberries. Serve.

YIELD 2 servings

NUTRITION ANALYSIS PER SERVING 150 calories, 16 g carbohydrate, 8 g protein, 5 g fat, 2 g dietary fiber

27 Papaya

Benefits

The papaya was the first fruit tree to have its genome mapped. Originally cultivated in Mexico and South America, papayas are now grown in almost all tropical countries. Papayas are a rich source of antioxidants and anti-inflammatories, including lutein, alpha- and beta-carotene, and vitamin C. They also provide folate, pantothenic acid, potassium, magnesium, and fiber.

Papayas contain the enzyme papain, which breaks down protein fibers and is used to tenderize tough meats, and which may also help with digestion. This ability to break down proteins allows papain to help relieve the pain of insect and jellyfish stings and bites, because the toxins in these venoms are also proteins. But in November 2008, the FDA moved to ban topical (skin) treatments made with papain to avoid allergic reactions, which can be severe.

Papaya leaves were once brewed into a tea that was thought to prevent malaria, but there is no scientific evidence that the tea has the desired effect. Papaya has also played a role as a folk medicine contraceptive. In some animal studies, large amounts of green papaya fruit seem to negatively affect fertility in both males and females, possibly by suppressing the hormone progesterone.

> **NUTRITIONAL COMPOSITION** One medium raw papaya provides 119 calories, 29.8 g carbohydrate, 1.9 g protein, 0.4 g fat, 5.5 g dietary fiber, 863 IU vitamin A, 188 mg vitamin C, 1 mg niacin, 116 mcg folic acid, 781 mg potassium, 9 mg sodium, 15 mg phosphorus, 73 mg calcium, and 30 mg magnesium.

PAPAYA

The papain in papaya can help extract nutrients from your food. So can eating more slowly—allowing 20 chews for each bite. Chewing food thoroughly increases the production of saliva, which contains amylase, the first step of digestion. Eating more slowly also allows you to appreciate and savor the tastes of your food, as your body absorbs more of its value. As a bonus, chewing also stimulates the parotid glands in front of each ear. These glands are part of your immune system, and stimulating them can give you a health boost.

Bringing It Home

Papayas are ripe when their skins are fully red-orange and the fruit feels soft. Avoid papayas that seem bruised or that are too soft, but a few black spots are acceptable. If the fruit still has a few patches of yellow color, it will ripen in a few days at room temperature. Papayas will ripen in the presence of ethylene, so you can speed up the process by putting them in a paper bag with a banana. But papayas that are green or hard won't get juicy and sweet, because there's a limit to how much they can ripen once they've been picked. Green papayas can be used in cooking, especially in some Asian dishes. Ripe papayas will keep in the refrigerator for a day or two. Fully ripened papayas provide the most antioxidant punch. Papaya is also available frozen.

Livit Recipe

Peachy Papaya Smoothie

  1 cup unsweetened soy milk
  1 container peach soy yogurt
1½ cups frozen papaya
  5 frozen strawberries
  5 ice cubes
¼ cup 100% fruit juice (pineapple, mango, orange, apple)
  1 small banana

- Pour the soy milk and soy yogurt into a blender jar. Add papaya, strawberries, and ice. Blend for a few seconds to break up the frozen fruit and ice. Add the fruit juice and the banana. Process on low until smooth.

- VARIATION Try ice cubes made with coconut water for an extra tropical taste!

YIELD 2 servings

NUTRITION ANALYSIS PER SERVING 234.2 calories, 50.9 g carbohydrate, 8.9 g protein, 3.8 g fat, 5.8 g dietary fiber

28 Peaches

Benefits

Peaches are a low-calorie, very juicy fruit and a good source of "portable water" for hot days. Another hot weather benefit is their high potassium content, which helps regulate hydration and can therefore help you avoid muscle cramps. Peaches are also a good source of vitamins A and C, beta-carotene, and lutein—all beneficial to preserving vision. Peaches also have a reputation as a laxative, courtesy of the combination of high fiber and high water content.

In the lab, extracts from peaches have slowed the growth of some types of breast and colon cancer cells. In a National Cancer Institute study, people who consumed more peaches and related fruits, such as nectarines and plums, were less likely to develop cancers of the mouth, throat, or larynx.

NUTRITIONAL COMPOSITION One medium raw peach provides 37 calories, 9.7 g carbohydrate, 0.6 g protein, 0.1 g fat, 2 g dietary fiber, 465 IU vitamin A, 6 mg vitamin C, 3 mcg folic acid, 171 mg potassium, 4 mg calcium, 10 mg phosphorus, and 6 mg magnesium.

Bringing It Home

There are more than two thousand varieties of peaches, ranging from a nearly white color to a rich golden yellow and red. According to a 2006 Texas A&M study, the more strongly colored peaches had more anthocyanins, polyphenols, and antioxidants, and yellow-fleshed peaches had more carotenes. This is not surprising, since these nutrients also add color to fruit.

Some peaches are "clingstone"—where it takes a little effort to separate the edible flesh from the pit. Others are "freestone," with pits that are easily removed. To take the pit out, make a longitudinal slice all the way around the peach, down to the stone, then twist the halves in opposite directions.

Because peaches grow in many parts of the country, and different varieties ripen at different points in the season, you can find fresh peaches from spring to late summer. The peak season is July and August. Choose peaches by smell and by feel—because there is such a range of colors, the shade doesn't tell you as much about ripeness. But a ripe peach should have a sweet smell. It should be firm but yielding. Peaches bruise easily and will turn bad at the bruised spot, so treat them gently.

Peaches are perishable, lasting at most three or four days at room temperature and not much longer refrigerated, so buy conservatively, and wash them just before you eat them.

Livit Recipe

Instant Peach Frozen Yogurt

½ cup nonfat plain yogurt
1 to 2 tablespoons peach schnapps
½ teaspoon vanilla extract
1 package (16 ounces) unsweetened frozen peaches (about 2 cups)
½ cup sugar, preferably superfine

- In a small bowl, stir together the yogurt, schnapps, and vanilla.
- Combine the peaches and sugar in a food processor or blender jar, and pulse until they are finely chopped. With the machine running, gradually add the yogurt mixture through the auxiliary ingredient opening. Blend until all is smooth and creamy. You may need to scrape down the sides of the container once or twice to get everything incorporated. By using frozen peaches, you are able to create a dessert that's already frozen.
- Scoop the mixture into chilled dessert dishes to serve.
- NOTE You can make this treat up to four days ahead of time and store it, covered, in your freezer. Let it soften for 20 minutes in the refrigerator before serving.

YIELD 6 servings

NUTRITION ANALYSIS PER SERVING 113 calories, 27 g carbohydrate, 1 g protein, 0 g fat, 1 g dietary fiber

29 Pears

Benefits

Pears are rich in vitamins B$_2$, C, E, and K, as well as copper and potassium, and they are a great source of fiber. Pears are the least acidic of common fruits, so they are recommended for both babies and adults with gastric reflux or a tendency to heartburn. An Australian project on the influence of foods on asthma found that pears (along with apples) seemed to protect the young adults studied both from asthma attacks and from developing asthma. And although any food may cause an allergy in a person sensitive to it, pears are so rarely allergenic that they are included in the allergen-restricted diets used to determine and control food allergies.

Red-hued pears, such as Red Anjou and Red Bartlett, have more antioxidant anthocyanins than the green, yellow, and brown varieties.

> **NUTRITIONAL COMPOSITION** One medium pear provides 103 calories, 27.5 g carbohydrate, 0.68 g protein, 0.21 g fat, 5.5 g dietary fiber, 41 IU vitamin A, 7.5 mg vitamin C, 0.28 mg niacin, 8 mcg vitamin K, 16 mg calcium, 12 mg magnesium, 20 mg phosphorus, and 212 mg potassium.

Bringing It Home

Pears are widely cultivated in cool temperate regions of the earth and grow across the northern half of the United States. There are many varieties, so we have lots of fresh choices throughout the late summer and early fall. Some are brown, others blush red, and still others are ready to eat when green in color. Pears left to ripen on the tree sometimes develop gritty starch crystals, so they are commonly picked when somewhat unripe and allowed to ripen in storage. Fully ripe pears are very perishable, so they are usually shipped to the store still relatively hard. They will ripen at room temperature in a few days. You can speed the process by putting them in a paper bag. The pears will have more antioxidant value if you eat them when fully ripe.

Livit Recipe

Pecan Pear Chutney

Great to dress up grilled chicken or a sandwich!

  ¼ cup pecans, chopped
  1 cup white grape juice OR apple juice
  4 firm, ripe Bosc pears, peeled, cored, and coarsely chopped
  ¼ cup apple cider vinegar
  1½ teaspoons peeled and minced fresh ginger OR ½ teaspoon ground ginger

½ teaspoon ground cinnamon
½ teaspoon mustard seed
¼ teaspoon red pepper flakes

- In a small, heavy skillet, toast the pecans over medium to low heat until they are crisp and lightly aromatic. Stir constantly and watch them carefully, because once they are heated through they can go from brown to burnt very quickly. Shake them out of the skillet and into a dish so that they don't continue to cook. Set aside.

- In a saucepan over high heat, bring the juice to a boil. Reduce heat to low, and simmer until the juice is reduced by half, about 5 to 10 minutes. Add the pears, vinegar, ginger, cinnamon, mustard seed, and red pepper flakes to the reduced juice. Increase heat to medium and bring the mixture to a boil. Reduce heat and simmer, uncovered, stirring occasionally, until the pears are tender and the juices have thickened, about 20 minutes. Remove from heat and let cool to room temperature. Stir in the toasted pecans.

- Store in the refrigerator in a covered container. Bring to room temperature before serving.

- NOTE Chutney will stay fresh in the refrigerator for up to a week.

YIELD 2 cups

NUTRITION ANALYSIS PER SERVING 81 calories, 15 g carbohydrate, 1 g protein, 3 g fat, 2 g dietary fiber

30 Persimmons

Benefits

The common, or American, persimmon is native to the eastern United States and is one of the Virginia foods described by Captain John Smith in 1612. Red-orange in color, persimmons are a good source of antioxidants and carotenes, vitamins A and C, and both soluble and insoluble fiber.

The Japanese persimmon originated in China and is grown throughout Asia, as well as in California. Larger than the American version, it contains many of the nutrients of its American cousin but has less vitamin C and calcium per gram. Asian persimmon varieties are divided into two groups: astringent and non-astringent. Astringent persimmons (such as the Hachiya) are high in tannins, which can serve as antioxidants but also render unripe fruit inedible. The non-astringent varieties (such as the Fuyu) contain fewer tannins and lose them earlier in the ripening process, so these pears can be consumed either while still firm or when soft.

In traditional Chinese medicine, the Japanese persimmon is believed to regulate ch'i, the vital energy. Raw, they are used to treat constipation. Cooked, they are used to treat diarrhea. Some varieties are high in the antioxidant tannins catechin and gallocatechin.

NUTRITIONAL COMPOSITION (AMERICAN PERSIMMON) One medium raw American persimmon provides 32 calories, 8.4 g carbohydrate, 0.2 g protein, 0.1 g fat, 1.6 g dietary fiber, 17 mg vitamin C, 78 mg potassium, 7 mg calcium, and 7 mg phosphorus.

NUTRITIONAL COMPOSITION (JAPANESE PERSIMMON) One medium raw Japanese persimmon provides 118 calories, 31.2 g carbohydrate, 1 g protein, 0.03 g fat, 6 g dietary fiber, 12.6 mg vitamin C, 270 mg potassium, 13 mg calcium, and 29 mg phosphorus.

UNRIPE PERSIMMONS

Unripe persimmons contain a tannin called shibuol that can contribute to the unusual medical problem called a bezoar. The tannin combines with the acid in the stomach to become a kind of glue, which can then collect fruit seeds, skins, and fiber, forming a lump that may need to be surgically removed.

Bringing It Home

Choose persimmons that have good, bright color and whole, shiny skins with no cracks or leaks. Fully ripe persimmons will feel thin-skinned and full of juice. Handle them carefully.

American persimmons are native to eastern North America and can even be found wild from Virginia to Wisconsin. Because freezing helps to ripen the fruit, American persimmons can be harvested from September through December, even after frost. Persimmon festivals are held in North Carolina and Illinois in November, and in Indiana in late September.

Japanese persimmons have been grown in California since the 19th century, and their season is slightly longer than that of the American version. Orange County, California, holds a persimmon festival in November, celebrating the California fruits. Japanese immigrants brought with them a traditional method of drying persimmons that results in a dried fruit called *hoshigaki*. Dried persimmons are also available in other, less specialized forms.

Persimmons can go from ripe to overripe in a very short period of time, so enjoy ripe persimmons within a day or two, or buy persimmons that are still firm and ripen them at room temperature in a paper bag. Once they are ripe, store them in the refrigerator. Take advantage of the fact that persimmons can be ripened by freezing: Freeze them overnight, then thaw them for eating. This "ripening" also converts the tannins to a more edible form.

Because ripe persimmons are so fragile, specialty farmers and some food stores carry canned or frozen persimmon pulp for year-round use.

Persimmon Yogurt Parfait

1 tablespoon brown sugar
2 cups nonfat vanilla yogurt
2 persimmons, peeled and cut into 16 thin slices
1 cup fresh raspberries
1 cup low-fat granola

- In a small bowl, stir together the brown sugar and yogurt until they are well blended.
- Set out four 8-ounce dessert glasses. Spoon ¼ cup of the sugared yogurt mixture into each glass. Layer each with 4 persimmon slices, 2 tablespoons of the raspberries, and 2 tablespoons of the granola. Repeat the layers, finishing with granola. Serve immediately.

YIELD 4 servings

NUTRITION ANALYSIS PER SERVING 276 calories, 57 g carbohydrate, 9 g protein, 2 g fat, 4 g dietary fiber

31 Pineapple

Benefits

Pineapples are another food, like papayas, that contains an enzyme that breaks down proteins. In the case of pineapples, the enzyme is bromelain. In addition to making pineapple a good meat tenderizer, bromelain helps block some metabolic products that contribute to inflammation, making it a good anti-inflammatory. Isolated bromelain has been used to treat sports injuries, digestive problems, swelling, and other problems involving inflammation. Its action on proteins has also been found to reduce blood clots, especially in arteries.

Pineapple is a good source of manganese, vitamin B_1, and vitamin C.

NUTRITIONAL COMPOSITION One cup of raw pineapple pieces provides 76 calories, 8.4 g carbohydrate, 0.2 g protein, 0.1 g fat, 2.3 g dietary fiber, 17 mg vitamin C, 78 mg potassium, 7 mg calcium, and 7 mg phosphorus.

Bringing It Home

Pineapples don't ripen after they are picked, so don't expect that a hard or too-green pineapple will improve. A ripe pineapple should smell sweet, especially at the stem end. Avoid fruit with soft spots, bruises, or dark spots. Also steer clear of any that smell musty, sour, or fermented.

Pineapple will keep at room temperature for a day or two. To keep it for more than two days, wrap it in plastic and store it in the refrigerator, or cut up the pineapple and refrigerate the chunks in an airtight container. Adding a little juice to the container will help the cut pieces stay moist and juicy.

Pineapple's sweetness can raise blood glucose levels fairly quickly—so balance it out with a handful of nuts to provide more fiber and protein.

Livit Recipe

Pineapple Stir-Fried Chicken

See Safe Handling of Poultry on page 211.

Rice

> 2¼ cups water
> 1 cup brown rice

Chicken in marinade

> 1 teaspoon reduced-sodium soy sauce
> 1 teaspoon brown rice vinegar (not seasoned)
> ½ teaspoon grated fresh ginger
> ½ pound boneless, skinless chicken breast, cut into 1-inch cubes

Sauce

> 2 garlic cloves, minced
> 1 teaspoon grated fresh ginger
> 3 tablespoons unsweetened pineapple juice
> 1 teaspoon rice vinegar
> 1½ tablespoons reduced-sodium soy sauce
> 1½ tablespoons cornstarch

Assembly

> 1 small carrot, thinly sliced into diagonal strips
> 1 red bell pepper, chopped into ½-inch pieces (about 1 cup)
> 1 small head bok choy, chopped into bite-sized pieces (about 1 cup)
> 2 to 3 ounces snow peas (about 1 cup)
> ½ cup sliced green onions
> 1 tablespoon peanut oil
> 1 cup canned unsweetened pineapple chunks

- *To prepare the rice:* Bring water to a boil in a heavy 1-quart saucepan. When the water has come to a boil, add the rice. Bring the water back to a boil, stir, and then reduce heat until the rice is just simmering. Cover and cook for 50 minutes to an hour, until the kernels begin to open. While the rice is cooking, prepare the other ingredients.

- *To prepare the chicken in marinade:* In a small bowl, whisk together the soy sauce, rice vinegar, and ginger. Put the chicken and the marinade into a plastic zipper bag. Seal and refrigerate until it's time to stir-fry.

- *To prepare the sauce:* In a small bowl, whisk together the garlic, ginger, pineapple juice, rice vinegar, soy sauce, and corn starch. Set the sauce aside.

- *To assemble the dish:* Prepare the carrot, bell pepper, bok choy, snow peas, and green onions before you start cooking, each in a separate container, so that they can be added to the pan individually, at just the right time. One of the secrets to good stir-frying is to cook each item only as long as it needs to be cooked.

- In a large wok or deep, wide frying pan, heat ½ tablespoon of the peanut oil over medium-high heat. Add the carrot slices and red pepper squares and stir-fry for 2 to 3 minutes. Add the bok choy and pineapple and stir-fry for 1 minute. Add the snow peas and onions and stir-fry for 1 additional minute. Transfer all vegetables from the wok to a large bowl and set them aside.

- Return the wok to the burner. Add the remaining ½ tablespoon of peanut oil and the chicken cubes. Stir-fry for about 3 minutes, or until the chicken is cooked through. It should be white or lightly browned with no traces of pink. Return the cooked vegetables to the wok. Stir-fry everything together for 1 minute more.

- Whisk the sauce mixture until the cornstarch is completely dissolved. Add the sauce to the wok and bring to a boil. Cook, stirring gently, about 1 additional minute, until the sauce thickens and becomes clear and shiny. Serve over prepared brown rice.

YIELD 4 servings

NUTRITION ANALYSIS PER SERVING (with ⅓ cup brown rice) 257 calories, 35 g carbohydrate, 17 g protein, 5 g fat, 4 g dietary fiber

PURPLE—THE HEALTHIEST COLOR?

The color in purple fruits and vegetables comes from a group of powerful anti-oxidant pigments called anthocyanins, and research strongly suggests that the health benefits of eating purple foods such as berries are also due, at least in part, to the same anthocyanins.

These purple pigments have shown potential in the laboratory to fight cancer, aging and neurological diseases, inflammation, diabetes, and even bacterial infections. In cancer research, anthocyanins have been shown to inhibit the growth and proliferation of several types of cancer cells, via a variety of mechanisms, including causing cancer cells to die faster, reducing the inflammations that may spark their production, slowing the growth of the blood vessels to the tumors, and minimizing the damage to healthy cells' DNA. Research continues to confirm the potential for these compounds to contribute to health and long life in humans.

Purple fruits and vegetables include blueberries, blackberries, black cherries, black raspberries, black currants, plums, elderberries, bilberries, figs, raisins, eggplants, purple carrots, purple cabbage, beets, and pomegranates.

32 Plums

Benefits

Plums grow in many parts of the world, including North and South America, Europe, and Asia. More than 140 types of plums are available in the United States. Varieties that originated in Europe tend to be purple-skinned, but there are other varieties that are white-, yellow-, green-, or red-skinned. Inside, the flesh of plums can be white, green, orange, purple, pink, black, or red. The more purple the plum, the more anthocyanins it is likely to contain, and the more purple parts will be richest in them—so eat the skins! But plums have lots of other nutritional value as well. They are a good source of calcium, magnesium, potassium, vitamins A and C, lutein, and beta-carotene. Plums are also a significant source of the trace mineral boron, which is helpful in converting calcium to bone and may therefore play a role in preventing osteoporosis.

Plums, along with prunes, have earned their reputation as a remedy for constipation. In addition to a healthy dose of fiber, they contain sugars, including sorbitol, a sugar alcohol that draws water from the intestine to produce a laxative effect, and isatin. Some sources say that most of the sorbitol and isatin is in the plum skin and advise peeling the fruit to avoid this side effect.

Although plums are quite sweet, they don't cause blood sugar to spike, probably because of the fiber, fructose, and sorbitol that all contribute to slowing down absorption of the sugars.

> **NUTRITIONAL COMPOSITION** One medium raw plum provides 36 calories, 8.6 g carbohydrate, 0.5 g protein, 0.4 g fat, 0.9 g dietary fiber, 213 IU vitamin A, 6 mg vitamin C, 1 mcg folic acid, 114 mg potassium, 3 mg calcium, 7 mg phosphorus, and 5 mg magnesium.

Bringing It Home

Fresh plums are available all summer, from May through October. Plums do not ripen much after picking, so buy them ripe and eat them within a day or two. They will keep at room temperature for only a day or two, slightly longer if refrigerated.

A good, ripe plum has a rich color and a smooth, full-feeling, intact skin with no holes, bruises, soft spots, or leakage. Plums may have a whitish, slightly waxy substance on the skin: This is called "bloom" and is a sign that the fruit has not been over-handled. The darkest purple plums, like Black Friars, have the most anthocyanins, but other colors may have more carotenes. Choose a variety of plums throughout the season for the most benefit.

Livit Recipe

Cooling Plum Sorbet

See Add Zest! on page 34.

> 12 plums, halved, pitted, and sliced
> 1 cup organic fresh squeezed orange juice
> 1 tablespoon agave nectar
> 1 tablespoon orange zest
> Orange slices, as garnish

- Combine the plums, orange juice, agave nectar, and orange zest in a blender jar. Process until smooth. Pour the mixture into a loaf pan and freeze for at least 4 hours.

- Thirty minutes before serving, remove it from the freezer and blend it again. Return the mixture to the freezer until serving. Serve the sorbet in dessert dishes garnished with orange slices.

YIELD 9 servings

NUTRITION ANALYSIS PER SERVING 63 calories, 15 g carbohydrate, 1 g protein, 0 g fat, 2 g dietary fiber

Carbohydrates:
Fruits
· · · · ·
51

33 Prunes (Dried Plums)

Benefits

Also see SuperFood 32, Plums.

Prunes are rich in anthocyanins, as well as a good source of calcium, magnesium, potassium, vitamins A and C, lutein, and beta-carotene. They are a significant source of the trace mineral boron, which is useful in converting calcium to bone and may play a role in preventing osteoporosis. Prunes have many of the same health benefits as plums (their fresh counterparts), with more concentrated sugars and fiber, due to the drying.

Prunes have recently undergone an image-improvement campaign, thanks mainly to Sunsweet, a growers' cooperative that produces about two thirds of the world's prunes. Prunes are dried plums, although there are specific varieties that are grown especially for drying, to retain more sweetness and better texture. Some varieties of plum have traditionally been called "prune" even when fresh.

Prunes, as well as plums, have earned their reputation as a remedy for constipation. In addition to a healthy dose of fiber, plums and prunes contain sugars, including sorbitol, a sugar alcohol that draws water from the intestine to produce a laxative effect, and isatin. Prune juice contains some of the prune skin because unlike the juices of fresh fruits, it is made by softening dried prunes and then pureeing them.

Although prunes are quite sweet, they don't cause blood sugar to spike, probably because of the fiber, fructose, and sorbitol that contribute to slowing down absorption of the sugars.

NUTRITIONAL COMPOSITION Five dried prunes provide 100 calories, 26 g carbohydrate, 1.1 g protein, 0.2 g fat, 3 g dietary fiber, 834.5 IU vitamin A, 1.5 mg vitamin C, 0.8 mg niacin, 1.5 mcg folic acid, 313 mg potassium, 21.5 mg calcium, 1.5 mg sodium, 33 mg phosphorus, 1.04 mg iron, and 19 mg magnesium.

Bringing It Home

Although prunes are a dried fruit, they should still be soft when you buy them, and they should look shiny and plump. Don't buy prunes that appear to have dried out completely or that have signs of mold. Try to avoid prunes processed with sulfites or other preservatives. Stored in an airtight container away from heat and light, they will keep for several months. In the refrigerator, prunes may keep as long as six months if they are not allowed to dry out.

As part of the effort to "update" the prune's image, they are now being sold individually wrapped as a snack food. But you can pack a few in a plastic zipper bag for your own high-fiber snack.

Livit Recipe

Chicken Lettuce Wraps with Prune Sauce

See Safe Handling of Poultry on page 211.

    1 tablespoon sesame oil
    1 pound boneless, skinless chicken breasts, cut into small pieces
    1 tablespoon grated fresh ginger
    2 cups prune juice
    ¼ cup agave nectar OR honey
    2 tablespoons reduced-sodium soy sauce
    2 tablespoons rice vinegar
   16 small leaves of butter lettuce
       Chopped peanuts, as garnish
       Cilantro leaves, as garnish
       Sliced green onion tops, as garnish

• In a medium skillet, heat the sesame oil. Add the chicken pieces, and cook over medium heat, stirring frequently, for 5 minutes, or until browned and cooked through. Add the ginger and cook for 1 minute more. Remove from heat and set aside.

• In a medium saucepan, combine the prune juice, agave nectar, soy sauce, and rice vinegar. Cook over medium-high heat for 20 minutes, or until the mixture has thickened somewhat. It will continue to thicken as it cools. Add about half of this sauce to the cooked chicken, stirring to coat the chicken pieces well. Return the skillet with glazed chicken to the heat, and cook it for an additional 5 minutes.

- To serve, put 4 lettuce leaves on each plate, and spoon about one fourth of the chicken mixture onto each lettuce leaf. Serve the remaining sauce on the side, along with chopped peanuts, cilantro, and green onions as garnish.
- VARIATION Use another of the green leaf lettuces for a slightly different taste.

YIELD 4 servings

NUTRITION ANALYSIS PER SERVING 223 calories, 43.8 g carbohydrate, 5.7 g protein, 3.7 g fat, 1.6 g dietary fiber

34 Pomegranates

Benefits

The pomegranate is a fruit so unusual and delicious that it has attracted attention throughout history, having been cultivated throughout the Mediterranean since ancient times. Because Persephone ate pomegranate seeds while in the underworld, she was doomed to spend part of each year there, resulting in the origin of winter in Greek mythology. The ancient Egyptians used pomegranate for its medicinal powers, even including the fruit in their elaborate burials. It's mentioned in the holy books of Judaism, Christianity, and Islam. Ayurvedic medicine uses all parts of the pomegranate—fruit, leaves, bark, and flowers. Pomegranate flowers, because of their astringent properties, were used in 19th-century English medicine to treat skin irritations, sore throats, and diarrhea.

Pomegranate juice is high in potassium and a good source of vitamin C, vitamin B_5 (pantothenic acid), and many polyphenols and antioxidants, some of them unique to this fruit. It has demonstrated potential in the laboratory, including in preliminary human trials, for reducing several risks related to oxidation and atherosclerosis that are involved in heart disease. As an antioxidant, it has a moderate ORAC of 2,860 units per 100 grams.

The seed-juice sacs of a pomegranate, called "arils," are a significant source of linolenic acid, which has shown some potential for combating insulin resistance. Pomegranate seed oil has also been effective against breast cancer cells in the lab.

NUTRITIONAL COMPOSITION One medium raw pomegranate provides 105 calories, 26.4 g carbohydrate, 1.5 g protein, 0.5 g fat, 0.9 g dietary fiber, 9 mg vitamin C, 9 mcg folic acid, 399 mg potassium, 5 mg sodium, 12 mg phosphorus, and 5 mg magnesium.

Bringing It Home

Pomegranates keep amazingly well for a fruit—two to three weeks at room temperature and two to three months in the refrigerator. So when they are in season, from October through December, stock up! Because it's all about the juice, choose a pomegranate that feels heavy in the hand and has a skin free of cracks and brown spots.

To make your own pomegranate juice from a fresh fruit, roll the pomegranate back and forth on a table with your palm, pressing gently. Then cut the pomegranate in half and squeeze out the juice.

When purchasing pomegranate juice, choose a juice that is 100 percent pomegranate juice and not from concentrate. It's delicious mixed with sparkling water and ice for a refreshing, and lighter, drink.

Livit Recipe

Pomegranate Arugula Salad

    3 tablespoons apple cider OR red wine vinegar
 1½ tablespoons aged balsamic vinegar
    ¼ teaspoon kosher salt
    ⅛ teaspoon freshly ground pepper
    2 tablespoons extra-virgin olive oil
    2 medium bunches arugula, rinsed and with stems removed
    ⅓ cup coarsely chopped toasted pecans
    1 medium pomegranate, arils (seeds and juice) only (about ½ cup)

· In a medium bowl, whisk together the vinegars, salt, and pepper. Gradually drizzle in the olive oil, whisking until the dressing is emulsified.

· Toss the arugula with just enough of the vinegar mixture to coat. Sprinkle with pecans and pomegranate arils. Serve.

YIELD 4 servings

NUTRITION ANALYSIS PER SERVING 167 calories, 10.6 g carbohydrate, 1.6 g protein, 14.2 g fat, 1.4 g dietary fiber

35 Quinces

Benefits

Quinces originated in the Caucasus region, and Turkey remains the largest producer, although they are grown throughout the Middle East as well as in Chile, Uruguay, and Argentina. Though quinces were once grown widely in the United States, they have been subject to insects and blights, and now most of the quinces available in the United States come from Argentina.

Quinces are especially high in pectin, a soluble fiber that helps lower blood cholesterol. Quinces are a good source of vitamin A and iron, and they provide moderate amounts of potassium, vitamin C, and calcium. Quinces' high acid content is thought to help with the digestion of fatty meals. Research on the closely related Chinese quince shows potential for preventing stomach lesions and combating some viruses.

The high pectin content of quinces accounts for their common use in jams and jellies. Quinces were traditionally used to produce an extract for treating coughs and sore throat, as well as for digestive problems. They also have a pleasing sweet smell and have long been used as the base for pomanders.

> **NUTRITIONAL COMPOSITION** One medium raw quince provides 52 calories, 14.1 g carbohydrate, 0.4 g protein, 0.1 g fat, 1.7 g dietary fiber, 37 IU vitamin A, 14 mg vitamin C, 3 mcg folic acid, 181 mg potassium, 4 mg sodium, 16 mg phosphorus, 10 mg calcium, 7 mg magnesium, and 0.12 mg iron.

Bringing It Home

You're likely to find quinces in Middle Eastern, Armenian, and other ethnic markets, because quinces are a staple of Middle Eastern and Caucasian cuisine. Both fresh and preserved quinces are available.

Most types of quinces have a high tannin content and, like persimmons, must go through a ripening or freezing process to convert the tannins before they can be eaten. Fresh quinces usually can't be eaten raw—they are simply too hard and acidic—but when cooked they turn pink and develop a pleasant tartness and texture. Peeling and sweetening the cooked quince, or mixing it with sweeter or blander ingredients, makes it even more palatable. In European cooking, quinces tend to be used in desserts and jellies. In Mediterranean cuisines, they are often added to stews and meat dishes.

A ripe quince is yellow all over, hard as a winter squash, and looks like a large, lumpy pear. It gives off a characteristic sweet quince aroma. Quince will keep up to two months in the refrigerator.

Apple Quince Pie

Quince adds a sweet harvest flavor to this luscious and healthy apple pie.

1 9-inch whole wheat pie crust, unbaked

Pie filling

2 medium quinces, sliced (about 3 cups)
½ cup unsweetened apple juice
5 medium tart apples, sliced (about 5 cups)
¼ cup agave nectar
3 tablespoons all-purpose flour
1 teaspoon ground allspice
½ teaspoon ground cinnamon
¼ teaspoon salt
¼ teaspoon ground nutmeg

Crumble topping

⅓ cup quick-cooking oats
2 tablespoons all-purpose flour
2 tablespoons organic brown sugar
¼ teaspoon ground cinnamon
1 tablespoon non-hydrogenated margarine

- Preheat oven to 350°F.
- Prepare pie crust in a 9″ pie plate; flute the edges.
- *To prepare the pie filling:* In a large saucepan, combine the quinces and apple juice, and bring them to a boil. Reduce heat, cover, and let the quinces simmer for 12 to 15 minutes, until they are crisp-tender. Uncover the pan, and simmer for another 8 to 12 minutes, until the liquid has reduced to about 2 tablespoons. Remove from heat and allow the quinces to cool for 5 minutes.
- In a large bowl, combine the sliced apples, agave nectar, flour, allspice, cinnamon, salt, and nutmeg. Gently stir the quince mixture into the apple mixture. Spoon the filling into the crust.
- *To prepare the crumble topping:* In a small bowl, combine the oats, flour, brown sugar, and cinnamon. Cut in the margarine until the mixture is crumbly. Sprinkle topping over the pie filling.
- Bake for 50 to 60 minutes, or until the apples are tender and the crust is golden brown. Cool on a wire rack.

YIELD 8 servings

NUTRITION ANALYSIS PER SERVING 240 calories, 44.3 g carbohydrate, 1.9 g protein, 7.2 g fat, 3.4 g dietary fiber

36 Raisins

Benefits

Raisins are dried grapes, but their extensive history puts them in a special class. Raisins are nearly 80 percent carbohydrate, most of which is sugar, but they also provide significant fiber, as well as minerals like potassium, calcium, and fluoride.

In an experiment designed to test the effectiveness of relatively minor lifestyle changes, researchers found that women who ate a cup of raisins a day for six weeks lowered their blood pressure, reduced their waist size, reduced signs of inflammation, and lowered their blood cholesterol and triglycerides.

It appears raisins may also help with oral health: Polyphenols extracted from raisins suppressed the growth of some germs that attack the mouth and gums, including some that set the stage for oral cancers. Raisins also appear to be one of the main sources of boron in the American diet. This trace mineral may have a role in calcium metabolism and preventing osteoporosis.

NUTRITIONAL COMPOSITION One-quarter cup of seedless raisins, packed, provides 123 calories, 32.7 g carbohydrate, 1.3 g protein, 0.2 g fat, 1.5 g dietary fiber, 0.95 mg vitamin C, 1.5 mg vitamin K, 0.32 mg niacin, 4.6 mg choline, 20.5 mg calcium, 0.78 mg iron, 13.3 mg magnesium, 41.8 mg phosphorus, and 309 mg potassium.

Bringing It Home

Choose organic raisins that have not been treated with sulfites, if possible. One-quarter cup of raisins is an easy, sweet way to increase your daily intake of fruit.

Livit Recipe

Apple Raisin Risotto

2 tablespoons packed brown sugar	⅛ teaspoon salt
1 tablespoon safflower oil	½ teaspoon ground cinnamon
1 medium apple, cored and diced	¼ cup dry Marsala wine
¼ cup raisins	1 cup apple cider OR apple juice
1 cup uncooked arborio rice	4 cups water

· In a large nonstick skillet, heat sugar and oil over medium heat. Add apple and raisins to the skillet and sauté, stirring constantly, until they are slightly soft. Add the rice, salt, and cinnamon. Cook, stirring constantly, for 2 to 3 minutes. Add the wine and stir until the rice has absorbed it. Increase heat to medium high and stir in the cider. Cook, uncovered, stirring frequently, until the juice is absorbed. Add the water, 1 cup at a time, stirring in each cup and allowing it to be absorbed, until the rice is tender and the mixture has a creamy consistency (allow approximately 25 to 30 minutes). Serve immediately.

YIELD 8 servings

NUTRITION ANALYSIS PER SERVING 156 calories, 31 g carbohydrate, 1 g protein, 2 g fat, 1 g dietary fiber

37 Raspberries

Benefits

Raspberries are frequently studied for their health effects, because they are a significant source of anthocyanins, antioxidants, and phytochemicals. Raspberries are one of the few berries with the potential to inhibit the formation of cancer tumors, according to experiments involving human subjects. Raspberries contain ellagic acid, quercetin, and kaempferol, as well as anthocyanins. They have an ORAC of 4882, one of the highest among rated foods.

Because raspberries are aggregate fruits, made up of many small beads of fruit, each containing a seed, they are very high in fiber.

NUTRITIONAL COMPOSITION One cup of raw raspberries provides 60 calories, 14.2 g carbohydrate, 1.1 g protein, 0.7 g fat, 8.4 g dietary fiber, 160 IU vitamin A, 31 mg vitamin C, 32 mcg folic acid, 187 mg potassium, 15 mg phosphorus, 27 mg calcium, 22 mg magnesium, and 1.25 mg manganese.

Bringing It Home

There are red, purple, black, and yellow varieties of raspberries. Choose berries that are not leaking juice. If there are signs of mold, pick out and discard the moldy berries before storing the rest. Don't wash them until you are ready to eat them. Instead, store unwashed berries in the refrigerator and then eat them within a day or two. Don't try to keep them at room temperature, for they will spoil very quickly. Fresh raspberries are highly perishable, subject to bruising and mold as well as simply not having a very long shelf life. Treat them gently, and eat them promptly!

On the plus side, raspberries freeze very well. You can purchase frozen raspberries or freeze your own. Wash them gently, dry them gently with a paper towel, and arrange them in a single layer on a flat pan or cookie sheet. Put them in the freezer until they are frozen, then transfer them to plastic zipper bags for longer-term freezer storage.

Livit Recipe

Raspberry Sauce for Poultry

Pour this sauce on chicken or turkey for a high antioxidant flavor boost.

> 1 pint (16 ounces) organic raspberries, rinsed and patted dry
> ¼ cup raw sugar
> 2 teaspoons fresh lemon juice

- In a small saucepan, combine berries, sugar, and lemon juice. Cook over medium heat, crushing the berries with the back of a wooden spoon, until the mixture is soft and begins to boil. Remove from heat, and allow the mixture to cool slightly. Force the mixture through a fine sieve or a strainer lined with cheesecloth. Serve over chicken or turkey.

YIELD 1 cup

NUTRITION ANALYSIS PER SERVING 79 calories, 19.8 g carbohydrate, 0.6 g protein, 0.3 g fat, 4.2 g dietary fiber

38 Strawberries

Benefits

Although strawberries don't pack the anthocyanin punch of some of the purple fruits and berries, they do contain at least two anthocyanins, and they are an excellent source of a variety of other flavonoids, including catechin, quercetin, and kaempferol, as well as vitamin C, potassium, beta-carotene, lutein, and ellagic acid. This makes strawberries potential cancer fighters. Fisetin, another flavonoid found in strawberries, has been shown to improve long-term memory in mouse studies, although researchers warn that humans would have to eat ten pounds a day to get an equivalent effect.

NUTRITIONAL COMPOSITION One cup of raw strawberries provides 45 calories, 10.5 g carbohydrate, 0.9 g protein, 0.6 g fat, 3.4 g dietary fiber, 40 IU vitamin A, 84 mg vitamin C, 26 mcg folic acid, 247 mg potassium, 1 mg sodium, 28 mg phosphorus, 21 mg calcium, and 15 mg magnesium.

Bringing It Home

The sweetest and tastiest strawberries are usually the smallest ones, and this is one fruit where the farmer's market will definitely outshine the supermarket, because the most popular commercial varieties are a compromise between sturdiness in transport and taste. Choose the brightest red berries, with caps that look green and fresh, not dry. Fresh strawberries should have a distinctive sweet strawberry smell. If they are not fragrant, they were probably picked too soon. Avoid mushy, leaky, or moldy berries, and be sure to check the underside of the container for telltale juice stains.

Strawberries are best when consumed promptly or frozen. In an airtight container, they may keep for two to three days in the refrigerator. To freeze, wash the berries gently, dry them, and remove the leafy caps. Set the berries in a single layer on a shallow pan or cookie sheet and freeze. Once frozen, they can be transferred to a plastic zipper bag and stored in the freezer for up to six months.

Strawberry Cinnamon Muffins

2 eggs OR 6 tablespoons pasteurized liquid egg whites
⅔ cup sugar
½ cup nonfat milk
¼ cup nonfat Greek-style yogurt OR ¼ cup nonfat plain yogurt, drained

1 teaspoon vanilla
¼ cup non-hydrogenated margarine, melted
2 cups all-purpose flour
1 tablespoon baking powder
¼ teaspoon salt
¼ teaspoon cinnamon
1½ cups strawberries, hulled and cut into chunks

- Preheat oven to 375°F.
- Line muffin tins with 12 paper baking cups.
- In a large mixing bowl, whisk the eggs and sugar together until the mixture becomes light. Add the milk, yogurt, vanilla, and margarine to the eggs and whisk them together gently.
- In a separate bowl, combine the flour, baking powder, salt, and cinnamon.
- Add the dry ingredients to the milk mixture and stir just until the flour disappears. Gently fold in the berries.
- Spoon the batter into muffin cups, filling each cup to the top. (The strawberries will shrink in baking, so the muffins won't overflow.) Bake for 25 minutes, or until a toothpick comes out clean. Remove the muffins from the pan, and cool them on a wire rack. Serve warm.
- NOTE You can freeze these muffins in plastic zipper bags. Reheat frozen muffins in the oven at 350°F for 10 minutes.
- VARIATION For a low-fat variation, use ¼ cup of unsweetened applesauce instead of margarine.

YIELD 12 muffins

NUTRITION ANALYSIS PER SERVING 177.4 calories, 29.2 g carbohydrate, 4.1 g protein, 4.9 g fat, 1 g dietary fiber

39 Tangerines

Benefits

Like other members of the citrus family, especially the oranges that they most resemble, tangerines are full of vitamin C and a great source of beta-carotene. They also provide potassium, magnesium, and many B vitamins, including B_1, B_2, B_6, folic acid, and pantothenic acid. Tangerines have the highest concentration of pectin, a soluble fiber helpful in reducing cholesterol, among the commonly eaten citrus fruits. They also contain lutein, which may help prevent macular degeneration, and hesperidin, which helps keep blood vessels healthy and has shown potential for fighting osteoporosis.

NUTRITIONAL COMPOSITION One medium raw tangerine provides 37 calories, 9.4 g carbohydrate, 0.5 g protein, 0.2 g fat, 1.9 g dietary fiber, 773 IU vitamin A, 26 mg vitamin C, 17 mcg folic acid, 132 mg potassium, 1 mg sodium, 8 mg phosphorus, 12 mg calcium, and 10 mg magnesium.

Bringing It Home

Tangerines, clementines, and tangelos are all types of mandarin oranges. Although the season for classic tangerines may be limited to December and January, there are similar fruits available nearly all fall and winter.

Tangerines should have glossy, rich orange skins, though a few green patches are acceptable. They will keep in the refrigerator for about a week. There is no reliable way to predict which tangerines will have many seeds and which will have only a few.

Because they are easy to peel and divide into sections, tangerines are a quick snack. Adding tangerines to salads, fruit cups, and even salsas served with fish or chicken is a quick and easy way to include more citrus fruit in your meals. Be sure to remove the seeds.

Livit Recipe

Citrus Salmon

- 2 teaspoons non-hydrogenated margarine
- 2 scallions, thinly sliced (about ¼ cup)
- ½ teaspoon minced fresh ginger
- ½ teaspoon reduced-sodium soy sauce
   Cooking oil spray
- 2 boneless salmon fillets, 5 to 6 ounces each, with skin removed
- 3 medium tangerines, peeled and sectioned (about 1 cup), with seeds removed
   Italian parsley, chopped, as garnish

- Preheat oven to 350°F.
- Melt the margarine in a small pan, then remove from heat. Add the scallions, ginger, and soy sauce to the melted margarine and stir to make a sauce. Set aside.
- Spray a 9″ × 13″ baking pan lightly with oil. Put the salmon fillets in the pan. Arrange the tangerine sections on the fillets. Pour the sauce over the salmon and tangerines. Cover pan loosely with foil. Bake for 20 minutes, or until the salmon is opaque and cooked through.
- Garnish with parsley and serve hot.

YIELD 2 servings

NUTRITION ANALYSIS PER SERVING 378 calories, 15.3 g carbohydrate, 40.8 g protein, 16.7 g fat, 3.3 g dietary fiber

40 Watermelon

Benefits

Vietnamese legend says that the watermelon originated there in answer to the prayer of an exiled prince. But this fruit is so easy to love that it has been cultivated wherever it has traveled—watermelon seeds were found in Tutankhamen's tomb, North African traders brought it to Europe by the 13th century, and it appears to have been adopted by Native Americans early in the history of their contact with Europeans.

As captured in its name, watermelon is mostly water—making it a refreshing treat and a somewhat portable source of hydration. It provides vitamin A, vitamin C, potassium, and some B vitamins.

Watermelon is also a rich source of lycopene, which is a phytochemical found in some red fruits and vegetables. (Lycopene is often regarded as the likely agent in the tomato's apparent prevention of some cancers.) Watermelon rinds are a significant source of citrulline, which helps lower blood pressure by relaxing blood vessels.

> **NUTRITIONAL COMPOSITION** One cup of raw watermelon pieces provides 51 calories, 11.5 g carbohydrate, 1 g protein, 0.7 g fat, 0.8 g dietary fiber, 586 IU vitamin A, 15 mg vitamin C, 4 mcg folic acid, 186 mg potassium, 3 mg sodium, 14 mg phosphorus, 13 mg calcium, and 18 mg magnesium.

Bringing It Home

There are many types of watermelon available. In general, melons with deep color will have more carotenoids, but a deep green exterior does not always guarantee a deep red interior. When buying a cut melon, check the color of the flesh and go for the rich dark reds. When buying watermelon whole, choose one with a shiny, rich green skin and without bruises, dents, or blemishes. A paler patch where the fruit has rested on the ground means that the melon ripened in the sun—a good sign as long as the patch is neither mushy nor dry. The melon should feel firm and heavy.

Wash the outside of the watermelon before cutting into it. You can store a whole watermelon in the refrigerator for a day or two. If you cut the watermelon into slices or cubes, store them in an airtight container in the refrigerator, where they will keep for three or four days.

For a quick, refreshing cold soup, purée watermelon, cantaloupe, and kiwi together. (Remove the skins and seeds first!) Swirl in a little nonfat plain Greek-style yogurt and serve!

Mix watermelon cubes with thinly sliced red onion, salt, and black pepper for a great summer salad. Watermelon is a wonderful addition to any fruit salad.

Livit Recipe

Watermelon Refresh Smoothie

2 cups watermelon chunks, with seeds removed
1 tablespoon agave nectar OR honey
1 tablespoon fresh mint leaves
1 cup lemon yogurt
Cinnamon

• In the container of a food processor or blender, puree the watermelon, agave nectar, and mint, using short bursts to avoid overblending. (Because watermelon is 92 percent water, it will disintegrate under too much pressure.) Add the yogurt and cinnamon to the watermelon mixture. Pulse in short bursts, just until smooth. Serve.

YIELD 2 servings

NUTRITION ANALYSIS PER SERVING 181 calories, 37.8 g carbohydrate, 8 g protein, 1.9 g fat, 0.9 g dietary fiber

Carbohydrates:
Fruits
· · · · ·
63

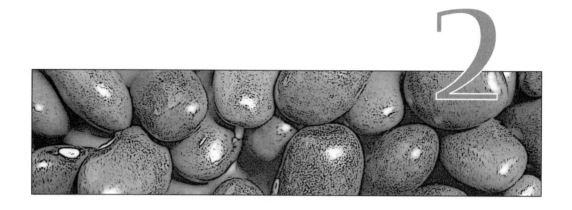

Carbohydrates: Starchy Vegetables

Many of the starchy vegetables occupy a middle ground between fruits and true vegetables, acting as both a carbohydrate and a significant source of vitamins, minerals, antioxidants, and sometimes protein. Although this is not true in every case, most starchy vegetables release their energy relatively slowly, so that they maintain more stable blood sugar levels than some of the sweeter fruits. They tend to be high in fiber and, in some meals, can take the place of a grain even while providing a wider range of nutrients.

41 Acorn Squash

Benefits

Acorn squash is one of the winter squashes, which in temperate climates are harvested in the autumn when their seeds have matured and their outer skins have hardened into a rind. They're called "winter" squashes because, before refrigeration, they could be kept and eaten through the winter.

As you might guess from the acorn squash's orange flesh, it is a good source of antioxidant carotenes. It also provides the minerals magnesium, manganese, potassium, and calcium, and vitamins A and C.

· · · · ·

NUTRITIONAL COMPOSITION One-half cup of baked acorn squash cubes provides 57 calories, 14.9 g carbohydrate, 1.1 g protein, 0.1 g fat, 4.5 g dietary fiber, 437 IU vitamin A, 11 mg vitamin C, 19 mcg folic acid, 446 mg potassium, 4 mg sodium, 46 mg phosphorus, 45 mg calcium, and 44 mg magnesium.

Bringing It Home

Acorn squash are relatively small. One squash is often just large enough to provide two servings. Their skin is dark green, though it often has some yellow-orange areas. A fully ripe acorn squash should feel hard, solid, and heavy, with no breaks or soft spots in the shell. A squash that is shiny may have been picked early or it may be waxed. If you are not sure which, you will want to ask. Squash that are picked early lack the sweetness of fully ripened ones. Stored in a cool, dark, dry environment (including the refrigerator, although sometimes the refrigerator is too damp for extended storage), acorn squash can keep for two months or more. Discard them if they get soft spots or develop mold, and keep them from freezing.

Be careful when cutting acorn squash. The pointed shape, hard rind, and small size can make them dangerous. Break or cut away the stem and set them stem-side down on your cutting board (that's the closest they come to having a "flat" side). Then cut carefully from the pointed tip down. It may help to lightly steam an acorn squash to help soften it before cutting.

Livit Recipes

Acorn Squash with Tempeh Stuffing

2 medium acorn squash	8 ounces plain soybean tempeh,
½ cup pine nuts	coarsely crumbled
1 tablespoon canola oil	¼ cup agave syrup
½ sweet onion, diced	¼ cup maple syrup
1 carrot, diced	1 teaspoon olive oil
1 to 2 stalks celery, diced	Minced parsley, as garnish

- Preheat oven to 400°F.
- Line a 9″ × 12″ baking sheet with parchment paper.
- Cut the acorn squash in half lengthwise; scoop out the seeds and pulp. Slice just enough off the rounded side of the squash halves that they will rest on the baking sheet without rocking. Set the squash halves, cut side up, on the baking sheet. Cover with aluminum foil and bake for 15 minutes. Remove from the oven, uncover, and set aside.
- Toast the pine nuts in a small skillet, shaking it constantly, until they are lightly browned. Watch them carefully, because they can go from raw to burnt very quickly. Once they are toasted, transfer the pine nuts to a small dish so that they don't continue to cook.
- Oil a large skillet with canola oil. Add onion, and heat over medium heat until the onion begins to soften, about 2 minutes. Add the carrot and celery and sauté another 2

minutes. Reduce heat to low, and stir in pine nuts and tempeh. Cook, stirring constantly, for another 5 to 7 minutes, and remove from heat.

- Fill the center of each squash half with tempeh filling.
- In a small bowl, whisk together the agave syrup, maple syrup, and oil. Drizzle about half of this mixture over the squash and filling.
- Cover the pan with foil again, and bake for 15 minutes. Remove the foil, drizzle with the rest of the syrup mixture, and bake for another 20 to 25 minutes, until the flesh of the squash is tender and the filling is browned.
- Garnish with parsley. Serve.

YIELD 4 servings

NUTRITION ANALYSIS PER SERVING 452 calories, 62.6 g carbohydrate, 12.3 g protein, 21.1 g fat, 4.9 g dietary fiber

Acorn Squash Bisque

1 large acorn squash (about 2 pounds)
Cooking oil spray
½ cup baby carrots
1 bunch leeks, white and light green parts only, cleaned and trimmed
1 yellow onion, quartered

1 quart low-sodium vegetable broth
1 cup nonfat Greek-style yogurt
¼ cup maple syrup
½ teaspoon cayenne pepper
½ teaspoon nutmeg
½ teaspoon cinnamon

- Preheat oven to 400°F.
- Cut the acorn squash in half lengthwise; scoop out the seeds and pulp.
- Spray a 9″ × 13″ baking dish with cooking oil spray. Arrange the squash halves, cut side down, in the pan, together with the carrots, leeks, and onion. Add water to a depth of about 1 inch.
- Bake the vegetables for about 30 minutes, or until the squash and carrots are soft enough to be pierced easily with a fork. Remove the vegetables from the oven and allow them to cool. When they are cool enough to handle, separate the flesh of the squash halves from their skin.
- In a blender, puree the squash flesh with the other vegetables until smooth. You may need to add some broth to get a smooth texture from the vegetables. Using a medium-fine strainer, strain the vegetable puree and discard the solids. This will reduce the fiber content of your soup, but it will make a more elegant dish.
- In a large saucepan or medium stockpot, combine the vegetables with the vegetable broth. Simmer over medium heat, stirring frequently, until heated through. In a small bowl, add a little of the hot soup to the yogurt, whisk until blended, and repeat until the mixture in the bowl is about half yogurt and half soup. This tempering of the yogurt will help keep it from curdling in the soup. Add the tempered yogurt to the main pot of soup, whisking until it is completely blended. Add the maple syrup and whisk again thoroughly. Add cayenne, nutmeg, and cinnamon to taste. Serve.

YIELD 8 servings

NUTRITION ANALYSIS PER SERVING 270.8 calories, 60.6 g carbohydrate, 9.2 g protein, 0.7 g fat, 7.2 g dietary fiber

42 Artichokes

Benefits

Before the health benefits of the Mediterranean diet were well-known, there was probably no single food more emblematic of Mediterranean cuisine than the globe artichoke. And indeed, artichokes contain fructans, such as inulin; cynarin, which appears to help lower cholesterol and protect liver cells; and luteolin, an antioxidant that may also be involved in healthy carbohydrate metabolism.

The edible part of the artichoke is the flower bud. The feathery part known as the "choke" is the immature flower. If it is allowed to bloom, the flower resembles a thistle, with a purple feathery top. Artichoke hearts are well worth the effort of nibbling away the leaves and peeling back the choke, for they are very rich in antioxidants. A cup of artichoke hearts has as high an Oxygen Radical Absorption Capacity (ORAC) rating as a cup of blackberries.

Artichokes are a good source of the minerals magnesium, chromium, manganese, and potassium, as well as vitamins A and C, folic acid, niacin, riboflavin, thiamine, and biotin. They also provide dietary fiber.

> **NUTRITIONAL COMPOSITION** One medium boiled artichoke provides 150 calories, 33.5 g carbohydrate, 10.4 g protein, 0.5 g fat, 16.2 g dietary fiber, 531 IU vitamin A, 30 mg vitamin C, 3 mg niacin, 153 mcg folic acid, 1062 mg potassium, 285 mg sodium, 258 mg phosphorus, 135 mg calcium, 3.87 mg iron, 180 mg magnesium, and 1.47 mg zinc.

Bringing It Home

The best artichokes are a deep green color and do not look dry. The leaves should appear tight, closely packed, and somewhat shiny.

You can keep raw artichokes in a plastic bag in the refrigerator for about five days. Cooked, they will keep for about a week. When preparing artichokes, use lemon juice or water with lemon to help keep the cut parts from turning brown.

An artichoke by itself is a balanced snack: It provides protein, fiber, and carbohydrates, and it contains 150 calories—the optimal number of calories to get the thermic effect of food that will help increase your metabolism. For a great unique snack, have a steamed artichoke with your favorite flavoring (mayo, hummus, or Italian dressing) as the fat source.

Livit Recipe

Garlichokes

4 medium artichokes OR 2 large artichokes
3 to 4 cloves garlic, minced
2 tablespoons hummus OR low-fat Italian dressing OR reduced-fat mayonnaise

- Rinse the artichokes thoroughly, opening up the leaves to make sure any dirt is cleaned out from between them.
- On a cutting board, trim the stems to ½ inch in length, and cut ½ inch to 1 inch off each artichoke bud. With kitchen scissors, snip about ¼ inch off each leaf, removing the sharp, rough tips. Force a little minced garlic under each leaf.
- Fill a large steamer pot with water just up to the steamer insert so that your artichokes don't sit in the water while cooking. Carefully set the artichokes into the steamer insert, stem side down, and cover the pot. Heat over medium heat until the water boils, reduce to a simmer, and cook the artichokes for 30 to 45 minutes, until the leaves pull off easily. Be careful not to overcook. Artichokes should not be mushy—just tender enough to bite the meat off every leaf.
- Serve with hummus, dressing, or mayonnaise for dipping.
- NOTE My favorite part is the base of the artichoke, called the "heart," hidden below the spiny "choke." Pull the choke away, and spread the heart with your dip. It's delicious— and it may be the best source of antioxidants.

YIELD 2 servings

NUTRITION ANALYSIS PER SERVING 153 calories, 30.9 g carbohydrate, 9.9 g protein, 1.8 g fat, 14.8 g dietary fiber

BEANS!

According to the Livitician, beans are the healthiest food on earth!

Low in fat, rich in fiber, and with a skin full of antioxidants, beans contribute to lowering cholesterol and reducing the risk of heart disease, type 2 diabetes, and some cancers. Beans are a great source of proteins and minerals, including the heart-healthy electrolytes calcium, magnesium, and potassium that are vital for controlling blood pressure and keeping you hydrated. They also provide folic acid and B_6, which help your heart by reducing levels of the stress hormone homocysteine.

As part of the Nurses' Health Study II, which involved more than 90,000 women, researchers found that women who ate beans and lentils at least twice a week had a 24 percent lower risk of breast cancer. And beans was the only food in the study—which also looked at blueberries, tea, and other healthy foods—that showed such a potent protective effect. Some beans, including small red beans, red beans, and pinto beans, showed antioxidant capacity as good as, or better than, some of the most powerful antioxidant fruits and vegetables, including blueberries, cranberries, and artichokes.

In one study, eating half a cup of pinto beans per day for eight weeks lowered the participants' cholesterol by 8 percent. A review of 19 years of data from the National Nutrition and Health Examination Survey found that people who eat beans four times or more per week were significantly better protected against heart disease than those who ate them once a week or less.

A study using four years of data from the same survey found that beans might also keep you thin. Adults who averaged a serving and a half of beans (three-quarters of a cup) every day ate less total and saturated fat than non-bean eaters, and were 22 percent less likely to be obese. Teenagers and adults who ate beans had waist sizes that were smaller, too—a full inch for the teens, and three-quarters of an inch for the adults. The overall diets of the bean-eaters were one-third higher in fiber, and participants who were bean-eaters weighed about seven pounds less than those who did not eat beans.

Because much of the fiber in beans is of the soluble type, it can help stabilize blood sugar and keep cholesterol from accumulating in your system. The fiber, protein, and minerals combine to give beans a low glycemic index and keep you feeling full for several hours.

With all that going for them, it appears that the main reason people don't embrace the bean more fully is … gas. There are two culprits: complex sugars called oligosaccharides and fiber. The complex sugars require digestive enzymes to break them down that humans don't have—so when those sugars get to your large intestine, microbes do the work, releasing gas. Increasing fiber, though it has many health benefits for most people, does change the speed at which foods pass through the digestive system—again meaning more sugars may arrive intact in the large intestine, where the gas-producing microbes have their way.

Many people find that the flatulence is worst when they are first introducing, or increasing, the amount of beans in their diet, and that over time their bodies adjust. Others report that eating fewer fruits or sweets with their bean meals can help. Navy and lima beans may have the worst effect, so it may help to try some of the other types of beans instead.

According to the California Dry Bean Board, a growers' industry group, you can minimize the oligosaccharides without sacrificing nutrients by using the "hot-soak" method: In a 2½-quart or larger pot, heat five cups of water. Add one cup of beans. Bring the water to a boil, and let the beans boil two to three minutes. Remove from heat, cover, and let soak for at least four hours. The longer the beans soak, the more the complex sugars are dissolved. When the beans have soaked long enough and it's time to cook them, discard the soaking water; don't use it for cooking. After the beans have been cooked, you can reduce the oligosaccharides still more by rinsing the beans.

If that's too much effort, perhaps the best advice is what your mother probably told you—chew them thoroughly, and don't swallow a lot of air when you eat.

The older a dried bean is, the more slowly it cooks—if a bean is stale enough, it may never soften up enough to eat. Try to buy dried beans in stores where they are popular and don't sit too long—health food stores and ethnic groceries may have fresher beans.

Canned beans are the ultimate healthy convenience food. To reduce the flatulence-causing capacity of canned beans, drain and rinse them before cooking.

Acidic ingredients such as vinegar, tomatoes, and lemon juice can slow down cooking times, so leave these additions for the end of the cooking process, when the beans are already tender. The use of salt with beans is controversial: The California Dry Bean Board says that adding it to the pre-soak boil can help the beans absorb the water more evenly, but many cooks maintain that salt will lengthen the cooking time, as acids do. You can preserve the maximum amount of nutrients in beans by cooking them in a pressure cooker or steaming them. Beans are done when you can crush them easily with the back of a spoon against the side of the pot. Since beans can cook unevenly, you should test more than one.

43 Black (Turtle) Beans

Benefits

Although there are several kinds of beans that are black, the black beans most widely used in American cuisine are those that are sometimes called turtle beans. Their dark color indicates a high concentration of anthocyanins, flavonoids known for their antioxidant effect. A half-cup serving of black beans has an ORAC score similar to that of plums, cranberries, grapes, and apples.

Black beans, like most other beans, are rich in fiber, protein, and minerals. They are also an especially good source of molybdenum.

NUTRITIONAL COMPOSITION One-half cup of boiled black beans provides 113.5 calories, 20.4 g carbohydrate, 7.6 g protein, 0.5 g fat, 7.5 g dietary fiber, 5 IU vitamin A, 128 mcg folic acid, 305.5 mg potassium, 1 mg sodium, 120.5 mg phosphorus, 23 mg calcium, 1.8 mg iron, 60 mg magnesium, and 0.96 mg zinc.

Bringing It Home

Dried black beans should be a rich black-brown color, with smooth skins. When buying canned black beans, seek out organics and those with the least salt. When cooking black beans, remember that steaming and pressure-cooking preserve more antioxidants than conventional boiling.

For a complete protein, balance beans with grains like brown rice, tortillas, whole grain pasta, or corn. Black beans and corn are the basis of a delicious Southwestern salad, and a black bean and rice burrito may be one of the healthiest fast foods you can find.

Livit Recipe

Quick Black Bean Soup

1 tablespoon extra-virgin olive oil	½ teaspoon ground cumin
1 large onion, diced	½ teaspoon dried oregano
3 or 4 cloves garlic, minced	2 tablespoons finely minced fresh parsley
4 cans (16 ounces each) organic black beans, rinsed and drained	Freshly ground black pepper
	1 quart water
½ lemon, juice only	2 green onions, thinly sliced, as garnish

- In a large soup pot, heat the oil over medium heat. Sauté the onion for 3 to 4 minutes, until it becomes translucent. Add garlic, and sauté onion and garlic together for another 3 to 4 minutes, until the onion is golden in color. Add the beans, lemon juice, cumin, oregano, parsley, pepper, and water to the pot. Bring the soup to a simmer. Remove about 1 cup of the soup to a small bowl. Using a potato masher or a wooden spoon, crush the beans in the bowl and return them to the pot. This will give some extra body to the soup. Cover, and let the soup simmer gently for 10 minutes.

- Top with green onions. Serve hot.

- VARIATION In addition to the onions, try topping the soup with nonfat plain Greek-style yogurt, soy yogurt, or ricotta cheese.

YIELD 8 servings

NUTRITION ANALYSIS PER SERVING 252 calories, 43.2 g carbohydrate, 15.6 g protein, 2.7 g fat, 15.3 g dietary fiber

44 Butternut Squash

Benefits

Butternut squash is another winter squash. It has a dense, smooth, orangey-colored flesh, evidence of its rich supply of carotenoids. Indeed, half a cup of baked butternut squash provides 9,368 mcg of beta-carotene. It is high in fiber; in the vitamins A, B_6, C, and folate; and in the minerals manganese, magnesium, and potassium.

Butternut squash is a package of antioxidants and anti-inflammatories—good for your heart, metabolism, and immune system. Its sweet taste and high fiber make it a filling and sustaining addition to fall and winter meals.

NUTRITIONAL COMPOSITION One-half cup of baked butternut squash provides 41 calories, 10.7 g carbohydrate, 0.9 g protein, 0.1 g fat, 2.87 g dietary fiber, 7141 IU vitamin A, 15 mg vitamin C, 1 mg niacin, 20 mcg folic acid, 290 mg potassium, 4 mg sodium, 28 mg phosphorus, 42 mg calcium, and 30 mg magnesium.

Bringing It Home

As with other winter squash, you want a butternut squash that feels heavy and hard, with a creamy skin that is not shiny and lacks soft spots or dark spots. Remember that shiny squash were picked too soon, before they ripened to full sweetness.

As a winter squash, butternut keeps exceptionally well in cool, dark, dry, well-ventilated places. The refrigerator may be too humid, which could encourage mold or rot. Once a butternut squash has been cut open, it will keep for about a week in the refrigerator if you wrap it in plastic.

Butternut squash is also available both frozen and canned, and both these forms spare you the work of cutting and peeling. Be sure to read the package and opt for plain squash, not prepared side dishes or pie filling, which come already seasoned and may have other ingredients, such as butter or condensed milk. Some groceries also sell fresh pre-peeled squash cubes—a great time-saver!

For a balanced meal, serve butternut squash as your high fiber starch, with a piece of grilled chicken or fish and some steamed broccoli or green beans.

Livit Recipe

Maple Butternut Squash

1 butternut squash (about 2 pounds)	2 teaspoons agave syrup
3 tablespoons water	1 teaspoon cinnamon
2 tablespoons maple syrup	

- Preheat oven to 350°F.
- Wash the outside of the whole squash and carefully cut it in half. Scoop out the seeds and pulp (for butternut squash, these are usually only in the globe at the base—not in the long neck), and peel it. Cut the squash flesh into 1-inch cubes.
- In a 9" × 13" glass baking dish, distribute the squash cubes evenly. Add water to the dish to provide moisture while the squash bakes.
- In a small bowl, combine the maple and agave syrups. Pour the syrup mixture over the squash cubes, and use a spatula to turn the cubes until all are well covered with syrup. Sprinkle with cinnamon.
- Cover the pan with aluminum foil and steam-bake in the oven for 30 minutes, or until the squash cubes are tender and easily pierced with a fork. Serve hot.

- VARIATION This recipe can also be made with pre-peeled, pre-cubed squash, either fresh or frozen. You will need about 1¼ pounds of squash. It should be thawed, rinsed, and drained before being put into the baking dish.

YIELD 4 servings

NUTRITION ANALYSIS PER SERVING 128 calories, 33.4 g carbohydrate, 2 g protein, 0.2 g fat, 6.7 g dietary fiber

45 Corn (Maize)

Benefits

Corn plays two important roles: It is both a grain and a vegetable. Although some heirloom species can serve as a vegetable when harvested young (at the "milk" stage) and also serve as a grain when allowed to ripen further and dried, most of the corn we eat today has been bred for one use or the other. The sweet corn we eat as a vegetable, either in kernels or on the cob, has a relatively high sugar content, which helps it retain its sweet taste even if it has to travel far from the field. This corn is a good source of B vitamins, including thiamine, pantothenic acid, and folates; vitamins A, C, and E; and the minerals magnesium and phosphorus. It is also a relatively good source of some amino acids, though it is not a complete protein.

The word "corn" originally meant any type of grain, and in England and many other parts of the world, it still does. In those settings, the word "maize" is used for what we in the United States call "corn." When English visitors first arrived in North America, they called the grain the Native Americans grew "Indian corn." In the United States, this term eventually shortened to "corn," the term in general use today. Increasingly, as people rediscover the more colorful heirloom varieties, the term "Indian corn" has been used to apply to them.

Since many of the antioxidant and anti-inflammatory phytochemicals in foods are found in their pigments (anthocyanins in blue and purple foods, lycopenes in red ones), corn's various colors provide intriguing nutritional possibilities. The common yellow corns are rich in carotenes, but red, pink, black, white, and blue corn varieties may be found to have different "secret weapons" to benefit health. Some types of corn even have different colored kernels on the same ears. Yellow sweet corn is an excellent source of lutein, a nutrient that is also found in the retina and that may play a role in reducing the risk of age-related macular degeneration.

NUTRITIONAL COMPOSITION One-half cup of cooked corn provides 89 calories, 20.6 g carbohydrate, 2.7 g protein, 1 g fat, 2.3 g dietary fiber, 178 IU vitamin A, 5 mg vitamin C, 1.3 mg niacin, 38 mcg folic acid, 204 mg potassium, 14 mg sodium, 84 mg phosphorus, 2 mg calcium, and 26 mg magnesium.

Bringing It Home

If you ever have a chance to buy sweet corn from a farmer's own stand and take it home to cook immediately, you are in for a special experience—though it may ruin you for sweet corn acquired any other way. Although modern varieties hold their sweetness far better than they used to, the sugars in corn begin turning to starch the moment it is picked. Freshest is best. So grab it when it shows up in the farmer's market, and eat it the day you bring it home.

When buying fresh sweet corn, resist the temptation to strip the husk back and look at the kernels. I know everybody else at the produce table is doing it, but 90 percent of them don't know what they've looking for anyway. So let's set the record straight: It's the rare ear that has perfect kernels all the way up to the tip anyway, and the tiny kernels on a slightly immature ear are often the sweetest of all. You can run your thumb—gently, no need to crush the kernels!—over the closed husk to feel that the ear is full and plump. Husks should be green and fresh, cool to the touch like a green leaf. Dry husks mean dry ears. That's why the strip search is such a waste—it exposes the kernels to the drying effects of air unnecessarily.

So why do people do it? At one time, you had to check that corn borer parasites hadn't gotten to your chosen ear of corn ahead of you. Modern pest control methods and produce marketing virtually assure that you'll never see an ear that's been attacked. If you're worried about the worms, check the outside of the husk for irregular, black-edged holes that make it through all the layers of husk. They may be evidence that a bug chewed its way in.

If you can't cook and eat fresh sweet corn immediately, refrigerate it, in the husks, the minute it gets home. To steam fresh sweet corn, remove the husks and silk. (Try using a dry vegetable brush to get the silk out from between the rows.) Set the corn in a steamer rack above about an inch of boiling water. Steam for six to ten minutes—it should be both tender and crisp when you eat it. The best thing about fresh sweet corn is that it really doesn't need any butter or salt. It's delicious just the way it comes out of the steamer.

Corn is also available frozen—avoid the sauced kinds and go for the plain stuff. Fresh or frozen, the more cooking the corn gets, the more of its tasty sugar gets turned to starch. Steam frozen corn above the boiling water, not in it, for about five minutes.

Livit Recipe

Veggie Blast Soup

1 bag (10 ounces) spinach leaves OR 1 pound
    fresh spinach with stems, washed and trimmed
2 large tomatoes, cut into large chunks
2 medium zucchini squash, cut into large chunks
8 ounces frozen corn kernels
1 cup fresh green beans, ends trimmed

2 large carrots, cut into large chunks
½ cup frozen peas
2 cloves garlic, minced
Salt
Pepper
Onion powder

Carbohydrates:
Starchy
Vegetables

• • • • •

75

- Arrange the spinach, tomatoes, zucchini, corn, green beans, carrots, and peas in the basket of a steamer. If you don't have a steamer large enough, use a metal colander.

- In the bottom of a large pot that can accommodate your steamer or colander, bring an inch or two of water to a boil. When the water is boiling, set your steamer basket in the pot and cover. Steam the vegetables for 10 minutes.

- Working with a batch at a time, put steamed vegetables into a blender jar and puree each batch until it is smooth. Transfer the blended vegetables to a large saucepan. Add garlic and heat through. Season with salt, pepper, and onion powder to taste.

- NOTE This soup will keep in the refrigerator for up to three days. You can freeze any leftovers.

YIELD 10 servings

NUTRITION ANALYSIS PER SERVING 67 calories, 14 g carbohydrate, 4 g protein, 1 g fat, 2.8 g dietary fiber

WHEN CORN BECOMES SUGAR

High fructose corn syrup (HFCS) is a sweetener made from corn through an enzymatic process that converts corn syrup's glucose to fructose. HFCS has taken some heat for its role in sweetening so many foods. Due to corn subsidies and sugar tariffs, it is a less expensive sweetener in the United States than sugar, and since consumers like processed foods sweet, it turns up in a surprising number of places.

According to the Economic Research Service of the United States Department of Agriculture (USDA), per capita annual American HFCS consumption has grown from zero in 1966 to a peak of nearly 64 pounds in 1999. (Consumption has been falling since that time, down to 56.2 pounds in 2007.) Because Americans have become significantly more obese over the same time period, scientists have wondered about a correlation between HFCS and obesity.

Some studies did find some suggestive data. Soft drinks sweetened with HFCS had more of some compounds thought to cause complications in persons with diabetes, such as nerve damage, and large amounts of fructose appear to increase the liver's production of triglycerides. But other research has shown no significant differences between the health effects of HFCS and those of other sweeteners.

This may be in part because the forms of HFCS that are used in foods and beverages are actually about half fructose and half glucose, very similar to the ratio in table sugar. HFCS, it turns out, is only "high fructose" when compared to regular corn syrup, which is 100% glucose. So HFCS is unlikely to have the same effects as pure fructose and is much more likely to have effects similar to those of table sugar.

It now appears that if the increased use of HFCS had any effect on weight gain among Americans, it was probably simply that as a cheaper sweetener than sugar it may have made more high-calorie foods and beverages less expensive and more easily available. Between 1980 and 2000, Americans' consumption of sweetened soft drinks rose 40 percent, to about 16 ounces per day. Since there are 150 calories in a 12-ounce can (whether sweetened with sugar or HFCS), that's enough to raise your weight 18 pounds a year.

According to the Corn Refiners Association, an industry group based in Washington, D.C., HFCS is "nutritionally the same as table sugar and has the same number of calories, too. Studies comparing high fructose corn syrup and sucrose have found no significant differences in fasting blood glucose, insulin, leptin and ghrelin. Satiety studies of the two sweeteners have found no differences in appetite, feelings of fullness or short-term energy intakes."

So the bottom line may be this: Limit your use of sweeteners and learn to love the sweetness of whole foods, fruits, and vegetables!

46 Garbanzo Beans (Chickpeas)

Benefits

Garbanzo beans are a high-protein staple in many parts of the world, as the many names for them—including chickpea, ceci bean, and bengal gram—attest.

In addition to providing almost a third of the daily recommendation for protein, a cup of chickpeas provides about a third of the fiber, too. They are a good source of the minerals phosphorus, calcium, magnesium, iron, and zinc, and one cup provides 84.5% of the daily value for the trace mineral manganese. Garbanzos are also a significant source of folate, vital to circulatory and heart health. Garbanzo beans contain saponins, some of which may act as antioxidants.

Because they are such a good source of soluble fiber, garbanzo beans help regulate blood sugar and lower cholesterol. The fiber and protein combination means that garbanzos will keep you feeling full for a long time. They can be balanced with a whole grain to provide a more complete, high quality protein.

Although very few cases have been reported in North America, in countries where garbanzo beans form a significant part of the cuisine, such as India, allergies to them are relatively common, and the reactions can be severe or even life threatening.

Like many other dried legumes, garbanzos also are moderately high in oxalates, and people with a history of kidney stones or vulvar pain may wish to limit the amount of garbanzo beans they eat.

NUTRITIONAL COMPOSITION One-half cup of cooked garbanzo beans provides 134.5 calories, 22.5 g carbohydrate, 7.3 g protein, 2.1 g fat, 6.3 g dietary fiber, 22 IU vitamin A, 1 mg vitamin C, 141 mcg folic acid, 238.5 mg potassium, 5.5 mg sodium, 138 mg phosphorus, 40 mg calcium, 2.37 mg iron, 39.5 mg magnesium, 1.25 mg zinc, and 0.84 mg manganese.

Bringing It Home

Although studies have shown that dried foods can be stored for as long as 30 years if kept in an airtight container away from heat and light, dry legumes lose moisture over time and may require a very long cooking time after just a few years in normal storage conditions. Likewise, although canned foods as old as 100 years have been tested and found edible, it is recommended to keep canned garbanzos for no more than two years. They are too delicious not to use anyway! Cooked garbanzo beans can be kept in the refrigerator for three or four days, but the same nutrient banquet that makes them so good for us is also a tempting medium for microbes, so keep them covered and reheat them thoroughly.

Livit Recipe

Lean Hummus Spread

    1 can (15 ounces) garbanzo beans, drained and rinsed (reserve liquid)
    1 tablespoon tahini OR low-fat peanut butter OR yogurt
    1 or 2 cloves garlic, crushed
    1 fresh lemon, juice only
    ½ cup nonfat plain yogurt OR Greek-style yogurt
    1 teaspoon salt
    1 teaspoon ground cumin

· In a food processor or blender jar, combine the beans, tahini, garlic, lemon juice, and yogurt. Blend well. Add the salt and cumin, and blend again. If you want a thinner hummus, add a little of the liquid from the chickpeas, a teaspoon at a time, until it is the consistency you want.

· VARIATION The hummus can also be thinned with warm water or olive oil.

YIELD 2 cups

NUTRITION ANALYSIS PER SERVING 4.7 calories, 7.7 g carbohydrate, 2.3 g protein, 0.8 g fat, 1.4 g dietary fiber

47 Green Peas

Benefits

Peas are another food that is available in two forms—fresh or frozen, and dried. Fresh or frozen green peas are a great source of vitamin C and thiamine, as well as a good source of vitamin B_6, niacin, and folate. They are also a good source of the minerals iron, zinc, and phosphorus, and provide a reasonable amount of both protein and fiber. Green peas are also a very good source of lutein, which may help preserve eyesight and prevent the thickening of arterial walls. Combined with the B vitamins and fiber, this makes peas a good choice for keeping the heart and circulatory system healthy.

Another type of fresh pea has edible pods—snow peas and sugar snap peas. These have much the same nutrient profile as green peas, with the pods providing somewhat more vitamin C and potassium.

Dried peas become an even more important source of protein, while keeping much of their iron and folate value. A cup of dried split peas has more than 48 grams of protein and 50 grams of dietary fiber, but it will have lost its lutein and most of its vitamin C.

> **NUTRITIONAL COMPOSITION** One-half cup of cooked frozen peas provides 62 calories, 11.4 g carbohydrate, 4.1 g protein, 0.2 g fat, 4.4 g dietary fiber, 534 IU vitamin A, 8 mg vitamin C, 1.2 mg niacin, 47 mcg folic acid, 134 mg potassium, 70 mg sodium, 72 mg phosphorus, 19 mg calcium, 1.26 mg iron, and 23 mg magnesium.

Bringing It Home

Fresh green peas are another treat that should really be experienced straight from the garden—fresh-picked peas can be shelled straight into your mouth for a sweet treat. Get them at the farmer's market when you can, and use them within a day or two of purchase. Like corn, the sweetness in fresh peas begins turning to starch immediately after picking. Keep them in the refrigerator and shell them just before cooking. Snow peas and sugar snap peas don't need to be shelled, but the fibrous strings that run down each side of the pods should be removed. Snap the stem and use it to pull the strings off the pod.

Fresh green peas and edible-pod peas should be bright green and crisp, not rubbery or dry. Because peas have a short growing season, frozen ones are often your main choice. You can get both garden peas and edible-pod versions frozen.

Fresh or frozen, peas should be steamed for as short a time as possible—two to five minutes will do the job. Store fresh peas in the refrigerator and eat them within two days of purchase. Peas are a great—and fast—high-fiber carbohydrate to serve instead of rice, pasta, or bread.

Green Peas with Zest

1 pound frozen peas (about 3 cups)
2 tablespoons red wine vinegar
1 small shallot, diced (about 1 tablespoon)
1 teaspoon kosher salt
½ teaspoon black pepper, freshly ground

1 tablespoon extra-virgin olive oil
2 teaspoons finely minced fresh mint leaves
2 teaspoons finely minced fresh parsley
4 ounces Swiss cheese OR fresh mozzarella
   cheese, cut into ¼-inch cubes

- Prepare a large bowl of ice water for blanching the peas.

- In a steamer, steam the frozen peas for about 5 minutes, just until the iciness is gone. Remove from heat, drain, and plunge the peas into the ice water to stop the cooking process. (This technique is called blanching.) Drain the peas and set them aside.

- In a medium mixing bowl, whisk together the vinegar, shallots, salt, and pepper. While continuing to whisk the ingredients, slowly drizzle in the olive oil until the dressing is emulsified. Add the peas, mint, parsley, and cheese to the dressing in the bowl. Toss gently to distribute the ingredients evenly.

- Cover and refrigerate for 15 to 20 minutes to allow the flavors to blend before serving.

YIELD 6 servings

NUTRITION ANALYSIS PER SERVING 138 calories, 11.4 g carbohydrate, 9.2 g protein, 6.5 g fat, 3 g dietary fiber

Carbohydrates:
Starchy
Vegetables
· · · · ·

79

48 Kidney Beans

Benefits

Although long prized for their high protein and fiber content, kidney beans have gained new respect due to their high antioxidant content. In a study by the USDA, kidney beans showed nearly as much antioxidant capacity as wild blueberries.

Kidney beans are also a good source of folate, magnesium, iron, zinc, and molybdenum. Because they are high in fiber and protein, they help to stabilize blood sugar. Their panel of minerals, combined with the fiber, benefits the heart and circulation. And the potential value of antioxidants in preventing all kinds of age-related diseases, from heart disease to Alzheimer's, gives these beans a place on any list of SuperFoods.

NUTRITIONAL COMPOSITION One-half cup of cooked kidney beans provides 112.5 calories, 20.2 g carbohydrate, 7.7 g protein, 0.45 g fat, 6.5 g dietary fiber, 114.5 mcg folic acid, 356.5 mg potassium, 2 mg sodium, 125.5 mg phosphorus, 25 mg calcium, 2.6 mg iron, 40 mg magnesium, 0.95 mg zinc, and 0.42 mg manganese.

Bringing It Home

Kidney beans are available both dried and canned, and they have a shelf life of about two years in either form. To make your own convenience food, cook them and freeze them in single portions: Remove as much moisture as you can, and be sure to use airtight containers—plastic zipper bags are ideal. Balance the beans with a grain for a complete protein. Add cooked kidney beans to a salad with a whole wheat roll on the side, and you have a balanced, lean, vegetarian meal.

Livit Recipe

Frijoles Fiesta

½ cup brown rice	¼ teaspoon salt
1½ cups water	1 can (15 ounces) red kidney beans,
Canola oil	rinsed and drained
1 medium onion, diced	1 cup (4 ounces) shredded cheddar cheese
2 cloves garlic, minced	¾ cup nonfat milk
1 to 2 teaspoons chili powder	2 eggs, lightly beaten
1 teaspoon ground cumin	1 tablespoon non-hydrogenated margarine

- To prepare the rice, bring the water to a boil in a heavy saucepan. Once the water is boiling, add the rice. Bring the water back to a boil, stir, and reduce heat to a simmer. Cover, and cook for 45 minutes. While the rice is cooking, prepare the other ingredients.

- Preheat oven to 350°F.

- Oil the bottom of a 3-quart saucepan lightly with canola oil, spreading it with a paper towel. Heat the oiled saucepan over medium heat. When the pan is hot, add onion and garlic and sauté them together, stirring often, for about 2 minutes, or until the onion is translucent and the garlic is tender but not brown. Stir in the chili powder, cumin, and salt, and let them cook for about 1 minute with the onion and garlic. Add the beans, cooked rice, cheese, milk, and eggs.

- Lightly grease a 9″ × 9″ baking pan with margarine. Pour the bean and rice mixture into the baking pan, spreading it into an even layer. Bake, uncovered, for about 25 minutes, or until the center is firm. Remove from oven and let stand for 10 minutes before serving.

- NOTE Serve with low-sodium fresh salsa and a mixed green salad for a complete balanced meal.

YIELD 6 servings

NUTRITION ANALYSIS PER SERVING 237 calories, 22 g carbohydrate, 13 g protein, 11 g fat, 4.9 g dietary fiber

49 Lentils

Benefits

Lentils are among the legumes that are highest in protein, though they are low in two essential amino acids and need to be balanced by grains to provide complete protein. They look like split peas—the result of growing two in a pod, pre-split by nature.

In addition to providing protein and fiber, lentils are a good source of thiamine and other B vitamins, potassium, and iron. Because much of their fiber is soluble, they are helpful in stabilizing blood sugar and in lowering cholesterol.

NUTRITIONAL COMPOSITION One-half cup of cooked lentils provides 115 calories, 20 g carbohydrate, 9 g protein, 0.4 g fat, 7.8 g dietary fiber, 8 IU vitamin A, 1.5 mg vitamin C, 1 mg niacin, 0.63 mg pantothenic acid, 179 mcg folic acid, 365.5 mg potassium, 2 mg sodium, 178 mg phosphorus, 19 mg calcium, 3.3 mg iron, 35.5 mg magnesium, 1.25 mg zinc, and 0.49 mg manganese.

Bringing It Home

Lentils are available in brown, red, yellow, green, and black varieties. One of their great advantages over other dried legumes is that they do not need to be soaked, and they will cook in an hour or less, depending on the type. That's practically instant for a legume! Dried lentils will keep for about a year.

Livit Recipe

Soothing Lentil Soup

1 tablespoon canola oil	1½ cups dried lentils, rinsed and picked over
2 large onions, chopped	¼ to ½ teaspoon ground black pepper
3 carrots, peeled and coarsely grated	¾ cup (6 ounces) dry white wine
¾ teaspoon chopped fresh marjoram	⅓ cup finely minced fresh parsley OR
¾ teaspoon chopped fresh thyme leaves	2 tablespoons dried parsley flakes
1 can (28 ounces) diced tomatoes, with juice	4 ounces part-skim organic cheddar cheese, grated
7 cups low-sodium vegetable broth	

- Heat oil in a large soup pot. Add onions and carrots, then sprinkle marjoram and thyme over them. Sauté, stirring, for about 5 minutes. Add tomatoes, broth, and lentils, and bring to a boil. Reduce heat, cover, and let the soup simmer for about an hour, until the lentils become tender.

- Add the pepper, wine, and parsley, and allow to simmer for a few more minutes so the flavors can blend. Garnish with grated cheese. Serve.

YIELD 8 servings

NUTRITION ANALYSIS PER SERVING 168 calories, 17 g carbohydrate, 9 g protein, 5 g fat, 5.6 g dietary fiber

50 Lima Beans (Butter Beans)

Benefits

Lima beans, a great source of fiber and protein, are another legume that is eaten in both fresh and dried forms. A cup of cooked fresh lima beans provides 11.6 grams of protein and 9 grams of fiber, while a cup of cooked dried limas provides 14.7 grams of protein and 13.2 grams of fiber.

Lima beans are a good source of several minerals, including copper, iron, magnesium, manganese, molybdenum, phosphorus, and potassium, as well as the B vitamins folate and thiamine. Fresh limas also provide some vitamin A, vitamin C, and beta-carotene.

The magnesium and potassium help regulate blood pressure. Along with the folate and fiber, these beans are good for your heart.

One caution: Raw lima beans contain linamarin, a compound that can break down into the poison hydrogen cyanide in the human digestive tract. Cooking lima beans neutralizes the risk, and the varieties used for food are generally low in the substance. Linamarin may also contribute to glucose intolerance and diabetes, but studies have not been definitive.

Lima beans also contain protease inhibitors, which frustrate the development of cancerous cells.

> **NUTRITIONAL COMPOSITION** One-half cup of cooked lima beans provides 108 calories, 19.7 g carbohydrate, 7.4 g protein, 0.35 g fat, 6.6 g dietary fiber, 78 mcg folic acid, 477.5 mg potassium, 2 mg sodium, 104.5 mg phosphorus, 16 mg calcium, 2.2 mg iron, 40.5 mg magnesium, 0.9 mg zinc, and 0.22 mg copper.

Bringing It Home

Fresh lima beans come in pods, like peas. They have a limited season and may be hard to find, but frozen limas are widely available year-round. When you're buying them fresh, try to get them as close to the field as you can, and look for signs of freshness—good dark color, plump pods, and no sense of dryness. Keep them in the refrigerator until ready to cook, and cook them the day you get them for best flavor. Fresh lima beans are a lovely celadon green inside a shiny dark-green pod— a work of art all by themselves.

With frozen beans, you're more at the mercy of the packager, but since the beans are often frozen very close to the time of picking, frozen beans may in fact be the fresher choice.

Dried lima beans are somewhat more fragile than other dried legumes. Even so, they should keep for about six months in an airtight container that's kept away from heat and light.

Eat your limas once they're cooked! They do not last well, even when they're refrigerated.

Livit Recipe

Lima Bean Succotash

 2 tablespoons extra-virgin olive oil
 2 medium onions, diced
   Coarse kosher salt
 1 large clove garlic, minced
 1½ pounds tomatoes, coarsely chopped
 4 ears corn, 2 white and 2 yellow, kernels only (about 2 cups) OR 2¼ cups frozen corn kernels
 2 pounds fresh lima beans, shelled OR 10 ounces frozen lima beans
   Salt and pepper
 4 or 5 fresh basil leaves, sliced into thin strips

· In a large, heavy skillet, heat olive oil over medium heat. Add the onion to the oil and sprinkle it lightly with salt. Sauté the onion for about 5 minutes, until it is soft and translucent. Add the garlic and sauté it with the onion, stirring gently, until it is fragrant (about another minute).

· Add tomatoes, corn, and lima beans. Reduce heat to medium-low, cover, and allow the vegetables to simmer for about 20 minutes, stirring occasionally, until the corn and lima beans are tender and the tomatoes are soft. Season to taste with salt and pepper. Stir in the basil strips just before serving.

YIELD 6 servings

NUTRITION ANALYSIS PER SERVING 185 calories, 30.3 g carbohydrate, 6.8 g protein, 5.8 g fat, 6.7 g dietary fiber

51 Navy Beans

Benefits

Navy beans, also known as small white beans and pea beans, are among the most versatile beans to cook with. High in protein, they are also very high in fiber—even among the dried legumes. A cup of cooked navy beans provides 19 grams of dietary fiber! Navy beans are a very good source of folate and manganese and a good source of thiamine, as well as the minerals phosphorus, copper, magnesium, and iron.

NUTRITIONAL COMPOSITION One-half cup of cooked navy beans provides 129 calories, 24 g carbohydrate, 7.9 g protein, 0.5 g fat, 5.8 g dietary fiber, 2 IU vitamin A, 1 mg vitamin C, 127.5 mcg folic acid, 335 mg potassium, 1 mg sodium, 143 mg phosphorus, 63.5 mg calcium, 2.25 mg iron, 53.5 mg magnesium, 0.96 mg zinc, and 0.51 mg manganese.

Bringing It Home

Dried navy beans are small, white, oval beans. Keep them well sealed in a cool, dry, dark environment, and they will keep for a very long time, though after about two years they may take a very long time to cook. Fortunately, they are also available canned and ready to use. Navy beans can be used in almost any recipe that calls for a dried bean. Their flavor and texture blend well with many other ingredients. Navy beans play the starring role in many classic soups, and they are a delicious carbohydrate with protein to balance steamed vegetables and salads.

Livit Recipe

Greens with Navy Beans

    2 quarts low-sodium vegetable broth
    2 pounds dandelion greens, washed and trimmed
    1 medium onion, peeled and trimmed
    2 cloves garlic, minced
    3 sun-dried tomatoes, sliced into fine shreds
    1 can (15 ounces) navy beans, rinsed and drained

- In a 6-quart stockpot, bring the broth to boil. Add the greens and whole onion to the pot. Simmer the greens and onion in the broth, uncovered, until the greens are tender. (This takes about 10 to 15 minutes for dandelion greens; if you substitute other greens, the time may vary.) Drain the greens and set them aside. Discard the onion. Once the greens are cool enough to handle, chop them coarsely.

- In a large serving bowl, toss the greens with the garlic, tomatoes, and beans. Serve.

- NOTE If you use a spaghetti cooker with a colander insert, you can lift out the colander when the greens are cooked and then save the broth to use as the base of your next soup—full of yummy green flavor!

- VARIATION You can substitute kale, Swiss chard, turnip greens, mustard greens, or any other strong-flavored fresh, dark, leafy green.

YIELD 6 servings

NUTRITION ANALYSIS PER SERVING 139 calories, 25.5 g carbohydrate, 8.8 g protein, 0.8 g fat, 11.2 g dietary fiber

52 Pinto Beans

Benefits

Pinto beans are another healthy standby whose antioxidant power has only recently come to be appreciated. According to the United States Department of Agriculture, pinto beans have more antioxidant power than domestic blueberries.

Of course, they're also a great source of fiber, carbohydrate, protein, and minerals, including potassium, magnesium, and molybdenum, as well as folate. All this makes them particularly good at lowering the risk of some common chronic diseases, particularly heart disease and diabetes. Their soluble fiber lowers cholesterol; the folate helps reduce the risk of heart attack; and magnesium and potassium help regulate blood pressure. Molybdenum helps break down sulfites and may assist in antioxidant activities.

Like other beans, pinto beans combine with whole grains to provide complete protein, and their high fiber and protein content mean that their carbohydrate content is released relatively slowly into the bloodstream, which gives them a low glycemic index.

NUTRITIONAL COMPOSITION One-half cup of cooked pinto beans provides 126 calories, 22 g carbohydrate, 7 g protein, 0.9 g fat, 7.4 g dietary fiber, 1.5 IU vitamin A, 2 mg vitamin C, 147 mcg folic acid, 137 mg phosphorus, 41 mg calcium, 2.2 mg iron, 47 mg magnesium, and 0.93 mg zinc.

Bringing It Home

Pinto beans are the beans of American Southwestern cooking—the classic cowboy bean as well as the most common refrito. In many regions, pintos are the primary bean used for chili; elsewhere, they get competition from kidney beans. In the recipe below, the two work well together. Although they are speckled (the name "pinto" means "painted") when raw, when cooked they become a delicate pink color.

Livit Recipe

Vegetarian Chili

There's no need to stress over the long ingredient list. Most ingredients are seasonings—it isn't chili without the spice! See Handling Jalapeños! on page 86.

1¼ cups brown rice	Pinch of ground cloves
3¾ cups water	Pinch of ground allspice
1 tablespoon organic canola oil	2 teaspoons dried oregano
2 medium onions, chopped	2 tablespoons chili powder
3 large cloves garlic, minced	2 tablespoons ground cumin
1 green bell pepper, seeded and chopped	2 tablespoons brown sugar
1 fresh jalapeño pepper, seeded and minced	1 can (15 ounces) kidney beans,
1 can (28 ounces) chopped tomatoes, drained	rinsed and drained
1 can (15 ounces) tomato sauce	1 can (15 ounces) pinto beans,
½ teaspoon ground coriander	rinsed and drained

· To prepare the rice, bring the water to a boil in a heavy saucepan. Once the water is boiling, add the rice. Bring the water back to a boil, stir, and reduce heat to a simmer. Cover, and cook for 45 minutes. While the rice is cooking, prepare the other ingredients.

- Heat the canola oil in a large stock pot. Add the onions, garlic, green pepper, and jalapeño pepper, and sauté them over medium heat until they are tender, about 3 minutes. Add the tomatoes and tomato sauce, coriander, cloves, allspice, oregano, chili powder, cumin, brown sugar, and beans. Bring to a boil. Reduce heat, cover, and allow the chili to simmer for 30 minutes.
- Serve the chili over prepared brown rice.

YIELD 8 servings

NUTRITION ANALYSIS PER SERVING 251 calories, 48 g carbohydrate, 10 g protein, 4 g fat, 11.7 g dietary fiber

HANDLING JALAPEÑOS!

The kick in jalapeño peppers comes from capsaicin, an acidic compound that's strong enough to burn your skin. Always wear protective gloves when handling any cut jalapeño peppers. The best choice is disposable gloves, and if you are sensitive to latex, use latex-free ones. Keep your hands away from your eyes! And if you do get jalapeño juice on your skin, try neutralizing it with a gentle base. Many people swear by milk to soothe the burn.

The inner ribs and the seeds close to them have the most concentrated heat—if you want a less fiery taste, use less of the inner, more of the outer, pepper.

53 Potatoes

Benefits

The potato is an incredibly healthy food that has gotten a bad reputation, largely because it can be prepared in ways that counteract its benefits. Baked and served in its skin, a potato is a surprisingly good source of vitamin C, as well as potassium, fiber, vitamin B_6 and other B vitamins, copper, manganese, and even some lutein.

The key to getting the benefits of potatoes is to eat them baked rather than fried. But if you are absolutely having a French fry craving, go ahead and LIVIT—enjoy a few to satisfy the craving and to help prevent overloading on them when the craving gets out of control.

NUTRITIONAL COMPOSITION One medium-large potato with skin provides 220 calories, 51 g carbohydrate, 4.6 g protein, 4.8 g dietary fiber, 26 mg vitamin C, 3.3 mg niacin, 22 mcg folic acid, 1.12 mg pantothenic acid, 844 mg potassium, 16 mg sodium, 115 mg phosphorus, 20 mg calcium, 2.75 mg iron, and 55 mg magnesium.

Bringing It Home

Potatoes should be smooth and firm, without cut surfaces, soft spots, signs of mold, green areas, or sprouted eyes. If you will be baking more than one potato at a time, select potatoes that are about the same size and shape so that they will cook in the same amount of time.

Keep potatoes away from light, heat, and dampness. A closet or even a drawer works well. Kept cool (around 45°F to 50°F) and dark, potatoes will keep for several weeks, but at room temperature, they may last only a week. Light can cause them to sprout. Store potatoes separate from onions, because the two vegetables give off gases that can negatively affect each other's storage life. Don't refrigerate potatoes, as this changes the taste and may make them turn black when cooked.

Livit Recipe

Livitician's Best Baked Potato

2 medium baking potatoes, such as a russet, scrubbed and with the ends cut off
3 tablespoons water

Fresh salsa
Chives

- Preheat oven to 350°F.
- Put the potatoes into a glass baking dish, and add the water to maintain moisture. Bake for about 45 minutes, or until the potato is easily pierced with a fork.
- Serve potatoes in the skin, topping with salsa and chives for flavor. The salsa moistens the potato well and gives each bite some kick.
- NOTE Potatoes don't need the fats they're usually served with to be delicious!

YIELD 2 servings

NUTRITION ANALYSIS PER SERVING 168 calories, 37.1 g carbohydrate, 4.6 g protein, 0.2 g fat, 4 g dietary fiber

54 Pumpkin

Benefits

Pumpkins are closely related to squash and, like squash, have lots of alpha- and beta-carotenes and vitamin A, as evidenced by their rich orange color. Pumpkin also provides many of the B vitamins, including folate; some vitamin C; and the electrolyte minerals calcium, magnesium, and potassium. One cup of cooked mashed pumpkin also contains 2,484 mg of lutein. High in fiber, pumpkin is also somewhat sweeter than many other squashes, which allows it to be used in both sweet and savory dishes.

NUTRITIONAL COMPOSITION One cup of boiled, drained, and mashed pumpkin provides 49 calories, 12 g carbohydrate, 1.8 g protein, 0 g fat, 2.7 g dietary fiber, 12230 IU vitamin A, 11.5 mg vitamin C, 1 mg niacin, 22 mcg folic acid, 0.5 mg pantothenic acid, 564 mg potassium, 2 mg sodium, 74 mg phosphorus, 37 mg calcium, 1.4 mg iron, and 22 mg magnesium.

Bringing It Home

The pumpkins that are best to eat are usually not the same as the ones that make the best Halloween jack o' lanterns. The flesh of the smaller, sweeter pumpkins tends to be less stringy and more flavorful. Cooking pumpkins are often flatter in shape, and many have the word "sugar" in their names. They should still have a bright, rich orange color, and they should look plump and smooth, with no soft spots or signs of dryness. A four-pound pumpkin will yield about two pounds of edible flesh. If you are cooking the flesh as a vegetable or for pie filling, peel the pumpkin while it is whole, and then cut it into chunks. To preserve both nutrients and flavor, steam pumpkin rather than boiling it. It is also fun to use the whole pumpkin shell: You can bake it with a stuffing or use it to serve a soup.

For a quicker alternative, and when pumpkins are out of season, buy canned or frozen pumpkin chunks or puree. If buying canned, make sure to get plain pumpkin, not prepared pie filling.

Livit Recipe

Pumpkin Surprise Pie

1 package (10.5 ounces) organic silken tofu, packed in water, drained and rinsed
1 can (15 ounces) pureed pumpkin
¾ cup sugar
¼ teaspoon salt
1 teaspoon ground cinnamon
½ teaspoon ground ginger
¼ teaspoon ground cloves
1 9-inch pie shell, unbaked

- Preheat oven to 425°F.
- In a blender jar, puree the tofu until smooth. Pour it into a small bowl and set it aside.
- Put the pumpkin and sugar into the blender jar and blend them together. Add the salt, cinnamon, ginger, cloves, and the blended tofu to the pumpkin mixture. Process until all ingredients are thoroughly mixed and smooth. Pour the mixture into the pie shell.
- Bake for 15 minutes at 425°F. Reduce oven temperature to 350°F and bake the pie for an additional 40 minutes.
- Chill before serving.

YIELD 8 servings

NUTRITION ANALYSIS PER SERVING 219 calories, 32.9 g carbohydrate, 3.2 g protein, 6.4 g fat, 2.1 g dietary fiber

55 Quinoa

Benefits

Although quinoa may be unfamiliar to North Americans, it was a staple food for the Incas and has been grown in the Andes for more than 5,000 years. Technically a "pseudocereal," quinoa is often considered a grain, even though it is not a grass. It is more closely related to beets and spinach. Unlike wheat and other grains, it is gluten-free, but it can be substituted for grain in most recipes. Although primarily a carbohydrate, quinoa is relatively high in protein—one cup of cooked quinoa contains about 8 grams of protein—and it contains all of the essential amino acids. A good source of magnesium, manganese, and calcium, quinoa also provides vitamin B_2, vitamin E, iron, phosphorus, copper, and zinc. It is higher in fat than many true grains.

Quinoa is a source of oxalates, which may cause problems for those with a history of kidney stones or other conditions that require a low-oxalate diet.

The outside of raw quinoa is covered with saponins, which were traditionally used as a diuretic and laxative. If you don't want these effects, be sure to rinse your quinoa before cooking it.

> **NUTRITIONAL COMPOSITION** One cup of cooked quinoa provides 222 calories, 39.4 g carbohydrate, 8.1 g protein, 3.6 g fat, 5.2 g dietary fiber, 1 mg sodium, 281 mg phosphorus, 2.76 mg iron, and 0.2 mg riboflavin.

Bringing It Home

Quinoa is increasingly available packaged or as a bulk food. Be sure to buy seeds that are dry and free from moisture or discoloration. Because of its relatively high fat content, it keeps best in the refrigerator in an airtight container.

Since quinoa does act like a grain in many recipes, you may also be able to find quinoa pasta, quinoa breakfast cereal, and quinoa flour. Use these like their more familiar counterparts, but note that since quinoa lacks gluten, baked goods made with 100% quinoa flour will not rise properly. Use a mixture of half quinoa flour and half wheat flour for best results.

To remove the saponins on the outside of quinoa seeds, wash them in a strainer, making sure to rub the seeds against each other and circulate the water through them. When a test seed no longer tastes bitter, the saponins have been washed away.

Quinoa is a quick-cooking grain—it takes only about 15 minutes to prepare by boiling. Use one cup of seeds to two cups of water, bring to a boil, then reduce heat and simmer until the quinoa is fluffy, like rice. Quinoa more than doubles in volume during cooking.

Livit Recipe

Scarlet Quinoa

1½ cups quinoa seeds, washed and drained
2¼ cups water
　Pinch of salt
1 cup grated raw beets
½ cup finely minced fresh parsley
½ cup thinly sliced scallions

2½ tablespoons extra-virgin olive oil
2 or 3 lemons, juice only (about ½ cup)
3 cups baby salad greens
1 medium carrot, peeled and cut into
　fine ribbons

- In a large saucepan, combine the quinoa, water, and salt. Bring to a boil, then reduce heat and let it simmer until fluffy, about 15 minutes. Remove quinoa from heat, fluff the grains with a fork, and stir in the grated beets. When all the grains have turned scarlet, add the parsley, scallions, olive oil, and lemon juice. Gently toss ingredients until thoroughly combined.

- Prepare a bed of baby greens and carrot ribbons on either a serving platter or individual plates. Spoon quinoa mixture on top of the greens. Serve.

- NOTE The quinoa mixture can be served warm, at room temperature, or chilled.

- VARIATION Although making this dish with raw grated beets retains their maximum nutrition, if you prefer your beets cooked, steam whole beets in their skins for 45 minutes to an hour, until they can be pierced easily with a fork. Remove the skins before grating the beets.

YIELD 6 servings

NUTRITION ANALYSIS PER SERVING 242 calories, 58.1 g carbohydrate, 11.1 g protein, 10.6 g fat, 6.5 g dietary fiber

56 Red Beans (Small Red Beans)

Benefits

Small red beans have never been as well-known as their larger and meatier cousin, the red kidney bean. But they stepped into the spotlight in 2007 when the USDA discovered that small red beans had the highest antioxidant activity of all the foods tested.

Because many antioxidants are contained in plant pigments, it stands to reason that these small, dark-red beans would be a rich source of them. But scientists were surprised when these beans stole the show—small red beans showed higher antioxidant activity than wild blueberries.

Research at Colorado State University confirms that the phenol and anthocyanins that give bean coats their color have antioxidant properties and posits that there is a link between a darker seed coat and higher phenol levels.

Beans have long been known for their fiber, protein, and minerals, as well as their antioxidant properties. Small red beans are also a good source of phosphorus, magnesium, zinc, and B vitamins.

NUTRITIONAL COMPOSITION One-half cup of canned small red beans provides 100 calories, 17 g carbohydrate, 6 g protein, 0.5 g fat, 5 g dietary fiber, 39 mg calcium, and 65 mg sodium.

Bringing It Home

Small red beans are also known as Mexican red beans and, as half of the classic combo of Louisiana red beans and rice, they are sometimes called Louisiana red beans. Although they resemble kidney beans, they are smaller and darker in color. Either kidney beans or pinto beans can be substituted for them, and both were found to have nearly as powerful antioxidant effects. New Orleans cooks, however, say that the larger, meatier kidney bean does not provide the right taste.

Since the discovery of their antioxidant prowess, small red beans have become somewhat easier to find, and canned versions are no longer hard to come by.

Don't confuse these small red beans with red azuki beans popular in Asia, which have a different taste and nutrition profile.

Livit Recipe

Cajun Red Beans and Rice

1 cup brown rice	1 cup sliced celery
3 cups water	1 can (15 ounces) small red beans,
Vegetable oil spray	rinsed and drained
1 large onion, chopped	1 cup low-sodium spaghetti sauce
2 cloves garlic, minced	¾ teaspoon hot pepper sauce
1 medium green bell pepper, chopped	1 teaspoon dried thyme

- In a rice cooker or 1-quart saucepan, bring the rice and water to a boil. Reduce heat and simmer, covered, for 45 minutes.
- Lightly spray a 10-inch skillet with vegetable oil. Add onion and garlic to the skillet and cook them over medium-high heat, stirring frequently, for 3 minutes or until tender. Add green pepper, celery, beans, spaghetti sauce, hot pepper sauce, and thyme. Reduce heat and simmer, uncovered, for 15 minutes or until vegetables are crisp-tender, stirring occasionally.
- Serve over hot rice.

YIELD 4 servings

NUTRITION ANALYSIS PER SERVING 320 calories, 64.6 g carbohydrate, 12.3 g protein, 3.2 g fat, 12.3 g dietary fiber

THE DIFFERENCE BETWEEN SWEET POTATOES AND YAMS

Both sweet potatoes and yams are starchy tubers used for food. Both come in a variety of colors and are grown around the world. Yet they are not closely related, and they are most certainly not the same food.

According to the Science Reference Service of the United States Library of Congress, the confusion began because there are two types of sweet potatoes—soft and firm. Although both kinds were grown in the United States, when the softer ones were put into widespread commercial production, marketers borrowed the word "yam" to differentiate them from the firm varieties. African slaves had already been calling the soft sweet potatoes "yams" because they resembled the yams in Africa, so the name stuck.

Most often, it's the reddish-orange varieties of sweet potatoes that are mistakenly called "yams" today. These are the ones with vivid orange, sweet flesh, and a moist texture when cooked. The other common variety of sweet potato in the United States has a light yellow skin with pale yellow flesh; it has a dry, crumbly texture when cooked, more like a white baking potato, and is rarely referred to as a yam.

The true yam is less widely available in the United States. Older cookbooks still say that unless you have traveled out of the country, you have probably never seen a true yam, and while this is no longer true, yams usually must be sought in specialty and ethnic groceries. In general, while both sweet potatoes and yams are good sources of fiber, minerals, and antioxidants, yams are drier and starchier and they are not as rich in vitamins A and C.

57 Sweet Potatoes

Benefits

Sweet potatoes have been cultivated for more than 5,000 years. Originally from South America, sweet potatoes are now grown all over the world. Rich in fiber, protein, vitamins A and C, and the minerals iron and calcium, sweet potatoes are also packed with carotene and anthocyanins—the powerful antioxidants.

The Center for Science in the Public Interest ranked the baked sweet potato the most nutritious of all vegetables with a score of 184. That's 100 points higher than the runner-up, the baked white potato.

NUTRITIONAL COMPOSITION One medium sweet potato baked with skin provides 117 calories, 27.7 g carbohydrate, 2 g protein, 0.1 g fat, 3.4 g dietary fiber, 24877 IU vitamin A, 28 mg vitamin C, 26 mcg folic acid, 397 mg potassium, 11 mg sodium, 63 mg phosphorus, 32 mg calcium, and 23 mg magnesium.

Bringing It Home

Sweet potatoes should be dry and firm, with no mushy spots or sprouts. Although sweet potatoes can be cooked just about any way that white potatoes can, they do not store as well as white potatoes. They need the same cool, dry, dark conditions, but even so they may last only three to four weeks. If left at room temperature, they will last about a week. Don't refrigerate raw sweet potatoes.

Sweet potatoes are also available canned and frozen, but you must read labels carefully to avoid sugar- and fat-filled versions. The United States Department of Agriculture now requires that sweet potatoes be labeled as such rather than as yams, although the term "yam" can still be used along with it.

You can keep cooked sweet potatoes in a covered container in the refrigerator for four to five days. To freeze sweet potatoes, pack them in an airtight container, but leave some room for expansion. Frozen, they will keep up to ten months.

Livit Recipe

Mashed Sweet Potatoes

4 sweet potatoes, scrubbed and with the ends cut off
¼ cup water
1 teaspoon non-hydrogenated vegetable margarine
1 cup unsweetened soy milk
1 teaspoon agave nectar

- Preheat oven to 375°F.
- Put the potatoes and water into a 9″ × 13″ glass baking dish. Cover the dish with foil and bake for about 45 minutes, until the potatoes are soft and easily pierced with a fork at the thickest part of the potato.
- In a pot or a large bowl, mash the sweet potatoes with a potato masher. When they are smooth, add the margarine and soy milk. Continue to mash the mixture until the potatoes are moist. Sprinkle agave nectar over the potatoes and stir to distribute it well. Serve.

YIELD 4 servings

NUTRITION ANALYSIS PER SERVING 85 calories, 8.8 g carbohydrate, 2.7 g protein, 5.4 g fat, 3.4 g dietary fiber

58 Tomato Paste

Benefits

Tomatoes are the number one source of lycopene in the American diet, and cooking them makes this vital antioxidant up to four times more bioavailable, so tomato paste is actually higher in usable lycopene than fresh tomatoes. Just a tablespoon of tomato paste contains 4,602 mcg of lycopene.

Tomato paste is also a surprisingly good source of fiber and protein, vitamins A and C, and potassium.

> **NUTRITIONAL COMPOSITION** One-half cup of canned tomato paste provides 107 calories, 25.3 g carbohydrate, 4.8 g protein, 0.7 g fat, 5.4 g dietary fiber, 3203 IU vitamin A, 56 mg vitamin C, 4.2 mg niacin, 29 mcg folic acid, 1227 mg potassium, 115 mg sodium, 103 mg phosphorus, 46 mg calcium, 2.54 mg iron, 67 mg magnesium, 1.05 mg zinc, and 0.68 mg manganese.

Bringing It Home

Buy organic canned tomato paste if you can find it—not only for the organic tomatoes but because organic canners are more likely to use cans made without bisphenol A.

Many of the carotenoids found in tomatoes, including the lycopene, are fat-soluble. These are better absorbed if you eat foods containing them with a little olive oil or other high-quality fat source.

Despite its small size, a can of tomato paste is often more than a recipe requires. Freeze the leftover paste in an ice cube tray—measure one tablespoon into each compartment and freeze. When the tomato paste cubes have frozen solid, you can take them out of the tray and store them in a plastic zipper bag. The next time you need only one or two tablespoons, you won't have to open a new can!

Livit Recipe

Healthy Refried Bean Quesadilla

1 can (15 ounces) black beans, rinsed and drained
1 can (15 ounces) pinto beans, rinsed and drained
1 can (4 ounces) organic tomato paste
¼ teaspoon garlic powder
¼ teaspoon onion powder
¼ teaspoon chili powder
Dash of cayenne pepper
1 ounce shredded mozzarella cheese
4 whole wheat tortillas
1 tablespoon guacamole OR ⅛ avocado
1 tablespoon fresh salsa

· In a nonstick 1-quart saucepan, combine the black beans, pinto beans, tomato paste, garlic powder, onion powder, chili powder, and cayenne pepper. Heat over medium heat until it just begins to bubble. Remove from heat. Mash the beans with a potato masher.

- Sprinkle half of the cheese on each tortilla, and heat them in the oven or toaster oven at medium temperature until the cheese melts.
- Layer half of the bean mixture, guacamole, and salsa on each of 2 tortillas. Cover with the remaining 2 tortillas. Cut each quesadilla into 6 wedges. Serve

YIELD 6 servings

NUTRITION ANALYSIS PER SERVING 245 calories, 47 g carbohydrate, 14 g protein, 5 g fat, 13.7 g dietary fiber

59 Winter Squash

Benefits

Winter squash have that name because they kept well and were able to provide a source of vegetable nutrition through the winter before the era of refrigeration. Most winter squash are harvested in the autumn, by which time they have matured to have a hard rind. (Indeed, it used to be traditional to cut winter squash with the axe used to trim firewood!)

Some winter squash have already been listed individually earlier in this chapter—acorn squash, butternut squash, and pumpkin. Other winter squash include the buttercup, delicata, Hubbard, candy roaster, Lakota, Arikara, and spaghetti squash. Most varieties are good sources of beta-carotene, the B vitamins (including folate), vitamins A and C, potassium, copper, and fiber.

> NUTRITIONAL COMPOSITION One-half cup of baked winter squash provides 40 calories, 8.9 g carbohydrate, 0.9 g protein, 0.6 g fat, 2.9 g dietary fiber, 3628 IU vitamin A, 10 mg vitamin C, 0.7 mg niacin, 29 mcg folic acid, 446 mg potassium, 20 mg phosphorus, 14 mg calcium, and 8 mg magnesium.

Bringing It Home

There are many different kinds of winter squash. Probably the most common is the Hubbard, which comes in both blue and golden varieties. Squash should feel heavy and hard, with no soft spots. Some types have naturally warty skins, and others are smooth. The skin should be intact and unbroken in either case. Squash, even within the same variety, can vary widely in size. Pick the size that meets your needs.

Winter squash will keep three or more months if stored properly—and, not surprisingly, "properly" is a lot like the conditions in an old-time root cellar. Winter squash like a cool temperature (around 50°F) and relatively high humidity (70 to 75 percent) to prevent shriveling. If they are stored above 85 percent humidity, you may start to see problems with mold and rot. They also need good ventilation—don't stack them, and don't set them directly on the floor.

Winter Squash Casserole

4 pounds winter squash, peeled, seeded, and cut into 1-inch cubes
½ small onion, chopped
2 large leeks, coarsely chopped
3 garlic cloves, minced
2 teaspoons kosher salt OR sea salt
1 teaspoon freshly ground black pepper
¼ cup olive oil
1 pound whole grain pasta (ziti, penne, rotini)
1 cup apple juice OR hard cider OR white wine
⅓ cup grated Parmesan cheese
2 sprigs fresh parsley, finely minced, as garnish

- Preheat oven to 400°F.
- On a 9″ × 12″ baking sheet with a slight rim (such as a jelly roll pan), mix the squash cubes with the onion, leeks, garlic, salt, and pepper; drizzle with olive oil and toss gently until all the cubes are coated. Distribute the squash cubes so that they make an even layer in the pan. Roast them for 45 to 60 minutes, until the squash is soft and lightly browned.
- While the vegetables are roasting, cook the pasta according to package directions, drain, and set aside.
- When the vegetables are done, remove them from the oven and reduce the oven temperature to 350°F.
- Working in batches, put the roasted vegetables into a blender jar and puree until smooth. Transfer each pureed batch to a 2-quart pot. Add the juice to the pureed vegetables and cook over medium heat until the mixture has reduced slightly.
- In a 3- to 4-quart baking dish, combine the cooked pasta with the vegetable puree. Adjust seasonings if necessary. Sprinkle grated Parmesan over the casserole mixture and bake for 20 to 30 minutes, until the cheese is golden brown. Garnish with parsley. Serve.

YIELD 8 servings

NUTRITION ANALYSIS PER SERVING 427 calories, 82.8 g carbohydrate, 10.7 g protein, 8.4 g fat, 15.5 g dietary fiber

60 Yams

Benefits

Yams are a good source of vitamins B_6 and C and the minerals potassium and manganese, as well as dietary fiber. Vitamin B_6 is instrumental in breaking down homocysteine, lowering the risk of heart attack. The potassium and fiber in yams help control blood pressure. Yams have a lower glycemic index than true potatoes.

Some types of yams contain a steroid, diosgenin, that has been used by the pharmaceutical industry to synthesize human hormones, including cortisone, estrogen, and progesterone, but the body has not been shown to convert this steroid on its own. Still, there are some intriguing hormone connections. In studies on rats, the starch from Chinese yams has shown promise in reducing the levels of cholesterol and triglycerides in the blood.

> **NUTRITIONAL COMPOSITION** One-half cup of baked yams provides 79 calories, 18.8 g carbohydrate, 1 g protein, 0.1 g fat, 2.7 g dietary fiber, 8 mg vitamin C, 11 mcg folic acid, 456 mg potassium, 5 mg sodium, 33 mg phosphorus, 10 mg calcium, and 12 mg magnesium.

Bringing It Home

Choose firm yams with intact skins. Yams should not be refrigerated, as this changes the taste. Store them away from heat and light, and they will keep for up to ten days. Sunlight and warmth can cause them to sprout.

Yams are still somewhat scarce. You may need to seek them out in international groceries. (See The Difference Between Sweet Potatoes and Yams on page 92.)

Livit Recipe

Sliced Glazed Yams

    4 yams, scrubbed and sliced into ½-inch disks (discard the ends)
    ¼ cup water
    1 teaspoon agave nectar
    1 teaspoon non-hydrogenated margarine

- Preheat oven to 350°F.
- Put the yams and water in a 9" × 13" baking dish. Drizzle the yams with agave nectar and dot with margarine. Cover the dish with foil. Slit the foil in two or three places to allow some of the steam to escape. Bake for 30 minutes, until the yams are soft and easily pierced with a fork. Serve.

YIELD 4 servings

NUTRITION ANALYSIS PER SERVING 165 calories, 37.6 g carbohydrate, 2 g protein, 3.5 g fat, 5.4 g dietary fiber

61 Yellow (Wax) Beans

Benefits

Yellow wax beans, like green (snap) beans, are immature bean pods eaten as a vegetable. While it is possible to eat the young pods of nearly any common bean, special varieties have been developed that produce a succulent, fleshy young pod.

Yellow beans are a good source of lutein, beta-carotene, and vitamin A, so they are good for vision health. Lutein and beta-carotene have antioxidant effects that may help slow the effects of aging and prevent some cancers. Vitamin A may also be involved in maintaining epithelial cells—the cells that line the digestive tract and lungs. There is also a purple wax bean that may one day prove to be a good source of anthocyanins.

> **NUTRITIONAL COMPOSITION** One-half cup of cooked yellow wax beans provides 92 calories, 4.9 g carbohydrate, 1.2 g protein, 0.17 g fat, 2.1 g dietary fiber, 51 IU vitamin A, 6.1 mg vitamin C, 21 mcg folic acid, 187 mg potassium, 2 mg sodium, 24 mg phosphorus, 29 mg calcium, 0.8 mg iron, 16 mg magnesium, and 0.23 mg zinc.

Bringing It Home

With yellow wax beans, select crisp, young bean pods that are not dry, shriveled, or rubbery. Sort through and discard any moldy or woody beans. Snap off the ends and remove strings if they have them. (Most modern varieties don't.)

Even more than green beans, yellow beans can almost be eaten raw. You can steam them for a very short time—about five minutes—over an inch or less of boiling water. They should still have a bright color and be crisp for optimal nutrient retention. Add a drizzle of olive oil, oregano, rosemary, and black pepper.

Yellow beans are also available frozen, though you may have to hunt for them in this form. Canned beans tend to be overcooked and bland.

Livit Recipe

Yellow Bean, Asparagus, and Tomato Salad

    3 tablespoons balsamic vinegar
    3 tablespoons extra-virgin olive oil
      Salt and freshly ground black pepper
    2 tablespoons coarsely chopped fresh tarragon
    1 pound medium asparagus
    1 pound yellow wax beans, trimmed
    ½ pint red pear tomatoes OR cherry tomatoes
    ½ pint yellow pear tomatoes OR cherry tomatoes

- To prepare the dressing, whisk the vinegar with the olive oil in a small bowl and season to taste with salt and pepper. Add the tarragon. Set aside.
- In a large pot of boiling salted water, cook the asparagus until just tender, about 3 minutes. Use tongs to remove the asparagus to a colander, reserving the water. (If you use a spaghetti cooker with a colander insert, you can lift the asparagus out using the insert.) Rinse the asparagus under cold water to stop the cooking, and allow the asparagus to drain. Pat the asparagus dry with a paper towel and cut it into 3-inch lengths.
- Immerse the beans in the boiling water and cook them until they are tender, about 5 minutes. Remove the beans to a colander, rinse them under cold water, and drain. Pat them dry with paper towel.
- In a large serving bowl, toss the asparagus, beans, and tomatoes with the dressing. Serve.

YIELD 8 servings

NUTRITION ANALYSIS PER SERVING 85 calories, 8.8 g carbohydrate, 2.7 g protein, 5.4 g fat, 3.4 g dietary fiber

Carbohydrates:
Starchy
Vegetables
· · · · ·

Carbohydrates: "True" Vegetables

These "true" vegetables are very low in carbohydrate—most provide five grams or less for a serving—but they are high in fiber, vitamins, and minerals. This is not the same as the botanical definition of true vegetables, but it makes perfect sense if your goal is to balance your meals for optimal health!

A standard serving of one of these vegetables is one-half cup cooked, or a full cup raw, but you shouldn't limit yourself to such small quantities. Although these vegetables are not an efficient source of fuel, they are excellent sources of vitamins, minerals, and fiber. Try to eat vegetables at least twice a day. Include them, for example, at both lunch and dinner.

ABOUT CARBOHYDRATE EXCHANGES

To help control blood sugar, many persons who have—or are at risk for—type 2 diabetes adopt a carbohydrate-counting meal plan, because carbohydrates raise blood glucose. The American Diabetic Association suggests limiting carbohydrates to 45 to 60 grams per meal; other diet plans recommend less. As a general rule, a serving of fruit, starch, or milk products in such a plan is the amount that provides 15 grams of carbohydrate—for instance, one slice of white bread, one small piece of fruit, or two-thirds cup of plain fat-free yogurt.

> The vegetables listed here as "true" vegetables are low enough in carbohydrate per serving that they typically do not count against the carbohydrate limit in this type of food plan—providing, as a rule, no more than 5 grams of carbohydrate per serving.

62 Asparagus

Benefits

Asparagus is an excellent source of vitamin K; B vitamins, including folate, thiamine, riboflavin, niacin, and B_6; and vitamins A and C. It is a good source of the minerals iron, potassium, manganese, copper, and phosphorus. Asparagus provides plenty of fiber and, for a vegetable, a substantial amount of protein.

Asparagus contains asparagine, a non-essential amino acid that contributes to its protein content. It also contains asparagusic acid, which is unique to asparagus. One effect of asparagusic acid is that it causes an unusual smell in the urine of people who have eaten the vegetable. It is known in some folk medicine traditions for its diuretic properties, when this effect may be even more apparent! It has also been used for rheumatism and arthritis, and its effectiveness there suggests anti-inflammatory properties.

NUTRITIONAL COMPOSITION Six spears of cooked asparagus provide 22 calories, 3.8 g carbohydrate, 2.3 g protein, 0.3 g fat, 1.4 g dietary fiber, 485 IU vitamin A, 10 mg vitamin C, 1 mg niacin, 131 mcg folic acid, 144 mg potassium, 10 mg sodium, 49 mg phosphorus, 18 mg calcium, and 9 mg magnesium.

Bringing It Home

Asparagus is best in the springtime, when shoots are young and straight and the buds are tight. If you can, buy your asparagus at a store that keeps the stalks with their "feet" in a pan of water; the moisture helps keep asparagus fresh. To store asparagus at home, wrap the base of the bunch in a damp paper towel for the same effect, or put them in an inch of water in a tall container (a clean, empty quart yogurt container works nicely), covering with a plastic bag to keep the moisture in. Asparagus spears are often sandy or gritty, so be sure to wash them well before cooking.

Since asparagus is relatively expensive, rather than snapping off the relatively thick, woody bases of the stems, slice the very end off and then peel the stalks, starting at the wide base, for the bottom three inches or so. The top half of the stalk does not need to be peeled.

When steaming asparagus, you can either steam whole asparagus stalks upright in a specialized asparagus steamer (tall and narrow, with a basket for the stalks) or steam asparagus cut into inch-long pieces, using a slight diagonal cut to reduce cooking time. Steam asparagus only until it's tender enough to be easily pierced with a sharp knife—do not overcook!

Some cooks believe that the stalks stay greener and retain more flavor if they are quickly boiled rather than steamed. Fill a pot large enough to hold the asparagus stalks lying on their sides with enough water to cover the stalks in three inches of water. Bring the water to a boil, then plunge in the asparagus. Cover until the water comes back to a boil, then remove the cover and cook the asparagus until it is done, but still crisp and beautifully green. Remove it from the water immediately. You may want to plunge it into a bath of cold water to stop the cooking process.

An assortment of roasted vegetables with asparagus as the centerpiece can be a great appetizer. You can roast asparagus in the oven or on the grill in summer, but keep an eye on it, as it cooks quickly. Toss freshly cooked whole wheat pasta with asparagus, a little olive oil, and your favorite herbs—thyme, tarragon, and rosemary work well. Leftover steamed asparagus cut into bite-sized pieces makes a flavorful and colorful addition to omelets. Stir-fry asparagus with garlic, shiitake mushrooms, and tofu or chicken.

Livit Recipe

Cheesy Asparagus

See Add Zest! on page 34.

>   1 bunch medium asparagus (about 1 pound), cut diagonally into 1- to 2-inch pieces
>   1 tablespoon extra-virgin olive oil
>   2 tablespoons freshly grated Parmesan cheese
>   1 teaspoon fresh lemon zest
>   Salt
>   Freshly ground black pepper

- Fill a medium saucepan half full with water and bring it to a boil. Add the asparagus and reduce heat. Simmer for exactly 2 minutes. Drain.
- While the asparagus is still hot, transfer it to a medium serving bowl and toss it gently with the olive oil, Parmesan, and lemon zest. Add salt and pepper to taste. Serve warm or at room temperature.
- VARIATION For added zing, try squeezing some lemon juice over the asparagus before adding the cheese.

YIELD 4 servings

NUTRITION ANALYSIS PER SERVING 67 calories, 5.2 g carbohydrate, 3.6 g protein, 4.4 g fat, 2.4 g dietary fiber

DON'T BOIL!

When you cook vegetables, steam or stir-fry! Boiling and other longer-cooking methods leach the nutrients and flavor out of these wholesome foods. Many of the most powerful phytonutrients in vegetables are water-soluble, and boiling reduces their effectiveness. Cooked vegetables should be bright and crisp for best flavor and nutrition.

To steam vegetables, use a steamer insert in a pot large enough that the steamer and vegetables will fit with the pot tightly covered. Set your steamer in the pot and add water to a depth just below the bottom of the insert. Your goal is to keep the vegetables out of the water. Add the vegetables to the steamer, cover, and bring the water to a boil.

To "steam-fry" vegetables: You can stir-fry vegetables with just a little water in a pan or wok that has been seasoned properly, but you may need a little oil for most pans. Use an oil that can take high heat: Canola oil is good; olive oil works—but not the more delicate extra-virgin kind. Use just enough oil to shine the inside of the pan, spreading the oil with a paper towel. Bring the pan to a high heat, add the vegetables, and stir briefly. Add a small amount of water, reduce heat to low, and cover to give the vegetables a steaming, which will give you tender vegetables in a shorter time.

63 Beets

Benefits

Both the roots and the leaves of the beet are used for food. The roots, with their beautiful, rich red color, are a source of anthocyanins, which can be strong antioxidants. A 2008 study found that drinking beet juice lowered blood pressure, and researchers theorized that this was because of the nitrates in beets. This finding seems somewhat ironic, because nitrites and nitrates have long been suspected of creating carcinogenic nitrosamines in the stomach's acid environment. But nitrates and nitrites are also involved in a cycle that produces nitrous oxide, which relaxes blood vessels and lowers blood pressure. More research must be done to tease out the particulars.

Beet juice appears to help protect the integrity of cells lining the stomach and digestive tract. Thus it may benefit people taking aspirin and other non-steroidal anti-inflammatory drugs (NSAIDs), which are known to damage these cells. For the same reason, it may also help reduce adverse reactions to chemotherapy.

Beets provide the minerals phosphorus, sodium, magnesium, calcium, iron, and potassium, along with vitamins A and C, and the B vitamins folic acid, niacin, and biotin. They are rich in fiber, and although a half-cup serving of cooked beets contains more carbohydrate than most of the vegetables in this chapter, their unique benefits make them a powerful SuperFood.

Beet greens are in some ways even more nutritious than the root. A half cup of cooked beet greens has fewer carbohydrates, more protein, more fiber, more of vitamins A and C, and more potassium, calcium, iron, magnesium, and manganese than the beet root, and only about half its calories. What beet greens lack is the red pigment that may be the beet root's magic ingredient.

NUTRITIONAL COMPOSITION (COOKED BEETS) One-half cup of cooked fresh beets provides 37 calories, 8.5 g carbohydrate, 1.4 g protein, 0.2 g fat, 1.7 g dietary fiber, 30 IU vitamin A, 3 mg vitamin C, 68 mcg folic acid, 259 mg potassium, 65 mg sodium, 32 mg phosphorus, 14 mg calcium, 0.67 mg iron, 20 mg magnesium, and 0.28 mg manganese.

NUTRITIONAL COMPOSITION (COOKED BEET GREENS) One-half cup of cooked beet greens provides 19 calories, 3.9 g carbohydrate, 1.9 g protein, 0.2 g fat, 2.1 g dietary fiber, 5511 IU vitamin A, 17.9 mg vitamin C, 10 mcg folic acid, 654 mg potassium, 174 mg sodium, 30 mg phosphorus, 82 mg calcium, 1.37 mg iron, 49 mg magnesium, and 0.37 mg manganese.

Bringing It Home

Smaller beets are usually less tough than large ones. Choose beets that are smooth, without obvious dents or bruises, and with a rich, dark color. They should have at least a couple of inches of greens left on them; if you are going to eat the greens, choose small leaves, less than six inches or so in length.

Beets will last for two to three weeks in the refrigerator. Cut the leaves and stems away so they don't continue to feed on the root. If you plan to eat the greens, store them separately in a plastic bag in the refrigerator. Don't wash beets until you are ready to cook them.

Beets don't freeze well (the texture gets strange), and canned beets lose some of their protective nutrients in the heat of cooking, so this is a vegetable that is far better fresh.

To prepare beets, wash them carefully without breaking the skin. They can be steamed, baked, or roasted. Regardless of the cooking method used, let cooked beets cool enough to handle and remove the skins before serving (skins can be left on if beets are very young and fresh).

Livit Recipe

Caramelized Beets and Turnips

 Salt
1 tablespoon canola oil
5 ounces beets, peeled and quartered
5 ounces turnips, peeled and quartered

- Use a separate saucepan for each vegetable. Fill each saucepan half full with water, add a pinch of salt and ½ tablespoon of the oil to each pan, then add the beets or turnips. Cover both pans and simmer for about 20 minutes, until the vegetables are almost tender and most of the water has evaporated.

- Remove the covers and continue to cook the vegetables until they are shiny and glazed in juice. Remove from heat. Drain the beets and the turnips. Combine the beets and turnips in a serving bowl. Serve hot.

YIELD 2 servings

NUTRITION ANALYSIS PER SERVING 113 calories, 11.6 g carbohydrate, 1.8 g protein, 7.2 g fat, 2.7 g dietary fiber

64 Bell Peppers (Red/Yellow/Green/Orange)

Benefits

Bell peppers originated in Mexico, but they have traveled to all corners of the world and are essential to countless national cuisines. Bell peppers are the mild-mannered members of the capsicum family—not fiery, but sweet, which is what they are often called.

In addition to the relatively common colors of red, yellow, green, and orange, bell peppers can be found in many other colors from white to black, with purple, blue, maroon, and brown in between. As with other brightly colored fruits (peppers are technically a fruit, though they are used primarily as a vegetable in cooking), the pigments are a rich source of phytochemicals with antioxidant potential, including chlorogenic acid (which slows the release of glucose in the bloodstream), zeaxanthin (one of the two pigments, along with lutein, that are found in the retina), and coumaric acid (which may help prevent stomach cancer by inhibiting the formation of nitrosamines).

Green bell peppers are somewhat less sweet in taste and may have fewer phytochemical pigments than the other colors.

A good source of vitamins A and C, beta-carotene, and the B vitamins thiamine, B_6, and folic acid, peppers lower homocysteine levels in the blood (which reduces a known risk factor for heart attack) and provide support for eyes against retinal degeneration.

Peppers are low in calories, high in fiber, and 93 percent water by weight. They are one of the best vegetables for sustained release of hydration into the system— a kind of time-release water.

NUTRITIONAL COMPOSITION One-half cup of chopped raw bell peppers provides 14 calories, 3.2 g carbohydrate, 0.4 g protein, 0.1 g fat, 0.9 g dietary fiber, 316 IU vitamin A, 45 mg vitamin C, 11 mcg folic acid, 89 mg potassium, 10 mg phosphorus, 5 mg calcium, and 5 mg magnesium.

Bringing It Home

Peppers should be firm and richly colored, with no mushy or black spots. Peppers decay quickly if their skins are broken or if they sit in water, so don't wash them until you're ready to prepare them. Local peppers are usually available in the summer months, but they are grown around the world and are generally available year-round.

Handle peppers gently and keep them refrigerated. You can also buy frozen sweet peppers, usually conveniently diced or sliced into rings. Freeze whole peppers to preserve more of the nutrients and flavor.

Since insect pests can ruin peppers by breaking the skin and beginning the process of decay, peppers are among the foods on which pesticide residues are most frequently found. If you are intent on avoiding pesticides, purchase organic peppers if you can. Although washing helps reduce some pesticide residues, the United States Department of Agriculture (USDA) tests residue on foods that are already washed, and bell peppers still rank high in residues. To get the full benefit of these nutrition powerhouses, go organic.

Livit Recipe

Rainbow Sweet Pepper Soup

2 cups low-sodium vegetable broth
1 medium potato, peeled and cut into ½-inch cubes
2 tablespoons olive oil
1 small onion, diced
4 large bell peppers (green, red, orange, yellow), diced
1 teaspoon red pepper flakes
½ teaspoon salt
¼ cup plain yogurt
    Fresh herbs (dill, chives, scallion), minced, as garnish

- In a large saucepan, bring the broth and potatoes to a low boil, then reduce heat. Cover, and simmer for 20 minutes.
- In a sauté pan or wok, heat the olive oil. Add onion and sauté for 3 to 4 minutes. Add peppers and sauté for another 10 minutes, stirring with a wooden spoon, until the vegetables are soft.
- When the potato cubes are soft enough to be easily pierced with a fork, transfer the sautéed peppers and onion to the broth. Add red pepper flakes and salt.
- Working with a batch of the soup mixture at a time, put the soup into a blender jar and puree each batch until smooth. Transfer the soup back to the saucepan and heat through. If the soup is too thick for your taste, add a bit more vegetable broth or water. Taste, and adjust seasonings if necessary.
- Top with a tablespoon of plain yogurt and a sprinkling of fresh herbs on each portion. Serve hot.
- VARIATION This soup can also be served cold. To serve cold, remove it from the heat and chill it in the refrigerator for at least 20 minutes before serving.

YIELD 4 servings

NUTRITION ANALYSIS PER SERVING 162 calories, 22.4 g carbohydrate, 3.3 g protein, 7.3 g fat, 5 g dietary fiber

65 Bok Choy

Benefits

Bok choy, also called Chinese cabbage, is one of the cruciferous vegetables. This family of vegetables, which includes broccoli, cabbage, turnips, and kohlrabi, provides some important cancer-fighting nutrients that are being studied for their potential to not only help prevent some forms of cancer, but also possibly reverse and treat them.

Bok choy is a good source of vitamins A, B_6, and C, beta-carotene, the minerals calcium and potassium, and dietary fiber. The rich amount of beta-carotene (2,167 mcg in a half-cup of cooked bok choy) may even help reduce the risk of cataracts.

> NUTRITIONAL COMPOSITION One cup of shredded raw bok choy provides 9 calories, 1.5 g carbohydrate, 1.1 g protein, 0.14 g fat, 0.7 g dietary fiber, 3128 IU vitamin A, 31.5 mg vitamin C, 0.35 mg niacin, 0.06 mg pantothenic acid, 0.14 mg vitamin B_6, 46 mcg folic acid, 25.1 mcg vitamin K, 74 mg calcium, 0.56 mg iron, 13 mg magnesium, 26 mg phosphorus, 176 mg potassium, 46 mg sodium, and 0.13 mg zinc.

Bringing It Home

Bok choy ribs should be white and firm at the base, transitioning to pale celadon green leaves at the top. Bok choy should look fresh, without brown spots or wilted leaves. Baby bok choy, which has a cabbage head four to six inches long, can be delightful when cooked whole. Refrigerate bok choy in a plastic bag as soon as you get it home, and use it within three or four days. When you are ready to cook it, wash it well and make sure to remove any sand or grit between the stalks at the base.

Like its relatives, cabbage and broccoli, bok choy can develop an overpowering taste and limp texture if cooked too long. To avoid overcooking mature bok choy, cut both leaves and stalks into pieces. You can cut across the heads, because this cabbage has no hard core. Steam it as briefly as possible, and consider blanching it in cool water to stop the cooking while it is still crisp and delicate in flavor.

Bok choy is also delicious raw. You can use the leaves whole, broken, or shredded both in salads or as crudités for dipping in hummus or spicy flavored yogurt.

Livit Recipe

Citrus Bok Choy

- 1 teaspoon sesame seed oil
- 1 small onion, diced (about ½ cup)
- 1 medium head bok choy, washed and cut diagonally into ¼-inch slices
- 1 can (11 ounces) mandarin orange segments, drained (reserve juice)

- Lightly oil a medium frying pan or wok with sesame oil, using a paper towel to spread the oil evenly and absorb the excess. Heat the pan to medium-high heat. Add onion. Cook the onion until it becomes translucent, stirring often with a wooden spoon so that the onion doesn't stick or burn.
- Add the bok choy, the orange segments, and up to ¼ cup of the reserved juice from the oranges. Stir-fry briefly, 1 to 2 minutes, then cover and let steam for an additional 1 to 2 minutes. Remove cover. When the vegetables are crisp-tender, transfer them to a serving bowl. Serve hot.

YIELD 2 servings

NUTRITION ANALYSIS PER SERVING 211 calories, 41.4 g carbohydrate, 6.8 g protein, 3.1 g fat, 4.7 g dietary fiber

THE CRUCIFEROUS VEGETABLES

In addition to bok choy, the cruciferous vegetables (named for the X-shaped pattern of the ribs in most species), or Brassicae, include broccoli, cabbage, cauliflower, kale, Brussels sprouts, and mustard greens. Consumption of vegetables from this group has shown a strong correlation with reduced risk of cancer. Scientists are getting closer to knowing what makes the cruciferous vegetables such good cancer fighters.

These vegetables have been found to contain the chemical precursors that the body turns into powerful anti-carcinogens. Glucobrassicin, which the body turns into 3,3'-Diindolylmethane, is found in almost all the Brassicae. Researchers at the University of California at Berkeley are studying its potential as an anti-tumor agent and its possible action in response to oxidative stress. It has shown promise against breast and colon cancer cells in the laboratory. Sulforaphane, also found in these plants, appears to inhibit the growth of the bacteria that cause stomach ulcers, may work with diindolylmethane to resist cancers, and may also protect the skin from the effects of UV radiation. These compounds also appear to reduce inflammation, to help the body get rid of a form of estrogen that has been linked to breast cancer, and to help the liver neutralize some toxic compounds. They may inhibit the growth of human papilloma virus (HPV), which is implicated in cervical cancer.

With their wealth of vitamin C and soluble fiber, cruciferous vegetables also lower the risk of heart and circulatory diseases.

On the other hand, some of the powerful compounds in Brassica vegetables—thioglycosides and glucosinolates—may also interfere with the thyroid gland's use of iodine, in extreme cases causing goiters. People with healthy thyroid function who get sufficient iodine from their diet should not have a problem with these "goitrogens," but people for whom thyroid is an issue should consult their doctor about whether to limit intake of these foods.

Not only do the cruciferous vegetables develop an overpowering and unpleasant odor if overcooked, but they also lose their texture, flavor, and nutrients. Keep a watchful eye when cooking these vegetables to get their maximum benefit.

66 Broccoli

Benefits

Broccoli is an excellent source of the vitamins A, C, K, and folic acid; beta-carotene; and fiber. It's a good source of the minerals calcium, potassium, phosphorus, and magnesium, as well as vitamins B_6 and E, and it provides some selenium as well. Broccoli also provides a substantial amount of lutein, which can help preserve vision and has benefits for circulatory health. The tight-packed florets of broccoli are extra-rich in nutrition.

Although the cancer-fighting chemicals in broccoli are diminished by cooking (especially boiling), cooking increases the bioavailability of vitamin C and iron in this vegetable. Be sure to enjoy it both ways. The next time you sit down to eat, think about choosing broccoli as your SuperFood side dish!

NUTRITIONAL COMPOSITION One cup of chopped raw broccoli provides 24 calories, 4.6 g carbohydrate, 2.6 g protein, 0.4 g fat, 2.6 g dietary fiber, 1356 IU vitamin A, 82 mg vitamin C, 62 mcg folic acid, 286 mg potassium, 58 mg phosphorus, 24 mg sodium, 42 mg calcium, and 22 mg magnesium.

Bringing It Home

Broccoli is a vegetable so hardy that even before refrigerated trucking it was shipped cross-country, packed in ice. Although it was traditionally a late-harvest vegetable, it is now available year-round. The best broccoli is a rich, dark green, with a blue or even purplish cast to the florets. The florets should be tightly closed buds. If they are turning yellow or appear to be opening into flowers, the broccoli is past its prime. Any leaves should be dark and green, and the stalks should be relatively thin.

Fresh broccoli does not keep well, so store it in the refrigerator for no more than three days before using. This vegetable needs room to breathe, so don't seal it up in plastic—use a perforated plastic bag. Cooked broccoli lasts a day or two in the refrigerator, but it quickly gets mushy.

Many people dislike the stems of broccoli, but if you peel them, they are tender and delicious, and they complement the florets beautifully. Don't peel the stems until you're ready to cook them, because peeled stems will dry out in the refrigerator.

Frozen broccoli is also available, or you can freeze your own. To freeze broccoli, wash it, peel the stems, and cut it into pieces. Steam briefly, blanch in cold water, let it drain, and seal it in plastic zipper bags. With a package or two in your freezer, you can easily add it as a last-minute enhancement to soups and casseroles.

Livit Recipe

Steamed Cheesy Broccoli

1 bunch broccoli (1 to 1½ pounds), trimmed and separated into florets
1 clove garlic, minced
½ teaspoon lemon pepper
1 ounce part-skim white cheddar cheese, grated

· Put the broccoli into a steamer basket and sprinkle it with the minced garlic, pressing some of the garlic bits into the flower heads. Sprinkle lemon pepper over the broccoli. Set aside.

· In a covered saucepan that will accommodate the steamer basket, heat about 1 inch of water to boiling. Set the steamer basket over the boiling water, cover, and steam for about 5 minutes. The cooked broccoli should be bright green and crisp; check it at 4 minutes and every minute thereafter. When it is just tender, remove the broccoli from the steamer and put it into a medium serving bowl.

· Sprinkle the broccoli with grated cheddar. Serve hot.

- NOTE If you are using more than an inch or so of the stalk below the floret heads, peel the stalks from the bottom up.

YIELD 4 servings

NUTRITION ANALYSIS PER SERVING 78.2 calories, 11.4 g carbohydrate, 5.8 g protein, 2.4 g fat, 5.2 g dietary fiber

67 Brussels Sprouts

Benefits

Brussels sprouts are the mid-range members of the cruciferous vegetable line and are an excellent source of vitamins A and C, beta-carotene, and fiber.

Brussels sprouts have the potential to be especially good for supporting the health of your colon. As well as being high in fiber, Brussels sprouts are an especially rich source of sinigrin, which has been shown to prevent the formation of cancer cells.

> **NUTRITIONAL COMPOSITION** One-half cup of cooked Brussels sprouts provides 30 calories, 6.8 g carbohydrate, 2 g protein, 0.4 g fat, 2 g dietary fiber, 561 IU vitamin A, 48 mg vitamin C, 47 mcg folic acid, 247 mg potassium, 16 mg sodium, 28 mg calcium, 44 mg phosphorus, 16 mg magnesium, and 0.94 mg iron.

Bringing It Home

Individual Brussels sprouts have a diameter of one to two inches. Brussels sprouts should be firm, deep green, and compact, showing no wilting or yellowing and no soft places. Try to get sprouts of uniform size so that they will cook evenly.

It can be especially fun to bring home a stalk of sprouts from the farmer's market, though you'll have to remove them for cooking. A stalk is two to three feet tall and covered with tiny cabbage heads like a vegetable *croquembouche*!

Perhaps because of their high sinigrin content, Brussels sprouts seem to be especially vulnerable to developing an overly strong, unpleasant taste and smell. Keep them refrigerated, but don't attempt to keep them for very long. Use Brussels sprouts within two or three days, and be especially careful not to overcook these delicate bundles of leaves.

If you want to serve them raw, try them sliced in half with a savory dip. Try braising Brussels sprouts in a vegetable broth infused with your favorite herbs and spices. Because they're small and compact, cooked Brussels sprouts make a great snack food that can simply be eaten as is or seasoned with salt and pepper.

Livit Recipe

Tangy Brussels Sprouts

    1 tablespoon extra-virgin olive oil
    2 cups Brussels sprouts, halved lengthwise
    ¼ cup balsamic vinegar
      Salt and pepper

- Preheat oven to 400°F.

- In a cast-iron skillet, gently heat the oil. Add the Brussels sprouts in a single layer, cut side down. Let them cook until the edges brown and develop a crust; do not stir them in the skillet.

- Transfer the skillet to the oven, with the sprouts still cut-side down. Allow the Brussels sprouts to roast for 4 minutes in the oven. Remove the skillet from the oven and use tongs to turn each sprout over carefully.

- Add the balsamic vinegar to deglaze the pan, gently shaking the skillet until there is no excess vinegar in it. The skillet should retain enough heat for this process, but if it does not, set the skillet back over low heat. Season to taste with salt and pepper. Serve immediately.

YIELD 4 servings

NUTRITION ANALYSIS PER SERVING 65.9 calories, 7.5 g carbohydrate, 2 g protein, 3.8 g fat, 2 g dietary fiber

68 Cabbage (Green/Red)

Benefits

Cabbage is the flagship of the cruciferous vegetables. One of the best non-fruit sources of vitamin C, it is also rich in folate and fiber, and it's remarkably low in calories.

As early as 1949, researchers were studying the effect of cabbage juice on gastric ulcers. It appeared that the juice helped the ulcers to heal faster. Since we now know that most ulcers are caused by a bacterium, further study is needed to see why the cabbage juice appeared to be so effective, and whether cabbage juice alone possesses the healing property. (It's possible that a quart a day of almost any high-antioxidant vegetable juice might promote healing just as much!) Cabbage has long been recognized for its anti-inflammatory properties and its positive effect on overall health.

NUTRITIONAL COMPOSITION One cup of shredded raw red cabbage provides 18 calories, 4.2 grams carbohydrate, 1 g protein, 0.2 g fat, 1.4 g dietary fiber, 28 IU vitamin A, 40 mg vitamin C, 14 mcg folic acid, 144 mg potassium, 8 mg sodium, 30 mg phosphorus, 36 mg calcium, and 10 mg magnesium.

Bringing It Home

Choose cabbage that is brightly colored, firm, and heavy, with fresh-looking leaves. Be on the lookout for worms, because they leave holes in the leaves that will introduce rot. If you suspect that your cabbage is buggy, soak the head in either salt water or a mixture of water and vinegar for 15 to 20 minutes. Once you've done that, you should rinse the cabbage and cook it immediately, as the moisture will interfere with its keeping qualities. Unwashed, cabbage will keep in the refrigerator for up to two weeks. Sliced cabbage will keep in the refrigerator for nearly a week if stored in a perforated bag.

Some of the firmer cabbages were developed as winter keepers and will keep for months in a cold but humid place, though the smell gets unpleasantly strong. The looser-leaved cabbages do not store as well.

For the best taste and nutrition, respect cabbage's cruciferous nature and don't overcook it. If you get a craving for a dish that must cook for a long time, such as cabbage stew or corned beef and cabbage, consider cooking the cabbage separately and adding it at the end.

Livit Recipe

Curried Cabbage and Arame

1 cup dried arame
1 cup cold water
2 teaspoons sesame oil
½ pound of cabbage, shredded (about 2 cups)
1 tablespoon shoyu soy sauce
1 tablespoon curry powder
1 small bunch of fresh parsley, minced (about ¼ cup)

- Rinse the arame and put it into a medium bowl. Add the water and soak the arame for about 5 minutes to reconstitute. Drain the liquid from the arame into a separate bowl. You will be using it later in the recipe. The arame will have approximately tripled in size. Chop the arame into bite-size pieces.

- In a large saucepan, heat the oil. Add the arame and sauté for 3 to 5 minutes. Add cabbage, arame soaking water, and soy sauce. Cover, and allow to simmer for 5 minutes. Add the curry powder. Cover, and heat for another 5 minutes. Add the parsley just before serving.

YIELD 4 servings

NUTRITION ANALYSIS PER SERVING 37.1 calories, 3.6 g carbohydrate, 1 g protein, 2.4 g fat, 2.1 g dietary fiber

69 Carrots

Benefits

Carrots are where carotene gets its name, and with good reason: One medium carrot contains 5,054 mcg of beta-carotene, 2,121 mcg of alpha-carotene, and a whopping 10,191 IU of vitamin A. One cup of carrots provides roughly 686 percent of the recommended dietary allowance (RDA) for vitamin A. A diet high in carotenes has been associated with significant decreases in the incidence of some cancers, including cancers of the bladder, cervix, prostate, colon, larynx, esophagus, and post-menopausal breast cancer. Falcarinol is among the other substances in carrots being investigated for its potential cancer-preventive properties. Recent research suggests that getting carotenes from food is far more effective than consuming supplements. It is possible that beta-carotene from food sources can even be dangerous when consumed in excess. For example, it appears to increase the incidence of lung cancer in smokers.

It's more than a myth that carrots are good for your eyes. A carrot contains 1 mcg of lycopene and 156 mcg of lutein, both of which help protect and preserve the eye. A vitamin A deficiency can result in night blindness, though the connection between high carrot consumption and improved night vision is somewhat less solid.

NUTRITIONAL COMPOSITION One medium raw carrot provides 31 calories, 7.3 g carbohydrate, 0.7 g protein, 0.1 g fat, 2.2 g dietary fiber, 20253 IU vitamin A, 7 mg vitamin C, 10 mcg folic acid, 233 mg potassium, 25 mg sodium, 32 mg phosphorus, 19 mg calcium, and 11 mg magnesium.

Bringing It Home

Domesticated carrots were originally yellow, red, and purple in color. The familiar orange carrot was developed in Holland in the 17th century. As people become more interested in the different nutritional properties of various plant pigments, more colorful carrots are showing up in specialty markets, so keep an eye out for purple carrots!

Among orange carrots, the deeper the color, the more beta-carotene it contains. Carrots should be bright in color and firm. They should look fresh, not dry. Because the carrots we eat are roots that, when still in the field, exist to provide moisture and nutrients to the tops, be sure to remove the greens before you store your carrots so that the nutrients are kept in the root portion. Keep carrots in the coolest part of the refrigerator, wrapped in plastic.

Livit Recipe

Carrot, Cabbage, and Dried Fruit Salad

½ teaspoon sea salt
2 tablespoons red wine vinegar OR
　balsamic vinegar
2 fresh lemons, juice only
¼ teaspoon ground cumin
¼ teaspoon paprika

2 tablespoons extra-virgin olive oil
½ pound carrots, coarsely grated (about 1¼ cups)
¼ pound cabbage, grated (about 1¼ cups)
1 small bunch parsley, minced (about ¼ cup)
½ cup dried cherries OR blueberries OR cranberries
¼ cup roasted pumpkin seeds

- In a small bowl, combine salt, vinegar, lemon juice, cumin, and paprika. Whisk in the olive oil until the dressing is emulsified.
- In a large salad bowl, combine the carrots, cabbage, and parsley. Add the vinegar and oil dressing and toss lightly to coat the vegetables. Sprinkle the dried fruit and pumpkin seeds over the top. Toss gently to distribute the ingredients evenly. Serve.

YIELD 4 servings

NUTRITION ANALYSIS PER SERVING 129 calories, 15.1 g carbohydrate, 1.6 g protein, 7.8 g fat, 2.1 g dietary fiber

70 Cauliflower

Benefits

Cauliflower is one of the cruciferous vegetables, which have been shown to help reduce the risk of many types of cancers, including lung, colon, breast, ovarian, and bladder cancers. Cauliflower is very high in vitamin C, and it's a moderately good source of the B vitamins folate, B_6, and pantothenic acid. As with most other cruciferous vegetables, it is also a good source of fiber.

The familiar white cauliflower is unusual among the common crucifers in being relatively low in vitamin A and carotenes, so for someone who is concerned about getting too much vitamin A, cauliflower is a way to get the advantages of some of the Brassica diindolylmethane and sulforaphane while limiting vitamin A intake. The purple varieties are rich in anthocyanins, which give them their color. Green cauliflowers are slightly richer in nutrients than the white ones, with higher amounts of vitamin A and beta-carotene.

NUTRITIONAL COMPOSITION One cup of raw cauliflower pieces provides 26 calories, 5.2 g carbohydrate, 3 g protein, 0.2 g fat, 2.6 g dietary fiber, 20 IU vitamin A, 46 mg vitamin C, 58 mcg folic acid, 304 mg potassium, 30 mg sodium, 44 mg phosphorus, 22 mg calcium, and 16 mg magnesium.

Bringing It Home

Cauliflower's unique texture is called "curd." The florets aren't nearly as well defined or separate as they are on broccoli, and the stems are much shorter. Because both the flavor and texture of cauliflower are delicate, it must be purchased absolutely fresh and handled with care. Don't buy cauliflower that seems dull or is turning brown anywhere. Even if you trim away the brown spots, it is a sign that the cauliflower is past its prime.

To avoid overcooking cauliflower, bring the water to a boil before introducing the cauliflower. If you are steaming it, you may need as few as six minutes; if you are submerging it in boiling water, it may take just three.

Whether raw or cooked, cauliflower does not store well. You can keep raw cauliflower in the refrigerator in a perforated plastic bag for two to four days. Cooked cauliflower loses its texture in the refrigerator. So don't store it—eat it up!

Livit Recipe

Cauliflower Casserole All-in-One

A cup of this casserole, and you've got yourself a balanced meal.

- 12 ounces multi-grain elbow macaroni OR quinoa pasta (a gluten-free alternative)
- 1 head cauliflower (1 to 1½ pounds), trimmed and broken into small pieces
- 4 slices multi-grain bread
- 1 bunch fresh flat-leaf (Italian) parsley, minced
- 1 tablespoon safflower oil
- ½ teaspoon kosher salt
- ½ teaspoon black pepper
- 1 medium onion, diced
- 1 or 2 cloves garlic, minced
- ½ cup grated extra sharp cheddar cheese
- 1½ cups nonfat Greek-style yogurt
- ½ cup low-fat (1%) milk
- 1 tablespoon Dijon mustard
- Cayenne pepper, optional

- Preheat oven to 400°F.
- Cook the pasta according to package directions, drain, and set aside.
- Fill a large pot with water and bring it to a boil. Add the cauliflower pieces and let the water return to a boil. Cook the cauliflower for about 3 minutes. (Because it will be cooked again in the oven, it is better to undercook than overcook it at this stage.) Rinse the cooked cauliflower in cold water to stop the cooking. Set aside.
- Tear the bread into pieces, and pulse it in a food processor to make coarse crumbs. Add the parsley, 1 teaspoon of the oil, ¼ teaspoon of the salt, and ¼ teaspoon of the pepper to the bread crumbs in the food processor and pulse to combine them.

- In a large pot, heat the remaining 2 teaspoons of oil over medium heat. Add the onion, garlic, and the remaining ¼ teaspoons of the salt and pepper. Cook, stirring occasionally, for 5 to 7 minutes, just until the onion is soft. Remove from heat. Add the cooked pasta, cauliflower, cheese, yogurt, milk, and mustard to the onion. Add a pinch of cayenne pepper if you wish.
- Pour the cauliflower mixture into a 3-quart baking dish. Sprinkle the breadcrumbs over the top. Bake for about 12 to 15 minutes, until golden brown.

YIELD 4 servings

NUTRITION ANALYSIS PER SERVING 551 calories, 90.5 g carbohydrate, 26.9 g protein, 9.7 g fat, 13 g dietary fiber

71 Celery

Benefits

Celery is mostly fiber and water—by weight, celery is 1.6 percent dietary fiber and 95 percent water. It is an excellent source of vitamin C. Celery also provides the minerals potassium, calcium, molybdenum, manganese, magnesium, phosphorus, and iron, as well as the B vitamins thiamine, niacin, folate, and B_6.

Celery also provides some trace nutrients, including the male hormone androstenone and apiol, a substance that appears to affect the female hormonal system and was at one time used to induce miscarriage of unwanted pregnancies. The phthalides in celery help it to enhance flavor and richness in other foods, even when its own taste is overpowered. These compounds may also help arteries to dilate, reducing blood pressure.

Celery contains coumarins, the best known of which is the anti-coagulant warfarin. Others, such as auraptene, have been shown in animal studies to help prevent cancers of the skin, tongue, esophagus, liver, and colon. Ensaculin is being investigated for its potential in treating dementia. It has not yet been proven effective for this purpose in humans, but its main side effect—low blood pressure—could be a health advantage in the long run. These compounds may also help reduce the risk of blood clots and stroke. In the laboratory, other compounds appear to reduce the growth and proliferation of cancer cells.

The one drawback in celery's nutritional package is that because so much of this vegetable is water and fiber, there's just not a lot of room for these other nutrients—so you may have to eat a lot of celery to see its benefits.

Celery seed has an even longer medical history. It was at one time used as an analgesic, though modern testing has found no such effect.

A word of warning: For a small number of people, celery can cause a severe allergic reaction—including anaphylactic shock. There appears to be more of the allergen in celery root than in the stalks that are more commonly eaten in this country, with seeds containing the most. Cooking does not appear to destroy the allergen.

NUTRITIONAL COMPOSITION One raw stalk (7.5 inches long) of celery provides 6 calories, 1.5 g carbohydrate, 0.3 g protein, 0.1 g fat, 0.7 g dietary fiber, 54 IU vitamin A, 3 mg vitamin C, 11 mcg folic acid, 115 mg potassium, 35 mg sodium, 10 mg phosphorus, 16 mg calcium, and 4 mg magnesium.

Bringing It Home

Because celery has such a high water content, the biggest threat to its freshness is dehydration. It needs to be kept cool and moist. When buying celery, choose bunches that are firm and crisp-looking, with green leaves and no brown or dry spots. Celery will keep for a few days in the refrigerator in a loose plastic bag, but it will continue to lose moisture and is really best eaten fresh. The water content makes it a poor candidate for freezing. In fact, accidental freezing can damage it, so this is one vegetable that does not go in the coldest part of the refrigerator. If you have leftovers, use them to make soup or vegetable stock; they do not keep.

Wash celery carefully, as sand and mud can get between the stalks. To use the outer stalks, remove the strings by slicing into the base of the stalk with a small paring knife and then pulling the strings upward to remove.

Celery—both stalk and leaf—go almost everywhere: You can eat them raw, with or without a dip (peanut butter is classic); add them to salads; blend them with vegetable juices; add them to soups, stews, casseroles, or stir-fries. Salt-sensitive individuals can enjoy celery but should keep track of it when monitoring daily sodium intake.

Livit Recipe

Braised Celery and Radicchio

> 1 tablespoon vegetable oil
> 1 large onion, cut into ¼-inch slices
> 1 bunch celery (1 to 1½ pounds), separated into stalks, trimmed, washed, and sliced into 1-inch pieces (reserve the leaves)
> 1 or 2 heads radicchio (about 1 pound), outer leaves removed, with the remaining leaves separated, rinsed, and drained
> 1 teaspoon salt
> 1 teaspoon tarragon
> 1 cup vegetable broth
> ½ teaspoon black pepper
> 2 ounces chèvre OR other soft cheese, as garnish
> ½ cup walnut halves, as garnish

- Heat oil in a medium saucepan. Add the onion and cook, stirring, for just 1 or 2 minutes. Add the celery, celery leaves, radicchio, salt, and tarragon. Stir them together, reduce heat, and cover. Cook for about 15 minutes, stirring occasionally so that the vegetables don't burn.
- Add broth to the vegetables, cover, and cook for 20 to 25 minutes, until all the vegetables are tender.
- Remove cover. Cook for a few more minutes to reduce and thicken the liquid. Add pepper and remove from heat.
- Garnish with cheese and walnuts. Serve.

YIELD 4 servings

NUTRITION ANALYSIS PER SERVING 215 calories, 17.2 g carbohydrate, 6.5 g protein, 15.1 g fat, 4.9 g dietary fiber

72 Collard Greens

Benefits

Collard greens, also referred to as collards, are a member of the cruciferous vegetable genus Brassica, which is rich in cancer fighters diindolylmethane and sulforaphane, as well as fiber. Collard greens provide antioxidant vitamins A, C, and E; vitamin K and niacin; and carotenoids, including a substantial amount of lutein. They are also a good source of zinc, manganese, calcium, and magnesium.

Collard greens are among a small number of foods that contain measurable amounts of oxalates, so over-consumption can cause problems for those with kidney disease, gout, vulvar pain, rheumatoid arthritis, or other conditions that may require a low-oxalate diet.

NUTRITIONAL COMPOSITION One cup of chopped and boiled collards provides 35 calories, 7.8 g carbohydrate, 1.7 g protein, 0.2 g fat, 3.6 g dietary fiber, 3491 IU vitamin A, 15 mg vitamin C, 0.4 mg niacin, 8 mcg folic acid, 168 mg potassium, 20 mg sodium, 10 mg phosphorus, 29 mg calcium, 9 mg magnesium, and 0.20 mg iron.

Bringing It Home

Greens should be green! Collards are large-leafed and dark, and they should not seem wilted, soft, yellow, or dried out. Leave them unwashed and wrap them in a damp paper towel inside a paper bag. If you keep the paper towel damp, the greens will keep up to a week. They also freeze well, or they can be purchased frozen. If you freeze your own, submerge them in boiling water for two minutes, then plunge them in ice water to stop the cooking. Let them drain, and pack them in plastic zipper bags. They will keep for about six months in the freezer.

When you are ready to cook them, wash the collards carefully. Both dirt and bugs can cling to the leaves. Like other members of the genus Brassica, collards should not be overcooked.

Collard greens, like other large greens, can be bitter. The traditional Southern method of simmering them in broth mediates the flavor and results in a traditional "pot likker" that can be a good base for soups. It's also a great way to recapture nutrients that may have escaped from the greens. If you want to add even more to the nutrient value of your broth, consider putting the stems in a cheesecloth bag and cooking them in the water or broth with the collard leaves.

Damage to the leaves is believed to trigger the conversion of inactive compounds to the isothiocyanates that have health benefits, so you may want to let the cut leaves and stems sit for a few minutes before cooking in order to allow time for more of this reaction to take place.

Livit Recipe

Mediterranean-Style Collard Greens

    1 pound collard greens, washed and trimmed
    1 medium clove garlic, minced
    ½ fresh lemon, juice only
    1 tablespoon extra-virgin olive oil
       Sea salt
       Black pepper
    1½ tablespoons sunflower seeds

- Cut the leaves of the collard greens away from the stems. Slice the leaves into ½-inch strips and then cut them crosswise. Cut the stems into ¼-inch slices.

- Fill a steamer or large pot with water to a depth of 2 inches. Bring the water to a boil over medium heat. Once the water is boiling, place the collard leaves and stems in a steamer basket over the boiling water. Steam them for no more than 5 minutes.

- In a serving bowl, toss the collards with the garlic, lemon juice, oil, salt, and pepper. Sprinkle sunflower seeds over the top.

YIELD 4 servings

NUTRITION ANALYSIS PER SERVING 87.1 calories, 8.1 g carbohydrate, 3.5 g protein, 5.6 g fat, 4.5 g dietary fiber

ANTI-INFLAMMATORY FOODS: THEIR ROLE IN DISEASE PREVENTION

Recent research has uncovered the role of inflammation in the progress of chronic diseases, especially cancers, lung disease, and cardiovascular disease. Many of the foods emphasized in this book were chosen for their anti-inflammatory qualities.

Inflammation is the body's response to irritation, injury, and infection. One kind of inflammation is seen when a cut gets red and swollen. Internal inflammation of blood vessels, breathing passages, and other organs, however, can eventually damage tissues. For example, prolonged inflammation in blood vessels is one of the factors that contribute to thickening of artery walls (atherosclerosis), which contributes to heart disease and stroke.

Unfortunately, certain foods and eating patterns can increase inflammation. The saturated fats from animal products (meat and dairy), trans-fatty acids (found in hydrogenated oils), and high blood sugar (sweets, refined starches, and other foods with a high glycemic load) have all been found to contribute to vascular inflammation, as has cigarette smoking.

To reduce inflammation, limit intake of full-fat animal products, avoid trans-fats, and avoid blood-sugar spikes. In addition to avoiding foods that promote inflammation, increase your consumption of foods that are believed to reduce it. Antioxidant foods are believed to help reduce inflammation because they scavenge and neutralize the oxygen free radicals that are among its causes. Foods that may reduce inflammation include the following:

- Monounsaturated fats, including extra-virgin olive oil, avocados, nuts, and seeds
- Antioxidant-rich fruits and vegetables
- Red wine in moderation
- Unsweetened cocoa (Just don't use it as an excuse to add high-fat dairy and sugar!)
- Fish oils that are high in omega-3 fatty acids (The proper balance between omega-3 and omega-6 acids is thought to help cardiac health. On its own, too much omega-6 is thought to increase inflammation.)

In general, fresh foods prepared at home are lower in fats, salt, and sugars than prepared and processed foods. You can control the amount you add to your meals. Substituting beans and legumes for animal protein and substituting whole grains for refined carbohydrates help reduce inflammation by providing more soluble fiber, which takes cholesterol—a known source of blood-vessel irritation—out of the bloodstream. Some seasonings appear to have an anti-inflammatory effect, including garlic, ginger, onions, and turmeric.

Some research also indicates that plant sterols may help reduce inflammation, but other studies have suggested that these phytosterols may accumulate the way cholesterol does. The jury remains out on their overall benefit.

You can reduce inflammation by substituting plant proteins, fish, and omega-3–enhanced eggs for meat as the centerpiece of at least one meal a day.

73 Cucumber

Benefits

Cucumbers are more than 95 percent water and nearly 4 percent carbohydrate by weight. They provide vitamins A, C, and K; folate and other B vitamins; carotenes; and the minerals calcium, potassium, and magnesium. They are an excellent hot weather snack, because they provide both water and electrolytes to help with hydration and blood pressure.

The compound that makes cucumber slices a kitchen remedy for puffy eyes is believed to be caffeic acid. Found in many plants, it is especially accessible in cucumbers and has been shown to be an antioxidant. It has also shown potential to inhibit the growth of cancer cells in laboratory studies.

> **NUTRITIONAL COMPOSITION** One cup of raw cucumber slices, with the peel, provides 16 calories, 3.8 g carbohydrate, 0.7 g protein, 0.1 g fat, 0.5 g dietary fiber, 109 IU vitamin A, 3 mg vitamin C, 7 mcg folic acid, 153 mg potassium, 25 mg phosphorus, 17 mg calcium, and 14 mg magnesium.

Bringing It Home

Cucumbers should be firm, with no soft or mushy spots, and a bright, dark green color. Try to find cucumbers that have not been waxed, because waxed cukes will need to be peeled, especially if you plan to cook them. Cucumbers will keep for several days in the refrigerator. When storing a cucumber that has been cut, be sure to wrap the cut end tightly. Cucumbers wilt at room temperature, so if you are preparing them in advance of the meal, remember to put them back in the refrigerator to chill until time to serve.

Use cucumber slices as mini-plates for vegetable salads, bits of soft cheese, or hummus. Mix diced cucumbers with sugar snap peas and mint leaves and then toss with brown rice vinegar or apple cider vinegar.

Livit Recipe

Almost-Instant Gazpacho

1 cucumber, cut into chunks
1 fresh tomato, cut into chunks
1 green bell pepper, seeded and cut into chunks
1 small onion, cut into chunks
1 clove garlic, minced
½ lemon, juice only

1 cup tomato juice
¼ teaspoon cumin
Salt
Pepper
¼ cup nonfat plain yogurt, as garnish

- In a blender jar, combine the cucumber, tomato, pepper, onion, garlic, lemon juice, tomato juice, and cumin. Add salt and pepper to taste. Puree until smooth. Pour into bowls and garnish with a tablespoon of yogurt in the center of each bowl. Serve cold.

YIELD 4 servings

NUTRITION ANALYSIS PER SERVING 56 calories, 12.2 g carbohydrate, 2.8 g protein, 0.4 g fat, 2.1 g dietary fiber

74 Eggplant

Benefits

Eggplant is a very good source of dietary fiber, potassium, manganese, copper, and thiamine (vitamin B_1). It is also a good source of vitamin B_6, folate, magnesium, and niacin.

Although eggplant got its name from varieties that were white or yellow in color, the most common eggplant in North American cuisine is purple. That rich purple skin is the source of an interesting anthocyanin called nasunin. Nasunin has antioxidant properties, is a scavenger of free radicals, and has been shown in the laboratory to protect cell membranes, including brain cells, from oxidative damage.

Another eggplant nutrient, chlorogenic acid, is an antioxidant and works to slow the release of glucose into the bloodstream after eating. In fact, it's sold in some countries as a weight-loss supplement.

Eggplant is among a small number of foods that contain measurable amounts of oxalates, so over-consumption can cause problems for those with kidney disease, gout, vulvar pain, rheumatoid arthritis, or other conditions that may require a low-oxalate diet.

NUTRITIONAL COMPOSITION One-half cup of boiled eggplant provides 13 calories, 3.2 g carbohydrate, 0.4 g protein, 0.1 g fat, 1.2 g dietary fiber, 31 IU vitamin A, 1 mg vitamin C, 7 mcg folic acid, 119 mg potassium, 11 mg phosphorus, 3 mg calcium, and 6 mg magnesium.

Bringing It Home

Eggplant should be glossy, richly colored, and heavy. The skin should seem taut and the flesh should have some resilience. Larger is not better when it comes to eggplant. Both large and small eggplants can be dry or overly seedy inside. Brown or soft spots mean that the flesh underneath is subject to decay. Eggplant becomes bitter when stored in the refrigerator, but it does not keep well above about 50°F. If possible, cook it on the same day you buy it.

Although eggplant itself is low in fat, it is famous for soaking up cooking oil, so if you wish to limit fat intake, it is best to cook eggplant by baking, roasting, or cooking in soup. You can reduce the amount of oil it absorbs by salting and draining it: Slice the eggplant and sprinkle the surface with salt, then set it in a colander or on a few sheets of paper towel for about 30 minutes. To speed up the draining, press the eggplant slices or put a weight on top of them (a plate works well). This process adds sodium to the eggplant, however (rinsing the salt off after draining doesn't really work). If you should avoid excess salt, blanch the eggplant instead: Drop cubes or slices of eggplant into boiling water for a minute or two, then drain.

Livit Recipes

Baba Ghanoush

1 eggplant (about 1½ pounds)	1 lemon, juice only
1 clove garlic, minced	1 tablespoon olive oil
3 tablespoons tahini	1 teaspoon salt

- Preheat oven to 400°F.
- Prick the eggplant all over with a fork. Place it in a shallow pan or cookie sheet. Bake the eggplant for 40 minutes, or until very soft. Cut the baked eggplant in half and scoop the soft flesh out of the skin.
- In a blender jar, puree the eggplant, garlic, tahini, lemon juice, olive oil, and salt. Serve as a dip or on sandwiches.

YIELD 2 cups

NUTRITION ANALYSIS PER SERVING 32.6 calories, 2.6 g carbohydrate, 0.8 g protein, 2.4 g fat, 1 g dietary fiber

Ratatouille

2 tablespoons olive oil	4 large tomatoes, peeled and diced
2 cloves garlic, minced	3 small zucchini, cut into ½-inch cubes
1 large onion, diced	1 teaspoon dried basil
1 large eggplant, peeled and cut into ½-inch cubes	½ teaspoon dried oregano
2 green bell peppers, seeded and diced	2 tablespoons red wine vinegar
	Salt and pepper

- In a large, heavy Dutch oven, heat the oil over medium heat. Add the garlic and onions. Cook for about 5 minutes, or until softened, stirring frequently. Add the eggplant and peppers, and stir to coat them with oil. Cover, and cook for 10 minutes, stirring occasionally.
- Stir in the tomatoes, zucchini, basil, and oregano. Cover, and let the vegetables simmer for another 10 minutes, until tender. Remove from heat.
- Stir in the red wine vinegar, and add salt and pepper to taste. Serve immediately.

YIELD 4 servings

NUTRITION ANALYSIS PER SERVING 135 calories, 17.5 g carbohydrate, 2.8 g protein, 7.2 g fat, 5.8 g dietary fiber

75 Green Beans

Benefits

Green beans are low in calories, high in fiber, and full of nutrients. They provide antioxidant vitamins A and C, as well as vitamin K and the B vitamins thiamine, niacin, riboflavin, and folate. Minerals found in green beans include manganese, potassium, iron, calcium, copper, and phosphorus. This wealth of nutrients gives green beans great potential in preventing cancers, heart disease, and other illnesses in which inflammation plays a role.

Green beans are, however, another food that has measurable amounts of oxalates, so over-consumption can cause problems for those with kidney disease, gout, vulvar pain, rheumatoid arthritis, or other conditions that may require a low-oxalate diet.

NUTRITIONAL COMPOSITION One-half cup of boiled green beans provides 22 calories, 4.9 g carbohydrate, 1.2 g protein, 0.2 g fat, 2 g dietary fiber, 413 IU vitamin A, 6 mg vitamin C, 21 mcg folic acid, 185 mg potassium, 2 mg sodium, 24 mg phosphorus, 29 mg calcium, and 16 mg magnesium.

Bringing It Home

Choose green beans that are smooth, firm, brightly colored, and unbruised. Store them in a plastic bag in the vegetable drawer of the refrigerator. Whole beans will keep for about seven days. Don't wash green beans until you're ready to cook them. To trim green beans, snap off the stems and any brown parts. They can be cooked by steaming in just five or six minutes.

Livit Recipe

Healthy Green Bean Casserole

　　Vegetable oil spray
1　pound green beans, trimmed and washed
⅓　cup all-purpose flour
¼　teaspoon salt
1　large onion, thinly sliced, with rings separated
1　tablespoon vegetable oil
1　can (10½ ounces) low-sodium cream of mushroom soup OR reduced-fat cream of mushroom soup
¾　cup skim milk
　　Salt and pepper

• Preheat oven to 350°F.
• Spray the inside of a 9″ × 9″ baking dish with vegetable oil.

- Add 1 inch of water to a steamer pot and bring it to a boil. Once the water is boiling, put the green beans into the steamer insert. Steam for about 6 minutes, until they are bright green but still crisp. Remove from heat and drain.
- In a pie plate or shallow dish, mix the flour and salt. Toss the onion rings in the flour and salt mixture until they are well coated.
- In a large nonstick skillet, heat the oil over medium-high heat and add the coated onions. Cook for 4 to 5 minutes, until they are golden brown and crispy, turning them once or twice. If they start to stick, spray them lightly with oil. Set aside.
- In a large bowl, mix the green beans, soup concentrate, milk, and half of the crisped onions. Season to taste with salt and pepper. Pour into the prepared baking dish and bake for 10 minutes. Top with the remaining crisped onions and return to the oven for another 5 minutes.

YIELD 4 servings

NUTRITION ANALYSIS PER SERVING 191.7 calories, 34.2 g carbohydrate, 6.4 g protein, 3.5 g fat, 6.1 g dietary fiber

76 Hot Peppers

Benefits

What makes hot peppers hot is a group of six acids called capsaicinoids, primarily capsaicin. These compounds likely evolved because they discourage animals from eating the peppers and act as anti-fungal agents. But they have such a powerful and unique effect on the nerves and tissues of mammals, including humans, that they are being studied for a variety of possible health benefits.

Both in the laboratory and in animal studies, capsaicin has been shown to kill prostate cancer cells and to inhibit the onset of tumor growth and cell mutations that might lead to cancer. Some studies have also suggested that capsaicin may have a role to play in curbing obesity and treating type 1 diabetes, because it appears to reduce the amount of insulin needed to lower blood sugar after a meal. It also appears to inhibit the growth of Helicobacter pylori, the bacterium that causes 80 percent of stomach ulcers. Because of its profound effect on nerves, it is used in a variety of pain-relief therapies. And because it acts on Substance P, which is involved in the body's inflammatory response, it may turn out to be a strong anti-inflammatory. Studies have shown that countries where the cuisine includes a lot of hot pepper have lower rates of heart disease and stroke.

Hot peppers are also high in vitamins A and C, the B vitamins (especially B_6), and the minerals potassium, magnesium, and iron.

NUTRITIONAL COMPOSITION One raw hot chili pepper provides 18 calories, 4.3 g carbohydrate, 0.9 g protein, 0.1 g fat, 0.7 g dietary fiber, 347 IU vitamin A, 109 mg vitamin C, 11 mcg folic acid, 153 mg potassium, 3 mg sodium, 21 mg phosphorus, 8 mg calcium, 11 mg magnesium, and 0.14 mg zinc.

Bringing It Home

Whether your hot peppers are red, yellow, or green, choose peppers that are glossy and have tight, richly colored skins, with no soft or blackened spots. Keep them in the refrigerator in paper bags or wrapped in paper towels—not in plastic, which tends to allow them to become damp and spoil.

When handling chili peppers, especially the hottest varieties, wear disposable latex (or non-latex, if you are allergic) gloves, and be careful not to get your fingers near your eyes. The hottest parts of the peppers are the central ribs and the pith surrounding the seeds, so if you want a milder dish, trim those parts away. If you're going for fire, be sure to include them!

Livit Recipe

Chicken Fire

See Safe Handling of Poultry on page 211.

> 3 to 6 fresh red chili peppers, halved and seeded
> 1 small fresh ginger root (about 1 inch long), peeled and cut in half
> ½ lemon, zest only
> 4 skinless, boneless split chicken breasts (3 to 4 ounces each), cut into ¼-inch strips
> 6 cups water
> 6 small red onions OR shallots, thinly sliced
> 4 cloves garlic, crushed
> Salt and pepper

- In the bowl of an electric mixer, combine the peppers, ginger root, and lemon zest. Mix for 1 to 2 minutes, until they are well blended. Remove the bowl from the mixer. Add the chicken pieces to the bowl. Using your hands or a wooden spoon, turn the chicken in the seasoning mixture until it is well coated.

- Put the chicken and seasonings into a 3-quart saucepan and pour the water over it. Add most of the onions (reserving a small amount for garnish) and the garlic. Season with salt and pepper. Cook over high heat for 5 minutes, or until the water is reduced and the chicken is cooked through. Transfer to a serving bowl. Garnish with the remaining onion slices. Serve.

YIELD 4 servings

NUTRITION ANALYSIS PER SERVING 197 calories, 15.3 g carbohydrate, 29.7 g protein, 1.8 g fat, 2.7 g dietary fiber

77 Jicama

Benefits

Jicama is mostly water. It is a good source of dietary fiber, potassium, and vitamin C. It also contains inulin, which is partly responsible for its sweet taste. In addition, inulin increases the absorption of calcium, and possibly of magnesium. Combined with the fiber and water found in jicama, these nutrients help both hydration and blood pressure. Although it is a sweet-tasting source of fiber, it does not appear to raise blood sugar or triglyceride levels.

> **NUTRITIONAL COMPOSITION** Three and one-half ounces of raw jicama provides 46 calories, 10.6 g carbohydrate, 0.86 g protein, 0.11 g fat, 5.8 g dietary fiber, 19 IU vitamin A, 24 mg vitamin C, 8 mcg folic acid, 135 mg potassium, 4 mg sodium, 16 mg phosphorus, 11 mg calcium, and 11 mg magnesium.

Bringing It Home

Jicama is an edible root, tan in color, and shaped somewhat like a turnip. Although it can grow quite large, the crisp, sweet taste is best in jicama about the size of a grapefruit. It should be firm and dry. Rootlets should be dry, and the tuber should have no soft or dark spots. Jicama will keep in the refrigerator for about two weeks.

Jicama can be eaten raw and is an interesting addition to salads, salsas, and stir-fries.

Livit Recipe

Jicama Antioxidant Boost

1 fresh lime, juice only
1 teaspoon salt
1 teaspoon chili powder
½ teaspoon cayenne pepper
1 pound jicama, peeled and diced
1 can (11 ounces) mandarin oranges, drained
2 scallions, minced
1 cup raspberries

- In a large bowl, mix the lime juice, salt, chili powder, and cayenne. Add the jicama, oranges, and scallions. Toss together gently until the jicama is coated. Transfer to a serving bowl.

- Just before serving, gently rinse and drain the berries, and arrange them evenly over the top of the jicama mixture. (Raspberries are too fragile to mix in with the other ingredients; they would be crushed.) Serve cold.

YIELD 4 servings

NUTRITION ANALYSIS PER SERVING 85 calories, 20.3 g carbohydrate, 1.7 g protein, 0.3 g fat, 8.6 g dietary fiber

78 Kale

Benefits

Kale is a leafy member of the Brassica genus. As a dark, green leafy vegetable, it is rich in vitamin K. In addition to the benefits typical of the cruciferous vegetables, kale also provides a flavonoid called kaempferol that appears to reduce the risk of heart disease. In one 8-year study, kaempferol, in combination with the flavonoids quercetin and myricetin, reduced the risk of pancreatic cancer by 23 percent.

Kale is rich in the antioxidant vitamins A and C, as well as several carotenoids, including beta-carotene, lutein, and zeaxanthin. These compounds help protect vision and lower the risk of cataracts and age-related macular degeneration. It is also a good source of B vitamins, including thiamine, riboflavin, and B_6, and the minerals calcium and iron.

Kale is one of a small number of foods that contain measurable amounts of oxalates, so over-consumption can cause problems for those with kidney disease, gout, vulvar pain, rheumatoid arthritis, or other conditions that may require a low-oxalate diet.

NUTRITIONAL COMPOSITION One-half cup of cooked, chopped kale provides 21 calories, 3.7 g carbohydrate, 1.2 g protein, 0.3 g fat, 1.3 g dietary fiber, 4810 IU vitamin A, 27 mg vitamin C, 9 mcg folic acid, 148 mg potassium, 15 mg sodium, 18 mg phosphorus, 47 mg calcium, and 12 mg magnesium.

Bringing It Home

Kale should have firm, very dark green leaves with no brown or dry spots. Smaller leaves will be less tough and strong-flavored than large ones. Kale is available at farmer's markets in the eastern United States near the end of summer and through the winter in California. Like many greens, it is better fresh, but travels well.

Don't wash kale before storing it in the refrigerator. It will keep for a few days, though the flavor becomes more bitter the longer it is stored. For a less bitter experience, trim away not only the stems but the central vein on each leaf.

Kale, collard greens, mustard greens, Swiss chard, and dandelion greens can all be used more or less interchangeably in recipes. See the entries on those vegetables for more ideas on how to handle and enjoy these nutritional powerhouses.

Livit Recipe

Raw Sweet Kale Salad

1 lemon, juice only
1 tablespoon apple cider vinegar
1 teaspoon extra-virgin olive oil
¼ cup dried cranberries
1 tablespoon pine nuts
1 bunch kale (about ¾ pound with stems), rinsed, with stems and central veins
    trimmed away, and leaves cut into 1-inch strips
1 can (11 ounces) mandarin oranges, drained

- In a small bowl, whisk together the lemon juice and apple cider vinegar. Whisk the olive oil in slowly until the dressing is emulsified. Add the dried cranberries and pine nuts to the vinegar and oil.

- In a large salad bowl, combine the kale with the mandarin oranges. Add the dressing. Toss gently.

- NOTE You can make enough to last through the week, but keep the kale separate from the oranges and dressing. Combine just before eating for a great quick veggie side to any meal.

YIELD 4 servings

NUTRITION ANALYSIS PER SERVING 125 calories, 24.4 g carbohydrate, 2 g protein, 3 g fat, 2.3 g dietary fiber

79 Kelp

Benefits

Kelp is included here as an example of the "sea vegetables"—oceanic plants that are eaten in many parts of the world, from Ireland and the Canadian Maritimes to Japan and Korea. They are especially rich in minerals, including calcium, iodine, iron, magnesium, and trace minerals. They also contain vitamin A.

Because of the mineral-rich environment of the sea, kelp provides the broadest range of minerals of any food. Kelp is an excellent source of vitamin K, and provides the B vitamins folate, riboflavin, and pantothenic acid. People who eat kelp have been found to have a lower risk of intestinal and breast cancers. Sea vegetables are an excellent source of iodine, necessary to healthy thyroid function and the prevention of goiter. If you have stopped using ordinary iodized table salt, you may wish to add sea vegetables to your meals to provide this essential mineral. You can even keep a container of kelp flakes on the dinner table and use it instead of table salt for seasoning foods.

NUTRITIONAL COMPOSITION Three and one-half ounces of raw kelp provides 43 calories, 9.6 g carbohydrate, 1.7 g protein, 0.6 g fat, 1.3 g dietary fiber, 116 IU vitamin A, 3 mg vitamin C, 180 mcg folic acid, 89 mg potassium, 42 mg phosphorus, 233 mg sodium, 168 mg calcium, 2.85 mg iron, 121 mg magnesium, and 1.23 mg zinc.

Bringing It Home

Although kelp is listed as the SuperFood, there are many other sea vegetables, including nori, dulse, hijiki, kombu, wakame, and arame. All are worth exploring. Virtually all seaweeds are sold dried, in tightly sealed packages. They will last for several months if kept tightly sealed at room temperature.

Make homemade vegetable sushi rolls by wrapping rice and your favorite vegetables in sheets of nori. Slice nori into small strips to sprinkle on top of salads. When cooking beans, put kelp in the cooking water. It will expedite the cooking process and improve beans' digestibility by reducing the chemicals that can cause flatulence.

Because of their high sodium content, however, be sure to drink a lot of water to balance out the sodium when eating kelp or other sea vegetables.

Livit Recipe

Miso Soup

This recipe calls for two kinds of seaweed. You can also garnish it with powdered kelp.

> 1 piece kombu (dried kelp), 8″ × 3″, brushed clean
> ½ cup dried wakame
> ¼ cup shiro miso (white fermented-soybean paste)
> ½ pound soft tofu, drained and diced into ½-inch cubes
> 3 or 4 scallions (green tops only), thinly sliced

- Fill a deep 2-quart pot with water and soak the kombu in the water for about 30 minutes.
- Put the wakame into a medium bowl, and add warm water until it is covered by about 1 inch of water. Allow the wakame to soak for 15 minutes. Drain the wakame in a colander and set it aside.
- Place the pot containing the kombu over low heat. Cook until the water appears about to boil (with small bubbles along the edges). Remove the kombu from the broth.
- In a small bowl, mix the miso with ½ cup of broth until smooth.
- Increase heat under the pot of broth to moderately high. Once it is simmering, gently stir in the wakame and tofu. Simmer together for 1 minute, then remove from heat. Stir in the miso mixture and add the scallions. Serve.

YIELD 4 servings

NUTRITION ANALYSIS PER SERVING 55.8 calories, 3 g carbohydrate, 4.2 g protein, 2.3 g fat, 0.5 g dietary fiber

80 Leeks

Benefits

Leeks are popular in traditional European foods because these plants, close relatives of onions and garlic, could be left in the ground during the winter and harvested as needed, providing a rare source of fresh winter produce. The Allium family, to which leeks, garlic, and onions belong, have long been recognized for their cardiovascular benefits. Allicin, the compound that gives these vegetables their characteristic aromas, has antibacterial and anti-fungal properties, is an anti-inflammatory, and may help reduce fat deposits and hardening in blood vessels. Allicin breaks down into components that appear to be strong antioxidants. A diet rich in Alliums tends to lower both blood pressure and low-density lipoprotein (LDL), or "bad" cholesterol, reducing the risk of heart disease and stroke.

Leeks are a very good source of manganese and a good source of vitamin B_6, folate, vitamin C, and iron. This combination of nutrients helps stabilize blood sugar by slowing the absorption of sugars in the digestive tract and assisting in proper sugar metabolism.

Leeks are among the vegetables that contain measurable amounts of oxalates, which can cause problems for people with kidney disease, gout, rheumatoid arthritis, vulvar pain, or other conditions requiring a low-oxalate diet.

NUTRITIONAL COMPOSITION One-half cup of cooked chopped leeks provides 16 calories, 4 g carbohydrate, 0.4 g protein, 0.2 g fat, 0.6 g dietary fiber, 25 IU vitamin A, 2 mg vitamin C, 12 mcg folic acid, 46 mg potassium, 6 mg sodium, 8 mg phosphorus, 16 mg calcium, and 8 mg magnesium.

Bringing It Home

Leeks should be of medium size, firm, and bright green and white in color. Large leeks can be tough. True to their heritage as a winter vegetable, leeks are available year-round and are easiest to find in winter. Don't wash leeks before storing them in the refrigerator, where they will keep for about two weeks. Once they are cooked, they do not keep well; cook only what you will eat within a day or two.

Livit Recipe

Lean Leeks

2 pounds leeks, trimmed, with outer layers removed
1 tablespoon safflower oil OR canola oil
1½ cups plus 2 tablespoons water
2 small carrots, peeled and cut into ¼-inch slices
2 tablespoons uncooked brown rice
1½ teaspoons sugar
½ teaspoon salt
½ lemon, juice only, as dressing

- Slice the leeks into ½-inch disks, then wash them carefully in a bowl of water to remove the dirt that often lodges between the layers. Pat them dry with paper towels.
- In a medium nonstick pan, heat the oil with the 2 tablespoons of water over medium heat. Stir in the leeks and carrots. Cover, and cook for 30 minutes, stirring occasionally. After 30 minutes, stir in the rice, sugar, salt, and the 1½ cups of water. Cover, and allow the ingredients to simmer for another 30 minutes. Check occasionally to see if more water is needed. The final result should be neither watery nor dry.
- When the leeks and carrots are cooked, remove pan from the heat and allow it to cool. Transfer to a serving dish and dress with lemon juice. Serve cold.
- NOTE For a more balanced meal, serve a soup made from beans or lentils on the side, and add a whole wheat roll or sprouted grain toast.
- VARIATION To provide more complete protein, add some edamame (fresh steamed soybeans) to the final dish.

YIELD 4 servings

NUTRITION ANALYSIS PER SERVING 193 calories, 38 g carbohydrate, 3.8 g protein, 4.3 g fat, 4.9 g dietary fiber

81 Lettuce

Benefits

Almost all of the lettuces are low in calories and high in fiber, and provide vitamins A, C, and K; B vitamins thiamine, niacin, pantothenic acid, and folate; carotenes, including beta-carotene, lutein, and zeaxanthin; and the minerals manganese, potassium, and iron. The traditional iceberg lettuce is the least nutrient-dense of the lettuces. Romaine is probably the richest nutrient source among them; it is an excellent source of vitamins A, C, and folate, as well as the minerals manganese and chromium. It also provides vitamins B_1 and B_2, potassium, molybdenum, iron, and phosphorus. Many of the leaf lettuces offer nearly as good a nutrient profile as romaine, so you don't need to give up variety.

The mix of minerals, fiber, and antioxidants in romaine help it lower blood cholesterol and reduce the formation of fatty plaques in arteries. The potassium and other minerals help lower blood pressure, and the B vitamins help support and increase your metabolism.

NUTRITIONAL COMPOSITION One cup of shredded raw romaine provides 8 calories, 1.4 g carbohydrate, 1 g protein, 0.2 g fat, 1 g dietary fiber, 1456 IU vitamin A, 14 mg vitamin C, 76 mcg folic acid, 162 mg potassium, 4 mg sodium, 26 mg phosphorus, 20 mg calcium, and 4 mg magnesium.

Bringing It Home

Whatever lettuce you buy, it should be crisp, and it should not have wilted leaves or any mushy, dark, or slimy spots. In choosing a type of lettuce, keep in mind that the darker colored varieties, such as romaine, tend to be richer in nutrients than the paler ones, such as iceberg.

Romaine and leaf lettuces benefit from washing before they go into the refrigerator, as long as you also dry them well. Greens like arugula and watercress, which are sold with the roots still attached, should have those roots wrapped in a damp paper towel before they are stored in the refrigerator, but you should wait to wash them until just before they will be used.

Livit Recipe

Livit Designer Salad

- 1 package (6 ounces) baby romaine, washed and trimmed
- ½ cup grape tomatoes, halved
- 1 small avocado, diced
- 6 strawberries, sliced
- ½ English cucumber, cut into ¼-inch cubes
- 1 fresh lemon, halved
- 1 tablespoon slivered raw almonds
- ¼ cup dried cranberries

- Put the romaine, tomatoes, avocado, strawberries, and cucumber into a large salad bowl. Squeeze juice from the fresh lemon halves over the top. Add almonds and cranberries, and toss gently to combine. Serve.
- NOTE This is a side dish. Serve with 3 ounces of canned wild Alaskan salmon or tuna and ½ cup of mandarin oranges for a complete meal.
- VARIATION For a more complete meal, add a half cup of black beans, a half cup of defrosted frozen corn, and 1 ounce of sliced fresh mozzarella cheese to the salad. To add more flavor, you can add any of these ingredients without adding calories: apple cider vinegar or balsamic vinegar, lemon pepper, or your favorite herbal seasoning.

YIELD 4 servings

NUTRITION ANALYSIS PER SERVING 131.6 calories, 17.5 g carbohydrate, 2.9 g protein, 7.9 g fat, 6.3 g dietary fiber

82 Mushrooms

Benefits

There was a time when the only mushrooms you could get in United States supermarkets were white "button" mushrooms. Now, we have access to a wealth of different tasty fungi. Shiitake, straw, crimini, enoki, and portobello are among the most common. Most share similar nutrition profiles: Many species are high in fiber and protein and provide several B vitamins, including thiamine, riboflavin, and niacin. Brown mushrooms appear to provide more antioxidants.

White button mushrooms provide vitamin D, one of the very few non-animal sources for this vitamin. Vitamin D is essential to calcium metabolism and bone health. Deficiency in vitamin D is implicated in a variety of conditions, from chronic pain to Parkinson's disease, including coronary and cardiovascular disease. Vitamin D also appears to play a role in the immune system, and it produces a hormone that has been effective against cancer cells in laboratory tests. White mushrooms may provide some major components of vitamin B_{12}, though whether this is in a form that can be used by the body remains uncertain.

Shiitake mushrooms have a long history of medicinal use in China. Ming Dynasty physician Wu Juei wrote that shiitakes were a tonic against a variety of ills, including premature aging. In modern times, a compound found in shiitakes called lentinan has been investigated for its potential tumor-inhibiting capabilities, as well as its antiviral and antibacterial properties. It appears to stimulate the production of white blood cells and other components of the immune system used to fight disease. Another compound in shiitakes, lenthionine, keeps blood platelets from sticking together and may help prevent blood clots and stroke. Ergothioneine, found in shiitakes and several other mushrooms (notably oyster and maitake mushrooms), is an antioxidant, but it behaves differently than other sulfur-containing antioxidants (such as those in Allium and Brassica foods). Mushrooms are the richest source of this compound, which scavenges free hydroxyl radicals and may help protect against nitric oxides and regulate metal-carrying enzymes.

Shiitake mushrooms are an excellent source of selenium and a very good source of iron. They are also a good source of protein, dietary fiber, and vitamin C.

NUTRITIONAL COMPOSITION (RAW MUSHROOMS) One-half cup of raw mushrooms provides 9 calories, 1.6 g carbohydrate, 0.7 g protein, 0.1 g fat, 0.4 g dietary fiber, 1 mg vitamin C, 1.4 mg niacin, 7 mcg folic acid, 130 mg potassium, 36 mg phosphorus, 2 mg calcium, and 4 mg magnesium.

NUTRITIONAL COMPOSITION (DRIED SHIITAKE MUSHROOMS) One ounce of dried shiitake mushrooms provides 83 calories, 21.1 g carbohydrate, 2.7 g protein, 0.3 g fat, 3.2 g dietary fiber, 1 mg vitamin C, 4 mg niacin, 46 mcg folic acid, 430 mg potassium, 82 mg phosphorus, 3 mg calcium, and 37 mg magnesium.

Bringing It Home

Many grocery stores now carry several types of mushrooms, both fresh and dried. (Some people prefer the taste of dried, reconstituted shiitakes in soups and stews, where they may add a more "meaty" texture.) They are also easy to find in Asian groceries. Fresh mushrooms should be firm and plump, not withered or dry, but also not wet or slimy. Refrigerate, but allow them to breathe. They should last about a week.

Mushrooms can be cleaned with a mushroom brush under running water, or gently peeled with a paring knife. Trim away the woody bottom of the stems.

Livit Recipe

Savory Mixed Mushroom Ragout

　　1 tablespoon olive oil
　1½ pounds crimini mushrooms, cleaned, with stems removed and caps quartered
　　1 pound shiitake mushrooms, cleaned, with stems removed and caps quartered
　　1 portobello mushroom, cleaned, with stems removed and caps quartered
　　1 small onion, minced
　　1 tablespoon flour
　　¼ cup sherry
　　1 cup vegetable stock
　　1 cup mushroom stock
　1½ teaspoons salt
　　2 cloves garlic, minced
5 or 6 sprigs fresh parsley, trimmed, rinsed, dried, and minced
　　2 tablespoons minced fresh thyme OR 1 tablespoon dried thyme
　　1 teaspoon pepper

- In a large skillet, heat the oil over medium heat. Cover the bottom of the skillet with a single layer of mushrooms and sear them. Continue until you have seared all the mushrooms, adding oil if needed. Remove the mushrooms from the pan and set them aside.

- In the same pan, sweat the onion until it is soft. You may need to add more oil to keep the onions from sticking. Add the flour, stirring gently, and cook for a few minutes. Add the sherry to the floured onions. Cook over medium heat until the liquid is reduced by half. Add the stock, mushrooms, salt, and garlic. Simmer uncovered for 20 to 30 minutes, until the liquid is reduced to the consistency of a sauce. Season with the parsley and thyme, and add pepper.

- NOTE To cut fresh herbs, put them in a glass and use kitchen scissors to snip them until they are minced. If using all fresh herbs, you need about 4 tablespoons total. If using dried herbs, you need about 2 tablespoons total.

- VARIATION Instead of 1 cup vegetable stock and 1 cup mushroom stock, you may use 2 cups of vegetable stock.

YIELD 6 servings

NUTRITION ANALYSIS PER SERVING 143 calories, 20.2 g carbohydrate, 5.6 g protein, 5.1 g fat, 3.7 g dietary fiber

83 Mustard Greens

Benefits

Mustard greens are another leafy member of the Brassica genus. An excellent source of the three antioxidant vitamins, A, C, and E, mustard greens are also a very good source of magnesium, which helps with muscle cramps and may help keep the smooth muscles lining the airways relaxed, which can be helpful to persons with asthma. Mustard greens are known to play a vital role in keeping blood pressure low. They are also an excellent source of calcium. The balance of calcium and magnesium is important to maintaining hydration as well as to healthy bones and blood pressure. Like other green leafy vegetables, mustard greens are full of fiber, carotenes, and vitamin K.

> **NUTRITIONAL COMPOSITION** One-half cup of chopped, boiled mustard greens provides 11 calories, 1.5 g carbohydrate, 1.6 g protein, 0.2 g fat, 1.4 g dietary fiber, 2122 IU vitamin A, 18 mg vitamin C, 51 mcg folic acid, 141 mg potassium, 11 mg sodium, 29 mg phosphorus, 52 mg calcium, and 11 mg magnesium.

Bringing It Home

Choose mustard greens that are a rich green color, with no yellowing or dry spots. The best way to store them is to wrap the greens in a damp paper towel, then put them into a plastic bag to be stored in the refrigerator. They will keep three to four days, but as with other Brassica, the longer you keep them, the stronger and more bitter the flavor becomes.

Livit Recipe

Red Potato Comfort Greens

- ½ teaspoon salt
- 2 pounds small red potatoes, scrubbed but not peeled
- 1 pound mustard greens (8 cups), trimmed, washed, and cut into 1-inch pieces
- 1 tablespoon extra-virgin olive oil
- 2 cloves garlic, minced
- ½ cup fat-free buttermilk
   Salt and pepper

· Fill a large saucepan with water, add salt, and bring the water to a boil. Add the potatoes to the boiling water and cook them for about 15 minutes, until they are tender. Lift the potatoes out of the water with a slotted spoon and transfer them to a medium bowl. (Leave the water boiling on the stove.) Using a potato masher or the back of a large spoon, crush the potatoes and set them aside.

· Put the greens into the boiling water. Cook them for 2 to 3 minutes, until they are tender. Drain and set aside.

- Dry the pot, add the oil, and heat it over medium heat. Once the oil is warm, add the garlic and sauté for about 1 minute, until it is fragrant. Add the cooked greens to the pan and toss them with the garlic. Stir in the crushed potatoes and buttermilk. Season to taste with salt and pepper. Serve.
- NOTE This dish can be prepared up to an hour before serving. Keep it warm over a large pan of barely simmering water.

YIELD 8 servings

NUTRITION ANALYSIS PER SERVING 119 calories, 22 g carbohydrate, 4 g protein, 2 g fat, 4 g dietary fiber

84 Onions

Benefits

Onions are a very good source of vitamin C and chromium, and they also provide manganese, molybdenum, vitamin B_6, folate, potassium, phosphorus, and copper.

Onions, like leeks, garlic, and shallots, are members of the Allium family, a group of plants with a characteristic taste caused by sulfur compounds that also have some powerful benefits for human health. These sulfur compounds are being investigated for their anti-inflammatory, antioxidant, cholesterol-lowering, and cancer-fighting potential. Eating onions and other Allium vegetables regularly is associated with a lowered incidence of several types of cancers. The sulfur compounds are also known to help lower blood pressure and keep plaque from forming in blood vessels, and the B_6 that they provide helps reduce blood levels of homocysteine. Onions do a lot to help preserve cardiovascular health!

The chromium in onions is essential to the proper metabolism of sugar, and people at risk for diabetes may benefit from its glucose-regulating properties.

Another sulfur compound in onions that's come under study more recently may help prevent the absorption of bone, reducing the risk of osteoporosis.

Tests have suggested that the more pungent the onion, the more phenols and flavonoids it has—and the more likely it is to have a positive effect on your health. Eat the mild, sweet onions, too, but don't avoid the sharp ones. This is a vegetable worth risking the occasional watery eye for!

NUTRITIONAL COMPOSITION One-half cup of chopped raw onion provides 30 calories, 6.9 g carbohydrate, 0.9 g protein, 0.1 g fat, 1.4 g dietary fiber, 5 mg vitamin C, 15 mcg folic acid, 126 mg potassium, 2 mg sodium, 26 mg phosphorus, 16 mg calcium, and 8 mg magnesium.

Bringing It Home

Onions should be hard, not mushy, and the skins should be crisp and dry. Choose onions that have no hint of sprouting and no bruises. Store them away from heat, light, and moisture. All three are likely to make them start sprouting and turn mushy. Don't store whole onions in the refrigerator; it is too damp an environment for them. Kept cool and dry, onions will last for at least a month.

Don't store potatoes and onions together—they will both spoil!

To keep chopped onion on hand for use in recipes, seal some in plastic zipper bags and keep them in the refrigerator or freezer. Chopped onion will keep in the refrigerator for 30 days or in the freezer for about six months.

Livit Recipe

Traditional French Onion Soup Gone Healthy

3 or 4 slices whole wheat OR brown-rice bread (3.5 ounces), cut into 1-inch squares
1 teaspoon olive oil
1 pound white onions, thinly sliced
4 cups low-sodium vegetable broth
Salt
Freshly ground black pepper
4 ounces reduced-fat Swiss cheese OR low-sodium French Yogurt Cheese, cut into 4 slices

· Preheat oven to 350°F.

· Set the squares of bread on a cookie sheet, and lightly toast them in the oven for 5 to 10 minutes. Once they are toasted, remove them from the oven, but leave the oven on.

· Lightly oil a large skillet, using a paper towel to spread the oil evenly and absorb the excess. Place the oiled skillet over medium-high heat. Add the onions. Cook the onions until they have browned and caramelized, stirring constantly to keep them from sticking or burning. Add the vegetable broth. Add salt and pepper to taste. Stir well to deglaze, scraping the flavorful browned bits from the bottom of the pan. Reduce heat, and simmer for 3 to 4 minutes.

· Prepare for serving in 4 oven-safe soup bowls: Put 2 spoonfuls of the cooked onions into the bottom of each bowl. Divide the toast squares among the bowls, then add the rest of the soup, distributing broth and onions evenly among the 4 bowls. Top the soup with sliced Swiss cheese. Place the bowls in the oven. Bake until the cheese is melted and golden brown. Serve immediately.

· NOTE For a complete meal, serve with a mixed green salad and a whole wheat roll or slice of sprouted grain toast.

· VARIATION For more protein, add some white beans to the soup.

YIELD 4 servings

NUTRITION ANALYSIS PER SERVING 234 calories, 28 g carbohydrate, 5.5 g protein, 8.8 g fat, 3.7 g dietary fiber

85 Parsley

Benefits

Parsley is an excellent source of vitamins A, C, and K, as well as a good source of iron and folate. If eaten in quantities appropriate for a vegetable rather than a spice, it can provide calcium, potassium, magnesium, phosphorus, zinc, beta-carotene, and lutein. Parsley will also cleanse both your palate and your breath after a meal!

Parsley contains some interesting chemical compounds that warrant further study: volatile oils, including myristicin, limonene, eugenol, and alpha-thujene, and antioxidant flavonoids, including apiin, apigenin, crisoeriol, and luteolin. The volatile oils have shown potential to prevent the formation of cancerous tumors and may have positive effects on mood and cognition. Parsley has also shown potential for reducing inflammation in conditions such as rheumatoid arthritis.

These complex chemicals have not yet been fully studied, and some are known to have toxic effects when taken in large doses. For example, parsley also contains apiol, a substance that appears to affect the female hormonal system and was at one time used to induce miscarriage of unwanted pregnancies. For this reason, pregnant women should not use parsley seeds or essential oil of parsley in medicinal quantities.

Parsley also contains measurable amounts of oxalates, so over-consumption can cause problems for those with kidney disease, gout, vulvar pain, rheumatoid arthritis, or other conditions that may require a low-oxalate diet.

NUTRITIONAL COMPOSITION One-half cup of chopped fresh parsley provides 11 calories, 1.9 g carbohydrate, 0.9 g protein, 0.2 g fat, 1 g dietary fiber, 1560 IU vitamin A, 40 mg vitamin C, 46 mcg folic acid, 166 mg potassium, 17 mg sodium, 17 mg phosphorus, 41 mg calcium, 1.86 mg iron, and 15 mg magnesium.

Bringing It Home

Fresh parsley contains more vitamin C and volatile oils than the dried version. Use the dried form for flavoring when you have to, but if the parsley is a featured item on the menu, use fresh. Fresh parsley should have a rich green color; it should be crisp, without yellow or dry-looking leaves. Refrigerate fresh parsley in a plastic bag. A spritz of water before it goes into the refrigerator can help restore parsley that has wilted a bit in transit.

Parsley comes in two varieties: curly, which is familiar as a garnish, and flat-leaf, or Italian, which is more often used as an ingredient in Mediterranean and Middle Eastern dishes.

You can dry your own parsley, if you wish. The flat-leaf variety dries better than the curly, and that's what's most often used in cooking. Dry the flat-leaf parsley by laying it out in a single layer on a couple of thicknesses of clean paper towel. Once it has dried, keep it in an airtight container away from light, heat, and moisture. To preserve curly parsley, you're better off freezing it in a plastic zipper bag than drying it.

Livit Recipe

Parsley Tabbouleh

1 cup water	2 tablespoons olive oil
½ cup bulgur	2 bunches flat-leaf parsley, rinsed, trimmed, and minced
2 fresh lemons, juice only	3 or 4 sprigs fresh mint, rinsed, trimmed, and minced
1 small clove garlic, minced	2 medium tomatoes, diced
¼ teaspoon salt	1 small cucumber, peeled and diced
Freshly ground pepper	4 scallions, trimmed and sliced into thin rings

- In a small saucepan, bring the water and bulgur to a full boil. Once the water has come to a boil, remove from heat, cover tightly, and let stand for about 25 minutes, until the bulgur is soft and has absorbed all the water. Put the bulgur in a large serving bowl and set it aside to cool for about 15 minutes.
- In a small bowl, combine lemon juice, garlic, salt, and pepper. Whisk in the oil until it is emulsified.
- Add the parsley, mint, tomatoes, cucumber, and scallions to the bulgur in the serving bowl. Add the oil dressing to the bulgur and toss gently until the ingredients are distributed evenly.
- Serve at room temperature or chilled. If served chilled, it should be refrigerated for at least 1 hour.
- NOTE To mince parsley or mint, put a small handful of the fresh herb into a glass and use kitchen scissors to snip it until it is finely minced.

YIELD 4 servings

NUTRITION ANALYSIS PER SERVING 165 calories, 22 g carbohydrate, 4 g protein, 8 g fat, 6 g dietary fiber

86 Parsnips

Benefits

Parsnips are an excellent source of vitamin C, folic acid, pantothenic acid, copper, manganese, and fiber. They also provide vitamin E; the B vitamins niacin, thiamine, riboflavin, and B_6; and the minerals magnesium and potassium.

Parsnips are lower in calories and provide only about half as much protein and vitamin C as potatoes, but they contain more fiber and folic acid. Although closely related to carrots, they lack beta-carotene and, consequently, the orange color. Parsnips provide more potassium than carrots.

NUTRITIONAL COMPOSITION One-half cup of boiled parsnips provides 63 calories, 15.2 g carbohydrate, 1 g protein, 0.2 g fat, 3.1 g dietary fiber, 10 mg vitamin C, 45 mcg folic acid, 286 mg potassium, 8 mg sodium, 54 mg phosphorus, 29 mg calcium, and 23 mg magnesium.

Bringing It Home

Parsnips once played a more prominent role in European cuisine, but that role was largely taken over by potatoes once potatoes were exported from the Americas. Even in colonial America, parsnips were prominently featured in stews and soups. Parsnips can be left in the ground over the winter and harvested as needed, and their taste gets sweeter after a frost—both helpful attributes in the days before refrigeration.

Parsnips look like carrots, but they are often larger and have a pale golden color. Look for parsnips that are straight and firm. If they are rubbery or shriveled, they won't be tasty. Parsnips that are allowed to get very large start to lose their distinctive flavor and may have a woody core, which is flavorless. Parsnips need to be peeled before cooking; if they have gained a woody core, trim it away.

Store parsnips in the refrigerator in a perforated plastic bag, but don't wash them before storing. They will keep for four to five weeks. You can also freeze them: Wash, trim, and peel the parsnips, then cut them into chunks. Drop the chunks into boiling water and boil for three minutes. Remove them from the pot and cool them under cold water to stop the cooking. Drain well, and pack them in plastic zipper bags.

Parsnips are among the tastiest vegetables to roast in the oven. Try mixing parsnips with an equal number of carrots.

Livit Recipes

Butternut Squash and Parsnip Puree

1 butternut squash (1½ pounds), peeled and cut into 1-inch cubes
1 pound parsnips, peeled and cut into ½-inch thick slices
1 tablespoon tahini
½ teaspoon nutmeg
Salt

- Put the squash and parsnips into a large saucepan and add enough water to cover them completely. Bring the water to a boil and cook for about 10 minutes, until they are soft enough to puree.
- Drain the vegetables, reserving ¼ cup of the water in case you need it when blending.
- In a blender jar, process the squash and parsnips with the tahini and nutmeg. Add salt to taste. Puree until smooth.

YIELD 4 servings

NUTRITION ANALYSIS PER SERVING 171 calories, 38 g carbohydrate, 3.6 g protein, 2.5 g fat, 9.4 g dietary fiber

Whole Roasted Parsnips

1½ pounds whole parsnips, trimmed and peeled
1 tablespoon canola oil

- Preheat oven to 500°F.
- Put the parsnips in a baking pan that allows them to fit snugly in a single layer. Drizzle oil over the parsnips and roll them in it until they are coated on all sides. Roast in the oven for 15 minutes.
- Turn parsnips, using tongs. Return the pan to the oven. Roast for another 15 minutes.

YIELD 4 servings

NUTRITION ANALYSIS PER SERVING 151 calories, 29 g carbohydrate, 2.2 g protein, 4 g fat, 6.1 g dietary fiber

8₇ Radishes

Benefits

Radishes, perhaps surprisingly, are yet another cruciferous vegetable. The familiar red, white, or purple radish seen in grocery stores is a spring or summer radish. It is rich in vitamin C, folic acid, and potassium, as well as a good source of vitamin B_6, riboflavin, magnesium, copper, and calcium. Radishes are also relatively high in fiber.

Radish greens are said to have six times the vitamin C of the roots, and they provide calcium as well. The Oriental radish, also known as daikon, is a larger, winter radish. It is also a good source of vitamin C.

As with the other cruciferous vegetables, radishes contain compounds that show potential in fighting cancer. Daikon also contains an enzyme called myrosinase that is believed to help in digestion and that, in the presence of water, converts to thiocyanates and isothiocyanates, some of which may be involved in the radish's anti-cancer benefits.

NUTRITIONAL COMPOSITION (SUMMER RADISHES) Ten medium raw summer radishes provide 8 calories, 1.6 g carbohydrate, 0.3 g protein, 0.2 g fat, 0.7 g dietary fiber, 4 IU vitamin A, 10 mg vitamin C, 12 mcg folic acid, 104 mg potassium, 11 mg sodium, 8 mg phosphorus, 9 mg calcium, and 4 mg magnesium.

NUTRITIONAL COMPOSITION (ORIENTAL RADISH) One raw Oriental radish (daikon) provides 61 calories, 13.9 g carbohydrate, 2 g protein, 0.34 g fat, 5 g dietary fiber, 74.4 mg vitamin C, 95 mcg folic acid, 767 mg potassium, 71 mg sodium, 78 mg phosphorus, 91 mg calcium, and 54 mg magnesium.

Bringing It Home

Look for spring and summer radishes at farmer's markets. Choose brightly colored radishes that are smooth and firm and not too big. If you can find them fresh with the green tops on, all the better. Trim off the greens, and store the greens and bulbs separately in the refrigerator. Eat the greens within a day or two; the bulbs will keep up to a week. Radishes don't need to be peeled. Just scrub them before eating.

Daikon and other winter radishes should be smooth and hard, with no soft spots or bruises; they are usually white.

Livit Recipe

Radish Salad

20 small colorful radishes, trimmed, scrubbed, and thinly sliced
1 green bell pepper, seeded and sliced into fine slivers
2 tablespoons apple cider vinegar
4 teaspoons reduced-sodium soy sauce
1 tablespoon agave nectar

- In a salad serving bowl, combine radishes and green pepper.
- In a cup, whisk together the cider vinegar, soy sauce, and agave nectar. Drizzle this dressing over the radishes and peppers. Toss gently until they are well coated. Serve.

YIELD 4 servings

NUTRITION ANALYSIS PER SERVING 18 calories, 4 g carbohydrate, 0.7 g protein, 0.1 g fat, 0.6 g dietary fiber

88 Rhubarb

Benefits

Rhubarb is a good source of vitamin C, fiber, and calcium, and it also provides some potassium. Rhubarb is very low in calories, and half of its carbohydrates are dietary fiber. Since it is very tart, rhubarb is usually sweetened with sugar when cooked. Its unusual flavor has led to its use in traditional medicine in many regions. It is known for its laxative effect, and the roots were initially cultivated for use as a purgative or cathartic.

More recently, researchers have been investigating rhubarb's potential as a cancer-fighting food. Anthraquinones in rhubarb appear to attack cancer cells in several different ways, including starving tumor cells by interfering with their ability to take in glucose, limiting their proliferation, and preventing metastasis (the traveling of cancer cells to other parts of the body). One rhubarb extract may also help relax blood vessels, lowering blood pressure. Another appears to help constrict blood vessels, useful for stopping bleeding. Rhubarb also appears to have antioxidant and anti-inflammatory properties.

Rhubarb, however, is a food that not only contains measurable amounts of oxalates, but is actually quite high in them. The leaves are so high in oxalic acid that they are regarded as poisonous, and although they were used in some traditional soups, it is better to avoid eating them altogether. The leaves also contain a second toxin, possibly anthraquinone glycoside, which is thought to be related to its laxative effect. The stalks contain much less oxalate, and these can be eaten by those who are not at risk. However, rhubarb can cause problems for those with kidney disease, gout, vulvar pain, rheumatoid arthritis, or other conditions that may require a low-oxalate diet.

NUTRITIONAL COMPOSITION One cup of frozen raw rhubarb provides 29 calories, 7 g carbohydrate, 0.8 g protein. 0.2 g fat, 2.5 g dietary fiber, 147 IU vitamin A, 7 mg vitamin C, 11 mcg folic acid, 148 mg potassium, 3 mg sodium, 266 mg calcium, 16 mg phosphorus, and 25 mg magnesium.

Bringing It Home

Fresh local rhubarb is often available at farmer's markets in late spring—sometimes as early as April. Because it's ready so early, there is sometimes a second crop around the beginning of July. Some varieties of rhubarb are still green in color when ripe, but the redder the stalks, the more anthocyanins it is likely to contain, so if you have a choice, buy red ones. Stalks should be firm, glossy, and crisp.

If you buy rhubarb stalks with the leaves on, remember that the leaves are toxic—only the stalks are edible. Cut the leaves off and discard them as soon as you get the rhubarb home. Stored in plastic zipper bags, rhubarb stalks will keep in the refrigerator for two or three weeks. Peel any tough outer strings before cooking.

To crisp rhubarb before cooking, stand the trimmed stalks in a glass of cold water.

Rhubarb freezes well. Wash and trim the stalks, then drop them into boiling water. Boil for one minute, then remove, rinse in cold water to stop the cooking, drain, and pack in plastic zipper bags.

Livit Recipe

Rhubarb-Banana Crumble

¼ cup non-hydrogenated margarine plus enough margarine to grease the dish
2 large bananas, peeled and cut into ¼-inch slices
1 pound raw rhubarb, washed, trimmed, and diced OR 10 ounces frozen rhubarb, thawed
2 tablespoons brown sugar
¼ teaspoon cinnamon
Dash of nutmeg

½ cup whole wheat pastry flour
½ cup graham cracker crumbs (about 6 squares)
1½ teaspoons baking powder
1 egg, lightly beaten
¼ cup skim milk

- Preheat oven to 400°F.
- Using a small amount of margarine, grease the inside of a 9″ pie plate or a shallow glass or ceramic baking dish.
- In a medium bowl, combine the bananas, rhubarb, sugar, cinnamon, and nutmeg. Spoon this mixture into the greased baking dish.
- In another medium bowl, combine the flour, graham cracker crumbs, and baking powder. Cut in the ¼ cup margarine until the mixture is crumbly.
- In a small bowl, lightly beat the egg, then add the milk. Mix them together and add the milk mixture to the dry ingredients.
- Drop the batter by spoonfuls over the top of the fruit mixture, covering the top as evenly as possible. Bake for 25 to 30 minutes. Serve warm or at room temperature.

YIELD 6 servings

NUTRITION ANALYSIS PER SERVING 217.6 calories, 31.1 g carbohydrate, 4.2 g protein, 9.6 g fat, 3.4 g dietary fiber

89 Rutabaga

Benefits

Rutabagas are believed to have begun as a cross between a cabbage and a turnip, both cruciferous vegetables. They are also known as "Swedish turnips," sometimes shortened to "swedes." Rutabagas are an excellent source of vitamin C and a good source of vitamin A and potassium. They are also high in fiber.

Rutabagas are loaded with phytochemicals, including carotenoids, terpenes, flavonoids, coumarins, indoles, phenolic acids, and isothiocyanates. Many of these chemicals are believed to act as antioxidants and cancer fighters; they may also help preserve vision and lower blood pressure.

Cooked rutabagas are somewhere in between our "starchy vegetable" and "true vegetable" categories. They provide about 35 calories per half-cup serving. But they can also be eaten raw, which preserves more of their vitamins A and C, so try them in thin slices as an addition to salads.

NUTRITIONAL COMPOSITION One-half cup of boiled rutabaga cubes provides 33 calories, 7.4 g carbohydrate, 1.1 g protein, 0.2 g fat, 1.5 g dietary fiber, 477 IU vitamin A, 16 mg vitamin C, 13 mcg folic acid, 277 mg potassium, 17 mg sodium, 48 mg phosphorus, 41 mg calcium, and 20 mg magnesium.

Bringing It Home

Rutabagas are a vegetable that has historically stored well over the winter. They should be firm and heavy, without soft spots or signs of shriveling. Rutabagas will keep in the refrigerator for three to four weeks. If you want to freeze rutabagas, cook and mash them first.

Livit Recipe

Smooth Rutabaga Soup

1 rutabaga (2 pounds), peeled and cut into 1-inch cubes
1 cup organic skim milk OR 1% milk
¼ teaspoon nutmeg

- Put the rutabaga into a medium saucepan and add cold water to cover the rutabaga. Bring the water to a boil, then reduce heat and simmer for about 20 minutes, until the rutabaga is tender. Drain the rutabaga and discard the water.
- In the container of a food processor or blender, puree the cooked rutabaga.
- Heat the milk in the saucepan over low heat. Once the milk is warm, stir in the rutabaga. Add nutmeg. Cook, stirring, for another 1 to 2 minutes. Serve in soup bowls.

YIELD 4 servings

NUTRITION ANALYSIS PER SERVING (made with 1% milk) 76 calories, 14.4 g carbohydrate, 3.7 g protein, 0.9 g fat, 3.5 g dietary fiber

90 Salsa

Benefits

Traditionally, salsa is made of tomatoes, hot peppers, onions, lemon or lime juice, and cilantro, but you can add any number of fruits or vegetables to it for variety. In diet terms, it is a "free" condiment, that is, the calorie content is so low for the quantities at which it is normally eaten that it's not worth counting.

Ironically, for something that tastes so good, almost all the ingredients have significant health benefits. The tomatoes bring vitamin C and lycopene, the peppers add capsaicin, and the onions bring their Allium-family goodness. Salsa is full of anti-inflammatory, antioxidant, cholesterol-lowering, and cancer-fighting compounds. This is one treat it's hard to overdose on!

NUTRITIONAL COMPOSITION One-quarter cup of a typical salsa provides 10 calories, 2 g carbohydrate, 0 g protein, 0 g fat, 0 g dietary fiber, 125 mg sodium, 54 IU vitamin A, 9 mg vitamin C, 1 mg calcium, and 30 mg phosphorus.

Bringing It Home

If you are buying salsa, choose one that's low in sodium—less than 140 mg per serving. The salsas sold in the refrigerator case will have more fresh goodness and zing than those that are sold in jars on the shelves. The refrigerated salsas are usually uncooked—or less cooked—than what is sold in shelf-stable jars, and they may also have fewer preservatives. But salsa is even more wonderful when you make it yourself. Try adding diced jicama, oranges, pears, or berries!

If refrigerated, fresh salsa lasts about a week.

Livit Recipe

Kick It Up Salsa

See Handling Jalapeños! on page 86. Remember to keep your hands away from your eyes!

     3 medium fresh tomatoes, diced
    ½ red onion, diced
     1 jalapeño pepper, with stems and seeds removed, finely diced (reserve trimmed pepper ribs)
     1 serrano pepper, with stems and seeds removed, finely diced (reserve trimmed pepper ribs)
     1 lime, juice only
    ½ cup chopped fresh cilantro
        Salt
        Pepper
        Oregano, optional
        Cumin, optional

- In a medium bowl, combine the tomatoes, onion, peppers, lime juice, and cilantro. Add salt and pepper to taste; add the oregano and cumin, if using. Taste. If the salsa isn't hot enough, dice some of the reserved pepper ribs very finely (remember to put gloves back on) and add just a little at a time to the salsa.
- Let the salsa sit in the refrigerator for at least an hour to allow the flavors to blend.
- NOTE Sometimes the flavor gets hotter as the salsa sits, so don't go overboard with adding pepper right away.

YIELD 32 servings (2 tablespoons each), or about 3 to 4 cups

NUTRITION ANALYSIS PER SERVING 3.6 calories, 0.8 g carbohydrate, 0.1 g protein, 0 g fat, 0.2 g dietary fiber

91 Scallions

Benefits

Scallions are also known as spring onions or green onions. Some scallions found in stores are young onions of the standard yellow or white cooking variety, harvested before they have had time to develop full round bulbs. There are also varieties that are specifically bred as green onions. The green tops are often used along with the bulb, so scallions may provide more of vitamins A, C, and K than their more mature relations. They are also a source of folate, calcium, and potassium.

NUTRITIONAL COMPOSITION One medium scallion (4⅛ inches long) provides 4.8 calories, 3.9 g carbohydrate, 0.7 g protein, 0.2 g fat, 0.4 g dietary fiber, 150 IU vitamin A, 28 mg vitamin C, 31.1 mcg vitamin K, 9.6 mcg folic acid, 41.4 mg potassium, 10.8 mg calcium, 5.6 mg phosphorus, and 3 mg magnesium.

Bringing It Home

Look for fresh local scallions at your farmer's market as well as at the grocery store. They should seem crisp, with bright green leaves and firm white bulbs. They will keep in the refrigerator for up to a week. Don't wash them until you're ready to eat them. To clean green onions, rinse them, trim off the roots, and strip away any wilted outer layers. The flavor of green onions is so delicate that they are usually best served raw, or just lightly stir-fried.

Livit Recipe

Fueling Scallions

This dish provides a high-fiber carbohydrate fuel plus a vegetable all in one dish.

   1 cup raw brown rice
2½ cups low-sodium chicken broth OR vegetable broth
   1 tablespoon non-hydrogenated margarine
   2 tablespoons extra-virgin olive oil
  ½ pound mushrooms, thinly sliced
   4 medium scallions (including the tops), thinly sliced
  ¼ teaspoon salt
  ¼ teaspoon black pepper

- In a large, heavy saucepan, bring the rice, broth, and margarine to a boil over high heat. Reduce heat, cover, and simmer for about 45 to 50 minutes, until the rice is tender and the broth is absorbed. Fluff it with a fork and keep it warm until the rest of the ingredients are ready.
- In a large heavy skillet, heat olive oil over moderate heat for 1 minute. Add mushrooms and scallions and stir-fry until golden, about 5 minutes. Remove pan from heat and add rice, salt, and pepper. Toss gently until all is well distributed.

YIELD 4 servings

NUTRITION ANALYSIS PER SERVING 273 calories, 38.4 g carbohydrate, 5.8 g protein, 11.1 g fat, 3.7 g dietary fiber

92 Shallots

Benefits

Shallots are one of the more elegant members of the Allium family. They provide vitamins A and C, folic acid, potassium, calcium, and iron, as well as fiber. In at least one study, shallots were found to have more phenols and higher antioxidant activity than most of the commercially available varieties of onions. This means that they may be even better than the other Alliums at lowering blood pressure, preventing atherosclerosis, and inhibiting the onset and proliferation of cancers.

NUTRITIONAL COMPOSITION One tablespoon of chopped raw shallots provides 7 calories, 1.7 g carbohydrate, 0.3 g protein, 0 g fat, 0 g dietary fiber, 1248 IU vitamin A, 1 mg vitamin C, 3 mcg folic acid, 33 mg potassium, 1 mg sodium, 6 mg phosphorus, 4 mg calcium, and 2 mg magnesium.

Bringing It Home

Shallots should be dry, firm, and plump—not wrinkled, mushy, or sprouting. Also watch for any signs of black mold. Most of the shallots available in the supermarket have been dried and can be kept for a month or more.

Shallots are a little like onions and a little like garlic—they have tops and a papery skin, but they also have cloves. Remove the outer skin to separate the cloves. Shallots can be used raw or cooked. They add a subtle onion taste to dishes, and they caramelize well.

Try freezing minced shallots in ice cube trays. Measure two tablespoons of minced shallots into each compartment. Once they're frozen solid, you can transfer the cubes into plastic zipper bags and store them in the freezer for up to eight months. Freezing breaks down the cell membranes somewhat, so the frozen shallots are best used for cooking.

If you have fresh shallots with the greens still attached, you can use the tops like chives or scallions. In fact, in some countries, "scallion" is used to mean shallot tops.

Finely diced shallots are a wonderful addition to salad dressings, or you can add them directly to the salad. Use minced shallots in soups, stews, and sauces. Use shallots in place of onions in delicately flavored dishes such as quiche and omelets.

Livit Recipe

Brussels Sprouts with Caramelized Shallots

4 tablespoons olive oil
½ pound shallots, thinly sliced
   Coarse kosher salt
   Black pepper
2 tablespoons apple cider vinegar
1 teaspoon sugar
1½ pounds Brussels sprouts, trimmed and cut into ⅛-inch slices
1 cup water

Carbohydrates:
"True"
Vegetables
· · · · ·
151

- In a medium skillet, heat 2 tablespoons of the olive oil over medium heat. Once the oil is hot, add the shallots. Sprinkle with salt and pepper. Sauté about 10 minutes, until the shallots are soft and golden. Add vinegar and sugar. Cook for about 3 more minutes, stirring constantly, until the shallots are brown and glazed. Set aside.

- In a large skillet, heat the remaining 2 tablespoons of oil over medium-high heat. Once the oil is hot, add the Brussels sprouts. Sprinkle the Brussels sprouts with a little salt and pepper. Sauté them for about 6 minutes, until they are brown at the edges. Add 1 cup of water. Sauté another 3 minutes, until most of the water has evaporated and the sprouts are tender but still bright green.

- Transfer to a serving bowl and add the shallots. Season to taste with salt and pepper. Serve.

YIELD 6 servings

NUTRITION ANALYSIS PER SERVING 159 calories, 17.5 g carbohydrate, 4.8 g protein, 9.4 g fat, 4.3 g dietary fiber

93 Spinach

Benefits

Popeye the Sailor was ahead of his time! Spinach provides vitamins A, C, and K; B vitamins including folate and riboflavin; and the minerals iron, calcium, magnesium, manganese, potassium, copper, phosphorus, zinc, and selenium. Vitamin C helps the body make use of the iron found in spinach. Although cooking reduces the vitamin C, it helps make the iron more bioavailable in other ways, so spinach is a better source of iron when cooked. Consider serving it with an additional source of vitamin C to enhance iron absorption.

Spinach is also rich in antioxidants and even provides some omega-3 fatty acids. It is an excellent source of lutein, which appears to protect the eye from sun damage. People whose diets are high in spinach were found to have reduced their risk of both cataracts and age-related macular degeneration.

Spinach is one of the foods that contains measurable amounts of oxalates, so over-consumption can cause problems for those with kidney disease, gout, vulvar pain, rheumatoid arthritis, or other conditions that may require a low-oxalate diet. The oxalates in spinach may also interfere with the body's absorption of some of the minerals spinach provides.

NUTRITIONAL COMPOSITION One-half cup of boiled spinach provides 21 calories, 3.4 g carbohydrate, 2.7 g protein, 0.2 g fat, 2.2 g dietary fiber, 7371 IU vitamin A, 9 mg vitamin C, 131 mcg folic acid, 63 mg sodium, 419 mg potassium, 122 mg calcium, 50 mg phosphorus, 78 mg magnesium, and 3.21 mg iron.

Bringing It Home

Spinach is available in the supermarket nearly year-round, but if you can find it at a farmer's market in season, it is a much more tender and flavorful treat. Spinach should be a deep, rich green, with no yellowing, wilting, or bruising. Don't buy spinach that shows evidence of slimy leaves.

Keep spinach in the refrigerator in a roomy plastic bag. If possible, sort through and remove any questionable leaves before you refrigerate it, but don't wash the spinach until you are ready to use it. When you wash it, be sure to get all the sand and grit out of it.

Frozen spinach is a great convenience food and allows you to add this great vegetable to almost any cooked dish. Steam frozen spinach for four to eight minutes, until the frost is gone, and use it wherever you would use fresh spinach.

A quarter cup of orange sections or sliced strawberries in a spinach salad will add the vitamin C that helps your body absorb the iron in spinach. When cooking spinach, a quick steam is usually better than a long boil for retaining nutrients, texture, and flavor.

Livit Recipe

Cheesy Spinach Squares

Canola oil
1 whole egg
2 egg whites
6 tablespoons whole wheat pastry flour
10 ounces frozen chopped spinach, thawed and drained OR
   1 pound fresh spinach, washed, drained, trimmed, and coarsely chopped
16 ounces (2 cups) low-fat cottage cheese
6 ounces cheddar cheese, grated
¼ teaspoon ground black pepper
⅛ teaspoon cayenne pepper
Pinch of nutmeg, optional
3 tablespoons raw wheat germ

- Preheat oven to 350°F.
- Grease a 13″ × 9″ baking pan lightly with canola oil, using a paper towel to spread the oil and soak up the excess.
- In a large bowl, beat the egg and egg whites with the flour until the mixture is smooth. Add the spinach, cottage cheese, cheddar cheese, pepper, and cayenne. Add nutmeg, if using. Mix the ingredients well.
- Pour the spinach and cheese mixture into the baking pan. Sprinkle wheat germ over the top. Bake for 45 minutes. Remove from oven and let stand for about 10 minutes. Cut into 1½″ squares and serve.
- NOTE Frozen spinach may be defrosted by steaming it lightly (4 minutes or less). Drain well in a colander, pressing with a wooden spoon to get all the water out.

YIELD 10 servings

NUTRITION ANALYSIS PER SERVING 166 calories, 7 g carbohydrate, 14 g protein, 8 g fat, 1.5 g dietary fiber

94 Summer Squash

Benefits

The summer squashes include yellow squash, yellow crookneck, and pattypan, as well as zucchini, which is so numerous it gets its own entry! Tender, yellow summer squash provides vitamins A and C; the B vitamins B_6, riboflavin, niacin, and folate; and the minerals potassium and magnesium. They are a good source of fiber and, at 93 percent water, low in calories and helpful for staying hydrated in the summer heat. They also provide lutein and zeaxanthin, two carotenoids that help preserve vision.

> NUTRITIONAL COMPOSITION One cup of sliced raw summer squash provides 12 calories, 5.2 g carbohydrate, 1.2 g protein, 0.4 g fat, 2.4 g dietary fiber, 440 IU vitamin A, 10 mg vitamin C, 30 mcg folic acid, 276 mg potassium, 2 mg sodium, 42 mg phosphorus, 28 mg calcium, and 28 mg magnesium.

Bringing It Home

Yellow summer squash is available in the supermarket almost year-round, but the sweetest and most flavorful are local squash bought in season, so keep an eye out for them at your farmer's market. Pattypans are a bit less common, but they should be available at least in the summer.

Yellow summer squash should be strong, bright yellow, firm, and unbruised. The smaller ones are better; the big ones can be bland and woody tasting. Pattypans, or cymlings, are a delicate pale green with ruffled edges; they are best when no larger than 3 inches in diameter. Their skins should be thin and delicate, and they should feel heavy. Neither type should look withered or dry.

Keep summer squash in the refrigerator in a plastic bag; it will keep for three or four days. This squash is so full of water that it does not freeze well, either raw or cooked.

You can use most summer squash raw, or steam it very lightly for a simple, low-calorie vegetable side dish. Sprinkle grated summer squash on top of salads and sandwiches. Enjoy an easy seasonal ratatouille by sautéing summer squash, onions, bell peppers, eggplant, and tomatoes and simmering the mixture in tomato sauce. Season to taste. Serve raw summer squash cut into strips or bite-sized pieces with your favorite dips.

Livit Recipe

Summer Squash Bread

Canola oil
¾ cup sugar
½ cup unsweetened applesauce
1 egg
6 tablespoons pasteurized liquid egg whites
1 teaspoon vanilla extract
1¾ cups organic all-purpose flour
1 cup whole wheat pastry flour
¼ teaspoon salt
1 teaspoon baking soda
½ teaspoon cinnamon
2 cups shredded summer squash
½ cup chopped nuts

- Preheat oven to 350°F.
- Grease a 9″ loaf pan with canola oil, using a paper towel to distribute the oil evenly and soak up any excess.
- In a large mixing bowl, beat together the sugar, applesauce, egg, egg whites, and vanilla.
- In a separate bowl, sift together the all-purpose flour, wheat pastry flour, salt, baking soda, and cinnamon.
- Add the flour mixture to the applesauce mixture and stir to combine. Gently stir in the squash and nuts. Pour the batter into the greased loaf pan and bake for 50 to 60 minutes.

YIELD 12 slices

NUTRITION ANALYSIS PER SERVING 206 calories, 36.3 g carbohydrate, 6.9 g protein, 4.4 g fat, 2.6 g dietary fiber

95 Swiss Chard

Benefits

Swiss chard is a green that is closely related to beets. The same betacyanins and betaxanthins found in beets are found in chard. Swiss chard also contains antioxidant phenols and flavonols, which have been shown in the laboratory to inhibit the growth of some types of cancer cells.

Chard is an excellent source of vitamins C, E, and K, and the minerals potassium, magnesium, iron, and manganese. It also provides the B vitamins B_6, thiamine, niacin, and folic acid, and the minerals calcium, selenium, and zinc. It is a good source of carotenes and fiber. With 27.4 percent of the recommended daily value for potassium and 47 percent of the recommended daily value for magnesium in a one-cup serving, chard helps keep blood pressure down.

Swiss chard does contain measurable amounts of oxalates, so over-consumption can cause problems for those with kidney disease, gout, vulvar pain, rheumatoid arthritis, or other conditions that may require a low-oxalate diet.

NUTRITIONAL COMPOSITION One-half cup of boiled, chopped Swiss chard provides 18 calories, 3.6 g carbohydrate, 1.7 g protein, 0.1 g fat, 1.8 g dietary fiber, 2762 IU vitamin A, 16 mg vitamin C, 8 mcg folic acid, 483 mg potassium, 158 mg sodium, 29 mg phosphorus, 51 mg calcium, 2 mg iron, and 76 mg magnesium.

Bringing It Home

Look for Swiss chard in season at farmer's markets. This leafy green is delicious when young and tender, as well as later in the season, when the leaves are larger and the ribs are tougher. It should be a deep, dark green, without yellowing or browning, and the leaves should show no signs of wilting.

Store chard in the refrigerator in a plastic bag. It will keep for three to five days. Do not wash it until you are ready to use it.

Prepare the chard by washing it well to remove all the grit. If you have tender baby chard, you can cook it stems and all. If you have older, tougher chard, trim the leaves away from the stems and central ribs and cook the leaves separately from the stems and ribs. The stems and ribs taste slightly of beets.

You can stuff chard leaves the way you would cabbage leaves, with a filling of whole grain and seasoned ground turkey or tempeh. Try tossing pasta with olive oil, lemon juice, fresh garlic, and steamed Swiss chard, or add steamed chard to omelets and frittatas. You can use chard in place of spinach in many dishes.

Livit Recipe

Swiss Chard and Creamy Pasta

  6 ounces dry fettuccine
  1 tablespoon olive oil
  1 pound Swiss chard, washed, trimmed, and cut into ¼-inch strips
  2 cloves garlic, minced
  ½ small onion, chopped
  2 large tomatoes, chopped
  ½ cup plain low-fat yogurt OR plain nonfat yogurt
  ½ cup 1% milk
  ¼ cup grated Parmesan cheese
  ⅛ teaspoon salt
  ⅛ teaspoon black pepper

- Cook the pasta according to package directions. Drain and set aside.
- In a 2-quart saucepan, heat the oil over medium-high heat for 1 to 2 minutes. Once the oil is hot, add the Swiss chard, garlic, and onion. Cook for 1 to 2 minutes, stirring occasionally. Reduce heat, and add the tomatoes, yogurt, milk, and Parmesan cheese. When the cheese has melted, add the cooked fettuccine. Add salt and pepper, and stir well. Serve warm.

YIELD 6 servings

NUTRITION ANALYSIS PER SERVING 187 calories, 28.4 g carbohydrate, 10 g protein, 5 g fat, 3.4 g dietary fiber

96 Tomatoes

Benefits

Tomatoes are one of nature's best sources of lycopene. Cooking tomatoes makes the lycopene more available, but that doesn't mean you need to avoid raw ones. One cup of raw tomato still provides plenty of lycopene, as well as lutein, vitamins A and C, carotenes, anthocyanins, and potassium.

It is the lycopene, however, that has made tomatoes a SuperFood. It may be the best substance for quenching oxygen free radicals, and it helps protect the skin from the aging effects of ultraviolet light. Lycopene has been researched for its potential in combating several types of cancers, including prostate, breast, pancreatic, and intestinal cancers. Interestingly, however, in some studies lycopene alone did not convey the same protection as eating a diet rich in tomatoes. So there are certainly more health-protecting treasures inside this versatile food.

A study in 2007 found that broccoli and tomatoes together were better at fighting prostate cancer than either vegetable was alone. Although the study was done on rats, the tomato-broccoli combination was effective enough to have strong implications for humans as well.

The fiber and antioxidants in tomatoes have been shown to lower cholesterol levels and stabilize blood sugar levels. In at least one study, a high dietary intake of tomato products significantly reduced both low-density lipoprotein (LDL), or "bad" cholesterol, and total cholesterol levels, while making the cholesterol less vulnerable to oxidation.

NUTRITIONAL COMPOSITION One raw red tomato provides 26 calories, 5.7 g carbohydrate, 1 g protein, 0.4 g fat, 1.4 g dietary fiber, 766 IU vitamin A, 23 mg vitamin C, 18 mcg folic acid, 273 mg potassium, 11 mg sodium, 30 mg phosphorus, 6 mg calcium, and 14 mg magnesium.

Bringing It Home

Tomatoes come in all shapes and sizes. Choose tomatoes that have the deepest color, with a smooth skin that has no cracks or holes. Tomatoes that are ripe and ready to eat have a distinct tomato smell. If you can't smell them, they won't have much flavor, either.

To get the benefit of everything that tomatoes have to offer, seek out heirloom varieties as well as the familiar red ones. Yellow, orange, and even purple tomatoes all bring different phytochemicals to the table. With many of the heirloom varieties, the tomato may be multi-colored without being unripe.

Lycopene is fat soluble, so it is more bioavailable if you eat your tomatoes with a little fat, such as olive oil or cheese. If you're trying to eat broccoli with your tomatoes, try an omelet filled with broccoli and tomatoes cooked in olive oil. Add a side dish of lightly steamed broccoli florets and shredded mozzarella to a bowl of tomato soup at lunchtime. Or make it a pasta dish, with chunky tomato sauce, steamed broccoli, and mozzarella on whole wheat pasta.

Livit Recipe

SuperFood Marinara Sauce

    1 can (28 ounces) peeled Italian plum tomatoes
    2 teaspoons olive oil
    4 large cloves garlic, finely minced
    1 can (6 ounces) tomato paste
 1¼ teaspoons dried oregano
       Salt
       Pepper
    1 bunch fresh basil, trimmed, with leaves cut into tiny ribbons

- In the container of a food processor or blender, puree the tomatoes.
- In a medium saucepan, heat the oil and add garlic. Sauté the garlic, stirring, for 15 seconds; do not let it brown. Add the pureed tomatoes, tomato paste, and oregano. Add salt and pepper to taste. Bring the sauce to a boil, reduce heat, and simmer for 20 minutes. Remove sauce from heat. Stir in fresh basil. Serve over whole wheat or quinoa pasta.
- VARIATIONS For a balanced meal, add protein to the sauce: Stir in some ricotta cheese or blend silken soft tofu with a little water to add to the sauce. Try mixing steamed broccoli into the sauce to get the tomato-broccoli one-two punch!

YIELD 4 servings

NUTRITION ANALYSIS PER SERVING 102 calories, 19 g carbohydrate, 4.3 g protein, 2.8 g fat, 4.5 g dietary fiber

97 Turnip Greens

Benefits

Turnips—both the root and the greens—are cruciferous vegetables. Although the root has a long history as a staple food, the tops are much richer in vitamins, minerals, and fiber. The green leaves are a good source of vitamins A, C, and K, as well as folate, copper, and calcium. They are high in lutein and beta-carotene, which help protect eyesight and preserve the linings of blood vessels.

Turnip greens are packed with antioxidants, and the B_6 and folate help reduce levels of homocysteine in the blood, protecting the walls of blood vessels and helping prevent atherosclerosis.

NUTRITIONAL COMPOSITION One-half cup of boiled, chopped turnip greens provides 14 calories, 3.1 g carbohydrate, 0.8 g protein, 0.2 g fat, 2.5 g dietary fiber, 3959 IU vitamin A, 20 mg vitamin C, 85 mcg folic acid, 146 mg potassium, 21 mg sodium, 21 mg phosphorus, 99 mg calcium, and 16 mg magnesium.

Bringing It Home

Turnip greens are not necessarily sold separately from the turnips themselves. If you're buying turnips for the greens, make sure the leaves are crisp and a deep green color. Remove the leaves from the roots and store them separately. In a plastic bag in the refrigerator, turnip greens will keep for about four days. Although they are more delicately flavored than collards, turnip greens can be used in many of the same recipes. The turnip root is similar to a rutabaga and can be substituted for it in most recipes.

Livit Recipe

Turnips with Greens

4 turnips, peeled and cut into ½-inch cubes
1 tablespoon olive oil
1 large clove garlic, minced
¼ cup low-sodium vegetable broth OR chicken broth
¼ teaspoon salt
  Dash of pepper sauce
1 pound turnip greens, washed and trimmed, with leaves sliced down the middle, then cut crosswise into strips

- In a medium saucepan, bring about four cups of water to a boil. Once the water is boiling, drop the turnips into the water and boil them for 5 to 8 minutes, until tender. Drain and set aside.
- In a large pot, heat the oil over medium heat. Add the garlic and cook until soft. Add the broth, salt, and pepper sauce, and stir to combine. Add the turnip greens and turnips, and stir to combine. Cover the pot, and cook for 8 to 12 minutes, until the greens are just tender.
- NOTE This dish is traditionally served with vinegar on the side.

YIELD 4 servings

NUTRITION ANALYSIS PER SERVING 103 calories, 16.4 g carbohydrate, 2.9 g protein, 3.8 g fat, 5.8 g dietary fiber

98 Watercress

Benefits

Watercress provides vitamins A, B_6, folic acid, C, and K; the minerals iron, calcium, iodine, and manganese; and beta-carotene and lutein. Watercress is related to cabbages and mustard greens and provides some of the same sulfur compounds that have been found to be protective against some forms of cancer and heart disease. It is more than 95 percent water and extremely low in calories.

> NUTRITIONAL COMPOSITION One cup of chopped watercress provides 4 calories, 0.4 g carbohydrate, 0.8 g protein, 0 g fat, 0.6 g dietary fiber, 1598 IU vitamin A, 14 mg vitamin C, 4 mcg folic acid, 112 mg potassium, 14 mg sodium, 20 mg phosphorus, 40 mg calcium, and 8 mg magnesium.

Bringing It Home

Watercress is a semi-aquatic plant and is often grown hydroponically. This allows it to be available year-round. Watercress should be firm and crisp, with no signs of wilting, and it should be a rich green color.

If the watercress still has its roots attached, wrap them in a wet paper towel and store the watercress in a plastic bag in the refrigerator. It will keep for up to five days, but true to its Brassica relations, it has a better flavor and texture if you eat it the day it is purchased. Do not wash it until you are ready to eat it, but then wash it carefully, as it can hold on to grit tenaciously. Watercress can be eaten raw or cooked.

Livit Recipe

Watercress Fusilli

½ pound whole wheat fusilli	1 red bell pepper, seeded and sliced into thin strips
2 tablespoons pine nuts	1 bunch watercress, washed and trimmed
1 tablespoon olive oil	1 teaspoon basil, optional
2 cloves garlic, minced	¼ cup freshly grated Parmesan cheese

- In a large pot, bring 3 to 4 quarts of water to a boil. Once the water is boiling, add the pasta and cook until al dente (about 8 minutes, depending on the pasta). Drain the pasta, reserving 1 cup of the pasta water, and set the pasta aside.

- Toast the pine nuts in a dry skillet over medium heat until they just begin to turn golden brown. Watch carefully and stir them constantly, as they can burn very quickly. Transfer the pine nuts to a small bowl to cool.

- In a medium skillet, heat the oil over medium heat. Once the oil is hot, add the garlic. Cook, stirring frequently, for 1 to 3 minutes, until it is lightly browned. Add peppers and cook for another 2 minutes. Add watercress to the pan with ¼ cup of the reserved pasta water. Simmer for an additional 4 to 6 minutes, until the peppers are soft. Add the pasta to the sauce and toss gently to combine. Add basil, if using. Cook together for 1 minute, stirring often.

- Transfer to a serving bowl. Sprinkle Parmesan and pine nuts over the top, tossing gently to combine. Serve.

YIELD 4 servings

NUTRITION ANALYSIS PER SERVING 291 calories, 38 g carbohydrate, 12.8 g protein, 9.3 g fat, 7.1 g dietary fiber

99 Zucchini

Benefits

Zucchini provides vitamins A and C, folate, potassium, manganese, lutein, and beta-carotene. Although it is 95 percent water and 4 percent carbohydrate, zucchini is a low-calorie source of antioxidants and anti-inflammatories, as well as some of the phytonutrients that help protect vision.

The manganese in zucchini (one cup provides 38 percent of the recommended daily value of this mineral) is a vital cofactor in a number of enzymes, including some that help cells maintain their shape and others that are essential to metabolic processes. Manganese ions are essential to the process of neutralizing superoxide free radicals, which are quite toxic.

NUTRITIONAL COMPOSITION One cup of sliced raw zucchini provides 18 calories, 3.8 g carbohydrate, 1.6 g protein, 0.2 g fat, 1.6 g dietary fiber, 442 IU vitamin A, 12 mg vitamin C, 28 mcg folic acid, 322 mg potassium, 4 mg sodium, 42 mg phosphorus, 20 mg calcium, and 28 mg magnesium.

Bringing It Home

The best zucchini is small to medium in size, with a shiny, thin, deep green skin. Because most of the carotenes are in the skin, it's best to get zucchini with skins that are thin enough to eat. Zucchini should be handled carefully to avoid punctures. It will keep for about seven days if stored in a plastic bag in the refrigerator.

Livit Recipe

Zucchini Lasagna

¼ cup whole wheat pastry flour
   Freshly ground black pepper
4 medium zucchini, with ends cut off, cut lengthwise into ¼-inch strips
1 tablespoon canola oil
1 large container (15 ounces) part-skim ricotta cheese
1 egg
1 egg white
1 teaspoon dried oregano
4 tablespoons grated Parmesan cheese
2 cups spaghetti sauce
½ pound part-skim mozzarella cheese, shredded

- Preheat oven to 350°F.
- In a shallow pan or pie plate, mix the flour with the pepper. Dip both sides of each zucchini strip into the seasoned flour.
- Heat the oil in a large, nonstick skillet over medium heat. Working in batches, fry the zucchini slices in a single layer until they are golden, turning them once. Remove zucchini to a platter covered with a paper towel to drain. Set aside.
- In a medium bowl, combine the ricotta, egg, egg white, oregano, and 3 tablespoons of the Parmesan. Set aside.
- Spread half of the spaghetti sauce in a 9″ × 13″ baking pan. Layer it with half of the zucchini slices, then half of the ricotta mixture, then half of the shredded mozzarella. Repeat the layers. Sprinkle the remaining 1 tablespoon of Parmesan over the top. Bake for 45 minutes, or until bubbly. Remove from oven and let stand for about 10 minutes before serving.

YIELD 6 servings

NUTRITION ANALYSIS PER SERVING 286 calories, 15.9 g carbohydrate, 21.3 g protein, 16.3 g fat, 2 g dietary fiber

Carbohydrates: Grains

When I ask my patients to name their favorite food, the most common answer is "Bread." Pasta runs a close second. But the most common thing my patients say about these foods is "I can't eat them! They make me fat!"

Low-carbohydrate diets encourage this attitude, with their emphasis on avoiding breads and grains. But there's a difference between the refined, white-flour versions of these foods and the nutritious whole grains that are a vital part of balanced eating. Unfortunately, while people are avoiding carbs, they're also neglecting whole grains. A 2000 study found that 42 percent of adults in the United States ate no whole grains at all on a typical day.

Yet whole grains—as part of a menu that includes fruits and vegetables—are a key component in preventing, delaying, and reducing the effects of some of the most common chronic diseases, including heart disease, stroke, type 2 diabetes, several forms of cancer, and some gastrointestinal disorders.

Indeed, fiber-rich whole grains have been shown to help prevent weight gain and obesity. Carbohydrates are the body's fuel; we can't live without them. So choose the most satisfying, sustaining fuel for your body: Eat whole grains at least twice a day. They will help you feel full longer, which is key to achieving and maintaining an optimal body weight. They are full of fiber, vitamins, and antioxidants such as magnesium, copper, and vitamin E.

To keep your carbohydrate intake in the right proportion to other foods you eat, choose either whole grains or fruit with every meal or snack. For example, have a fist-sized portion of whole wheat pasta at lunch with your protein source and veggies, then have a piece of fruit with your snack later.

What makes a grain "whole"? Whole grains include all three main parts of the grain kernel: bran, germ, and endosperm. When the label says "enriched" or "refined" flour, the bran and germ have been stripped out, removing the beneficial fiber, heart-health benefits, and significant nutrients. "Enriched" flours try to replenish some of those nutrients in the form of supplements, but they don't replace the full range of grain's benefits, and they don't replace the fiber.

Whole grains include brown rice, corn, oats, millet, whole wheat, buckwheat, barley, bulgur, amaranth, rye, and millet. (Quinoa is often included with whole grains, though we have grouped it with starchy vegetables in Chapter 2.)

Check labels for fiber content to make sure you're getting the most health value out of the bread and grains you eat. Look for three grams or more of dietary fiber in snack foods and five grams or more in a meal. Keep in mind that color alone isn't a reliable indicator of whether a food is whole grain. For example, a dark brown bread can get its color from ingredients such as molasses or spices; it's not necessarily whole wheat.

EATING GLUTEN-FREE

If you must avoid gluten-bearing grains (barley, rye, oats, and wheat), you can still get the benefits of whole grains from gluten-free alternatives, such as brown rice, wild rice, quinoa, millet, amaranth, and buckwheat. High-fiber, nutrient-dense starchy vegetables such as yams, butternut squash, acorn squash, spaghetti squash, winter squash, green peas, corn, and potatoes (if eaten with their skins) provide those benefits as well. Fruit, gluten-free breads, brown rice cakes, and gluten-free cereals can easily serve as your carbohydrate source in place of items containing gluten. If you try gluten-free cereals—corn flakes, puffed rice, millet, or corn—you might even want to increase the fiber by adding 1 or 2 tablespoons of ground flaxseeds to your bowl of cereal. Do make sure to drink plenty of water to help the fiber do its job.

100 Amaranth

Benefits

Amaranth is native to South America, Asia, and Africa. It grows easily and can be prolific in producing seeds. Its high-protein, gluten-free seeds are used as a grain, though technically amaranth is a pseudograin. For a plant source, it is also a relatively complete protein, because it includes lysine, an essential amino acid that grains often lack. The seeds are high in fiber and provide the minerals iron, magnesium, phosphorus, copper, and manganese.

In some countries, especially India and Africa, amaranth leaves are eaten as well. Although these greens are high in many vitamins and minerals, they are also high in oxalic acid. Both the flowers and leaves have been used in some forms of traditional medicine.

Amaranth seed appears to help reduce blood pressure and cholesterol, an effect not only of the seeds' fiber content but also of chemical substances called plant sterols. These sterols become stanols, some of which are known to reduce low-density lipoprotein (LDL), or "bad" cholesterol. Other stanols are used by the body to make steroids, which can have important anti-inflammatory properties.

NUTRITIONAL COMPOSITION One-quarter cup of organic whole grain amaranth provides 180 calories, 31 g carbohydrate, 7 g protein, 3 g fat, 7 g dietary fiber, 2.4 mg vitamin C, 8 mg calcium, 3.6 mg iron, 0.03 mg thiamine, 0.1 mg riboflavin, 0.8 mg niacin, 0.02 mg folate, and 200 mg phosphorus.

Bringing It Home

Amaranth seed is probably easiest to find at health food and natural food stores, where it is sometimes sold as a bulk grain. However, it is becoming more common to find it commercially packaged in conventional groceries. Because it is relatively rich in oils, there is a risk that it will go rancid if stored too long, so buy it from a store where the stock turns over relatively rapidly. At home, store it away from light, heat, and moisture.

Amaranth can be cooked like a grain or, with more water, as a hot cereal.

Pastas made with amaranth tend to be multi-grain, teaming it with rice or quinoa—a great way to add a variety of grains to your day. Amaranth-based pastas cook more quickly than wheat pastas, usually in a mere four to six minutes. You definitely don't want to overcook this pasta, because it gets mushy. You may want to drain it immediately and rinse with cold water to stop the cooking.

Livit Recipe

Amaranth Pilaf

2 cups water
1 cup low-sodium vegetable broth
1 cup amaranth seeds
½ teaspoon salt
½ teaspoon dried thyme leaves
2 tablespoons non-hydrogenated margarine
⅛ teaspoon pepper

- In a medium saucepan, combine water, broth, amaranth, salt, and thyme. Bring to a boil, then reduce heat and cover. Simmer for 20 to 25 minutes, until the water is absorbed. Remove pan from heat. Let it stand for 15 minutes, covered, to finish cooking. Stir in margarine and pepper. Serve.

YIELD 6 servings

NUTRITION ANALYSIS PER SERVING 224 calories, 31.8 g carbohydrate, 7 g protein, 7 g fat, 7 g dietary fiber

101 Barley

Benefits

Barley was one of the first grains cultivated by humans. Whole barley contains all eight essential amino acids, making it a complete protein. Raw barley is also a good source of niacin and vitamin B$_6$, as well as the minerals phosphorus, iron, magnesium, and zinc. One cup of barley provides 14.2 percent of the recommended daily value for niacin. Barley also provides some lutein, which may help preserve vision.

Barley is very rich in fiber—nearly 16 percent dietary fiber by weight. Fiber helps prevent constipation, and it helps the colon stay healthy by helping intestinal flora produce butyric acid. Dietary fiber also reduces blood cholesterol levels, and whole grain barley contains enough soluble fiber that the Food and Drug Administration (FDA) has recognized it as a food that can reduce the risk of heart disease. Taken together, barley's fiber and its B vitamins, which help preserve the health of blood vessels, make barley an especially heart-healthy grain.

Barley provides magnesium, a mineral that acts as a co-factor for more than 300 enzymes, including enzymes involved in glucose metabolism and the production of insulin. Studies have shown that barley may be even more effective in stabilizing glucose and insulin responses than oats. It appears to regulate blood sugar for up to 10 hours.

Health benefits of barley were observed as long as 2,400 years ago by Indian physicians who recommended substituting barley for white rice, along with losing weight and increasing activity, to treat the disease we now identify as type 2 diabetes. Barley is even mentioned by Islam's founding prophet, Muhammad, as effective against seven diseases—including grief.

Most of the benefits of barley come from the whole grain form—called "hulled" barley, because only the inedible husk has been removed. Hulled barley retains the healthful bran and germ. Unfortunately, the more widely available "pearled" barley has been steamed and polished to remove the bran. To get the benefits of barley, you'll have to seek out the hulled, whole grain form.

NUTRITIONAL COMPOSITION (COOKED BARLEY) One cup of cooked, pearled barley provides 193 calories, 44.3 g carbohydrate, 3.5 g protein, 0.7 g fat, 6 g dietary fiber, 11 IU vitamin A, 3.2 mg niacin, 25 mcg folic acid, 146 mg potassium, 5 mg sodium, 85 mg phosphorus, 17 mg calcium, 2.09 mg iron, 35 mg magnesium, and 1.29 mg zinc.

NUTRITIONAL COMPOSITION (RAW BARLEY) One-quarter cup of raw, hulled barley provides 163 calories, 33.8 g carbohydrate, 5.7 g protein, 1.1 g fat, 8 g dietary fiber, 10 IU vitamin A, 2.1 mg niacin, 9 mcg folic acid, 208 mg potassium, 6 mg sodium, 121 mg phosphorus, 15 mg calcium, 1.66 mg iron, 61 mg magnesium, and 1.27 mg zinc.

Bringing It Home

Make it a point to buy hulled barley, which is the least processed version. You may only be able to find it in health food and natural food stores. Pearled barley is more commonly found in supermarkets. Store barley away from moisture, heat, and light. In warmer months, keep it in a tightly covered glass jar in the refrigerator.

Livit Recipe

Barley Breeze

It's a breeze to make!

> 1 cup hulled barley, rinsed
> 2 cups water
> 1 cup low-sodium vegetable broth
> 1 teaspoon olive oil
> 1 small onion, diced
> 1 clove garlic, minced
> 1 medium green bell pepper, seeded and diced
> 1 medium carrot, peeled and diced
> ½ cup diced fresh tomato
> ½ cup fresh spinach, washed and coarsely chopped
> ½ teaspoon salt
> ¼ teaspoon freshly ground black pepper
> 1 small bunch fresh parsley, minced
> Seasonings of choice (basil, onion powder, oregano, thyme), optional

- In a medium saucepan, combine the barley, water, and broth. Bring to a boil, then reduce heat. Cover tightly and allow to simmer for about 45 minutes. Check it at 30 minutes. If all liquids have been absorbed, add up to ¼ cup water. The barley is done when it reaches a chewy texture.
- While the barley is cooking, lightly oil a nonstick pan. Use a paper towel to distribute the oil and soak up any excess. Add onion and garlic, and sauté over medium heat until the onion is translucent. Add the bell pepper, carrot, tomato, and spinach. Continue sautéing until the vegetables are tender, stirring often to keep them from sticking and to allow them to cook evenly. Sprinkle salt and pepper over the vegetable mixture. Add the parsley. Add other seasonings, if using. Stir to combine. Cover the skillet and remove it from the heat.

- Once the barley has finished cooking, add the sautéed, seasoned vegetables to the cooked barley. Toss with a fork to distribute the vegetables and fluff up the grain. Serve hot.
- NOTE To mince parsley, put it in a glass and, using kitchen scissors, snip the parsley until it is finely minced.
- VARIATION For a more balanced dish, add lentils, garbanzo beans, or white beans for added protein. Adding hummus or part-skim cheese provides more fat.

YIELD 6 servings.

NUTRITION ANALYSIS PER SERVING 138 calories, 27 g carbohydrate, 5 g protein, 1.6 g fat, 6.7 g dietary fiber

102 Brown Rice

Benefits

Rice has gotten a bad rap, partly because it is somewhat calorie-dense and partly because even brown rice turns out to have a surprisingly high glycemic index. But if you eat it with extra fiber and keep your portion size below one cup, rice is an acceptable food, even if you have diabetes. Balance brown rice with a protein food and lots of steamed vegetables, and it takes its rightful place in a healthy, nutritious meal.

Brown rice is the whole grain version of rice, with more fiber and more nutrients than its paler counterpart. Just one cup of brown rice will provide you with 88 percent of the recommended daily value for manganese. This mineral is involved in the metabolism of protein and carbohydrates, as well as the synthesis of a number of enzymes, proteins, fatty acids, and hormones. Brown rice is also a good source of selenium, a trace mineral that is involved in many antioxidant reactions in the body and that plays a role in thyroid health. Brown rice is high in fiber, which helps you feel full after eating and speeds the passage of foods through the digestive tract. This may help maintain both a healthy body weight and a healthy colon.

In the late 19th century, it was observed that people who ate brown rice were less likely to get beriberi than those who ate exclusively white, polished rice. This led to an analysis of the differences between the two and helped lead to the discovery of vitamins.

NUTRITIONAL COMPOSITION One cup of cooked long grain brown rice provides 216 calories, 44.8 g carbohydrate, 5 g protein, 1.8 g fat, 3.5 g dietary fiber, 8 mcg folic acid, 84 mg potassium, 10 mg sodium, 162 mg phosphorus, 20 mg calcium, 84 mg magnesium, 1.23 mg zinc, and 1.77 mg manganese.

Bringing It Home

Most whole grains, including brown rice, contain more oils than refined white grains, so there is a greater risk that they will become rancid. Therefore, it is important to keep track of the "use by" date on brown rice or, if buying it in bulk, buy it from a store where the turnover is high enough that the rice is relatively fresh. At home, keep it in a tightly closed container, away from heat, moisture, and light. Stored properly, it should keep about six months. In warmer months, you may wish to move your rice to the refrigerator. Just make sure it's in a tightly sealed container, to keep the moisture out.

Livit Recipe

Balanced Black Beans and Rice

1½ cups water
½ cup brown rice
1 teaspoon canola oil
1 small onion, minced
1 clove garlic, minced

1 can (15 ounces) organic black beans, rinsed and drained
1 can (14.5 ounces) Mexican-style tomatoes OR Italian-style stewed tomatoes, with liquid
1 ounce yogurt cheese

- Bring 1½ cups of water to a boil in a medium saucepan with a tight-fitting lid. Once the water is boiling, add ½ cup of brown rice. Allow the water to return to a boil, then reduce heat to a simmer, cover, and cook over low heat for 45 to 55 minutes, until the liquid is absorbed.
- Heat the oil in a medium saucepan. Add the onion and garlic, and sauté until the onions are translucent and the garlic is tender but not brown. Add the beans and the tomatoes with their liquid. Bring to a boil, then reduce heat. Cover, and allow to simmer for about 5 minutes. Remove from heat. Add the yogurt cheese, and stir until the cheese has melted.
- To serve, scoop a heaping ⅓ cup of rice onto each plate. Make a well in the center of the rice, and fill it with a quarter of the black bean mixture.
- NOTE For a more balanced meal, add steamed vegetables on the side.

YIELD 4 servings

NUTRITION ANALYSIS PER SERVING 256 calories, 48 g carbohydrate, 11 g protein, 2 g fat, 10.5 g dietary fiber

103 Buckwheat

Benefits

Buckwheat has a long culinary history in Eastern Europe and Central Asia, where the groats are used in the staple dish kasha. Technically, buckwheat is a pseudograin and not related to wheat at all, with seeds (the groats) that are similar to sunflower seeds. Buckwheat is commonly used in noodles in Japanese, Korean, and Northern

Italian cuisine. It lacks gluten but is high in protein, antioxidants, vitamins B_1 and B_2, and the minerals iron, zinc, and selenium.

Buckwheat contains rutin, a glycoside related to quercetin. Like quercetin, rutin appears to have properties that protect blood vessels, inhibiting platelet aggregation and acting as an antioxidant. It is being investigated for its potential in protecting the eyes from diabetic retinopathy, a serious complication of diabetes that can lead to blindness. Rutin helps lower the risk of heart disease as well. One cup of buckwheat provides almost 86 milligrams of magnesium—a mineral that relaxes blood vessels, improving blood flow and nutrient delivery while lowering blood pressure—the perfect combination for a healthy cardiovascular system.

Buckwheat also contains a form of inositol that appears to lower cholesterol and increase insulin sensitivity. This compound is being studied for its potential role in fighting polycystic ovary disease (PCOD) and type 2 diabetes.

NUTRITIONAL COMPOSITION One cup of cooked buckwheat groats provides 182 calories, 39.5 g carbohydrate, 6.7 g protein, 1.2 g fat, 5.3 g dietary fiber, 28 mcg folic acid, 174 mg potassium, 8 mg sodium, 139 mg phosphorus, 14 mg calcium, 101 mg magnesium, and 1.21 mg zinc.

Bringing It Home

Buckwheat is available in many forms: whole buckwheat, hulled buckwheat groats, buckwheat flour, buckwheat noodles, buckwheat flakes, and even buckwheat waffle mix! Buckwheat is also a common component of multi-grain products. Buckwheat groats, noodles, and pancakes turn up in every corner of the world. Enjoy experimenting with Japanese soba, Russian blini, Polish kasha, and Acadian ployes.

Keep buckwheat away from light, heat, and moisture. Whole buckwheat will keep about a year. Buckwheat flour's lifespan is shorter, but it will keep for four to six months if stored in the refrigerator.

Livit Recipe

Tex-Mex Buckwheat

1 tablespoon soybean oil OR canola oil	1 can (35 ounces) chopped tomatoes,
1 large onion, diced	with liquid
1 stalk celery, diced	1 teaspoon dried oregano
1 large green bell pepper, seeded and	½ teaspoon cumin
diced	1 teaspoon mild chili powder
1 clove garlic, minced	Freshly ground black pepper
¾ cup whole buckwheat groats	3 ounces Monterey Jack cheese, coarsely grated

· In a large skillet with a tight-fitting lid, heat the oil. Once the oil is hot, add the onion, celery, pepper, and garlic. Sauté for about 5 minutes, until the onion is soft.

- Stir in the buckwheat groats and the tomatoes with their liquid. Add the oregano, cumin, chili powder, and black pepper. Bring to a boil, then reduce heat. Cover, and allow to simmer for 10 to 15 minutes, until all the liquid is absorbed and the groats are tender but chewy.
- Sprinkle the cheese over the top, replace the cover, and let the dish stand for about 1 minute to allow the cheese to melt. Serve.

YIELD 4 servings

NUTRITION ANALYSIS PER SERVING 284 calories, 37.7 g carbohydrate, 12.1 g protein, 11.5 g fat, 6.6 g dietary fiber

104 Bulgur Wheat

Benefits

Bulgur wheat is the groat form of wheat. It differs from cracked wheat in that it has been parboiled and dried. The most common types of bulgur have also had the bran removed, but whole grain bulgur is available, and this type has by far the best nutrition profile. Whole grain bulgur has a lower glycemic index than brown or white rice and buckwheat. It is not a gluten-free grain, however, since it is a form of wheat.

Bulgur is an excellent source of several B vitamins—thiamine, riboflavin, niacin, B_6, and folate—that are essential to metabolism and that help convert homocysteine into less harmful chemicals; this helps lower blood pressure and protect the heart. It also provides the minerals iron, zinc, magnesium, phosphorus, and selenium, and it is high in fiber. The protein in bulgur is not complete. Like other grains, it lacks sufficient lysine, and therefore it should be eaten with foods such as beans or seeds that can provide this essential amino acid.

> **NUTRITIONAL COMPOSITION** One cup of cooked bulgur provides 151 calories, 33.8 g carbohydrate, 5.6 g protein, 0.4 g fat, 8.2 g dietary fiber, 33 mcg folic acid, 124 mg potassium, 9 mg sodium, 73 mg phosphorus, 18 mg calcium, 58 mg magnesium, 1.75 mg iron, 1.04 mg zinc, and 1.11 mg manganese.

Bringing It Home

Bulgur is found in the international food section of the supermarket or with other grains, though it is unlikely that whole grain bulgur will be found there. For whole grain bulgur, you will likely have to seek out a health food store. Store bulgur away from heat, light, and moisture. Cooked bulgur will keep about four days in the refrigerator.

Livit Recipe

Quick Fuel Salad

½ cup bulgur wheat
1½ cups boiling water
½ lemon, juice only
1 teaspoon olive oil
2 sprigs parsley, minced

1 tomato, diced
1 green bell pepper, seeded and diced
1 small cucumber, peeled and diced
½ cup cooked corn
Salt

- Put the bulgur in a medium bowl, then pour the water over the bulgur. Let the bulgur soak for about 30 minutes, then drain. Rinse the bulgur in cold water to cool it.
- In a small bowl, whisk together the lemon juice and olive oil. Add the parsley.
- In a salad serving bowl, combine the bulgur, tomato, pepper, cucumber, and corn. Add salt to taste. Add the oil dressing and toss gently until it is well distributed. Serve.
- NOTE To mince parsley, put it in a glass and, using kitchen scissors, snip it until it is finely minced.

YIELD 2 servings

NUTRITION ANALYSIS PER SERVING 231.6 calories, 48.1 g carbohydrate, 7.8 g protein, 3.6 g fat, 10.6 g dietary fiber

105 Corn Tortilla

Benefits

Corn is included as a vegetable in Chapter 2, yet corn's history as a grain is far longer. As a grain, corn is allowed to mature and is dried. People long ago learned to treat the corn with slaked lime (an alkali) to remove the outer hulls and soften the grains enough to make them more palatable. This treatment also improves the nutritional value of dried corn by converting the niacin into a form that the body can more easily absorb. Depending on the process used, such a treatment may also increase the amount of certain minerals in the corn.

In addition to the improved availability of niacin, corn tortillas offer some other B vitamins necessary to metabolism—thiamine, pantothenic acid, and folate.

NUTRITIONAL COMPOSITION One corn tortilla provides 70 calories, 14 g carbohydrate, 2 g protein, 1 g fat, 1.5 g dietary fiber, 2 mg calcium, and 0.36 mg iron.

Bringing It Home

Because of the oils found in whole grains, whole grain corn tortillas are found in the refrigerator section in most groceries. Blue corn tortillas have some additional antioxidants due to the blue color, and they are a fun variation. Check the "sell by" date on the package to make sure that the tortillas are fresh. Store them in a sealed plastic bag in the refrigerator, and they will keep up to about a week.

Livit Recipe

Tortilla Soup

See Safe Handling of Poultry on page 211.

See Safe Handling of Poultry on page 211.

2 corn tortillas, sliced into ¼-inch strips
½ pound boneless, skinless chicken breasts
4 cups low-fat chicken broth
2 cloves garlic, minced
¼ teaspoon ground cumin
3 or 4 scallions, minced
1 small bunch fresh cilantro, minced
1 fresh lime, cut into quarters

- Toast the strips of tortilla in a toaster oven until crisp. Set aside.
- Put the chicken in a medium skillet and add enough water to cover. Bring the water to a simmer, cover, and let the chicken poach over low heat for about 10 minutes, until the chicken is cooked through. Remove the chicken from the water and allow it to cool.
- In a medium saucepan, bring the broth, garlic, and cumin to a boil. Reduce heat, and simmer for 10 minutes. Stir in the scallions and cilantro.
- When the chicken has cooled, shred the meat with a fork and add it to the soup. Add the toasted tortilla strips, and simmer for 5 minutes. Serve immediately with a wedge of lime.
- NOTE To mince fresh cilantro, put it into a glass and, using kitchen scissors, snip the cilantro until it is finely minced.

YIELD 4 servings

NUTRITION ANALYSIS PER SERVING 130 calories, 6 g carbohydrate, 18 g protein, 3.5 g fat, 1 g dietary fiber

106 Millet

Benefits

Millet is not really one single plant, but rather a group of plants that produce small grains. The kind normally sold as food in the United States is proso, or common millet. Other millets sometimes used for food include foxtail millet, pearl millet, and finger millet. Millets are gluten-free grains. Although they are not very closely related to wheat, they have a similar protein content, about 11 percent by weight. Like many other grains, millets are a good source of B vitamins, including niacin, B_6, and folic acid, as well as the minerals calcium, iron, potassium, magnesium, phosphorus, manganese, and zinc.

In recent studies, a protein extract from a Korean foxtail millet appeared to effectively increase the amount of adiponectin, a protein hormone that modulates a number of metabolic processes, including glucose regulation and fatty acid catabolism. Mice that were fed a millet extract had higher levels of high-density lipoprotein (HDL), or "good" cholesterol, and lower levels of blood glucose than those that were not. While this research is very preliminary, and the millet extract was highly concentrated, it raises the possibility that millet may have a role to play in fighting insulin resistance, type 2 diabetes, and cardiovascular disease.

NUTRITIONAL COMPOSITION One-half cup of cooked millet provides 143 calories, 28.4 g carbohydrate, 4.2 g protein, 1.2 g fat, 1.5 g dietary fiber, 1.6 mg niacin, 23 mcg folic acid, 74.5 mg potassium, 2.5 mg sodium, 120 mg phosphorus, 3.5 mg calcium, 0.75 mg iron, 53 mg magnesium, and 1.09 mg zinc.

Bringing It Home

Whole grain millet should be stored away from light, heat, and moisture. It will keep for up to a year. Millet flour goes rancid very quickly, however, so if you are going to bake with millet, consider grinding the flour immediately before use. If you cook millet in a relatively small amount of liquid, it will come out light and dry; if you use a lot of water, it comes out thick and mushy, more like mashed potatoes. Many traditional recipes begin with toasting the millet to add to its flavor.

Livit Recipe

Kim's Autumn Golden Millet Bowl

½ cup millet, rinsed and drained
1½ cups low-sodium vegetable broth OR water
½ small butternut squash, peeled and cut into ½-inch cubes
1 green apple, cut into ½-inch cubes
½ teaspoon dried sage
2 tablespoons low-sodium soy sauce
2 tablespoons honey
¼ cup toasted pumpkin seeds, as garnish

- Heat a large nonstick skillet over medium heat. Add the millet. Toast it until it just begins to change color, stirring constantly so that it doesn't burn. Add the broth, squash, apple, sage, and soy sauce. Allow the broth to come to a boil, then reduce heat. Cover, and allow the millet to simmer for about 20 minutes, until the millet is soft and the liquid is mostly absorbed. If the millet is soft enough but there is still liquid in the pan, cook it, uncovered, for an additional 5 minutes over medium heat.

- Transfer to bowls. Drizzle with honey and garnish with pumpkin seeds. Serve.

- NOTE To rinse and drain the millet, use a sieve and allow it to stand long enough to drain completely.

YIELD 4 servings

NUTRITION ANALYSIS PER SERVING 199.4 calories, 43.4 g carbohydrate, 4.3 g protein, 1.9 g fat, 3.7 g dietary fiber

107 Multi-Grain Cereals/Pilaf

Benefits

One great thing about the increased concern with healthy eating is that there are products available to make it easier. One of the best things you can do for your health is simply to eat a greater variety of foods, including grains. If you don't have time to cook multiple grains for every meal, there are prepared products that include several grains in every bite. Look for them in health food stores as well as the supermarket.

Multi-grain products are a way to try out unfamiliar grains, get the benefits of several grains at once, add a variety of tastes to your day, and give you more satisfaction per chew, since they are so high in fiber.

> **NUTRITIONAL COMPOSITION** One-half cup of cooked multi-grain pilaf provides 170 calories, 30 g carbohydrate, 6 g protein, 3 g fat, 6 g dietary fiber, 2 mg calcium, and 1.4 mg iron.

Bringing It Home

Choose higher-fiber multi-grain products—5 or more grams of dietary fiber per serving—to help you feel satisfied longer. If you prefer one of the lower-fiber blends, you can add a tablespoon of ground flaxseed to increase the fiber.

Livit Recipe

Veggie Pilaf

2 cups buckwheat	Pinch of salt
½ cup whole peanuts	2 tablespoons water
2 teaspoons toasted sesame oil	½ red bell pepper, seeded and diced
2 small cloves garlic, diced	2 sprigs fresh cilantro, coarsely chopped
1 small red onion, diced	2 tablespoons low-sodium soy sauce
¼ teaspoon cumin	1 tablespoon brown rice vinegar
¼ teaspoon coriander	1 teaspoon grated fresh ginger root
⅓ cup raisins	½ teaspoon crushed red chili flakes
1 small carrot, scrubbed and sliced into matchsticks	1 teaspoon sugar OR evaporated cane juice crystals
½ cup diced red cabbage	

- Cook the buckwheat according to the directions on the package and set aside.
- Dry toast the peanuts in a small skillet until golden brown. Remove from heat and set aside.
- Heat the oil in a large skillet. Add the garlic and onion, and sauté until they are limp. Add the cumin, coriander, raisins, carrots, cabbage, salt, and water. Stir well. Reduce heat, cover, and simmer for 3 minutes. Remove from heat.

- In a large mixing bowl, combine the sautéed mixture with the cooked buckwheat, toasted peanuts, bell pepper, and cilantro. Mix well.
- In a small bowl, whisk together the soy sauce, vinegar, ginger, chili flakes, and sugar. Add this dressing to the pilaf, and toss gently so that all ingredients are evenly distributed.

YIELD 8 servings

NUTRITION ANALYSIS PER SERVING 180 calories, 25 g carbohydrate, 6 g protein, 7 g fat, 4 g dietary fiber

108 Multi-Grain Crackers/Bread (Whole Grain)

Benefits

Add variety to your day's grain intake just by opening up a box of multi-grain crackers or having a slice of multi-grain bread. Make sure the crackers and breads that you choose are whole grain, high in fiber, and low in fat. For extra nutritional punch, choose one that includes seeds!

NUTRITIONAL COMPOSITION Fourteen multi-grain crackers provide 150 calories, 22 g carbohydrate, 2 g protein, 6 g fat, 3 g dietary fiber, 2 mg calcium, and 1.4 mg iron.

Bringing It Home

You'll feel satisfied longer if you choose crackers that have 3 or more grams of dietary fiber per serving. That will also help you avoid eating an entire box of crackers in one sitting! All multi-grain and whole wheat crackers are not created equal. Some have less than 1 gram of fiber, so always check the fiber content to be sure that you'll really be satisfied and sustained by what you eat.

Livit Recipe

Fruit, Cheese, and Crackers Snack

8 multi-grain and flaxseed water crackers
2 ounces soft goat cheese
½ cup fresh blueberries OR strawberries OR raspberries

- Spread each cracker with soft goat cheese. Top each cracker with 1 tablespoon of berries.
- VARIATION Frozen berries may also be used; thaw and drain them ahead of assembly.

YIELD 2 servings

NUTRITION ANALYSIS PER SERVING 155.7 calories, 17 g carbohydrate, 6.4 g protein, 7.2 g fat, 2 g dietary fiber

109 Oat Bran/Oatmeal

Benefits

Oats, oat bran, and oatmeal are famous for providing soluble fiber, which has been shown to help lower cholesterol levels, thus lowering the risk of heart disease. Although oats are not the only source of soluble fiber, they are an excellent source and a familiar, easily available food.

Studies have found that eating 3 grams of soluble oat fiber per day can help some people with high cholesterol lower their cholesterol levels by 8 to 23 percent. Since it's estimated that each 1 percent drop in serum cholesterol translates to a 2 percent decrease in the risk of developing heart disease, oats have become a part of many health programs.

Oats are known for their external soothing properties, so perhaps it's not surprising that they also provide some special antioxidants. Avenanthramides help prevent free radicals from damaging LDL cholesterol, helping to reduce the risk of cardiovascular disease. Like many other whole grains, oats are a good source of magnesium, a mineral involved in many of the reactions vital to human metabolism.

Beta-glucan is a component of the soluble fiber in oats that is also found in some seaweeds, mushrooms, and brewer's yeast. Beta-glucan is believed to help fight bacterial infections. Patients with type 2 diabetes who were given foods rich in beta-glucans experienced much lower rises in blood sugar than those who were given white rice or white bread.

Most of the special nutritional benefits of oats are concentrated in the bran. Oat bran cereal can be an efficient way to maximize those benefits. Oat bran provides about 50 percent more fiber—both soluble and insoluble—than quick oats, and it contains more protein.

NUTRITIONAL COMPOSITION One-half cup of cooked oat bran provides 44 calories, 12.6 g carbohydrate, 3.5 g protein, 0.9 g fat, 6 g dietary fiber, 7 mcg folic acid, 101 mg potassium, 131 mg phosphorus, 11 mg calcium, 44 mg magnesium, and 1.06 mg manganese.

Bringing It Home

Oat bran, being higher in fat than rolled oats, is more susceptible to rancidity. When buying oat bran, only buy what you need for the short term, and make sure that it is fresh and has no perceptible rancid smell. All oat products should be stored away from heat, light, and moisture. Rolled and steel-cut oats will keep about two months. When buying instant oatmeal, take a careful look at the ingredients, because many are packed with salt and sugar.

Eat oat bran as a hot cereal or add it to baked goods to increase your intake of soluble fiber.

Livit Recipe

Satisfying Oatmeal Raisin Cookies

1 cup non-hydrogenated margarine
1 cup firmly packed brown sugar
½ cup granulated sugar
1 egg
3 tablespoons egg substitute
1 teaspoon vanilla extract

1½ cups all-purpose flour
1 teaspoon baking soda
1 teaspoon cinnamon
½ teaspoon salt, optional
3 cups uncooked rolled oats
1 cup raisins

- Preheat oven to 350°F.
- In a large bowl, beat together the margarine and sugars until creamy. Add egg, egg substitute, and vanilla. Beat well.
- In a separate bowl, stir together the flour, baking soda, cinnamon, and salt, if using. Add the flour mixture to the sugar and eggs, and mix thoroughly. Stir in the oats and raisins. Mix well.
- Drop by rounded tablespoonfuls onto an ungreased cookie sheet.
- Bake for 10 to 12 minutes, or until golden brown.
- Allow the cookies to cool for 1 minute on the cookie sheet before removing them to a serving plate.
- VARIATION For bar cookies, spread the batter into an ungreased 13″ × 9″ baking pan. Bake for 30 to 35 minutes. Allow to cool slightly and cut into bars.

YIELD 5 dozen cookies

NUTRITION ANALYSIS PER SERVING 80.4 calories, 12.4 g carbohydrate, 1.2 g protein, 3 g fat, 0.6 g dietary fiber

110 Popcorn

Benefits

Popcorn has a secret identity. Loaded with butter and salt, it's a heart attack waiting to happen, but treated properly, popcorn is a great high-fiber snack.

NUTRITIONAL COMPOSITION Three and one-half cups of plain, air-popped popcorn provide 107 calories, 21.8 g carbohydrate, 3.4 g protein, 1.2 g fat, 4.2 g dietary fiber, 55 IU vitamin A, 6 mcg folic acid, 84 mg potassium, 1 mg sodium, 84 mg phosphorus, 3 mg calcium, and 37 mg magnesium.

Bringing It Home

Plain, raw popcorn kernels are the best bargain and the best nutritional choice. It's wise to stay away from flavorings and additives. Look for popcorn with a one-word ingredient list: Popcorn. Health food stores carry organic popcorn, and you can also find some exotic varieties—such as red or black popcorns—that are just more fun. Since what makes popcorn pop is the moisture inside the kernels, it's important to store your popcorn in an airtight container so that it doesn't dry out. Don't refrigerate it. If you have an air popper, you can pop your corn without any additives at all.

Livit Recipe

Homemade Popcorn

3 tablespoons canola oil OR other oil with a high smoking point
⅓ cup high-quality popcorn kernels
2 tablespoons butter
  Salt

- In a large saucepan, heat oil over medium-high heat. To test that the pan is hot enough, put 3 or 4 popcorn kernels into the oil, cover the pan, and wait for them to pop.
- Once the test kernels pop, add the rest of the popcorn to the oil. Cover the pan and remove it from the heat for 30 seconds. (This gets all the kernels ready to pop.) Return the pan to the heat. As the popping gets under way, gently shake the pan, continuously, so that the popped corn doesn't burn. When the popping slows down so that there are seconds between the pops, remove the pan from the heat, take off the lid, and pour the popcorn at once into a large bowl.
- Melt the butter and drizzle it over the popped corn. Add the salt last. Serve.
- NOTE Many cooks believe that adding salt to popcorn too soon results in tough corn.
- VARIATION For popcorn with more taste and less fat, reduce or eliminate the butter and add Spanish smoked paprika, nutritional yeast, cayenne pepper, chili powder, curry powder, or cumin—or your favorite combination of the above!

YIELD 4 servings

NUTRITION ANALYSIS PER SERVING 205 calories, 12.5 g carbohydrate, 2 g protein, 16.9 g fat, 2.4 g dietary fiber

111 Spelt and Spelt Pasta

Benefits

Spelt is a close relative of wheat and was widely cultivated in the Middle Ages, though over time it lost out to other wheats. When harvested, spelt has a tough hull on the grains that must be removed before it can be milled into flour.

Spelt provides potassium, phosphorus, magnesium, manganese, and the B vitamins niacin, thiamine, and riboflavin. As a close relative of wheat, its nutrition profile is much the same, though it appears to provide more niacin. Spelt also contains gluten, making it inappropriate for people with celiac disease or on gluten-free diets.

NUTRITIONAL COMPOSITION One and one-half cups of cooked organic whole spelt pasta provide 190 calories, 40 g carbohydrate, 8 g protein, 1.5 g fat, 5 g dietary fiber, and 1.8 mg iron.

Bringing It Home

Spelt is available as whole grain, flour, pasta, bread, and sprouted grain bread. Like other whole grains, spelt should be kept away from light, heat, and moisture. The flour is more vulnerable to rancidity and loss of nutrients, so it should be stored in the refrigerator.

Livit Recipe

Spelt Pasta Primavera

½ pound spelt pasta
1 tablespoon olive oil
¼ cup water
1 carrot, peeled and cut into 2-inch × ½-inch strips
1 medium zucchini, cut into ¼-inch slices
½ small eggplant, cut into ¼-inch slices
½ red onion, cut into ¼-inch slices
½ bell pepper, any color, seeded and cut into thin strips
¼ cup pasta sauce OR marinara sauce
2 or 3 cloves garlic, minced
½ teaspoon Italian seasoning OR herbes de Provence
Salt and pepper
1 pint cherry tomatoes, halved
Grated Parmesan cheese, optional

- Bring a large pot of water to a boil. Add the pasta, and cook according to the package directions until it is al dente. Try to time it so that the pasta will be ready very shortly after the vegetables are cooked.

- In a large skillet, heat the oil and water over medium heat. Add the carrot, zucchini, eggplant, onion, and pepper. Stir to coat them with oil and water. Cook the vegetables for about 10 minutes, stirring only occasionally, until they are just heated through and soft enough to eat. They should still be crisp and colorful. Turn off heat, but leave the pan on the burner.

- Add pasta sauce to the vegetables. Add another ¼ cup of water to thin the sauce, if necessary. Add garlic and Italian seasoning. Add salt and pepper to taste.

- When the pasta is al dente, drain it and add it directly to the skillet with the vegetables. Adjust the seasoning, if needed. Transfer to a serving bowl.

- Just before serving, gently stir in the cherry tomatoes. Sprinkle with Parmesan cheese, if using. Serve.

YIELD 6 servings

NUTRITION ANALYSIS PER SERVING 209 calories, 40.1 g carbohydrate, 7.9 g protein, 3.8 g fat, 6.1 g dietary fiber

112 Spelt Pretzels

Benefits

Also see SuperFood 111, Spelt and Spelt Pasta.

Spelt pretzels are another great high-fiber, easy snack. Pretzels are baked, so pretzels in general are a healthier snack than deep-fried chips. Spelt pretzels give you the additional benefits of whole grains.

NUTRITIONAL COMPOSITION Eighteen spelt pretzels provide 110 calories, 21 g carbohydrate, 4 g protein, 1.5 g fat, 4 g dietary fiber, 240 mg sodium, and 0.36 mg iron.

Bringing It Home

If possible, find unsalted spelt pretzels. You should be able to find them at your local store or online. Because spelt is high in sodium, be sure to drink lots of water with spelt pretzels and other spelt products to help counteract the high sodium content.

Livit Recipe

Spelt Pretzel Snack

¼ cup organic peanut butter
2 cups celery sticks
18 spelt pretzels

- Put the peanut butter in a small bowl in the center of a plate. Arrange the celery sticks and spelt pretzels around it.
- NOTE Although spelt pretzels are a quick snack on their own, you can make a more balanced snack by adding protein and a fruit or vegetable.

YIELD 2 servings

NUTRITION ANALYSIS PER SERVING 266 calories, 22.2 g carbohydrate, 10.6 g protein, 16.6 g fat, 4.5 g dietary fiber

113 Sprouted Grain Bread

Benefits

Eating sprouted grains is like eating a whole little plant—combining the nutrition of a grain with that of a green vegetable. Some breads made with sprouted grains also include sprouted legumes; some have no flour; some are made without yeast. Most sprouted grain breads are made with ingredients as unrefined as possible. Sprouted grain breads tend to have a low glycemic index and to be low in saturated fat.

The sprouted grains used most often for these breads are wheat, millet, and spelt. The breads that incorporate legumes use sprouted lentils and sprouted soybeans, making the bread a complete protein.

NUTRITIONAL COMPOSITION One slice of typical sprouted grain bread provides 80 calories, 15 g carbohydrate, 8 g protein, 0.5 g fat, 3 g dietary fiber, 75 mg sodium, 80 mg potassium, 0.72 mg iron, 0.12 mg thiamine, 0.03 mg riboflavin, 0.4 mg niacin, 0.08 mg vitamin B_6, 24 mg magnesium, and 0.6 mg zinc.

Bringing It Home

Sprouted grain breads are generally low in sodium, so you may not need to go to the extreme of getting the "low-sodium" version, which is sometimes lacking in flavor.

Sprouted grain breads are rich in nutrients but low in preservatives, so mold grows on them very quickly. It is best to put them in the freezer immediately. Bread can be toasted directly out of the freezer, combining thawing and toasting in one step. To simply defrost it, wrap the bread in foil and put it in the toaster oven for about three minutes.

Sprouted grain cheese toast makes a quick out-the-door breakfast for the entire family, or try toasted sprouted grain bread topped with ¼ cup of part-skim ricotta cheese and a little cinnamon. This is especially yummy on sprouted grain cinnamon raisin bread.

Livit Recipe

Sprouted Grain Cheese Toast

    4 slices sprouted grain bread
    4 slices (1 ounce each) reduced-fat cheddar cheese
    1 medium tomato, sliced

- Preheat oven to 350°F.
- Lay the slices of bread on a baking sheet. Top each slice of bread with 1 slice of cheese and 1 slice of tomato.
- Heat in the oven until the cheese is melted, about 1 or 2 minutes.
- NOTE This recipe can be made in a toaster oven as well, which is an especially good choice if you're making just one or two servings. If you start out with frozen bread, wrap the slices individually in foil and warm them in a conventional or toaster oven for 2 minutes to thaw.

YIELD 4 servings

NUTRITION ANALYSIS PER SERVING 156.5 calories, 17.4 g carbohydrate, 12.3 g protein, 5.1 g fat, 3.3 g dietary fiber

114 Sprouted Grain English Muffin/ Whole Wheat English Muffin

Benefits

Sprouted grain or whole wheat English muffins are a great, high-fiber replacement for white bread English muffins—and much more satisfying. This is a fantastic staple starch to keep on hand as the basis for a quick breakfast, lunch, or dinner. For a more balanced meal, add a protein source and vegetables.

> **NUTRITIONAL COMPOSITION** One half of a sprouted grain English muffin provides 80 calories, 15 g carbohydrate, 4 g protein, 0.5 g fat, 3 g dietary fiber, 80 mg sodium, and 75 mg potassium.

Bringing It Home

Like the sprouted grain breads, these should be put into the freezer immediately. If you prefer to eat just half an English muffin at a time, cut them in half and pack them in plastic zipper sandwich bags before putting them into the freezer.

These muffins can be toasted right out of the freezer, combining defrosting and cooking in one easy step. To simply defrost a muffin, wrap it in foil and put it in the toaster oven for about three minutes.

Livit Recipe

Egg "McLivit" Muffin

Say good-bye to the fast-food version and hello to a healthier heart!

    1 slice part-skim mozzarella cheese
    1 sprouted grain English muffin, sliced in half
    ¼ teaspoon non-hydrogenated margarine
    1 egg OR 6 tablespoons egg whites

- Preheat oven to 350°F.
- Place the slice of cheese on one half of the muffin. Toast both halves in the oven until the cheese has melted and the plain half is browned.
- Lightly grease the inside of a nonstick frying pan with margarine, using a paper towel to distribute the margarine and absorb any excess.
- Fry the egg in the pan until the whites are solid. Sandwich the egg between the two halves of toasted English muffin, with the cheesy half on top. Serve.

YIELD 1 serving

NUTRITION ANALYSIS PER SERVING 235 calories, 17.4 g carbohydrate, 17.1 g protein, 11.5 g fat, 3 g dietary fiber

115 Sprouted Grain Tortilla

Benefits

Sprouted grain tortillas are a high-fiber, versatile staple food to keep in your refrigerator for a quick breakfast, lunch, or dinner. These tortillas are great to use for wraps, egg burritos, and vegetarian burritos.

NUTRITIONAL COMPOSITION One sprouted grain tortilla provides 150 calories, 24 g carbohydrate, 6 g protein, 3.5 g fat, 5 g dietary fiber, 150 mg potassium, 140 mg sodium, 4 mg calcium, 1.8 mg iron, 0.22 mg thiamine, and 40 mg magnesium.

Bringing It Home

Always check the "use by" date when buying packaged tortillas and try to give yourself at least a couple of weeks to use them. If you think you won't use them up by the "use by" date, store them in the freezer. Keep the tortillas sealed either in the original package or in a plastic zipper bag. To reheat or defrost, wrap a tortilla in foil and heat it in the toaster oven at 350°F.

Livit Recipe

Quick Bean and Cheese Burrito

1 sprouted grain tortilla OR whole wheat tortilla OR corn tortilla
½ cup canned black beans OR pinto beans, drained and rinsed
1 ounce shredded part-skim mozzarella cheese
⅛ avocado, thinly sliced
  Salsa

- Set the toaster oven to 350°F.
- Put the tortilla on the toaster oven tray. Cover the tortilla with beans. Sprinkle cheese over the top. Fold the tortilla over the beans and cheese, and heat in the toaster oven for about 5 minutes, until the cheese melts.
- Put the burrito on a plate, open the tortilla, and add avocado and salsa. Fold the tortilla back over the mixture. Serve.
- NOTE For a more balanced lunch or dinner, serve a mixed green salad on the side.

YIELD 1 serving

NUTRITION ANALYSIS PER SERVING 314 calories, 44 g carbohydrate, 17 g protein, 8 g fat, 10.2 g dietary fiber

116 Teff

Benefits

Teff is the tiny grain from which Ethiopian injera bread is made. Teff is also popular in India and Australia, and it is now being grown in the United States, primarily in Idaho. Teff is so small that the bran and germ—the parts in most grains that contain most of the nutritional value—make up almost the entire grain. As a result, teff is exceptionally high in fiber. Teff also provides all eight essential amino acids, making it a complete protein. It is a gluten-free grain.

Teff is a good source of several minerals, including calcium, phosphorus, iron, copper, aluminum, barium, magnesium, boron, and zinc. The iron in teff is in a form that is relatively easy for the body to absorb (unlike many other plant-based iron sources). Teff also provides thiamine, and more lysine than either wheat or barley.

> **NUTRITIONAL COMPOSITION** One-quarter cup of dry whole grain teff provides 160 calories, 33 g carbohydrate, 6 g protein, 1 g fat, 6 g dietary fiber, 10 mg sodium, 80 mg calcium, and 3.6 mg iron.

Bringing It Home

Teff is available as a whole grain or as flour, and it comes in a range of colors, including ivory, red, and brown. Store teff in the refrigerator in an airtight container. Don't rinse it before cooking; if you do, it will turn into a gel. That gel-like property makes it effective for thickening sauces and other foods, like puddings.

Teff porridge is a great substitute for your morning oatmeal. Serve it with agave nectar, raisins, nuts, fruit, or cinnamon for extra flavor and nutrients.

Livit Recipe

Teff Cocoa Pudding

2 cups water
½ cup teff
3 tablespoons cocoa

2 tablespoons maple syrup
2 teaspoons vanilla extract

- In a small saucepan, combine the water and teff and bring to a boil. Cover, reduce heat, and allow to simmer for 15 to 20 minutes, stirring occasionally, until the water is absorbed. Once the water is absorbed, remove the teff from the heat and allow it to cool to room temperature.
- In a blender jar, combine the cooked teff, cocoa, maple syrup, and vanilla. Blend until smooth and light—if the mixture is too thick, add a little water.
- Pour the pudding mixture into serving bowls and chill. Serve cold.

YIELD 4 servings

NUTRITION ANALYSIS PER SERVING 121.4 calories, 25.7 g carbohydrate, 3.8 g protein, 1.1 g fat, 4.3 g dietary fiber

117 Triticale

Benefits

Triticale was developed as a wheat-rye hybrid to take advantage of rye's hardiness and wheat's high yields. Triticale is also high in protein and has twice the lysine of wheat. High in fiber as well, triticale also provides potassium, phosphorus, magnesium, manganese, and B vitamins.

> **NUTRITIONAL COMPOSITION** One-half cup of whole grain triticale flour provides 219 calories, 47.7 g carbohydrate, 8.5 g protein, 1.2 g fat, 9.5 g dietary fiber, 48 mcg folic acid, 303 mg potassium, 208.5 mg phosphorus, 23 mg calcium, 99.5 mg magnesium, 1.73 mg zinc, and 2.72 mg manganese.

Bringing It Home

Triticale is available as a whole grain, as flour, and as an added ingredient in some cereals and multi-grain breads and snacks. It should be stored in an airtight container, away from sunlight, heat, and moisture.

Adding triticale flour to baked goods gives them an unexpected new flavor. Triticale also can be sprouted and added to salads.

Livit Recipe

Triticale Home-Style Biscuits

1 cup unbleached flour	3 tablespoons safflower oil
¼ cup triticale flour	¼ cup 1% buttermilk
2½ teaspoons baking powder	½ teaspoon margarine
¼ teaspoon salt	

- Preheat oven to 450°F.
- In a medium mixing bowl, combine the flours, baking powder, and salt. Stir in the oil and buttermilk and mix thoroughly.
- Knead dough with floured hands about 10 times, until it becomes thick and sticks together.
- On a lightly floured surface, pat the dough to a thickness of about ½". Using a drinking glass or cookie cutter, cut 2"-diameter biscuits.
- Lightly grease a cookie sheet with margarine. Set the biscuits close together on the greased cookie sheet so that they almost touch. Bake for 10 to 12 minutes.
- VARIATION To reduce the fat content of these biscuits, use unsweetened applesauce in place of the oil.

YIELD 6 biscuits

NUTRITION ANALYSIS PER SERVING 159.3 calories, 20.9 g carbohydrate, 3.2 g protein, 7.2 g fat, 1.4 g dietary fiber

118 Wheat Germ

Benefits

Wheat germ provides vitamin E, folate, phosphorus, thiamine, zinc, and magnesium. It is also a good source of fiber. Wheat germ contains more iron and potassium than almost any other food. A 3.5-ounce portion contains 9.5 mg of iron, 827 mg of potassium, 2 mg of vitamin B_1, and 4.2 mg of vitamin B_3.

The active elements in wheat germ are vitamin E and the essential fatty acids. One of the fatty acids in wheat germ, octacosanol, appears to help increase endurance and improve the utilization of oxygen during exercise. It may also help reduce cholesterol in the blood and be useful in treating Parkinson's disease. Oil derived from wheat germ improves strength and increases longevity.

NUTRITIONAL COMPOSITION Two tablespoons of wheat germ provides 48 calories, 6.4 g carbohydrate, 4.1 g protein, 1.2 g fat, 1.6 g dietary fiber, 17 IU vitamin A, 51 mcg folic acid, 143 mg potassium, 147 mg phosphorus, 7 mg calcium, 41 mg magnesium, and 2.08 mg zinc.

Bringing It Home

Buy raw wheat germ if at all possible, because it provides the best nutrient profile. It is also high in oils and should be stored in the freezer to protect against rancidity. Toasted wheat germ has a more nutlike flavor and is good added to cereal or baked goods, as well as on cooked vegetables or fruit. It doesn't have to be stored in the refrigerator, but it must be kept away from heat.

Many items are now available with wheat germ added. In addition to increasing the nutritional value of foods, it also adds sweetness and flavor. You can add it to your own baking by substituting it for one-half cup of the flour in any recipe. Use it to replace breadcrumbs in meat loaf and casseroles. It also makes a filling and satisfying breakfast cereal.

Livit Recipe

Morning Glory Muffins

Vegetable oil spray
1 egg
2 egg whites
½ cup apple butter
¼ cup vegetable oil
1 tablespoon vanilla extract
1½ cups all-purpose flour
½ cup whole wheat flour
1¼ cups white sugar

1 tablespoon ground cinnamon
2 teaspoons baking powder
½ teaspoon baking soda
½ teaspoon salt
2 cups grated carrots
1 medium apple, peeled, cored, and chopped
1 cup raisins
2 tablespoons finely chopped walnuts
2 tablespoons toasted wheat germ

- Preheat oven to 375°F.
- Lightly grease 18 muffin cups with vegetable oil spray.
- In a medium bowl, whisk together egg, egg whites, apple butter, oil, and vanilla.
- In a large bowl, stir together the flours, sugar, cinnamon, baking powder, baking soda, and salt. Stir in the carrots, apple, and raisins.
- Stir the apple butter mixture into the flour mixture until just moistened. Spoon the batter into the prepared muffin cups, filling them about three-quarters full.
- In a small bowl, combine walnuts and wheat germ. Sprinkle the mixture over the muffin tops.
- Bake for 15 to 20 minutes, or until the tops are golden and spring back when pressed lightly.

YIELD 18 muffins

NUTRITION ANALYSIS PER SERVING 197 calories, 37.9 g carbohydrate, 3.2 g protein, 4.3 g fat, 1.9 g dietary fiber

119 Whole Wheat Couscous

Benefits

Whole wheat couscous is a quick-to-make, satisfying, high-fiber starch. It is a great low-fat source of complex carbohydrates—the body's optimal fuel—and a nice alternative to rice and pasta. Made of bits of wheat moistened and rolled in wheat flour, this Middle Eastern food is not quite a grain and not quite a pasta.

> **NUTRITIONAL COMPOSITION** One-third cup of whole wheat couscous provides 190 calories, 43 g carbohydrate, 7 g protein, 1 g fat, 7 g dietary fiber, and 1.08 mg iron.

Bringing It Home

Choose whole wheat couscous over regular couscous for more fiber and a more filling and satisfying meal. Leave the seasoned couscous packets alone, because their sodium content is very high.

Livit Recipe

Couscous with Dried Cranberries

    4 cups unsweetened soy milk
    2 cups whole wheat couscous
    ½ cup dried cranberries

- In a large soup pot, bring the soy milk to a boil. Stir in the couscous, and immediately remove the pot from the stove. Stir until all the soy milk is absorbed. Let sit 5 minutes.
- Gently fold in the cranberries, and fluff with a fork. Serve.

YIELD 6 servings

NUTRITION ANALYSIS PER SERVING 286.5 calories, 59.8 g carbohydrate, 14.4 g protein, 4.3 g fat, 4.7 g dietary fiber

120 Whole Wheat Cracker/Flatbread/ Crispbread

Benefits

Whole grain crackers, flatbreads, and crispbreads provide a portable, crunchy whole grain with the convenience of a prepared food. High in fiber and low in fat, they come in a variety of flavors that feature different grains and seeds.

NUTRITIONAL COMPOSITION Five whole wheat crackers provide 115 calories, 19 g carbohydrate, 5 g protein, 2 g fat, 4 g dietary fiber, and 1.4 g iron.

Bringing It Home

Choose whole wheat crackers with a minimum of 3 grams of dietary fiber per serving for a snack that will keep you satisfied and keep you from extra late-night nibbling.

Livit Recipe

Crispbread Treat

¼ cup part-skim ricotta cheese
1 whole wheat crispbread cracker
   Dash of cinnamon
1 tablespoon all-fruit spread, any flavor

· Mound the ricotta on the crispbread, and sprinkle it with cinnamon. Drizzle the all-fruit spread over the ricotta.

YIELD 1 serving

NUTRITION ANALYSIS PER SERVING 163 calories, 21.9 g carbohydrate, 8.2 g protein, 4.9 g fat, 2.3 g dietary fiber

121 Whole Wheat Pasta

Benefits

Whole wheat pasta brings the benefits of whole grain to a familiar staple. Providing complex carbohydrates, fiber, manganese, and magnesium, whole wheat pasta lets you enjoy your favorite pasta dishes while helping to regulate blood sugar and protect intestinal health.

NUTRITIONAL COMPOSITION One cup of cooked whole wheat pasta provides 174 calories, 37.2 g carbohydrate, 7.5 g protein, 0.8 g fat, and 3.9 g dietary fiber.

Bringing It Home

If you are experimenting with whole wheat pasta for the first time, try the whole wheat angel hair. It's very thin, which helps to minimize the difference between whole wheat and white pastas, especially once tomato sauce is on top. Dry pasta has a very long shelf life, as long as it is kept dry. Cooked pasta without sauce keeps for three to four days in the refrigerator.

Livit Recipe

Mac and Cheese in a Breeze

  8 ounces whole wheat pasta shells
  2 tablespoons non-hydrogenated margarine
  1 tablespoon all-purpose flour
  2 cups nonfat milk OR unsweetened soy milk
  ½ teaspoon sea salt
  ½ teaspoon pepper
  1 tablespoon salt-free seasoning OR herbal blend
  ¾ cup grated reduced-fat cheddar cheese
  ½ cup grated fresh Parmesan cheese

- Cook the shells according to package directions. Drain and put into a large bowl. Set aside.
- In a medium saucepan over medium heat, melt the margarine. Stir in the flour. Cook, stirring constantly with a whisk, about 2 minutes, until the roux bubbles a bit—don't let it brown. Slowly add the milk, ½ cup at a time, while continuing to stir the roux. After all the milk has been added, increase heat to high and bring the sauce to a boil. Keep stirring until the sauce begins to thicken. Once the milk sauce has thickened, add the salt, pepper, and salt-free seasoning. Stir in the cheeses, and reduce heat. Cook, continuing to stir, for 2 to 3 more minutes, until the cheese is melted. Remove from heat.
- Pour the cheese sauce over the pasta shells. Mix gently with a wooden spoon. (If you're going to cool the sauce and save it to use later, cover the surface with wax paper so it doesn't develop a skin.)
- NOTE If you need to add thickness to the sauce, mix ½ tablespoon flour with 2 tablespoons cold water in a cup. Stir until all the lumps are gone. Slowly add just enough of this to your sauce, stirring constantly, to get the thickness you want.

YIELD 6 servings

NUTRITION ANALYSIS PER SERVING 248 calories, 33.5 g carbohydrate, 13.8 g protein, 6.3 g fat, 3.4 g dietary fiber

122 Whole Wheat / Whole Grain Pastry Flour

Benefits

Whole wheat pastry flour allows you to bake with whole grain in familiar recipes that call for white flour. The complex carbohydrates, bran, B vitamins, and minerals of whole grains remain intact. The lighter texture of pastry flour behaves more like all-purpose flour in most recipes.

NUTRITIONAL COMPOSITION One-third cup of whole wheat pastry flour provides 110 calories, 23 g carbohydrate, 4 g protein, 0.5 g fat, 3 g dietary fiber, 90 mg potassium, 20 mg calcium, and 1.08 mg iron.

Bringing It Home

Whole wheat pastry flour may require a trip to the natural food or health food store. This flour provides a finer texture and lighter consistency, as well as less gluten, than hard winter wheat flour, making it perfect for flaky pastries and light cakes. It also works well when making the roux for cream sauce.

Livit Recipe

Blissful Banana Bread

¼ teaspoon non-hydrogenated margarine	1 cup whole grain pastry flour
3 large, ripe bananas	1 cup unbleached flour
¼ cup organic unsweetened applesauce	¼ cup wheat germ
½ cup honey	¾ teaspoon salt
2 eggs	1 teaspoon baking soda
1 teaspoon vanilla extract	

- Preheat oven to 350°F.
- Lightly grease a 9″ × 5″ loaf pan with margarine, using a paper towel to spread the margarine and absorb any excess.
- In a medium bowl, mash the bananas with a fork. Add the applesauce, honey, eggs, and vanilla to the mashed bananas. Stir the mixture with a fork or metal whisk.
- In a large bowl, mix the flours, wheat germ, salt, and baking soda. Make a well in the dry ingredients and add the banana mixture. Stir until the dry ingredients are just moistened. Spoon the batter into the loaf pan. Bake for 40 to 45 minutes.
- The banana bread is done when it is golden brown. Loosen the loaf from the pan with a spatula and turn it out to cool on a wire rack. Serve.

YIELD 12 servings

NUTRITION ANALYSIS PER SERVING 169 calories, 36 g carbohydrate, 4 g protein, 2 g fat, 2.7 g dietary fiber

123 Wild Rice

Benefits

Wild rice is not really rice, although it is a close relative. It is a grass that grows in shallow water and is native to North America. A related species is native to Manchuria, in China. Cooked wild rice has a unique flavor and texture. It is high in protein and fiber, and it is gluten-free. Wild rice provides the B vitamins thiamine, niacin, and riboflavin, and the minerals potassium and phosphorus.

> **NUTRITIONAL COMPOSITION** One cup of cooked wild rice provides 166 calories, 35 g carbohydrate, 6.5 g protein, 0.6 g fat, 3 g dietary fiber, and 42.6 mcg folic acid.

Bringing It Home

Wild rice is usually sold as a dried grain, and it is almost black in color. Much "wild" rice is now cultivated in paddies, but many people prefer the truly wild version, harvested in canoes by Native Americans. The latter type is more expensive and increasingly hard to find. The cultivated type, however, is just as full of nutrients and flavor.

If wild rice is kept in a sealed container and away from heat, light, and moisture, it can be kept for a long time, but it is vulnerable to mold if it gets damp. Leftover cooked wild rice can be kept in the refrigerator for a day or two.

Livit Recipe

Wildly Gourmet Rice

2 cups low-sodium chicken broth OR vegetable broth	Freshly ground black pepper
1½ cups water	½ cup pine nuts
1⅓ cups wild rice (½ pound)	1 tablespoon non-hydrogenated margarine
½ cup dried currants	1 medium onion, finely chopped

- In a large saucepan, bring the broth and water to a boil. Once the water is boiling, add the wild rice and currants. Add black pepper to taste. Reduce heat, cover, and allow to simmer for 1 hour, or until the liquid is absorbed and the rice is tender. Add more water, if needed, to cook the rice fully.

- Meanwhile, in a small nonstick skillet, toast the pine nuts over low heat, tossing them constantly with a spatula, until they turn golden. Transfer the nuts to a small bowl. Set aside.

- In the same skillet, melt the margarine. Add the onion and sauté for about 3 minutes or until it is soft.

- In a serving bowl, toss the rice gently with the onion and nuts. Serve immediately.

YIELD 6 servings

NUTRITION ANALYSIS PER SERVING 298 calories, 46.7 g carbohydrate, 7.6 g protein, 9.5 g fat, 3.2 g dietary fiber

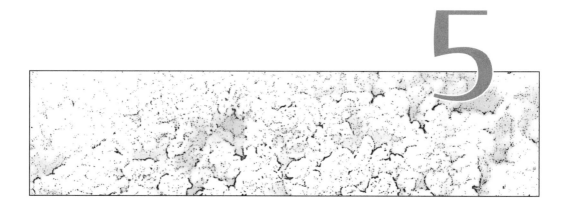

Carbohydrates: Dairy and Dairy Substitutes

Dairy has recently been blamed as a factor in weight gain and heart disease. But studies have consistently shown that consuming dairy products may instead contribute to maintaining a healthy weight. Milk drinkers tend to have better nutrition overall, and the calcium and vitamin D in milk may help the body burn more calories. Other nutrients in dairy products appear to help lower blood pressure.

The culprit in dairy food is its fat content. Milk is, by its very nature, a food for baby animals, and babies have a special nutritional need for energy to help them grow. The fat in whole milk is mainly saturated animal fat—the kind that raises blood cholesterol. Half of the calories from whole milk come from fat, while only 4 percent of the calories in nonfat milk are fat calories. By choosing nonfat or low-fat dairy products, you can avoid the pitfalls and gain the benefits of this unique food.

An eight-ounce glass of milk provides 30 percent of the recommended daily value of calcium, 25 percent of the daily value of vitamin D, and 16 percent of the daily value of protein. It provides several of the B vitamins, including B_{12}, riboflavin, and niacin, as well as the minerals potassium and phosphorus. Vitamin B_{12} is especially important, because it is impossible to get this vitamin from plant sources, and vitamin B_{12} is necessary for healthy functioning of the brain and nervous system. Vitamin B_{12} is also involved in basic cell metabolism, and it plays a role in regulating the circadian rhythm.

According to the Organic Trade Association, milk and dairy products certified as organic come from cows that have been fed organic feed raised on land certified as meeting national organic growing standards, raised in conditions that limit stress and promote health, cared for as individuals by dairy professionals who value animal health, and not routinely given antibiotics or growth hormones (although they may have been given antibiotics to address specific illnesses or infections).

Low-fat organic dairy products are an important part of healthy eating!

124 Greek-Style Yogurt

Benefits

Greek-style yogurt is strained to reduce the whey, making it creamier in texture without adding extra fat. This yogurt is also more stable as a cooking ingredient because it is less likely to curdle when heated. Per serving, there is more protein and less carbohydrate in Greek-style yogurt than in standard yogurts. Because of the reduced carbohydrates, there is more "room" in your carbohydrate count to eat fresh fruit with it. Definitely stick with the low-fat option—the whole-milk version has 20 grams of fat per serving!

> **NUTRITIONAL COMPOSITION** One cup of nonfat plain Greek-style yogurt provides 120 calories, 7 g carbohydrate, 22 g protein, 0 g fat, 0 g dietary fiber, 70 mg sodium, and 200 mg calcium.

Bringing It Home

Be sure to look for the 2 percent low-fat or nonfat versions of Greek-style yogurt. Keep it refrigerated, and pay attention to the expiration date.

Add a little cinnamon and a squirt of agave nectar to your Greek-style yogurt for a sweet, healthy treat.

Livit Recipe

Immune Boost Breakfast

¾ cup nonfat Greek-style yogurt   1 teaspoon cinnamon
1 cup fresh berries of your choice   1 tablespoon ground flaxseed

- Combine the yogurt, berries, cinnamon, and flaxseed in a bowl. Serve.
- NOTES You may also use frozen berries, but thaw and drain them before stirring them in. For an on-the-go snack, mix it in a wide-mouth vacuum bottle.

YIELD 1 serving

NUTRITION ANALYSIS PER SERVING 196.3 calories, 25.1 g carbohydrate, 18.7 g protein, 3 g fat, 11.6 g dietary fiber

125 1% Milk and Skim Milk

Benefits

A recent study found that calcium from dairy foods (1000 to 1400 milligrams per day) changes the way the body burns fat, increasing the metabolism of fat. This helps explain how skim milk not only provides sound nutrition, but may also help you lose weight.

Fat-free milk is high in protein, calcium, and the B vitamins, including B_{12}. If you are still drinking whole milk, switching to nonfat milk can be a significant move toward healthier living all by itself. Not only will you cut fat intake and calories, but you'll get more protein and vitamins in place of the fat. Start by switching from whole milk to 2 percent, then to 1 percent, and finally to skim milk.

> **NUTRITIONAL COMPOSITION** One cup of skim milk provides 86 calories, 12 g carbohydrate, 8 g protein, 0.5 g fat, 0 g dietary fiber, 500 IU vitamin A, 1 mcg vitamin B_{12}, 0.2 mg niacin, 1 mg pantothenic acid, 0.4 mg riboflavin, 3 mcg vitamin D, 302 mg calcium, 103 mg sodium, 247 mg phosphorus, and 382 mg potassium.

Bringing It Home

Some nutrients in milk are sensitive to light, so milk sold in clear glass bottles may have reduced amounts of riboflavin and vitamin A. Paper cartons offer the best protection from light damage.

Don't buy "raw" (not pasteurized) milk. Pasteurization was a great step forward for public health because it kills harmful bacteria that may be present in raw milk. Children, the elderly, and people whose immune systems are impaired are especially vulnerable.

Livit Recipe

Low-Fat Eggnog

1 cup sugar OR evaporated cane juice	4 cups organic skim milk
4 egg whites	2 teaspoons vanilla extract
½ teaspoon salt	½ to 1 cup brandy OR rum
⅓ cup water	Dash of nutmeg
¼ teaspoon cream of tartar	

- In the top half of a stainless steel (not aluminum) double boiler, whisk together the sugar, egg whites, salt, water, and cream of tartar.
- Put a small amount of water in the bottom of the double boiler, so that the top section will sit over the water but not in it (you want to heat the egg mixture, but not cook it). Bring the water to a simmer, then set the top of the double boiler over it. Beat the egg mixture with a hand mixer on medium for about 10 minutes, until the mixture is very thick and fluffy.

- Continue to beat for 3 more minutes. Remove the eggs from the heat. Continue beating the eggs until the mixture has cooled slightly.
- In a large serving bowl, stir the milk and vanilla together. Fold in the egg whites and add the brandy. Combine gently with a whisk. Serve chilled and dusted with nutmeg.

YIELD 8 servings

NUTRITION ANALYSIS PER SERVING 216 calories, 31 g carbohydrate, 6 g protein, 0.5 g fat, 0 g dietary fiber

126 Low-Fat or Nonfat Yogurt with Inulin

Benefits

Inulin in yogurt adds thickness and provides extra sweetness and fiber. Without inulin, most yogurt provides no fiber. Live yogurt cultures that are often present in yogurt with inulin act as prebiotics and probiotics to promote digestive tract health and strengthen your immune system.

> **NUTRITIONAL COMPOSITION** Six ounces of vanilla low-fat yogurt with inulin provides 130 calories, 22 g carbohydrate, 7 g protein, 1.5 g fat, 7 g dietary fiber, 105 mg sodium, and 300 mg calcium.

Bringing It Home

Choose organic yogurts. Desserts are part of a healthy relationship with food, and flavored yogurts are a quick, sweet snack of fuel and protein. If you start with plain yogurt and add your own fruit, cinnamon, or flavorings, you can limit the amount of sugar and still have a sweet treat.

Livit Recipe

Indulge Without the Bulge Yogurt Pie

A light, low-fat dessert that's easy to make!

  1 cup graham cracker crumbs (from crackers made without hydrogenated oils)
  ¼ cup non-hydrogenated margarine, melted
  2 tablespoons evaporated raw sugarcane juice OR brown sugar
  1 can (8 ounces) unsweetened crushed pineapple, drained (reserve juice)
  2 envelopes (4 teaspoons) unflavored gelatin
  3 cups plain low-fat yogurt
1½ teaspoons vanilla extract
  ¼ cup honey
  2 organic strawberries, sliced OR 1 organic kiwifruit, sliced, optional, as garnish

- In a small bowl, blend the graham cracker crumbs and margarine with the sugar. Pat the mixture into the bottom of an 8″ × 8″ baking pan. Chill in the freezer for 10 to 12 minutes.
- In a small saucepan, blend ⅓ cup of the reserved pineapple juice with the unflavored gelatin. Set the pan over medium-low heat and bring the mixture to a boil, stirring constantly with a wire whisk until the gelatin has melted. Remove from heat and let stand for about 5 minutes.
- In a mixing bowl, whisk together the juice mixture, yogurt, vanilla, honey, and crushed pineapple. Pour the filling into the baking pan on top of the crumb crust. Chill in the refrigerator until set.
- Cut into 9 squares. Garnish each square with a slice of fruit, if using. Serve.

YIELD 9 servings

NUTRITION ANALYSIS PER SERVING 203.3 calories, 29.5 g carbohydrate, 6.6 g protein, 6.7 g fat, 1 g dietary fiber

127 Low-Fat Cottage Cheese

Benefits

Cottage cheese is Little Miss Muffet's meal of curds and whey; it gets its name because it was often made at home, from milk that had already had some of its cream skimmed off for butter. As a result, it has long been made in skim and low-fat versions. It qualifies as a SuperFood because it concentrates the protein and other nutrients from milk but is low in fat.

Cottage cheese is made by adding a starter culture to the milk that causes it to separate. Most of the watery whey is drained off, leaving the curds, which are high in protein and calcium. Large-curd cottage cheese also contains rennet; the small-curd version does not.

Some low-fat cottage cheese includes active cultures like those in yogurt. These active cultures help digest lactose, making this cottage cheese a better option for people who have some degree of lactose intolerance. The active cultures may also make the calcium it provides easier for your body to absorb.

NUTRITIONAL COMPOSITION One-half cup of low-fat cottage cheese provides 100 calories, 4 g carbohydrate, 13 g protein, 2.5 g fat, 0 g dietary fiber, 200 IU vitamin A, 100 mg calcium, and 390 mg sodium.

Bringing It Home

For the most benefit, choose a cottage cheese that is both low in fat and contains live and active cultures. In general, low-fat cottage cheese is both filling and full of protein, and it substitutes well for higher-fat cheeses in both savory and sweet recipes. To lower the sodium in cottage cheese, try rinsing it in a strainer. The texture becomes more similar to feta cheese, and it's great on salads.

Livit Recipe

Cottage Cheese Toasties

4 slices whole wheat bread
1 cup low-fat cottage cheese
¼ teaspoon evaporated sugarcane juice OR sugar
½ teaspoon cinnamon
1 cup fruit slices or pieces (banana, peaches, apples, raisins, dates, goji berries)

- Toast the bread. Put ¼ cup of cottage cheese on each slice of toast, spreading it evenly.
- Mix the sugar and cinnamon together and sprinkle it on the cottage cheese. Top each slice of toast with one fourth of the fruit.
- Place the toast on a baking sheet, and place it under the broiler until just heated through. Serve warm.

YIELD 4 servings

NUTRITION ANALYSIS PER SERVING 187 calories, 31.2 g carbohydrate, 11.7 g protein, 2.8 g fat, 3.7 g dietary fiber

128 Low-Fat Unsweetened Kefir

Benefits

Kefir is a cultured or fermented milk beverage from the Caucasus region of Central Asia. The cultures are called "kefir grains" and include a mix of bacteria and yeasts. It takes kefir grains to make kefir grains, much like the sourdough starter process for bread. There are different strains and types of kefir grains, which give different qualities and health benefits to the beverage. Traditional kefir also has a low alcohol content.

Kefir's cultures are believed to help strengthen the immune system. They also make the milk more digestible for those with lactose intolerance. The "friendly" bacteria and yeast (and the alcohol) help eliminate more dangerous bacteria from the system. They may also encourage anti-cancer compounds and have been used to soothe skin disorders.

NUTRITIONAL COMPOSITION One cup of plain low-fat kefir provides 120 calories, 12 g carbohydrate, 14 g protein, 2 g fat, 3 g dietary fiber, 500 IU vitamin A, 2.4 mg vitamin C, 100 IU vitamin D, 125 mg sodium, and 300 mg calcium.

Bringing It Home

Choose organic kefir if possible. For a balanced snack, try a cup of unsweetened kefir with some berries added, or eat it like a fruit parfait. Sprinkle kefir with cinnamon for a different flavor.

Livit Recipe

Waldorf Salad Dressed with Kefir

½ tablespoon reduced-sodium tamari OR reduced-sodium soy sauce
2 teaspoons honey OR agave nectar
½ teaspoon spicy herbal salt OR salt
1 cup plain kefir
Dash of cayenne pepper, optional
¼ pound celery, cleaned, trimmed, and grated
1 or 2 firm apples, cored and coarsely grated
½ cup coarsely chopped walnuts

• In a medium bowl, gently combine the tamari, honey, herbal salt, and kefir. Fold in cayenne pepper, if using. Add celery, apples, and walnuts, and toss them gently in the kefir dressing. Refrigerate for at least 1 hour to enhance the flavor.

YIELD 4 servings

NUTRITION ANALYSIS PER SERVING 215 calories, 26.8 g carbohydrate, 5.1 g protein, 11.5 g fat, 4.4 g dietary fiber

129 Plain Low-Fat Yogurt

Benefits

Plain low-fat yogurt is a staple in healthy meal plans. The cultures in yogurt appear to support intestinal health and improve immune function. Low-fat yogurt is a very satisfying food and a good source of protein, calcium, and the B vitamins.

NUTRITIONAL COMPOSITION Eight ounces of plain nonfat yogurt provides 130 calories, 19 g carbohydrate, 13 g protein, 0 g fat, 0 g dietary fiber, 550 mg potassium, 170 mg sodium, 350 mg phosphorus, and 450 mg calcium.

Bringing It Home

To get the full benefit of yogurt, choose one that includes live, active cultures. Pay attention to the expiration date. Avoid yogurts with artificial colors, flavorings, thickeners, or sweeteners. Fruit yogurts tend to contain a lot of sugar, so buy plain yogurt and add your own fruit for a healthier treat.

Store yogurt in the refrigerator in its original container. If unopened, yogurt may keep for about one week past the expiration date.

Livit Recipe

Cucumber Yogurt Dip with Pita

16 ounces plain yogurt
 1 pound cucumber, peeled, seeded, and finely chopped
 2 teaspoons minced fresh dill plus 2 sprigs for garnish
 3 cloves garlic, minced
 1 tablespoon extra-virgin olive oil
 ½ lemon, juice only
   Salt
 4 pita breads, cut into wedges

- Line a large sieve with cheesecloth and place it over a bowl. Put the yogurt in the sieve and drain it, covered and chilled, for 6 hours. Discard the liquid.

- Squeeze the cucumber pieces between paper towels to reduce the moisture.

- In a medium bowl, stir together the drained yogurt, cucumbers, minced dill, garlic, oil, and lemon juice. Add salt to taste. Let the dip stand, covered and chilled, for at least 2 hours (and up to 8 hours) to allow the flavors to develop.

- Just before serving, stir the dip and garnish it with dill sprigs. Serve with pita wedges.

YIELD 4 servings

NUTRITION ANALYSIS PER SERVING 121 calories, 11.3 g carbohydrate, 7.1 g protein, 5.5 g fat, 0.8 g dietary fiber

130 Ricotta Cheese

Benefits

Ricotta cheese is a traditional Italian cheese, similar to cottage cheese but made from the whey left over from making other cheeses. The thin whey is left to continue to ferment in whatever starter was used to make the initial cheese; the additional fermentation increases the acidity of the whey, and when the acidic whey is heated, the remaining proteins precipitate into very fine curds. The name ricotta means "recooked," and refers to this second round of fermentation and heating. It's a way to squeeze more of the food value out of the milk, and the resulting cheese is high in protein and low in fat.

Ricotta has a different texture and taste than cottage cheese, with finer and drier curds. It works well in both sweet dishes and savory ones, and in Italian cooking is used in desserts as well as main courses.

Ricotta is higher in calcium and lower in sodium than cottage cheese. Even whole-milk ricotta cheese is relatively low in fat, so it's not necessary to choose a low-fat version.

NUTRITIONAL COMPOSITION One-half cup of part-skim ricotta cheese provides 171 calories, 6.4 g carbohydrate, 14.1 g protein, 9.8 g fat, 0 g dietary fiber, 38 mg cholesterol, 536 IU vitamin A, 16 mcg folic acid, 155 mg potassium, 155 mg sodium, 226 mg phosphorus, 337 mg calcium, 18 mg magnesium, and 1.66 mg zinc.

Bringing It Home

Ricotta cheese should be stored in the refrigerator immediately. Keep track of the expiration date and be sure to use the cheese before that date. For a high-calcium protein source that's even lower in fat, you can choose part-skim ricotta cheese. Ricotta cheese is a great replacement for sour cream and cream cheese. It's a great spread that you can make savory, with basil and tomato—or sweet, with cinnamon and fruit.

Livit Recipe

Scrumptious Veggie Lasagna

1 package (8 ounces) whole wheat lasagna noodles
1 package (10 ounces) frozen chopped spinach
1 package (10 ounces) frozen mixed vegetables (broccoli, zucchini, carrots)
1 egg
4 ounces small-curd low-fat cottage cheese
8 ounces low-fat ricotta cheese
2 cups shredded part-skim mozzarella cheese
1 large clove garlic, minced
¾ teaspoon dried oregano
¼ teaspoon black pepper
¼ teaspoon salt-free seasoning
¼ teaspoon nutmeg, optional
1 jar (24 ounces) organic spaghetti sauce OR marinara sauce

- Prepare noodles according to package directions.
- Preheat oven to 350°F.
- In a steamer, steam the spinach and mixed vegetables just to defrost, and drain them well.
- In a large bowl, beat the egg slightly, and add the cottage cheese, ricotta, 1 cup of the mozzarella, the spinach mixture, garlic, oregano, pepper, salt-free seasoning, and nutmeg, if using. Stir to combine.
- In a 13" × 9" baking dish, layer one third of the sauce, half of the noodles, and half of the vegetable mixture. Repeat the layers. Top with the remaining sauce. Sprinkle the remaining 1 cup of mozzarella cheese over the top. Cover tightly with foil and bake for 45 minutes. Remove the foil and cook for 15 minutes, until bubbly and golden brown. Let stand for 15 minutes before serving.

YIELD 8 servings

NUTRITION ANALYSIS PER SERVING 313 calories, 37.9 g carbohydrate, 18.7 g protein, 11.3 g fat, 6.8 g dietary fiber

131 Soy Milk (Unsweetened)

Benefits

Soy milk is low in carbohydrates, so you can eat it with your cereal without adding to your carbs. It's also low in fat and an excellent source of calcium. Soy milk is a great way to add the benefits of soy to your diet, reduce reliance on animal products, and possibly help lower cholesterol. As a milk replacement, soy milk is also supplemented with some vitamins and minerals to provide a more milk-like nutritional profile.

NUTRITIONAL COMPOSITION One cup of unsweetened soy milk provides 70 calories, 3 g carbohydrate, 7 g protein, 3.5 g fat, 1 g dietary fiber, 750 IU vitamin A, 120 IU vitamin D, 0.51 mg riboflavin, 3 mcg vitamin B_{12}, 70 mg sodium, 300 mg potassium, 300 mg calcium, and 1.8 mg iron.

Bringing It Home

Select refrigerated soy milk if it is available rather than the shelf-stable soy milk in a box, because the latter has been heat treated.

Livit Recipe

Breakfast Cereal Sustainer

1 cup high-fiber cereal (>5 g dietary fiber and <30 g carbohydrate per serving)
1 tablespoon ground flaxseeds
1 tablespoon shelled hemp seeds
1 cup organic unsweetened soy milk

• Pour the cereal into a bowl. Stir in ground flaxseeds and shelled hemp seeds. Add milk. Serve.

YIELD 1 serving

NUTRITION ANALYSIS PER SERVING 330 calories, 63.1 g carbohydrate, 21.5 g protein, 15 g fat, 21.2 g dietary fiber

THE THERMIC EFFECT

The very act of eating can increase your metabolism—digesting, absorbing, and transporting nutrients requires metabolic activity. It takes a minimum of 150 calories to get the thermic effect, so even if you're trying to watch your calories, make sure to eat at least 150 calories every time you snack—just to jump start your metabolism.

132 Soy Yogurt

Benefits

Soy yogurt provides calcium and live cultures without requiring the system to digest lactose or animal fat. Soy yogurt's live cultures help strengthen your immune system, and its relatively high fiber content—2 grams of dietary fiber per serving—will help satisfy you and lower your cholesterol. Soy isoflavones may help increase insulin secretion and improve glycemic control. Researchers speculate that soy yogurt, especially when served with fruit, may help regulate the enzymes that affect blood sugar levels in persons with diabetes.

> **NUTRITIONAL COMPOSITION** Six ounces of flavored soy yogurt provides 170 calories, 32 g carbohydrate, 6 g protein, 3.5 g fat, 2 g dietary fiber, 25 mg sodium, 300 mg calcium, and 1.08 mg iron.

Bringing It Home

Choose a soy yogurt made with whole soy milk rather than processed soy protein. If possible, choose one that has at least 2 grams of fiber. Store it in the refrigerator, and use it within a week of the "sell by" date. The 170 calories provided by a serving of soy yogurt is the perfect caloric intake for getting the thermic effect to increase your metabolism.

Livit Recipe

Escape to the Tropics Salad

Dressing

- 1 cup plain soy yogurt
- ¼ cup unsweetened soy milk
- ¼ cup agave nectar
- 1 fresh lemon, juice only
- 2 tablespoons chopped fresh mint

Salad

- 12 ounces soy deli slices, cut into thin strips
- ½ small cantaloupe, peeled, seeded, and diced
- ½ small honeydew melon, peeled, seeded, and diced
- ¾ pound seedless red grapes
- 1 head romaine lettuce, chopped into bite-sized pieces
- 2 kiwifruit, peeled and sliced into half-circles, as garnish

- *To make the dressing:* In a blender jar, combine the yogurt, soy milk, agave nectar, lemon juice, lemon zest, and mint. Blend until well combined, and chill until ready to use.

- *To assemble the salad:* In a large salad bowl, combine the soy deli slices, cantaloupe, honeydew, and grapes. Gently fold the dressing into the fruit mixture until all is well coated. Put a bed of lettuce on each plate. Mound the dressed fruit mixture in the middle. Garnish with sliced kiwi. Serve.

- NOTE If you will not be serving all six portions at one meal, divide the fruit mixture and the dressing before combining, as both the salad and dressing keep better separately. They will keep for about three days in the refrigerator.

YIELD 6 servings

NUTRITION ANALYSIS PER SERVING 212 calories, 15.7 g protein, 42.3 g carbohydrate, 2.8 g fat, 5.1 g dietary fiber

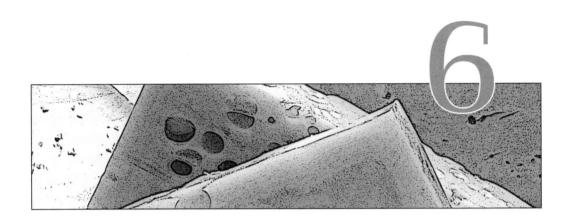

Proteins

In the past, some high-protein/low-carbohydrate diets led people to believe that the calories in proteins magically do not count. I often hear patients say, "I can eat as much meat as I want and still lose weight, right?"

But protein calories *do* count: Each gram of protein contains 4 calories. We need protein—it helps rebuild muscle and organs—but the typical American diet includes far more protein than most people's bodies require. Excess protein can stress the liver and kidneys and can precipitate dehydration.

So the key is to eat just the right amount of protein to keep your body healthy. The Recommended Dietary Allowance (RDA) for both men and women is 0.37 grams of protein per pound of body weight per day. Those who get a substantial amount of exercise may need more. Endurance exercisers such as walkers, joggers, and dancers may need 0.55 to 0.64 grams of protein per pound of body weight every day; those who do strength training, such as with weights, may need as much as 0.77 to 0.82 grams of protein per pound of body weight every day. Another way to estimate your protein needs is as a percentage of total calories: Aim for 20 to 25 percent of your total calories in a day to come from protein sources.

Eating protein foods at each meal or snack helps keep you satisfied longer, because protein foods are digested more slowly than carbohydrates. It takes from three to six hours to digest a high-protein food, compared to about one hour for a food that is mainly carbohydrates. And we do need protein every day—it's one of the basic building blocks of the body and makes up about 16 percent of our total body weight. Muscle, hair, skin, and connective tissue are mostly protein, and all the enzymes, hormones, antibodies, and neurotransmitters in your body are produced from protein.

Proteins are the body's building blocks, and amino acids are the building blocks of protein. Of the 20 "standard" amino acids required by the body, eight are considered "essential"—they must be provided by foods because the body cannot manufacture them. Protein from animal sources—including poultry, beef, pork, fish, milk, and eggs—contains the full complement of essential amino acids and are considered "complete" proteins. Egg protein is the highest biological value protein. It has the highest protein efficiency ratio and is used as the reference for comparing the relative protein values of other foods. Most plant sources of protein are not complete: They are low in (or lack) one or more of the essential amino acids. The idea of combining plant proteins to provide a complete protein in each meal was popularized in the 1970s by Frances Moore Lappé in her book *Diet for a Small Planet*. It is still optimal to balance the vegetable proteins within a meal, but later research indicates that it may be sufficient to balance your proteins within a day's menu.

Generally, non-meat protein sources can be divided into four categories based on which amino acids they have and which they lack: milk (including milk, yogurt, cheese, and fresh cheeses like cottage and ricotta), grains, legumes (dried beans, lentils, split peas, peanuts, and soy products, including tofu), and nuts and seeds. Although the milk category is a complete protein by itself, the concentration of some amino acids is low. The same is true for soybeans, which is the only bean that is considered a complete protein.

Grains lack the amino acids in which milk is high, so they are complemented by milk. Beans lack the amino acids that are abundant in grains. So the milk needs the grains and the grains need the beans. Here is a mnemonic to help you remember the groups that combine to provide the most balanced protein: My Grandmother Likes Nuts and Seeds—Milk goes with Grains; Grains go with Legumes; Legumes go with Nuts and Seeds. Some examples of food combinations that provide more complete vegetarian protein content are cereal and milk, pasta and cheese, bread and peanut butter, rice and beans, beans and corn, beans and a tortilla, and chickpeas with sesame seeds (for example, hummus with tahini).

Because soy is considered a complete vegetable protein, it is included here in the Proteins chapter. It comes in many forms and there are many ways to incorporate it into your meals, as evidenced by its appearance in four different SuperFood listings in this chapter: edamame, soy nuts, tempeh, and tofu.

Many protein-rich foods are included in other chapters of the book as well. Legumes other than soy are included in Chapter 2, Carbohydrates: Starchy Vegetables. Milk and some soy products are listed in Chapter 5, Dairy and Non-Dairy. Seeds and nuts are listed in Chapter 7, Fats, due to their rich monounsaturated and polyunsaturated fat content.

An overall Livit rule of thumb is that eating more plant foods and less meat will help you live younger, longer. A predominantly vegetarian diet confers phenomenal health benefits, providing more fiber, folic acid, vitamins C and E, potassium, and magnesium; a wider variety of plant-based phytochemicals to help reduce risk of chronic diseases; and less saturated fat, protecting the heart from some of its greatest dangers.

Convincing evidence shows that vegetarians have a greater life expectancy. Vegetarians have lower rates of coronary heart disease and lower low-density lipoproteins (LDL), or "bad" cholesterol; lower rates of hypertension and diabetes; and a lower prevalence of obesity. Vegetarians also have lower cancer rates, in particular, a lower risk of colorectal cancer.

So try to limit meat's role as the star of your meals. Of your two main meals each day, aim to make at least one of them vegetarian.

LOW-MERCURY FISH

Fish is an ultimate anti-aging SuperFood, as long as you eat predominantly low-mercury fish. They are, obviously, a source of animal protein. But they lack many of the harmful attributes of other animal foods—especially the saturated fats—and they are the richest source of omega-3 fatty acids, which appear to protect the heart and circulatory system by lowering blood pressure and triglyceride levels, thereby reducing the risk of heart attacks and some types of strokes. Salmon is an especially good source. Try to eat fish two or three times a week.

133 Almond Butter

Benefits

Almond butter is a great, high-protein, high-energy alternative to peanut butter. Almonds provide significant protein, calcium, fiber, magnesium, folic acid, potassium, and vitamin E. Because almond butter is rich in monounsaturated fats but extremely low in saturated fats (and it has no trans fats at all), it is a heart-healthy choice.

Almonds and almond butter are rich in plant sterols, which appear to have cholesterol-lowering benefits. One plant sterol, beta-sitosterol, appears to alleviate the symptoms of benign prostate hypertrophy—enlarged prostate—a condition that more than half of men over age 50 will experience. Two tablespoons of almond butter contains roughly 35 milligrams of beta-sitosterol.

NUTRITIONAL COMPOSITION Two tablespoons of organic creamy roasted almond butter provides 195 calories, 6 g carbohydrate, 8 g protein, 17 g fat, 3 g dietary fiber, 100 mg calcium, and 1.08 mg iron.

Bringing It Home

Choose organic almond butter with few additives. Some almond butters contain peanut oil, so if you are allergic to peanuts, check the label. Almond butter comes in roasted and non-roasted styles—many people find the roasted nuts make a richer-flavored butter. You can also find almond butter in both smooth and creamy styles.

Almond butter will keep on the shelf for a month or more if the jar has not been opened and it is protected from light and heat. Once you have opened the jar, however, it needs to be refrigerated. You may wish to stir the refrigerated almond butter occasionally to make it easier to spread when it's time to use it.

Some almond butter added to a breakfast shake will boost its protein content and give it a rich new taste.

Livit Recipe

Almond Butter Blondies

This recipe is gluten-free!

   1 teaspoon margarine
  16 ounces roasted almond butter
   1 cup agave nectar
   2 eggs
   ½ teaspoon salt
   1 teaspoon baking soda
   1 cup dark chocolate baking drops (73% cocoa solids)

• Preheat oven to 325°F.

• Grease a 9″ × 13″ baking pan with margarine.

• In a large bowl, stir the almond butter until it has a creamy texture (you may need a mixer or hand blender). Mix in the agave nectar and eggs. Still mixing, add the salt and baking soda. Mix well until thoroughly combined. Fold ½ cup of the chocolate drops into the batter. Pour the batter into the pan. Distribute the remaining ½ cup of chocolate drops evenly over the top of the batter.

• Bake for 35 minutes. Allow to cool, and then cut into bars. Serve.

YIELD 24 servings

NUTRITION ANALYSIS PER SERVING 228 calories, 22.1 g carbohydrate, 3.7 g protein, 15.7 g fat, 1.5 g dietary fiber

134 Cheese

Benefits

There are so many types of cheeses that it is hard to generalize about their content, let alone their health benefits. Cheeses can be made, for example, from cow's milk, goat's milk, sheep's milk, or the milk of water buffalos. Since milk is produced as the sole food for calves, lambs, and kids, it is already rich in protein and calcium. Cheese-making is a process that further concentrates this food into a solid, and the result may well include significant amounts of phosphorus, zinc, vitamin A, riboflavin, and vitamin B_{12}.

Unfortunately for those trying to live a healthier lifestyle, cheese-making also tends to concentrate the fats in the milk. Low-fat cheeses are available—in general, cheeses that are not aged tend to be lower in fat. Fresh mozzarella, farmer's, and chevre cheeses can be good choices, as well as harder cheeses that are specially made with low-fat milks. But cheese has so many milky benefits that it may also be the right place to "spend" some extra calories. Its high protein, mineral, and fat contents mean that it is digested slowly, and it will keep you feeling satisfied for several hours.

The high nutritional value of cheese and its beneficial roles in health make this food an important dairy food to include in a healthful diet.

NUTRITIONAL COMPOSITION One ounce of fresh mozzarella, given here as an example cheese, provides 70 calories, 0 g carbohydrate, 6 g protein, 5 g fat, 0 g dietary fiber, and 50 mg sodium.

Bringing It Home

Although it is best to choose light-colored white and yellow cheeses to avoid chemical food coloring (the milk doesn't come out of the cow orange!), many cheeses are colored with annatto (also called achiote), which is used as a seasoning in many Central and South American cuisines. Yogurt cheese brings both the benefits of yogurt and its slightly tart taste as well. Fresh mozzarella has the lowest fat and sodium content of any of the common cheeses. Fresh mozzarella comes in many sizes and shapes, usually packed in water. It has a lighter taste and texture than the pre-formed commercial mozzarella.

Livit Recipe

Fresh Tomato and Mozzarella Salad

This is a classic of Mediterranean cuisine.

> Low-fat vegetable oil spray
> ¼ cup chopped shallots
> 1 clove garlic, minced
> 1 teaspoon minced fresh thyme
> ¼ teaspoon salt
> ¼ teaspoon freshly ground black pepper
> 2½ cups cherry tomatoes OR grape tomatoes (red, yellow, orange, or a combination), rinsed and halved
> 1 cup fresh mozzarella cheese pieces (½-inch cubes)
> 1 tablespoon olive oil
> ½ tablespoon balsamic vinegar

- Spray a large skillet with low-fat vegetable oil. Add the shallots, garlic, thyme, salt, and pepper to the skillet, and sauté for 2 to 3 minutes, until the shallots are tender. Stir in the tomatoes, and cook for 1 to 2 minutes, until the tomatoes are just warmed. Remove from heat and transfer to a large bowl.

- Add the mozzarella to the tomato mixture and toss to combine. Drizzle olive oil and balsamic vinegar over the salad, and toss gently until the tomatoes and cheese are evenly coated.

YIELD   4 servings

NUTRITION ANALYSIS PER SERVING   139 calories, 7.5 g carbohydrate, 8.1 g protein, 8.7 g fat, 1 g dietary fiber

135 Chicken Breast Without Skin

Benefits

Boneless, skinless chicken breasts are the high-protein convenience food of many a diet. Four ounces of chicken breast meat provides two thirds of the recommended daily value for protein for the average adult. Chicken breasts are lower in fat than dark meat. With the skin removed, a chicken breast has less than half the fat of a chicken breast with the skin! Chicken is a very good source of niacin, a B vitamin that is involved in repairing DNA; vitamin B_6, which is important in several metabolic processes; and selenium, a mineral that plays a role in thyroid metabolism and is also an antioxidant. Research suggests that selenium may help prevent cancer.

NUTRITIONAL COMPOSITION (LIGHT MEAT)   Three and one-half ounces of roasted chicken (light meat without skin) provides 173 calories, 0 g carbohydrate, 30.9 g protein, 4.5 g fat, 0 g dietary fiber, 85 mg cholesterol, 29 IU vitamin A, 12.4 mg niacin, 0.97 mg pantothenic acid, 4 mcg folic acid, 247 mg potassium, 77 mg sodium, 216 mg phosphorus, 15 mg calcium, 27 mg magnesium, 1.06 mg iron, and 1.23 mg zinc.

NUTRITIONAL COMPOSITION (DARK MEAT) Three and one-half ounces of roasted chicken (dark meat without skin) provides 205 calories, 0 g carbohydrate, 27.4 g protein, 9.7 g fat, 0 g dietary fiber, 93 mg cholesterol, 72 IU vitamin A, 6.5 mg niacin, 1.21 mg pantothenic acid, 8 mcg folic acid, 240 mg potassium, 93 mg sodium, 179 mg phosphorus, 15 mg calcium, 1.33 mg iron, 23 mg magnesium, and 2.80 mg zinc.

WHITE MEAT OR DARK MEAT?

Which is healthier—dark meat or white meat? From the perspective of dietary fat and protein, white meat wins. But dark meat provides some extra minerals: Iron, zinc, and pantothenic acid levels are a little higher in dark meat.

Bringing It Home

Organic chicken has several benefits over conventionally farmed poultry. It is produced with fewer pesticides, antibiotics, and hormones, and the flesh has more flavor, which is especially nice when you're not eating the skin.

Chicken, whether sold whole or in parts, should feel pliable, but resilient. If you are buying chicken with the skin on, it should be opaque and uniform in color; the meat should be pinkish and slightly translucent. Poultry is one place where you can follow your nose—don't buy a chicken with any kind of bad smell, and don't buy one whose "sell by" date has expired (or will expire before you plan to use the meat).

Frozen chicken should not have visible ice crystals or freezer burn. If there is frozen liquid in the package, the chicken may have been defrosted and refrozen, which can compromise food safety as well as taste.

When buying chicken breasts for recipes, remember that a "whole" chicken breast is both sides of the chicken, normally yielding two servings, so the usual chicken breast portion is really a half-breast. Although removing the skin reduces the fat in your chicken, leaving the skin on while cooking helps hold in moisture and flavor, and removing the skin after cooking still takes away most of the extra fat.

Store chicken in the coldest part of the refrigerator, where it should keep for two to three days. You can store it in the package it came in, but if the package is leaky, rewrap the chicken before storing so that leaking juices don't contaminate the other foods.

To freeze raw chicken pieces, wash the chicken and pat it dry with a paper towel. Store each piece in its own plastic zipper bag, and press out as much air as you can while sealing the zipper. Frozen chicken can keep for as long as a year.

SAFE HANDLING OF POULTRY

Chicken has been associated with a number of food-borne bacteria, and it's important to handle this meat properly to avoid the risk of illness. According to the U.S. Department of Agriculture (USDA), the culprits include Salmonella enteritidis, Staphylococcus aureus, Campylobacter jejuni, and Listeria monocytogenes.

Keep the chicken cold until you are ready to cook it, then cook it thoroughly. Chicken is done when it registers an internal temperature of 165°F on a cooking thermometer—and this is really the only sure test. Don't partially cook chicken—for instance, in a microwave—unless you are going to finish cooking it immediately. Warming it up gives any bacteria a chance to start growing, and the only safe remedy is to finish thoroughly cooking the meat.

Because only thorough cooking can kill the bacteria that may be in chicken meat or juices, it's especially important to avoid contaminating other foods, especially those that won't be cooked again after exposure, such as baked goods or fruits and vegetables that will be eaten raw. Use plastic grocery bags when shopping and bringing food home, and keep the chicken in a separate bag from the other food. Store chicken in a sealed, leakproof container to keep juices from coming into contact with other foods in the refrigerator.

When preparing the chicken, wash your hands often. Use a separate cutting board and knife for chicken, and wash them—as well as any areas (counter, plates, pans, etc.) that the chicken may have touched—with hot, soapy water before you move on to preparing other foods. Clean up with disposable paper towels. If you use cloth towels for environmental reasons, always use a clean one, and then wash it in hot water before it's put back into use. Do not serve or store any food in a dish or container that has been used for raw chicken until the dish has been thoroughly washed in hot, soapy water. After you've marinated chicken, if you want to serve the marinade liquid as a sauce, boil it first to make sure any bacteria from the raw chicken are killed.

Cutting boards can be a particular hazard—it's all too easy to cut the chicken up, then move on to the vegetables. The USDA recommends having a separate cutting board that you use only for raw meats. That way, you raise the odds that raw meat juices won't end up on salad vegetables or baked goods. Sanitize work surfaces, cutting boards, and utensils with a mixture of one tablespoon of chlorine bleach to one gallon of clean water.

Remember: Although chicken has the worst reputation, food-borne bacteria can piggyback on any meat, fish, or shellfish—and even on some fruits and vegetables. You should strive to avoid cross-contamination with all of them.

Livit Recipe

Marvelous Mandarin Chicken

See Safe Handling of Poultry on page 211.

1 lemon, halved
½ cup organic orange juice
¼ cup water
¼ teaspoon paprika
¼ teaspoon lemon pepper
¼ teaspoon garlic powder
¼ teaspoon onion powder
3 skinless, boneless chicken breasts (6 breast halves)
½ cup canned mandarin orange segments, drained

- Preheat oven to 325°F.

- Squeeze the juice from ½ lemon into a small bowl; cut the remaining ½ lemon into thin slices and set it aside. Stir the orange juice and water into the lemon juice.

- In a small bowl, combine the paprika, lemon pepper, garlic powder, and onion powder.

- Rinse the chicken breasts and pat them dry with a towel. Put the chicken into a 9″ × 13″ casserole dish. Pour the juice mixture over the chicken. Sprinkle the spice mixture over the chicken. Lay the oranges and lemon slices on top.

- Bake, uncovered, for 20 minutes. Cover with foil and bake for an additional 25 minutes.

YIELD 6 servings

NUTRITION ANALYSIS PER SERVING 158 calories, 4 g carbohydrate, 26 g protein, 3 g fat, 0.3 g dietary fiber

MERCURY IN FISH

Although the levels of mercury in fish are a greater hazard to children and pregnant women, mercury can build up in adults as well, and they can be very harmful to human health. In general, larger fish and fish that live longer contain more mercury, because it accumulates in their systems over time from the smaller fish they eat. In 2004, the U.S. Food and Drug Administration (FDA) and the Environmental Protection Agency (EPA) issued an advisory to pregnant and nursing women, women who might become pregnant, and the caretakers of young children on the risks and benefits of eating fish.

The advisory states:

1. Do not eat shark, swordfish, king mackerel, or tilefish, because they contain high levels of mercury.
2. Eat up to 12 ounces (2 average meals) a week of a variety of fish and shellfish that are lower in mercury.
   - Five of the most commonly eaten fish that are low in mercury are shrimp, canned light tuna, salmon, pollock, and catfish.

- Another commonly eaten fish, albacore ("white") tuna, has more mercury than canned light tuna. When choosing your two meals of fish and shellfish, you may eat up to 6 ounces (one average meal) of albacore tuna per week.
3. Check local advisories about the safety of fish caught by family and friends in local lakes, rivers, and coastal areas. If no advice is available, eat up to 6 ounces (one average meal) per week of fish caught in local waters, but don't consume any other fish during that week.

Follow these same recommendations when feeding fish and shellfish to your young child, but serve smaller portions.

(from *What You Need to Know About Mercury in Fish and Shellfish,* March 2004)

136 Cod

Benefits

Cod have been commercially fished and traded since at least Viking times. They were an important export of the New England colonies from the time Europeans began to settle there, so this Atlantic fish has long played a role in European and Mediterranean diets. Taxes and limitations on the export of cod were among the grievances that sparked the American Revolution.

As a result of its long commercial history, the name "cod" has been applied to a number of fish, most of them white-fleshed and relatively light in taste. The name is now technically applied only to Atlantic cod, Pacific cod, and Greenland cod, related fishes that are in danger of overfishing, in part because their health benefits have long been apparent.

Cod are an excellent source of niacin, phosphorus, selenium, and vitamin B_{12}, and they also provide significant magnesium, potassium, thiamine, and vitamin E. A good source of omega-3 fatty acids—three ounces of cooked cod provides 0.1 gram—cod appear to greatly benefit the cardiovascular system, as they are linked to lower blood pressure. Cod liver oil was at one time recommended to provide vitamins A and D. It's now believed that the health benefits of the oil are probably related to the omega-3 fatty acids.

NUTRITIONAL COMPOSITION Three ounces of Pacific cod cooked by dry heat provides 89 calories, 0 g carbohydrate, 19.5 g protein, 0.7 g fat, 0 g dietary fiber, 40 mg cholesterol, 27 IU vitamin A, 3 mg vitamin C, 2.1 mg niacin, 7 mcg folic acid, 440 mg potassium, 77 mg sodium, 190 mg phosphorus, 8 mg calcium, and 26 mg magnesium.

Bringing It Home

The best way to find good fish is to find a good fish market—one that reliably gets good quality fresh fish. As fish has grown in popularity and air freight has become more commonplace for foodstuffs, fresh fish in good variety has become easier to find in the local supermarket.

It pays to be picky with fish, since it is so perishable. If the fish are whole, check the eyes—a fish that's been out of the water too long will have eyes that look dull and gray. The eyes, and the fish itself, should look shiny and clean; the gills should still be bright red. In general, any dulling of color or shine indicates a fish that's been out of the water too long.

Smell is probably the most important indicator. Fresh ocean fish should smell of the sea, and any type of bad smell is a reason to walk away. But it's not always possible to smell plastic-wrapped fish fillets. If the fillets have skin, the skin should be as shiny and metallic as that on a good whole fish. If there is liquid in the package, it should be clear. If the liquid is beginning to turn white, the fish is beginning to turn, too.

For best results, buy fish within a day or two of when you plan to eat it, and take it straight home. If you have a long trip or will be running errands, consider keeping a cooler of ice in your car to hold the fish.

Livit Recipe

Mediterranean Omega Cod

    1 can (14.5 ounces) crushed tomatoes
    1 teaspoon dried oregano
    ⅓ cup dry white wine
    1 lemon, juice only (about 2 tablespoons)
    3 ounces fresh baby spinach
    1 medium onion, thinly sliced
    1 pound cod fillets, cut into 4 pieces
    1 small zucchini, thinly sliced
    4 ounces crimini mushrooms, thinly sliced

- Preheat oven to 425°F.
- In a small bowl, combine the tomatoes, oregano, wine, and lemon juice.
- Place the spinach on the bottom of an 11″ × 7″ baking dish, and top it with the onion slices. Lay the cod on the bed of spinach and onions. Distribute the zucchini and mushroom slices over the fish fillets. Add the tomato mixture to the pan. Bake, covered, for 15 to 20 minutes, until the cod flakes easily with a fork.

YIELD 4 servings

NUTRITION ANALYSIS PER SERVING 175 calories, 16.7 g carbohydrate, 24.1 g protein, 1.3 g fat, 2.6 g dietary fiber

137 Edamame (Green Japanese Soybeans)

Benefits

Edamame are young, green soybeans in their pods, cooked by boiling, which make a great snack—high in fiber and protein, rich in calcium and potassium. Cooking the soybeans increases their available isoflavones, including daidzin, genistin, and genistein. Genistein has been investigated for its role in limiting the size and number of fat cells, possibly acting as an aid to preventing weight gain. Soy isoflavones may also reduce the risk of heart attack.

A cup of soybeans provides more than half of the daily recommended value of protein for the average adult—in less than 300 calories. Soybeans do, however, contain a fair amount of fat—11.6 grams per cup, of which 2.2 grams are saturated fat.

> **NUTRITIONAL COMPOSITION** One-half cup of boiled green soybeans provides 127 calories, 9.9 g carbohydrate, 11.1 g protein, 5.8 g fat, 3.8 g dietary fiber, 140 IU vitamin A, 15 mg vitamin C, 100 mcg folic acid, 485 mg potassium, 13 mg sodium, 142 mg phosphorus, 131 mg calcium, 2.25 mg iron, and 54 mg magnesium.

Bringing It Home

The fresh soybeans from which edamame is made are green pods found in the produce department. They should be firm and unbruised. Frozen parboiled pods are available year-round. If your supermarket or natural food store does not carry fresh or frozen edamame, try an Asian food market.

Store fresh edamame in the refrigerator, where it will keep for about two days. Frozen edamame will keep for two to three months.

To make the traditional edamame snack, wash fresh edamame pods and cut the ends off. Bring a large pot of water to a boil, add a tablespoon of salt, and toss in the edamame. Boil the pods for three to four minutes, then drain the pods and allow them to cool.

Livit Recipe

Sesame, Corn, and Edamame Salad

2 tablespoons toasted sesame oil
1 tablespoon rice vinegar
2 teaspoons tamari OR shoyu soy sauce
2 quarts water

2 cups frozen edamame
1 cup corn kernels
2 tablespoons toasted sesame seeds
Salt

- In a medium bowl, combine the sesame oil, rice vinegar, and tamari. Whisk to emulsify the dressing.
- Bring the water to a boil in a large saucepan. Once the water is boiling, add the edamame and boil for 3 minutes. Add the corn and boil for another 2 minutes. Drain the vegetables in a colander and run cold water over them to stop the cooking process.
- In a serving bowl, combine the dressing with the vegetables and toss gently. Add the sesame seeds and toss again. Add salt to taste.

YIELD 6 servings

NUTRITION ANALYSIS PER SERVING 253 calories, 20.1 g carbohydrate, 12.5 g protein, 14.4 g fat, 6.7 g dietary fiber

138 Eggs—Organic Omega-3

Benefits

Eggs have long been known as a good, inexpensive source of animal protein. They lost favor for a time when the role of cholesterol in heart disease was first identified, because egg yolks do contain a fairly high concentration of cholesterol (though the whites are cholesterol-free). Research since that time has determined that an egg a day will not raise the risk of heart disease for most people. Those who already have high cholesterol may want to limit their intake of yolks to two a week. Egg yolks are an excellent source of choline and lutein. Choline, an antioxidant, may be involved in reducing levels of homocysteine, thereby helping reduce the risk of heart disease. Lutein, found in the retina, may help prevent macular degeneration; it also has antioxidant properties. Eggs are also a good source of vitamin B_{12} and folate.

Hens fed a diet of flaxseed, which is itself high in omega-3 fatty acids, produce eggs that are also high in omega-3s. These eggs may have as much as seven times the omega-3 fatty acids of conventional eggs. They also contain more vitamin E.

NUTRITIONAL COMPOSITION One large whole egg provides 75 calories, 0.6 g carbohydrate, 6.2 g protein, 5 g fat, 0 g dietary fiber, 213 mg cholesterol, 318 IU vitamin A, 24 mcg folic acid, 61 mg potassium, 63 mg sodium, 89 mg phosphorus, 25 mg calcium, and 5 mg magnesium.

Bringing It Home

There are several brands of omega-3 eggs available, and the various brands likely have different concentrations of omega-3 fatty acids. They tend to be priced higher than conventional eggs. If you don't want to pay the higher price, consider eating the flaxseed itself!

Eggs are sized according to a national standard. Most recipes call for "large" eggs, but "medium" may be a better bargain in some cases. Look inside the carton and make sure none of your eggs are broken or cracked. They should also look relatively clean.

An egg's color depends on the breed of hen that laid it. Some sources say that differences in flavor and nutrition depend more on what the hen eats. But many people swear by brown eggs (laid by Rhode Island Reds), while others prefer white ones (laid by Leghorns).

There is no additional dietary value to eating fertilized eggs, and they are more likely to include blood spots, which renders them not kosher.

Eggs will keep in the refrigerator for about a month. Keep them in the carton or move them to an airtight container, so that they don't absorb odors from other food. Although many refrigerators have egg holders in the door, this is not the best place to store eggs, because that exposes them to warm air every time the refrigerator is opened. A shelf near the back is better for eggs.

Livit Recipe

Lean Toad in the Hole

- 2 slices sprouted grain bread OR whole wheat bread
- 1 teaspoon non-hydrogenated margarine
- 2 eggs
- 1 teaspoon 100% fruit spread, optional

- Using a drinking glass or a biscuit cutter, cut a 2"-diameter hole in the center of each slice of bread.
- Lightly grease a nonstick frying pan with margarine just until it shines, using a paper towel to distribute the margarine and absorb any excess. Lay the slices of bread in the pan side by side, over medium heat.
- Crack an egg into the center hole of each slice of bread. (You may want to crack the egg into a cup, then pour it into the pan.) When the egg is cooked on one side, carefully flip each slice of bread, together with its egg, to cook the other side until done.
- Place each slice of toast, with its egg in the center, on a plate. Serve with your favorite flavor of fruit spread, if using.

YIELD 2 servings

NUTRITION ANALYSIS PER SERVING 178 calories, 17.3 g carbohydrate, 10.3 g protein, 7.4 g fat, 3 g dietary fiber

139 Eggs—Pasteurized 100% Liquid Egg Whites

Benefits

A cup of egg whites contains 26.5 grams of protein—about half what the average adult needs in a day. Separated from the yolk, it has almost no cholesterol, so egg whites can be used in place of eggs in many places, increasing the protein content without adding cholesterol.

Egg whites have a very delicate taste and are much enhanced by the flavors of other foods, so they are especially good in vegetable omelets and baked goods. In addition to protein, egg whites provide potassium, calcium, magnesium, phosphorus, copper, zinc, iron, and B vitamins. Egg whites are somewhat high in sodium, however.

> **NUTRITIONAL COMPOSITION** The white of one large egg provides 17 calories, 0.3 g carbohydrate, 3.5 g protein, 0 g fat, 0 g dietary fiber, 47 mg potassium, 54 mg sodium, 4 mg phosphorus, 2 mg calcium, and 4 mg magnesium.

Bringing It Home

When buying prepared liquid egg whites, make sure they are 100% egg whites. They will keep in the refrigerator for two to three weeks.

Livit Recipe

Spinach Cheesy Egg White Omelet

A quick gourmet, optimally balanced breakfast—from mixing bowl to table in 10 minutes!

    6 tablespoons pasteurized 100% liquid egg whites
    1 teaspoon water
    ⅛ teaspoon salt
    ⅛ teaspoon freshly ground pepper
    2 teaspoons chopped fresh dill, optional
    ½ cup loosely packed fresh spinach, thinly sliced
    1 plum tomato, chopped
    2 tablespoons shredded nonfat cheddar cheese
      Low-fat vegetable oil spray

- In a medium bowl, whisk together the egg whites, water, salt, pepper, and the dill, if using, until the whites form soft peaks.

- In a small bowl, toss together the spinach, tomato, and shredded cheddar. Set aside 1 tablespoon of the spinach mixture for use as garnish.

- Spray an omelet pan or small skillet with oil. Set the pan over medium heat for 1 minute. Pour the egg mixture into the pan, and cook until the eggs begin to set. Cover half the omelet with the spinach mixture, leaving a ½" border. Gently lift the edge of the omelet nearest the handle and fold it over the filling, letting the filling peek out slightly. Cook for another 2 minutes.
- Slide the omelet onto a serving plate and garnish with reserved filling. Serve.
- NOTE For a more balanced meal, serve with a slice of whole wheat toast or some fresh berries to add some high-fiber fuel to the meal.

YIELD 1 serving

NUTRITION ANALYSIS PER SERVING 110 calories, 8 g carbohydrate, 18 g protein, 0.5 g fat, 1 g dietary fiber

140 Eggs—Powdered Egg Whites

Benefits

Powdered egg whites add the protein and minerals of eggs to a wide variety of foods.

> **NUTRITIONAL COMPOSITION** One tablespoon of dried egg white powder provides 50 calories, 0 g carbohydrate, 12 g protein, 0 g fat, and 0 g dietary fiber.

Bringing It Home

Select dried egg whites that are 100% egg whites, with no other ingredients. The powder will keep for about a year at room temperature. Reconstitute powdered egg whites for cooking or baking by using 2 level teaspoons of the powder and 2 tablespoons of water for each egg white called for in the recipe.

Livit Recipe

Vanilla Protein Shake

    5 ounces 1% fat milk
    ¼ teaspoon pure vanilla extract
    1 tablespoon honey OR agave nectar
    2 tablespoons powdered egg white

- In a blender jar, combine the milk, vanilla, honey, and powdered egg white. Process until smooth. Serve immediately.

YIELD 1 serving

NUTRITION ANALYSIS PER SERVING (made with honey) 227 calories, 25 g carbohydrate, 28.2 g protein, 1.5 g fat, 0 g dietary fiber

141 Flounder

Benefits

Low in calories and fat, and containing no carbohydrate or fiber, flounder is probably as close as we can get to the mythical "free" proteins of the low-carb diets. A three-ounce serving of cooked flounder has only 100 calories and nearly half the average adult's daily protein needs. It also provides a range of B vitamins, as well as some vitamin A and E.

> **NUTRITIONAL COMPOSITION** Three ounces of flounder cooked by dry heat provides 100 calories, 0 g carbohydrate, 20.5 g protein, 1.3 g fat, 0 g dietary fiber, 58 mg cholesterol, 32 IU vitamin A, 1.9 mg niacin, 2.1 mcg vitamin B_{12}, 8 mcg folic acid, 293 mg potassium, 89 mg sodium, 246 mg phosphorus, 15 mg calcium, and 49 mg magnesium.

Bringing It Home

Flounder has a delicate flavor and a slightly flaky texture, so it needs to be protected from strong tastes and from drying out, both in storage and in cooking.

Fresh flounder fillets may come in a range of colors, from tan to pink. On whole fish, the skin and eyes should look bright and shiny, the scales should appear tight, and the gills should be red. Any liquid or slime on the fish should be clear. Once it has turned white, the fish itself is starting to turn. Flounder should be transported in a cooler if your trip home from the market is long.

At home, unwrap the flounder, rinse it under cold water, and pat it dry with paper towels. For best storage, set it on a cake rack above a pan of ice, and cover with plastic wrap. Keep the fish in the coldest part of your refrigerator; it may keep for as long as two days.

Flounder also freezes well, and if securely wrapped it will keep for up to two months in the freezer. Thaw, unwrapped, in a covered pan in the refrigerator for 24 hours before use.

Flounder is good when poached in a mixture of white wine and lemon juice.

Livit Recipe

Cool and Spicy Flounder with Salsa

Flounder

- 4 flounder fillets (about 6 ounces each), rinsed and dried
- 1 teaspoon olive oil
  Lemon pepper
- 1 tablespoon white wine vinegar

Salsa

2 large tomatoes (about ½ pound each), seeded and chopped	2 teaspoons fresh lemon juice
½ cup minced scallions (2 or 3 scallions)	1 teaspoon olive oil
1 clove garlic, minced	¼ teaspoon raw sugar
1 tablespoon minced fresh parsley	Black pepper
	Salt, optional

- *To prepare the flounder:* Brush the fillets lightly with oil on both sides, then lightly oil a large skillet. Sprinkle the fish fillets with lemon pepper.
- Heat the pan for 30 seconds over moderately high heat. Lay the fillets in the pan, with room between them to allow for turning. Cook the fish for 1 minute. Turn them and cook the other side for about 1 minute, just until the fish is white and opaque but not yet dry or flaky.
- Arrange the cooked fish in a single layer on a serving platter. Sprinkle the fillets with vinegar, cover, and chill them for at least 20 minutes.
- *To prepare the salsa:* In a medium bowl, combine the tomatoes, scallions, garlic, parsley, lemon juice, oil, sugar, pepper, and salt, if using. Let the salsa stand at room temperature.
- Remove the fish from the refrigerator, pour the salsa over the fish, and let the dish come to room temperature. Serve.
- NOTE If preparing the dish in advance, refrigerate the salsa, and remove both the salsa and the fish from the refrigerator about 20 minutes before serving.

YIELD 4 servings

NUTRITION ANALYSIS PER SERVING 245 calories, 6 g carbohydrate, 42.1 g protein, 5.2 g fat, 1.4 g dietary fiber

142 Haddock

Benefits

Haddock is a terrific low-calorie, low-fat, high-protein fish. It provides several B vitamins, including niacin, B_{12}, and folic acid; vitamin A; and the minerals potassium, phosphorus, calcium, magnesium, and iron. Haddock is a low-mercury fish, although it is in danger of overfishing.

NUTRITIONAL COMPOSITION Three ounces of haddock cooked by dry heat provides 95 calories, 0 g carbohydrate, 20.6 g protein, 0.8 g fat, 0 g dietary fiber, 63 mg cholesterol, 54 IU vitamin A, 3.9 mg niacin, 1.2 mcg vitamin B_{12}, 11 mcg folic acid, 339 mg potassium, 74 mg sodium, 205 mg phosphorus, 36 mg calcium, 1.15 mg iron, and 43 mg magnesium.

Bringing It Home

Haddock is a very popular food fish, and in addition to being sold fresh, it is sold smoked, frozen, and dried. Haddock is often the type of fish used in British fish and chips.

Fresh haddock has a fine white flesh. When fresh, it will be firm and translucent. Any liquid or slime on the fish should be clear. Once it has turned white, the fish itself is starting to turn.

Livit Recipe

Easy Haddock

2 tablespoons margarine	¼ teaspoon pepper
1 egg, slightly beaten	1 pound haddock fillets
¼ cup low-fat milk	2 teaspoons fresh lemon juice
1 cup bread crumbs	2 tablespoons water
1 teaspoon oregano	2 tablespoons minced blanched almonds
¼ teaspoon salt	1 medium onion, minced

- Preheat oven to 425°F.
- Grease a 9″ × 13″ baking pan with 1 tablespoon of the margarine, using a paper towel to distribute it well and absorb any excess.
- In a shallow bowl or pie plate, whisk together the egg and milk.
- In a separate shallow bowl or pie plate, mix the bread crumbs, oregano, salt, and pepper.
- Dip each haddock fillet first into the egg mixture, then into the seasoned bread crumbs. Lay the coated haddock fillets side by side in the baking pan.
- Melt the remaining tablespoon of margarine and put it in a small bowl. Add the lemon juice and water to the margarine. Pour the lemon juice mixture over the haddock fillets.
- Sprinkle the tops of the fillets with almonds and onion.
- Bake, uncovered, for about 10 minutes, or until the fish is no longer translucent and flakes when tested with a fork. Serve.

YIELD 3 servings

NUTRITION ANALYSIS PER SERVING 397 calories, 31.4 g carbohydrate, 45.6 g protein, 8.8 g fat, 2.8 g dietary fiber

143 Halibut

Benefits

Halibut is a large flatfish found in the northern waters of both the Atlantic and the Pacific oceans. As one of the largest of the flatfish, it has a slightly higher mercury level than flounder and haddock. As a "moderate" mercury fish, halibut is still safe to eat, but don't have it more than six times a month. It has a very strong complement of vitamins and minerals.

NUTRITIONAL COMPOSITION Three ounces of halibut cooked by dry heat provides 19 calories, 0 g carbohydrate, 22.7 g protein, 2.5 g fat, 0 g dietary fiber, 35 mg cholesterol, 152 IU vitamin A, 6 mg niacin, 1.2 mcg vitamin B_{12}, 12 mcg folic acid, 490 mg potassium, 59 mg sodium, 242 mg phosphorus, 51 mg calcium, 0.91 mg iron, and 91 mg magnesium.

Bringing It Home

Halibut is a large fish, so you will usually find it as fillets, not as whole fish, which means that you won't be able to judge its freshness by its eyes or gills. As with other fresh fish sold as fillets, halibut should smell fresh, not fishy. The meat should be firm and translucent, not dark or cloudy, and should appear moist, not dried out. Frozen raw halibut should be frozen solid, with no soft spots.

Livit Recipe

Baked Fried Halibut

    Canola oil
⅓ cup coarse, fresh whole wheat bread crumbs
½ tablespoon grated skim-milk Parmesan cheese
⅛ teaspoon dried dill weed
⅛ teaspoon lemon pepper
3 tablespoons egg whites OR egg substitute
½ pound halibut
2 teaspoons non-hydrogenated margarine, melted
2 thin slices fresh lemon, as garnish
2 small sprigs fresh parsley, as garnish

- Preheat oven to 400°F.
- Lightly grease a small, shallow baking pan with canola oil, spreading the oil with a paper towel to cover the entire inside surface and absorb any excess.
- In a shallow dish or pie plate, combine the bread crumbs, cheese, dill, and lemon pepper.
- Beat the egg lightly in a separate shallow dish or pie plate.
- Dip the fish first in the egg, then in the seasoned bread crumbs. Repeat until all crumbs are used. Place the fish in the baking pan. Pour the melted margarine over the fish.
- Bake for about 15 minutes, or until the fish flakes when tested with a fork. Garnish with lemon slices and parsley. Serve.

YIELD 2 servings

NUTRITION ANALYSIS PER SERVING 268 calories, 29 g carbohydrate, 29 g protein, 9 g fat, 1.6 g dietary fiber

144 Hemp Seed

Benefits

Hemp seeds are a great source of omega-3 and omega-6 fatty acids, both known as "essential" fatty acids. Essential fatty acids are necessary for specific biological processes, but the body cannot make them. These fatty acids are believed to reduce various cardiovascular risks and may also help prevent some forms of cancer. Hemp seeds are a phenomenal source of protein—11 grams of protein in just 3 tablespoons of seeds. Hemp seeds provide calcium, iron, phosphorus, magnesium, zinc, copper, manganese, and vitamin E.

Although hemp comes from the same family as the plant commonly known as marijuana that is grown for its psychoactive and medicinal effects, the varieties of hemp that are used for food and fiber have a negligible amount of the psychoactive chemical THC.

> **NUTRITIONAL COMPOSITION** Three tablespoons of shelled hemp seed provides 160 calories, 7 g carbohydrate, 11 g protein, 9.8 g fat, 1 g dietary fiber, 57 mg calcium, 5 mg iron, 320 mg potassium, 3.6 IU vitamin E, 210 mcg folic acid, 360 mg phosphorus, 171 mg magnesium, 3 mg zinc, and 3 mg manganese.

Bringing It Home

Hemp seed can be purchased at natural food stores and from online vendors. Because it is so high in oils, it can turn rancid very quickly. Freeze hemp seeds immediately to best preserve them.

Eat two tablespoons of hemp seeds a day as an optimal energy sustainer. You can stir them into your morning cereal to add an easy protein source to balance your breakfast. They are also good mixed into sauces, such as marinara sauce, to give a protein boost to a pasta meal.

Livit Recipe

Veggie Loaf

This is a scrumptious vegetarian recipe.

1½ cups brown rice
3 cups water
Vegetable oil spray
1 red bell pepper, seeded and chopped
1 small white onion, chopped
2 cloves garlic, minced
1 tablespoon black pepper
1 egg OR 2 egg whites OR 3 tablespoons pasteurized egg whites

¼ cup hemp seed oil
1½ cups shelled hemp seed
2 teaspoons salt
2 tablespoons dried basil
½ cup organic ketchup OR fruit-sweetened ketchup

- In a rice steamer, prepare the rice by steaming it in the water, a process that will take about 50 minutes. Set aside.
- Preheat oven to 325°F.
- Lightly spray a 4″ × 8″ loaf pan with oil.
- In a blender jar, combine the red pepper, onion, garlic, black pepper, egg, and hemp seed oil. Blend on high until mostly smooth.
- In a large bowl, combine the shelled hemp seed, cooked rice, the blended pepper mixture, salt, and basil.
- Put the rice mixture into the loaf pan, mounding it slightly. Spread ketchup over the top.
- Bake for 1 hour.
- NOTES This loaf can be made with leftover cooked rice; you will need 4 to 5 cups of cooked rice. For a more balanced meal, serve the veggie loaf with a mixed green salad.

YIELD 8 servings

NUTRITION ANALYSIS PER SERVING 454 calories, 41.3 g carbohydrate, 20.6 g protein, 22.7 g fat, 3.9 g dietary fiber

145 Peanuts

Benefits

Peanuts are groundnuts—not true nuts, but legumes. A New World plant, they are native to Central and South America, but they are now grown and eaten around the world. The People's Republic of China is the greatest producer of peanuts. The United States is the fourth-largest producer, with production of about 1.7 million tons annually.

Peanuts, like other legumes, are a rich source of both protein and fiber. Although peanuts are relatively low in the amino acids cysteine and methionine, they are high in lysine, and they balance well with grains, which are high in methionine but low in lysine. A cup of peanuts provides 30 grams of protein. Nearly half of the carbohydrate in peanuts is dietary fiber—12.4 grams of fiber in one cup.

Peanuts are also a very good source of niacin and folate, and a significant source of pantothenic acid, magnesium, phosphorus, and zinc. Although peanuts are nearly half fat by weight, about half of that is monounsaturated, and only 13 percent is saturated fat.

Roasted peanuts may rival some berries for antioxidant content, including resveratrol and Coenzyme Q10.

The nutritional benefits of peanut butter depend on how it is made. All-natural, fresh-ground peanut butters are the most like peanuts, though you have to remember that any peanut butter is much more calorie-dense than whole peanuts. Peanut butters tend to have more sugars and fats but less fiber than whole peanuts, though they are still a high-quality source of protein, fiber, energy, vitamins, and minerals.

Despite their many health benefits and the longtime popularity of peanuts and peanut butter as staple foods for children, these days you are more likely to hear about peanuts causing allergies and being banned from schools. This is a serious issue, because for those who are allergic to peanuts, the reaction can be life-threatening anaphylactic shock. Research is ongoing, but it appears that roasting may increase the allergenic properties of peanuts. Most peanut butter is made from roasted peanuts. It's still controversial whether introducing peanuts to children at a young age is more likely to prevent the allergy or cause it. Raw peanuts also sometimes carry a mold called *Aspergillus* that can be dangerous to health.

NUTRITIONAL COMPOSITION Two tablespoons of unsalted all-natural peanut butter provides 210 calories, 6 g carbohydrate, 8 g protein, 16 g fat, 2 g dietary fiber, and 0.36 mg iron.

Bringing It Home

Avoid buying raw peanuts with any trace of mold, and keep them refrigerated once you have them home.

For a peanut butter with a nutritional profile closest to that of the peanut itself, buy an all-natural peanut butter or, better yet, the type that's ground in the store. To cut down on fat, let your peanut butter stand until the oil rises to the surface, then pour off half to three quarters of the liquid oil. You'll need to leave some of the oil so that the peanut butter can be stirred and spread. Keep any natural peanut butter in the refrigerator.

Peanut butter is a key ingredient for high-protein, easy snacks. Spread it on celery, apple slices, or whole wheat crackers. Enjoy a classic PB&J, slightly updated for better nutrition—a peanut butter and jelly sandwich made with whole grain bread and 100% fruit spread.

Livit Recipe

Peanut Butter Energy Bar

Vegetable oil spray
½ cup whole wheat flour
1 teaspoon cinnamon
½ teaspoon baking soda
⅛ teaspoon salt
½ cup natural-style smooth peanut butter
½ cup firmly packed brown sugar
⅓ cup honey

1 large egg
2 large egg whites
2 tablespoons safflower oil OR soybean oil
2 teaspoons vanilla extract
2 cups old-fashioned rolled oats
1 cup dried cranberries OR raisins
½ cup coarsely chopped walnuts OR almonds
½ cup semisweet chocolate chips

- Preheat oven to 350°F.
- Spray a 9″ × 13″ baking dish with oil.
- In a medium bowl, whisk together the flour, cinnamon, baking soda, and salt.
- In the large bowl of an electric mixer, beat together the peanut butter, sugar, and honey until well blended.
- In a small bowl, stir the egg and egg whites together with a fork.
- Add the eggs, oil, and vanilla to the peanut butter mixture, and beat until smooth. Using a rubber spatula, fold the flour mixture into the peanut butter mixture.
- Add the oats, cranberries, walnuts, and chocolate chips, and combine thoroughly. Scrape the batter into the baking dish and spread it into an even layer.
- Bake for 20 to 25 minutes, until lightly browned and firm to the touch. Cool the bars completely in the pan on a rack. Cut into 24 bars. Serve.
- NOTE For those who are allergic to peanut butter, this recipe can be made with soy nut butter or sunflower seed butter instead.

YIELD 24 bars

NUTRITION ANALYSIS PER SERVING 175 calories, 24 g carbohydrate, 4 g protein, 8 g fat, 2 g dietary fiber

146 Pollock

Benefits

There are two types of fish commonly called pollock available in United States markets: Atlantic pollock and Alaska—or walleye—pollock. Although related, the two fish are not of the same genus, and they have different spawning and fishing grounds.

Pollock is a gray- or white-fleshed fish, with a somewhat more distinctive taste than cod and haddock. Alaska pollock is milder and whiter than the Atlantic variety. Pollock has grown in popularity as other white fish have been subject to overfishing. The Alaska pollock fishery is strictly managed, although Greenpeace has now put Alaska pollock on its list of endangered fish.

Pollock is one of the lowest-mercury fish, so it is safe to eat frequently. Like many similar fish, pollock is very low in saturated fat and a very good source of protein, vitamin B_{12}, phosphorus, and selenium. It provides substantial riboflavin, niacin, vitamin B_6, magnesium, and potassium.

NUTRITIONAL COMPOSITION (ATLANTIC POLLOCK) Three ounces of Atlantic pollock cooked by dry heat provides 100 calories, 0 g carbohydrate, 21.2 g protein, 1.1 g fat, 0 g dietary fiber, 77 mg cholesterol, 34 IU vitamin A, 3.4 mg niacin, 3.1 mcg vitamin B_{12}, 3 mcg folic acid, 388 mg potassium, 94 mg sodium, 241 mg phosphorus, 65 mg calcium, and 73 mg magnesium.

NUTRITIONAL COMPOSITION (ALASKA POLLOCK) Three ounces of Alaska (walleye) pollock cooked by dry heat provides 96 calories, 0 g carbohydrate, 20 g protein, 0.95 g fat, 0 g dietary fiber, 82 mg cholesterol, 71 IU vitamin A, 1.4 mg niacin, 3.6 mcg vitamin B_{12}, 3 mcg folic acid, 329 mg potassium, 99 mg sodium, 410 mg phosphorus, 5 mg calcium, and 62 mg magnesium.

Bringing It Home

Pollock is available fresh and frozen. The frozen meat is good when poached and used in chowders. Be careful not to get fish that is freezer-burned, or the texture will not be as good. Fresh pollock should be translucent, though the Atlantic variety is grayish rather than white. The skin and eyes should be shiny and metallic, and the fish should have no smell other than that of the ocean.

Livit Recipe

Dill and Lemon Pollock

    Canola oil
⅓ cup coarse, fresh whole wheat bread crumbs
½ tablespoon grated skim-milk Parmesan cheese
⅛ teaspoon dried dill weed
⅛ teaspoon lemon pepper
3 tablespoons egg whites OR egg substitute
½ pound pollock
2 teaspoons margarine, melted
2 thin slices fresh lemon, as garnish
2 small sprigs fresh parsley, as garnish

- Preheat oven to 400°F.
- Lightly oil the inside of a small, shallow baking dish with oil, using a paper towel to spread the oil and absorb any excess.
- In a shallow dish or pie plate, combine the bread crumbs, Parmesan, dill, and lemon pepper.
- In a separate shallow dish or pie plate, lightly beat the egg. Dip the fish first in the egg, then in the seasoned bread crumbs, repeating until all the crumbs are used.
- Lay the fish gently in the baking pan. Pour the melted margarine over the top.
- Bake for about 15 minutes, or until the fish flakes when tested with a fork. Garnish with fresh lemon slices and parsley. Serve.

YIELD 2 servings

NUTRITION ANALYSIS PER SERVING 268 calories, 13 g carbohydrate, 29 g protein, 9 g fat, 1.6 g dietary fiber

ADDING FISH IS EASY

If you are not eating fish at least twice a week, you can begin improving your health by adding fish to your meal planning. Some fish can be grilled like steaks. Other types work well in sandwiches. You can keep tuna, canned or in pouches, on hand for a high-protein snack. Sardines are another easy snack food to keep on hand, and they can be eaten on crackers or in sandwiches. Start slowly by substituting fish or shellfish for another type of meal each week. Once that is an established part of your eating plan, increase to two seafood meals per week.

147 Salmon

Benefits

Salmon is a low-mercury, fatty fish that contains a very high level of omega-3 fatty acids, which are vital to healthy brain and circulatory function. It is also a good source of vitamin D and protein.

Salmon live in both the Atlantic and Pacific oceans, as well as in the Great Lakes. Although there are some concerns about overfishing some types of salmon—for example, commercial salmon fishing is very limited in California—wild Alaska salmon come from well-managed fisheries that still have adequate stocks of fish.

Salmon are also farmed. In fact, the vast majority of the Atlantic salmon available are farmed fish. Because these fish are fed a controlled diet, the balance of the omega-3 fatty acids may not be as good as it is in wild-caught fish. Farmed salmon may contain a somewhat lower level of omega-3 fatty acids overall. There is also a risk of higher levels of some contaminants, notably dioxins and PCBs, in the farmed fish. Salmon farming has been implicated in the introduction of harmful parasites to nearby wild salmon populations, leading to the decline and possible extinction of wild salmon in some areas.

The red color of salmon is the result of antioxidant carotenoids, including canthaxanthin and astaxanthin. (Atlantic salmon, however, do not contain canthaxanthin.) Astaxanthin appears to be a particularly powerful antioxidant, with positive effects throughout the body and special benefit to the brain and nervous system. Some farmed salmon are fed astaxanthin to improve their color.

NUTRITIONAL COMPOSITION Three ounces of wild salmon cooked by dry heat provides 155 calories, 0 g carbohydrate, 21.6 g protein, 6.9 g fat, 0 g dietary fiber, 60 mg cholesterol, 37 IU vitamin A, 8.6 mg niacin, 2.6 mcg vitamin B_{12}, 25 mcg folic acid, 1.6 mg pantothenic acid, 534 mg potassium, 48 mg sodium, 218 mg phosphorus, 13 mg calcium, and 31 mg magnesium.

Bringing It Home

For many reasons, wild-caught Alaska salmon may be the best choice, but it can also be expensive or hard to find. A 2006 review of studies on the presence and dangers of contaminants in fish, however, found that the overall benefits of eating salmon outweighed the potential risks encountered in the farmed version.

Another way to bring wild-caught salmon into your diet less expensively is to eat canned salmon, most of which is wild-caught Pacific salmon.

There are several varieties of salmon. Chinook, Coho, and Sockeye are among the more common Pacific salmon. Their flesh ranges from pink to orange to red, and some individual salmon may even be white-fleshed. Although the stronger color may indicate more carotenoids, a paler fish is not necessarily less healthy or flavorful.

Livit Recipe

Speedy Spicy Salmon

Canola oil spray
2 skinless salmon fillets (about 3 ounces each)
⅛ teaspoon cayenne pepper
⅛ teaspoon lemon pepper
1 fresh lemon, sliced into wedges
2 tablespoons fresh salsa
1 tablespoon hummus OR guacamole

- Preheat broiler.
- Lightly spray a broiler pan with oil.
- Rinse the salmon and gently shake off any excess water. Lay the fillets on the oiled broiler pan. Sprinkle the fillets with the cayenne and lemon pepper.
- Broil the salmon for 5 minutes on each side, using a broad spatula to carefully turn the fillets. When the fish is slightly golden at the edges, remove it from the broiler. Transfer the fillets to dinner plates. Garnish each fillet with a squeeze of fresh lemon juice, 1 tablespoon of fresh salsa, and ½ tablespoon of hummus.
- NOTE For a more balanced meal, add brown rice and steamed veggies.
- VARIATION Try this with other fish, or with other seasonings in place of the cayenne, such as minced garlic, onion powder, cumin, or all three!

YIELD 2 servings
NUTRITION ANALYSIS PER SERVING 163 calories, 3 g carbohydrate, 20 g protein, 7 g fat, 3.3 g dietary fiber

1**48** Sardines

Benefits

There are as many as 21 fish that can be called sardines: The name applies to a number of related small, oily fish, some of which are also called pilchards, and some of which are actually herring. Because sardines are typically smaller than four inches in length, they are especially low in mercury. The young fish eat mostly plankton, which is not a strong source of mercury. As oily fish, they are rich in omega-3 fatty acids, vitamin D, and protein. Since they are typically eaten bones and all, they are also a good source of calcium. In addition, they provide selenium, phosphorus, and iron.

Although in some parts of the world sardines are eaten fresh, they are the archetypical canned protein food. Ironically, many canned "sardines" are actually herring, a related fish. Herring have been studied for their high concentration of Coenzyme Q10, a nutrient involved in cell metabolism. Sardines, especially those that are really herring, share this characteristic.

> **NUTRITIONAL COMPOSITION** Four and three-eighths ounces of skinless, boneless sardines packed in water provides 120 calories, 0 g carbohydrate, 15 g protein, 6 g fat, 0 g dietary fiber, 60 mg calcium, and 2.25 mg iron.

Bringing It Home

Canned sardines are best for you if they are packed in water rather than oil, but they are also available packed in other liquids, such as tomato sauce and hot sauce. Choose sardines that have their heads and viscera removed before canning so they are easier to use as an instant snack.

If the "fishy" taste and smell of canned sardines is too powerful for you, try soaking them in milk before you eat them. (This also works with other preserved fish, such as anchovies, and it helps reduce the salt in dried fish.) Serve sardines on crackers with mustard and a squeeze of fresh lemon juice.

Livit Recipes

Quick Sardine Fish Cakes

1 egg
1 teaspoon freeze-dried minced onion
1 tin (4.37 ounces) sardines packed in water, chopped into medium-sized pieces
½ cup cracker crumbs
 Vegetable oil spray

· In a small bowl, beat the egg. Add the dried onion to the egg and let it reconstitute. Add the sardine pieces and cracker crumbs, and mix thoroughly.

- Spray a medium frying pan with oil. Drop the sardine mixture by large spoonfuls into the pan. Brown on each side. Serve.

YIELD 2 servings

NUTRITION ANALYSIS PER SERVING 207 calories, 20.6 g carbohydrate, 13.3 g protein, 7.4 g fat, 1.3 g dietary fiber

Sardine and Whole Oat Salad

⅓ cup hulled whole oats (oat groats)
1 cup water
1 small tomato, chopped (about ½ cup)
1 small cucumber, chopped (about ½ cup)
1 small red onion, chopped (about ½ cup)
1½ teaspoons vegetable oil
1 tablespoon lemon juice
4 to 6 large lettuce leaves
1 can (3.75 ounces) water-packed whole Maine sardines, drained OR Norwegian sardines, drained

- In a small saucepan, cook the oats in water for approximately 2 hours. Rinse to remove excess starch.
- In a medium bowl, toss together the oats, tomato, cucumber, onion, oil, and lemon juice.
- Make a bed of 2 or 3 lettuce leaves on each of 2 luncheon plates. Arrange half the oat mixture and half the sardines on each bed of lettuce.
- NOTE Leftover oats can be used in this recipe; you need 1 cup of cooked oats.

YIELD 2 servings

NUTRITION ANALYSIS PER SERVING 156 calories, 15 g carbohydrate, 12.7 g protein, 5.9 g fat, 2.2 g dietary fiber

149 Sole

Benefits

Sole is a name used for several white-fleshed flatfish. All are high in protein and low in calories and fat. With a delicate texture and a buttery flavor, sole is a fish that is easy to like, even for people who are not used to eating fish—a good "starter fish." It is low in mercury.

The nutritional profile of sole is similar to that of flounder. It is a good source of vitamins A, B_6, and B_{12}, as well as minerals, including selenium.

NUTRITIONAL COMPOSITION Three ounces of sole cooked by dry heat provides 100 calories, 0 g carbohydrate, 20.5 g protein, 1.3 g fat, 0 g dietary fiber, 58 mg cholesterol, 32 IU vitamin A, 1.9 mg niacin, 2.1 mcg vitamin B_{12}, 8 mcg folic acid, 246 mg potassium, 15 mg calcium, and 49 mg magnesium.

Bringing It Home

Sole is often sold in fillets with the skin removed. The fish should be a translucent white and have no discernible smell. As with all fish, it's best to purchase sole the day you plan to cook it. It will keep up to three days in the refrigerator.

Livit Recipe

Broiled Fillet of Sole

    Canola oil
1¼ pounds thin fillets of sole, without the skin
  2 teaspoons extra-virgin olive oil
1 or 2 tablespoons Dijon mustard
  ⅛ teaspoon ground black pepper
  2 tablespoons snipped fresh chives, as garnish
  1 fresh lime, cut in wedges, as garnish

- Preheat broiler.
- Lightly grease a baking sheet with canola oil, using a paper towel to spread the oil and absorb any excess. Arrange the fillets on the baking sheet, and brush them with olive oil. Spread half of the mustard evenly over each fillet, and sprinkle them with pepper.
- Broil the fillets about 4 inches from the heat for 2 to 3 minutes. When the fillets are golden brown at the edges and the flesh has turned opaque, remove them from the broiler. Transfer the fillets to plates. Garnish with chives and a wedge of lime. Serve.

YIELD 4 servings

NUTRITION ANALYSIS PER SERVING 222 calories, 2 g carbohydrate, 31 g protein, 9 g fat, 0.5 g dietary fiber

150 Soy Nuts (Roasted Soybeans)

Benefits

Soy nuts are a great way to satisfy the craving for a crunchy snack while still being good to your health. These roasted soybeans have all the benefits of soy, including lots of protein, folate, potassium, and fiber. The soybean is regarded as a complete protein, providing all the essential amino acids, and soybeans are one of the highest-protein legumes. Soybeans are about 20 percent oil.

One benefit of adding soy to your diet is that it can replace animal sources of protein that tend to have higher levels of cholesterol and saturated fats. In addition to adding less cholesterol than animal proteins, soy may even have a cholesterol-*lowering* effect. Soybeans contain isoflavones that are phytoestrogens—plant-based estrogens. Initially, phytoestrogens were hailed for their potential to relieve symptoms of menopause and reduce the risk of some cancers, heart disease, and osteo-porosis. Research has been shown to be inconclusive, however, as estrogen sup-plementation has been found to have a mix of health benefits and health hazards.

> **NUTRITIONAL COMPOSITION** One-fourth cup of roasted soy nuts provides 202 calories, 14 g carbohydrate, 15 g protein, 11 g fat, 7.6 g dietary fiber, 86 IU vitamin A, 1 mg vitamin C, 90.5 mcg folic acid, 632 mg potassium, 70 mg sodium, 156 mg phosphorus, 59.5 mg calcium, 1.7 mg iron, 62.5 mg magnesium, 1.3 mg zinc, and 0.93 mg manganese.

Bringing It Home

The primary danger with eating soy nuts as a snack is that they may have too much salt—as do many snacks—to be heart-healthy. Try to choose soy nuts that are low in sodium, and look for soy nuts with seasonings other than salt. You will get more fiber and other benefits if you choose soy nuts made from the whole soybean rather than from soy protein concentrate. If soy nuts are stored in a cool, dry place, they should last for six to eight months. They can also be frozen.

Livit Recipe

High-Protein Granola

        1 cup agave nectar OR honey
        1 tablespoon safflower oil
     1½ teaspoons vanilla extract
        6 cups old-fashioned rolled oats
        1 cup soy nuts
        1 cup wheat germ
        1 cup oat bran
        3 cups coarsely chopped dried fruit (cranberries, blueberries, dates, apricots,
            apples, mango)

- Preheat oven to 350°F.
- Line 2 baking sheets with parchment paper.
- In a large mixing bowl, whisk the agave nectar, oil, and vanilla together until thoroughly combined. Add the oats, soy nuts, wheat germ, and oat bran, mixing well. Spread the mixture evenly on the baking sheets.
- Bake for 20 minutes, or until golden brown.
- Remove the oat mixture from the oven and allow it to cool completely. Add the dried fruit, tossing to combine. Store in an airtight container in the refrigerator.
- NOTE This granola will keep for up to 2 weeks in an airtight container in the refrigerator.

YIELD 12 servings (4 ounces each)

NUTRITION ANALYSIS PER SERVING 372 calories, 65 g carbohydrate, 15 g protein, 7.6 g fat, 11 g dietary fiber

151 Tempeh (Fermented Soybean Cake)

Benefits

Tempeh is most commonly used as a meat replacement. It originated in Java, and one of its nicknames is "Java meat." It contains whole soybeans that have been cooked, fermented, and formed into a cake. The long tendrils of the tempeh mold help hold the tempeh together and give it a firmer texture than tofu. Because tempeh uses whole soybeans, it retains the fiber, mineral, and isoflavone benefits of soy, as well as the protein and fat. The fermentation may make it more digestible for some people and may make its mineral content easier to absorb. The mold used to ferment tempeh may also favor helpful intestinal flora over those that cause dysentery and other diseases.

> **NUTRITIONAL COMPOSITION** One-half cup of tempeh provides 165 calories, 14.1 g carbohydrate, 15.7 g protein, 6.4 g fat, 0 g dietary fiber, 569 IU vitamin A, 3.8 mg niacin, 43 mcg folic acid, 305 mg potassium, 5 mg sodium, 171 mg phosphorus, 77 mg calcium, 58 mg magnesium, 1.88 mg iron, 1.5 mg zinc, and 1.19 mg manganese.

Bringing It Home

Tempeh absorbs and benefits from the flavors of sauces and marinades. Especially if it is new to you, try it cooked in a favorite Asian recipe in lieu of the meat. It can also be crumbled and added to saucy pasta dishes, such as lasagna or macaroni and cheese. It can be sliced and fried, or cubed and added to stews. You can even grill it in kebabs!

In addition to tempeh with a 100 percent soybean content, some tempehs contain grains, coconut, and other ingredients to add variety to the taste and texture.

Tempeh is fermented, but it is still prone to spoilage. Keep it in the refrigerator, where it should last about three weeks unopened, or about a week once it has been opened. If you won't be using it soon, you can freeze it, though this may change the texture. Defrost frozen tempeh in the refrigerator.

Livit Recipe

Tempting Tempeh Fajitas

12 whole wheat tortillas
1½ pounds tempeh, sliced into ¼-inch strips
1 small white onion, thinly sliced
1 small red onion, thinly sliced
1 large red bell pepper, seeded and sliced into thin strips
1 large green bell pepper, seeded and sliced into thin strips

2 tablespoons vegetable oil
3 cloves garlic, minced
2 tablespoons chili powder
1 tablespoon ground cumin
¼ cup chopped cilantro, optional
Salt and pepper

- Preheat oven to 250°F.
- Stack the tortillas, wrap them in foil, and place them in the oven to warm.
- In a steamer basket set over boiling water, steam the tempeh for 5 minutes.
- In a medium bowl, combine the tempeh, onions, and peppers.
- In a large skillet, heat the oil over high heat. Add the tempeh mixture and sauté until the onions are translucent, about 5 minutes. Reduce heat to medium. Add garlic, chili powder, cumin, and cilantro, if using. Add salt and pepper to taste. Sauté for 3 minutes.
- Serve immediately with warm tortillas.

YIELD 6 servings

NUTRITION ANALYSIS PER SERVING 443 calories, 58 g carbohydrate, 28 g protein, 19 g fat, 5.2 g dietary fiber

152 Tofu

Benefits

Tofu is another soy-based protein source, made from dried soybeans that have been soaked and dried, then put through a process much like that used to make cheese. A coagulating substance is added, which curdles the soy milk, and then the mixture can be cut, strained, and pressed, producing tofus with different degrees of firmness. This range of textures allows tofu to take on many roles in cooking, bringing soy's high protein, minerals, and isoflavones to a variety of foods. Because of the degree of processing that the soybeans undergo, tofu has much less fiber than soy foods that use the whole bean.

NUTRITIONAL COMPOSITION One-half cup of raw, firm tofu provides 183 calories, 5.4 g carbohydrate, 19.9 g protein, 11 g fat, 2.9 g dietary fiber, 209 IU vitamin A, 37 mcg folic acid, 299 mg potassium, 18 mg sodium, 239 mg phosphorus, 258 mg calcium, 13 mg iron, 118 mg magnesium, 1.98 mg zinc, and 1.49 mg manganese.

Bringing It Home

Tofu comes in many forms. Soft and silken tofus are often used in desserts and recipes that need a creamy texture. Firmer tofus can be sliced or cubed, and sautéed, boiled, or deep-fried. "Medium firm" tofu has a good all-purpose texture. For a chewy, hard-fried texture, use a firmer tofu. You can also make a softer tofu firmer by freezing it, thawing it, and squeezing out the liquid.

Tofu is sold refrigerated in plastic tubs that are often opaque. Rely on the "sell by" date, and do not use tofu if it has any kind of sour smell or signs of mold. If you will not be using the whole package when you open it, it's a good idea to change the water in which the tofu is packed. By changing the water every day, opened tofu will keep in your refrigerator for about a week.

Livit Recipes

Rice Casserole Divine

1⅓ cups water
⅔ cup brown rice
1 tablespoon canola oil
1 small onion, chopped
1 clove garlic, minced
1 can (14.5 ounces) chopped Italian-style tomatoes, with liquids
1 teaspoon dried oregano OR basil
8 ounces soft silken tofu, drained
1 package (10 ounces) frozen chopped spinach, thawed and well drained OR
    10 ounces fresh spinach, rinsed and drained
½ teaspoon salt
¼ teaspoon pepper
½ cup shredded part-skim Swiss cheese
    Canola oil spray
1 tablespoon pine nuts OR toasted sesame seed

- Bring water to a rolling boil, and add brown rice. Once it returns to a boil, reduce heat to low, cover, and cook for about 45 minutes until all the water is absorbed. Set aside.
- Preheat oven to 350°F.
- In a large saucepan, heat the oil. Add the onion and garlic, and sauté until the onion is translucent and the garlic is tender but not browned. Add the tomatoes with liquids. Add the oregano, crushing the herbs between your fingers as you add them to the pot. Bring the tomato mixture to a boil. Reduce heat, and simmer for about 3 minutes, uncovered. Remove from heat.
- In a blender jar, whip the drained tofu until it is smooth, adding water if needed. Add the blended tofu to the tomato mixture. Stir in the cooked rice, spinach, salt, pepper, and ¼ cup of the Swiss cheese.
- Lightly spray a 2-quart rectangular baking dish with oil. Spoon the mixture into the baking dish and spread it evenly.
- Bake for 30 to 40 minutes, uncovered, until heated through. Before serving, sprinkle the pine nuts and the remaining ¼ cup of cheese over the top. Serve.
- NOTE This dish can be made with leftover rice; you need 2 cups of cooked brown rice.
- VARIATION You can make this dish with zucchini, yellow summer squash, chard, or other similar vegetables in place of the spinach.

YIELD 4 servings

NUTRITION ANALYSIS PER SERVING 258 calories, 35 g carbohydrate, 12 g protein, 8 g fat, 6.8 g dietary fiber

Barbecued Tofu Stir-Fry

  1 teaspoon canola oil
  1 package (12 ounces) organic extra-firm tofu, rinsed, drained, and cut into 1-inch cubes
  6 ounces prepared barbeque sauce
  ¼ cup water
  ¼ teaspoon garlic powder
  ¼ teaspoon onion powder
  ¼ teaspoon ground black pepper

· Lightly oil a nonstick pan with the canola oil, spreading the oil evenly with a paper towel. Heat the pan over medium heat. Add tofu, and stir-fry for about 5 minutes on each side, until it is golden brown. Add barbecue sauce, water, garlic powder, onion powder, and pepper. Simmer for 5 minutes, until the liquid has been reduced. Serve.

YIELD 4 servings

NUTRITION ANALYSIS PER SERVING 90 calories, 7 g carbohydrate, 7 g protein, 3 g fat, 0.9 g dietary fiber

Tofu in Disguise

  1½ cups (12 ounces) whole wheat pasta shells OR other small, shaped pasta
     Canola oil spray
  1 large onion, minced (about 1 cup)
  1 package (10 ounces) your choice of frozen vegetables, thawed, drained, and chopped into bite-sized pieces
  1 pound firm tofu, drained
  1 teaspoon salt
  ¼ teaspoon pepper
     Pinch of ground nutmeg
  ½ cup soy milk
  ½ cup shredded mozzarella cheese

· Cook pasta according to package directions. Transfer to a large bowl and set aside.
· Preheat oven to 350°F.
· Spray a large skillet with canola oil, and heat the skillet over medium-high heat. Add the onion and cook for about 5 minutes, until soft. Remove pan from heat. Add the chopped vegetables.
· In a blender jar, combine the tofu, salt, pepper, and nutmeg, and blend until smooth. Add the soy milk and process until mixed. Pour the tofu mixture into the vegetable mixture, and stir to combine.
· In a large bowl, combine the vegetable mixture with the cooked pasta, tossing to coat the pasta.
· Spray a 2-quart casserole dish with canola oil. Transfer the pasta mixture to the casserole dish. Top with the shredded mozzarella. Bake for 40 minutes, or until bubbly.

YIELD 6 servings

NUTRITION ANALYSIS PER SERVING 239 calories, 26 g carbohydrate, 16 g protein, 10 g fat, 10.4 g dietary fiber

153 Trout

Benefits

Trout are closely related to salmon, and they offer many of the same health benefits. They are an oily fish with a high level of omega-3 fatty acids. Trout provide calcium, phosphorus, potassium, and magnesium, as well as selenium, niacin, and vitamin B_{12}. They are low in mercury and, in one British study, trout were also found to have among the lowest levels of dioxins.

> **NUTRITIONAL COMPOSITION** Three ounces of trout cooked by dry heat provides 162 calories, 0 g carbohydrate, 22.6 g protein, 5.6 g fat, 0 g dietary fiber, 63 mg cholesterol, 57 mg sodium, 394 mg potassium, 47 mg calcium, 1.63 mg iron, 267 mg phosphorus, and 24 mg magnesium.

Bringing It Home

Trout are almost always sold whole, so you can usually judge their freshness by the brightness of the eyes and skin and the translucent look of the flesh. As a small fish, trout have a high proportion of bone. Ask the fish market to remove the bones.

Rainbow trout, and a trout relative called arctic char, are both successfully farmed in ways that do not significantly damage the environment or harm wild fish populations. Steelhead trout, however, are farmed in ways that expose wild fish to parasites and should be avoided. Lake trout have about twice the omega-3 fatty acids as a similarly sized portion of rainbow or brook trout, but they have also been found to have more mercury.

Livit Recipe

Trout with Fresh Herbs

4 trout fillets (about 6 ounces each)	2 teaspoons canola oil
¾ teaspoon salt	1 tablespoon fresh lemon juice
¼ teaspoon freshly ground black pepper	Canola oil spray
1½ tablespoons fresh herbs (parsley, chives, dill)	

- Slash the skin of the trout. Sprinkle the fillets with ½ teaspoon of the salt and the ¼ teaspoon pepper.
- In a medium bowl, combine the herbs, oil, lemon juice, and the remaining ¼ teaspoon salt.
- Lightly spray a large skillet with canola oil. Heat skillet over medium heat. Lay the fish in the skillet, skin side down. Cook until the skin is crisp, about 4 minutes. Gently turn the fish over and cook for 1 additional minute. Transfer the fillets to individual plates.
- Garnish each fillet with herbs. Serve.

YIELD 4 servings

NUTRITION ANALYSIS PER SERVING 219 calories, 1.9 g carbohydrate, 33.5 g protein, 8.8 g fat, 0.6 g dietary fiber

Benefits

Tuna is a large and oily fish, providing high amounts of vitamin D and omega-3 fatty acids, as well as selenium, niacin, and vitamins B_1 and B_6. It is an excellent source of protein and is relatively low in calories.

Because tuna is a large fish, some types are high in mercury. Canned "light" tuna is regarded as a low-mercury fish. Albacore or "white" tuna is regarded as somewhat higher in mercury content, such that pregnant women and young children should eat it no more than once a week. Both types of tuna are frequently cited as offering health benefits that far outweigh the risks of the small amounts of mercury they contain.

NUTRITIONAL COMPOSITION One-fourth cup of solid white tuna, drained, provides 80 calories, 0 g carbohydrate, 16 g protein, 1 g fat, 0 g dietary fiber, and 310 mg sodium.

Bringing It Home

Among types of canned tuna, light tuna packed in water is probably the best choice. If possible, choose a tuna whose ingredient list includes only tuna, water, and salt—or just tuna and water, if you are watching your sodium intake. Tuna is now also available in shelf-stable pouches. Either canned or pouch tuna provides a portable, high-protein food that is easy to keep on hand.

Tuna makes a simple snack served on crackers, and it is a classic addition to comfort foods like macaroni and cheese. A tuna melt on whole wheat bread or rolled in a whole wheat tortilla, served with lettuce and tomato, can provide a quick balanced meal.

Livit Recipe

Light and Easy Tuna Slaw

You can make this meal in a plastic zipper bag!

    1 can albacore tuna OR light tuna, packed in water, rinsed and well drained
    1 bag (12 ounces) broccoli slaw, rinsed and drained
    1 tablespoon organic Dijon mustard
    1 tablespoon apple cider vinegar
    1 teaspoon agave nectar
    1 tablespoon mayonnaise
    1 lemon, juice only
    2 tablespoons raisins
      Dash of lemon pepper OR salt-free herbal seasoning

- In a medium bowl, combine the tuna with the slaw, stirring until well mixed.
- In a small bowl, combine the mustard, vinegar, agave nectar, mayonnaise, and lemon juice. Stir to combine.
- Add the mustard mixture to the tuna mixture, stirring to combine. Add raisins and lemon pepper. Stir all the ingredients well with a large spoon. Serve.
- NOTES The ingredients can be combined in a 2-quart plastic zipper bag: Put the tuna and the slaw into the bag and shake to combine. Add the mustard, vinegar, agave nectar, mayonnaise, and lemon juice and shake to combine. Add the raisins and lemon pepper, shaking until all ingredients are evenly distributed. For a balanced quick and easy meal, add a piece of whole wheat pita bread or some whole wheat crackers.

YIELD 2 servings

NUTRITION ANALYSIS PER SERVING 162 calories, 15 g carbohydrate, 15.2 g protein, 5.4 g fat, 6.4 g dietary fiber

155 Turkey

Benefits

Turkey is a relatively low-fat source of high-quality animal protein. It is a very good source of selenium and vitamin B$_6$, two nutrients that are essential to healthy metabolism. Some studies have linked selenium deficiency to an increased risk of cancer, but it appears that in people with adequate selenium in their diets, increasing selenium had no further protective effect. More research is needed to pin down this mineral's anti-cancer potential. It does act as an antioxidant, and it is involved in proper thyroid function.

NUTRITIONAL COMPOSITION (TURKEY BREAST) One ounce of turkey breast provides 23 calories, 0 g carbohydrate, 4.7 g protein, 0.3 g fat, 0 g dietary fiber, 1.7 mg niacin, 1 mcg folic acid, 58 mg potassium, 301 mg sodium, 48 mg phosphorus, and 4 mg magnesium.

NUTRITIONAL COMPOSITION (TURKEY PATTY) One 4-ounce cooked ground turkey patty provides 193 calories, 0 g carbohydrate, 22.4 g protein, 10.8 g fat, 0 g dietary fiber, 4 mg niacin, 6 mcg folic acid, 221 mg potassium, 88 mg sodium, 161 mg phosphorus, and 20 mg magnesium.

Bringing It Home

Prepared, precooked turkey breast is a convenient source of good nutrition, but it does contain more salt than fresh turkey breast cooked at home. When buying cooked turkey breast, try to find turkey breast with the fewest additives and preservatives. Avoid nitrites, which are often used to preserve the color of cold cuts.

When buying ground turkey breast, note that packages marked "ground turkey" may include skin and dark meat—both of which contribute fat. "Ground turkey breast" contains only ground white meat, with a lower caloric load.

Fresh turkey should look plump and rounded and it should feel pliable. It should not have any hint of a bad smell. Don't push the "sell by" date—in the refrigerator, raw turkey will keep for only a day or two. Cooked, it will keep for about four days.

Frozen turkey should be free of ice crystals or frozen liquid in the package, both of which may indicate that the bird has been thawed and refrozen.

Organically raised turkeys have been fed an organic diet and are not given additional hormones or unnecessary antibiotics. Organic turkey has somewhat more flavor than conventionally raised birds, and heritage breeds are even tastier.

As with chicken, it's important to follow the rules for safe poultry handling. Don't partially cook a turkey and then hold it for further cooking—cook it thoroughly. If you stuff a turkey for cooking, remove all the stuffing and store any leftover meat and stuffing in separate containers.

Livit Recipe

Tasty Turkey Loaf

Canola oil spray
2 large cloves garlic, minced
2 large stalks of celery, finely chopped
1 small onion, finely chopped
2 medium red bell peppers, seeded and diced
8 ounces white mushrooms, trimmed and diced
1¼ pounds ground turkey breast
2 egg whites, lightly beaten
½ teaspoon freshly ground black pepper
Dash of nutmeg
½ cup fresh whole wheat bread crumbs
½ cup minced fresh parsley

- Preheat oven to 375°F.

- Spray a large nonstick skillet with canola oil. Heat the pan briefly, and add the garlic, celery, onion, and peppers. Sauté, stirring, for 3 to 5 minutes, or until slightly softened. Stir the mushrooms into the onion mixture and cover the pan to sweat the mushrooms. After about 3 minutes, remove the cover and resume sautéing the vegetables, stirring until all the liquid has evaporated. Remove from heat and set aside.

- In a large bowl, combine the turkey, egg whites, pepper, nutmeg, bread crumbs, and parsley. Add the sautéed vegetables, and stir to combine all the ingredients well.

- Spray an 8″ × 4″ loaf pan with canola oil. Transfer the turkey mixture to the pan. Center the loaf pan in a larger, shallow baking dish. Set the baking dish with the turkey loaf in it into the oven. Fill the outer baking dish with hot water to a depth of about 1 inch.

- Bake for 1 hour and 15 minutes.
- Let the loaf stand for about 15 minutes. Serve.

YIELD 6 servings

NUTRITION ANALYSIS PER SERVING 193 calories, 8 g carbohydrate, 32 g protein, 4 g fat, 2.7 g dietary fiber

156 Whitefish

Benefits

While many forms of white-fleshed fish with mild flavor are called "white fish," such as cod, haddock, hake, and pollock, "whitefish" also refers to a group of freshwater fish including the lake and round whitefish. Related to both salmon and trout, lake whitefish had been depleted by overfishing in the 1960s but have since recovered. They are fished commercially in the Great Lakes in both the United States and Canada.

NUTRITIONAL COMPOSITION Three ounces of whitefish cooked by dry heat provides 146 calories, 0 g carbohydrate, 20.8 g protein, 6.4 g fat, 0 g dietary fiber, 65 mg cholesterol, 111 IU vitamin A, 3.3 mg niacin, 14 mcg folic acid, 345 mg potassium, 55 mg sodium, 294 mg phosphorus, 28 mg calcium, 36 mg magnesium, and 1.08 mg zinc.

Bringing It Home

Lake whitefish may be sold under several different names, including Sault whitefish, whitefish, gizzard fish, and grande coregone. Round whitefish include Menominee whitefish, pilot fish, frost fish, and round fish.

Look for fish with eyes that are bright and clear, gills that are red and free from slime, and skin that is shiny and colorful. The best way to store fish is to take it out of the packaging, rinse it under cold water, and set it on a cake rack above a shallow pan full of crushed ice, covered, in the coldest part of the refrigerator. Whitefish will keep for up to two days.

Whitefish is also available frozen. Some recipes allow you to start cooking with frozen fish, or it can be safely thawed in the refrigerator.

Some Great Lakes fish have been found to be high in PCBs. For this reason, you may wish to remove the skin from whitefish before cooking, as contaminants are thought to accumulate in the fat and skin.

Livit Recipe

Lake Whitefish with Fingerling Potatoes

   3 tablespoons olive oil plus enough to oil the parchment paper
   ½ pound fingerling potatoes, cut into ½-inch slices
   3 cloves garlic, minced
   ½ cup minced fresh chives
      Salt and pepper
   ¾ cup dry white wine
   ¼ cup lemon juice
   1 tablespoon dried tarragon
   2 lake whitefish fillets (6 ounces each), with skin removed
   1 lemon, cut into thin slices, as garnish
      Sprinkle of paprika, as garnish

- Preheat oven to 400°F.
- Cover the bottom of an 11″ × 7″ baking pan with parchment paper. Rub the paper lightly with olive oil. Place the potatoes on top of the oiled parchment in a single layer.
- In a small bowl, combine 2 tablespoons of the oil, two thirds of the minced garlic, and the chives. Add salt and pepper to taste. Drizzle the mixture evenly over the potatoes.
- Bake for 20 minutes. Remove the potatoes from the oven and, using a wooden spoon, turn the potato slices over. Return them to the oven to bake for an additional 15 minutes, until the potatoes are tender.
- Meanwhile, in a shallow pan, combine the wine, the remaining 1 tablespoon of olive oil, lemon juice, dried tarragon, and the remaining one third of the minced garlic. Add salt and pepper to taste. Add the fish fillets, cover, and put the fillets in the refrigerator to marinate for 30 minutes.
- Remove the potatoes from the oven, and use a wooden spoon to push the potato slices to the sides of the pan, making room for the fish to lie flat. Gently add the marinated fish fillets to the baking pan with the potatoes, and return the pan to the oven. Bake for about 10 minutes, until the fish are opaque but still moist. Transfer to a serving dish.
- Garnish with lemon slices and sprinkle with paprika for color. Serve.

YIELD 2 servings

NUTRITION ANALYSIS PER SERVING 520 calories, 25 g carbohydrate, 37 g protein, 23 g fat, 2.3 g dietary fiber

Fats

What role do fats from food sources play in good health? Our understanding of this has changed significantly since the days when cutting out fat took center stage as the dietary cure-all. It's still true that too much fat—like too much of anything else—will put on the pounds. It's also still true that fat is the most calorie-dense of the basic macronutrients, weighing in at 9 calories per gram vs. 4 calories per gram for both carbohydrate and protein.

For two decades, the dietary focus was on low-fat meals, and yet more Americans grew more obese over that time. It's no wonder that scientists have revisited the issue. Recent studies comparing low-fat diets with simple calorie restrictions have found that low-fat diets offer no advantages over restricting calories, and they may not reduce the risk of heart disease at all.

Dietary fat is essential to good health. It is required for the digestion and absorption of the fat-soluble vitamins A, D, E, and K. It helps maintain skin and hair and regulate body temperature, and it plays a role in the immune system. In short, we need fats in our foods—but we need to choose them wisely.

Some fat sources are definitely better for you than others. Trans fats and saturated fats are associated with coronary heart disease. These fats raise the levels of low-density lipoproteins (LDL), or "bad" cholesterol, in the bloodstream. Saturated fats are also implicated in atherosclerosis. An important study published in the *New England Journal of Medicine* in 2006 concluded that even at relatively low levels of consumption, trans fats are the macronutrient that most negatively affects heart health.

· · · · ·

The fat sources we've included here are those that provide health benefits. Seeds and nuts, for example, appear to play a role in glycemic regulation as well as lowering LDL and raising high-density lipoproteins (HDL), or "good" cholesterol. Studies have shown that people who eat nuts regularly have a lower risk of heart disease. Seeds and nuts contain omega-3 fatty acids, vitamin E, and fiber, and they are good sources of protein.

157 Almonds

Benefits

Almonds are low in carbohydrates, and more than half their carbohydrate content, by weight, is dietary fiber. Though they are rich in fat, it is monounsaturated fat. Studies have suggested that almonds can lower LDL while raising HDL. Almonds are also rich in alpha-tocopherol vitamin E, the form most easily absorbed by the human body. They provide calcium, magnesium, and potassium—vital for electrolyte balance, which promotes cardiovascular health. Recent research is also finding beneficial polyphenols and antioxidants in the brown inner skins of almonds.

In Ayurvedic medicine, almonds are credited with improving intellect and adding to longevity.

NUTRITIONAL COMPOSITION One-fourth cup of raw almonds provides 206 calories, 7.8 g carbohydrate, 7.6 g protein, 17.7 g fat, and 4.4 g dietary fiber.

Bringing It Home

Almonds are available in many forms—in the shell, shelled, blanched, sliced, slivered, as almond butter (see Chapter 6, Proteins), roasted, and dry roasted. You can also get many of the benefits of almonds from almond beverages, which provide an interesting change from soy milk for those who must avoid dairy. Whole shelled almonds are probably the best compromise between convenience and nutrition.

Kept cold (under 40°F) and at low humidity (less than 65 percent), almonds can keep for up to two years. If you refrigerate them, keep them in an airtight container—plastic zipper bags work well—to help control the humidity, which will vary depending on what else is in the refrigerator and how often the door is opened. Because almonds are rich in fat, they have the potential to become rancid when exposed to heat and light. If they have any discernable smell other than a faint sweetness, discard them.

Recently, Spanish Marcona almonds have become popular. These almonds are less perfect-looking than the typical California almond, but they are rich in flavor and good for cooking. But beware—most are packed in oil, which significantly ups their fats and calories.

You can add whole or chopped almonds to both sweet and savory dishes. This works especially well if the almonds have been gently pan-toasted. Try them in salads, yogurt, and curries.

Livit Recipe

Almond Vegetable Stir-Fry

⅓ cup water
3 tablespoons reduced-sodium soy sauce
2 tablespoons cornstarch
1 tablespoon olive oil
2 cloves garlic, minced
2 teaspoons minced fresh ginger
½ cup whole almonds
½ pound carrots, peeled and thinly sliced
¼ pound broccoli, trimmed and cut into bite-sized pieces
4 bell peppers (green, red, orange, yellow), seeded and sliced into thin strips
1 pound summer squash (yellow squash, yellow crookneck, zucchini, pattypan), thinly sliced
½ pound green beans, trimmed and cut diagonally into 1-inch pieces
Salt and pepper
1 teaspoon toasted sesame oil

- In a small bowl, whisk together the water, soy sauce, and cornstarch until they are evenly blended.
- In a large nonstick skillet, heat ½ tablespoon of the olive oil. Add the garlic and ginger, and sauté for 4 minutes over medium heat. Remove the garlic and ginger from the pan. Add the almonds. Toast them, stirring constantly, for 8 minutes. Transfer the almonds to a small bowl to cool.
- Replenish the oil with the remaining ½ tablespoon of oil if needed, and increase the heat to high. Add the carrots, broccoli, peppers, squash, and green beans. Stir-fry them for about 5 minutes, until they are crisp-tender and bright in color, stirring constantly to keep them from burning or sticking to the pan. Reduce heat to medium.
- Return the garlic and ginger to the pan, and add the soy sauce mixture. Cook for 2 minutes, stirring gently. Season to taste with salt, pepper, and sesame oil. Transfer to a large serving dish. Garnish with toasted almonds. Serve.
- NOTE This stir-fry is delicious served with brown rice.

YIELD 4 servings

NUTRITION ANALYSIS PER SERVING 241.5 calories, 25.8 g carbohydrate, 8 g protein, 14.2 g fat, 8 g dietary fiber

Benefits

Avocados, high in monounsaturated fats, have been associated with lowered blood cholesterol. They appear to contain antioxidant compounds that relax blood vessels, which helps lower blood pressure.

Avocados are a good source of potassium, a mineral that helps regulate blood pressure as well as hydration. They are also low in sodium. Therefore, they are included in the health claim authorized by the U.S. Food and Drug Administration (FDA) that states, "Diets containing foods that are good sources of potassium and low in sodium may reduce the risk of high blood pressure and stroke."

One cup of avocado provides 23 percent of the recommended daily value for folate, and avocado is a good source of carotenoids including lutein, zeaxanthin, alpha-carotene, and beta-carotene. It's also rich in vitamin E.

In a laboratory study published in the *Journal of Nutritional Biochemistry,* an extract of avocado containing these carotenoids and tocopherols inhibited the growth of both androgen-dependent and androgen-independent prostate cancer cells.

> **NUTRITIONAL COMPOSITION** One medium avocado provides 306 calories, 12 g carbohydrate, 3.7 g protein, 30 g fat, 8.5 g dietary fiber, 1059 IU vitamin A, 14 mg vitamin C, 3.3 mg niacin, 113 mcg folic acid, 1097 mg potassium, 21 mg sodium, 73 mg phosphorus, 19 mg calcium, 2.04 mg iron, and 71 mg magnesium.

Bringing It Home

An avocado should be slightly soft and a rich dark green, with no dark sunken spots or cracks. You can ripen a less mature fruit at home in a paper bag. Don't refrigerate them until they are ripe. When you do refrigerate, refrigerate the whole avocado; once they're cut, they turn brown.

If you must refrigerate a portion of a cut avocado, sprinkle the cut surface with lemon juice and wrap it in plastic.

Livit Recipe

Quick Homemade Guacamole

Remember to wear disposable gloves when working with any hot pepper!

    2 avocados, peeled and pitted
    ½ small onion, diced
    6 cherry tomatoes, quartered
    1 lime, juice only
    1 jalapeño pepper, finely minced

- In a small bowl, mash the avocado flesh with a fork. Add the onion, tomatoes, lime juice, and jalapeño, stirring until all the ingredients are evenly combined. Serve.

YIELD 1½ cups

NUTRITION ANALYSIS PER SERVING 26.1 calories, 1.7 g carbohydrate, 0.4 g protein, 2.2 g fat, 1.1 g dietary fiber

159 Chestnuts

Benefits

At one time, one in every four hardwood trees in some parts of the United States was an American Chestnut. That situation changed with a blight that first arrived in 1904 on some Chinese Chestnut trees, which had resistance to the blight, though the American species did not. This blight virtually wiped out the American Chestnut by the 1940s. Today the chestnuts we eat are from a European variety, though efforts are ongoing to develop a blight-resistant American Chestnut so that the tree can be reintroduced to the United States.

Chestnuts are unusual nuts—they are low in fat and have a high starch content, and they provide vitamin C. They served as a staple food for the poor in many parts of Europe throughout the Middle Ages, when they were made into breads and soups as well as being eaten roasted.

Nutritionally, chestnuts are lower in calories than most nuts, primarily because they are lower in fats. They are a good source of carbohydrate, and they provide fiber and protein. Chestnuts are also a source of the minerals calcium, potassium, and iron.

NUTRITIONAL COMPOSITION One ounce of raw European chestnuts (2½ nuts) provides 60 calories, 12.9 g carbohydrate, 0.7 g protein, 0.6 g fat, 2.3 g dietary fiber, 8 IU vitamin A, 12 mg vitamin C, 18 mcg folic acid, 147 mg potassium, 26 mg phosphorus, 8 mg calcium, and 9 mg magnesium.

Bringing It Home

Chestnuts appear in markets around the winter holiday season, but they can be bought in jars year-round. They are also available as a canned puree, but be sure to buy the kind that contains just chestnuts and water rather than the sweet chestnut spread that is very high in sugar. Fully ripe chestnuts in the shell will feel a little loose inside the outer pericarp. The shells should be somewhat glossy and intact, with no signs of mold.

Keep chestnuts cool and dry. They should last for at least a week, but they do not have the keeping qualities of more hard-shelled nuts.

Roasted chestnuts are a wonderful snack and a traditional Christmas treat.

Livit Recipe

Roasted Chestnuts

10 chestnuts

- Preheat oven to 425°F.
- Cut an **X** in the convex side of each nut. A sharp paring knife will work, but one that is serrated may grip a little better.
- Put the chestnuts on a cookie sheet or jellyroll pan, in a single layer, flat side down. Sprinkle a bit of water over them.
- Put the pan of chestnuts on the oven rack closest to the heat. Roast them for 10 minutes. Using tongs, turn each nut over. Roast them for an additional 10 minutes. Serve hot.
- NOTE When hot, chestnuts are easy to peel. If you are using them for a recipe, peel them immediately. Wrap them in a thick towel if they must be kept warm.

YIELD 10 chestnuts

NUTRITION ANALYSIS PER SERVING 206 calories, 44.5 g carbohydrate, 2.7 g protein, 1.9 g fat, 4.3 g dietary fiber

COCONUT AND CANOLA OIL

Both coconut and canola oil would be on many lists of healthy foods—so why aren't they SuperFoods? There are mixed results in the research regarding both, so until the final verdict is in, we'll opt for caution.

The link between saturated fats and coronary heart disease is well established, and coconut oil is almost unique among vegetable oils for its high level of saturated fatty acids. These fatty acids are prime suspects in forming fatty deposits in human arteries—and coconut oil doesn't contain any of the mitigating linolenic acid. That indicates that research is increasingly ruling against coconut products, including coconut milk, coconut cream, and coconut oil. The picture is clouded by some positive findings for coconut: Its saturated fats appear to have antimicrobial properties that may attack bacteria, fungi, and other parasites that cause indigestion. Coconut oil also helps in the absorption of some nutrients.

Canola was developed in Canada in the late 1970s from rapeseed, which is a Brassica like cabbage, mustard, and kale, but with a very bitter taste. Canola oil is a version of rapeseed oil that was designed to be lower in erucic acid, the compound in rapeseed that is hard for humans to digest and that is responsible for the unpleasant flavor of the oil. Canola is 5 percent saturated fat, 57 percent oleic acid, 23 percent omega-6, and 10 to 15 percent omega-3. Though oils that are very high in omega-3 fatty acids break down when cooking at high temperatures, canola oil's omega-3 profile is good for cooking. Heating it can, however, produce unhealthy trans fats. Canola may also deplete the body of vitamin E.

Nonetheless, there is enough evidence that canola benefits the heart that the FDA allows the oil to carry the health claim that "Limited and not conclusive scientific evidence suggests that eating about 1½ tablespoons (19 grams) of canola oil daily may reduce the risk of coronary heart disease due to the unsaturated fat content in canola oil." But until the evidence is more consistent and conclusive, coconut and canola oil are not making the SuperFood list.

160 Flaxseed

Benefits

Flaxseed is high in fiber, omega-3 fatty acids, and phytochemicals called lignans. Flaxseed can help reduce total blood cholesterol and LDL levels and, as a result, may help reduce the risk of heart disease.

Flaxseed is rich in alpha-linolenic acid (ALA), an omega-3 fatty acid, and some research has suggested that for people who do not eat fish, flaxseed oil may provide a good alternative source of omega-3. Omega-3 fatty acids are used by the body to produce anti-inflammatory prostaglandins, and they may help reduce the inflammation that is a significant factor in conditions such as asthma, osteoarthritis, rheumatoid arthritis, migraine headaches, and osteoporosis.

We recommend ground flaxseed because it is easier for your body to digest. Whole seeds may pass through your system undigested.

> **NUTRITIONAL COMPOSITION** Two tablespoons of ground flaxseed provides 60 calories, 4 g carbohydrate, 3 g protein, 4.5 g fat, 4 g dietary fiber, 20 mg calcium, and 0.72 mg iron.

Bringing It Home

Buy ground flaxseed instead of whole if you want readily available, quick omega-3s. Alternatively, buy whole flaxseeds and grind them with a mortar and pestle or a spice grinder. Two tablespoons a day is recommended. When adding flaxseed to your diet, be sure to drink a lot of water because it's so high in fiber. Store the ground flaxseed in opaque packaging, tightly sealed, in the freezer.

You can add a tablespoon of ground flaxseed to yogurt, cereal, or a peanut butter sandwich.

Flaxseed Porridge

¼ cup flaxseed meal
½ cup boiling water
¼ cup ricotta cheese
Dash of cinnamon
½ cup fresh blueberries OR frozen blueberries, thawed and drained

- Put the flaxseed meal into a small bowl and pour the boiling water over it. Let it stand for about two minutes to allow the flaxseed meal to absorb the water.
- Stir in the ricotta, cinnamon, and berries. Serve.
- NOTE This is a very sustaining porridge and very high in fiber. Make sure to drink plenty of water with it.

YIELD 1 serving

NUTRITION ANALYSIS PER SERVING 244.4 calories, 20.6 g carbohydrate, 13.3 g protein, 14.4 g fat, 10.1 g dietary fiber

FLAXSEED OIL

The benefits of flaxseed oil have been somewhat overstated. Recent studies appear to show little correlation between consumption of flaxseed oil and a reduced risk of heart disease, stroke, or cancer. The oil has a very short shelf life before becoming rancid, and rancid oils contribute to the formation of free radicals—the very substances we eat antioxidants to combat. Although the whole seeds contain antioxidants, the extracted oil does not. Flaxseed oil does contain omega-3 fatty acids, but it doesn't have the beneficial fiber contained in the seeds.

161 Hazelnuts (Filberts)

Benefits

Hazelnuts are high in protein, carbohydrate, fiber, and monounsaturated fat. They are especially rich in vitamin E and provide significant amounts of the B vitamins thiamine, folate, and B_6, as well as the minerals iron and phosphorus. There is archaeological evidence that hazelnuts were a major component of the European diet from at least 7000 BCE.

NUTRITIONAL COMPOSITION One ounce of dry roasted hazelnuts provides 188 calories, 5.1 g carbohydrate, 2.8 g protein, 18.8 g fat, 2 g dietary fiber, 20 IU vitamin A, 21 mcg folic acid, 132 mg potassium, 92 mg phosphorus, 56 mg calcium, and 84 mg magnesium.

Bringing It Home

Hazelnuts are available in the shell, shelled, in pieces, and as a butter. They are particularly tasty when roasted. Hazelnuts will keep in the refrigerator for several months, and if kept in the freezer they will keep for a year or more.

Livit Recipe

Hazelnut Roasted Pears

 1 cup hazelnuts
1½ cups water
 1 cup sugar
 ½ cup maple syrup
 2 cinnamon sticks
 4 ripe pears, peeled, halved, and cored

- Preheat oven to 350°F.
- Spread the hazelnuts in a single layer on a shallow baking pan.
- Bake for 10 to 15 minutes, until the nuts are lightly browned and the skins have blistered. Wrap the nuts in a towel for 1 minute, then rub the nuts in the towel to remove the skins.
- Heat the water in a small saucepan over low to medium heat. Add the sugar, maple syrup, and cinnamon sticks, and simmer for 10 minutes. Add the toasted hazelnuts and soak them in the syrup for 4 minutes.
- Put the pears, cut side down, into an 8″ × 8″ baking dish. Pour the syrup off the hazelnuts into the dish with the pears. Roast the pears in the oven for 20 minutes, until they are soft and easily pierced with a fork.
- Line a baking sheet with parchment. Coarsely chop the hazelnuts, and spread the chopped nuts in a thin layer on the parchment. Toast the hazelnuts in the oven for 7 minutes, until golden brown.
- Garnish the pears with the toasted nuts. Serve.

YIELD 8 servings

NUTRITION ANALYSIS PER SERVING 303 calories, 53.6 g carbohydrate, 2.8 g protein, 10.6 g fat, 3.6 g dietary fiber

162 Hemp Seed Butter

Benefits

Nutritional hemp comes from the same species as marijuana, but from a different variety bred to have virtually none of the psychoactive chemical THC. Instead, nutritional hemp is bred to emphasize its array of essential fatty acids, especially the omega-3s. Hemp seeds provide a good balance between omega-3 fatty acids and omega-6 fatty acids. (It is thought that the typical Western diet contains too much omega-6 and too little omega-3.) They are also very high in protein, and the protein from hemp seed is considered to be a complete protein because it provides all of the essential fatty acids.

Hemp seeds are actually nuts, which is why you will sometimes see the butter called "hemp seed nut butter."

> **NUTRITIONAL COMPOSITION** Two tablespoons of hemp seed butter provides 160 calories, 7 g carbohydrate, 11 g protein, 9.8 g fat, 1 g dietary fiber, 10 mg sodium, and 3.6 mg iron.

Bringing It Home

Like many other nut butters, hemp seed butter is relatively high in calories and fat, so a small portion can provide a lot of taste, energy, and satisfaction. You can use it like other nut butters on breads or on crudités such as celery and sliced apples.

Livit Recipe

Tasty Hemp Seed Butter Spread

¾ cup hemp seed butter
1 tablespoon water
1 can (15 ounces) garbanzo beans, drained
3 cloves garlic
2 lemons, juice only

- In a blender jar, combine the hemp seed butter, water, garbanzo beans, garlic, and lemon juice. Process until smooth. You may need to add more water if the mixture is too thick. Serve.

- NOTE Spread on whole wheat crackers, sprouted-grain toast, or spelt pretzels, or make a thinner version with more water to use as a dip for veggies.

YIELD 16 servings (2 tablespoons each), or about 2 cups

NUTRITION ANALYSIS PER SERVING 68 calories, 8.8 g carbohydrate, 3.6 g protein, 2.2 g fat, 1.5 g dietary fiber

163 Hummus

Benefits

The main ingredient in hummus is garbanzo beans, which are high in fiber and protein but low in fat, and hummus shares their benefits. (See Chapter 2, Carbohydrates: Starchy Vegetables, for more on the benefits of garbanzo beans.)

Most hummus also includes tahini, a sesame seed paste, and olive oil. Both of these are high in monounsaturated fat, and consequently high in calories, but the amounts in hummus are relatively small. Hummus usually also contains lemon juice and garlic, and it may have cayenne pepper or other spices for variation. This mix of foods provides healthy fat, high protein, and lots of fiber.

> **NUTRITIONAL COMPOSITION** One-fourth cup of hummus provides 105 calories, 12.4 g carbohydrate, 3 g protein, 5.2 g fat, 3.1 g dietary fiber, 15.5 IU vitamin A, 5 mg vitamin C, 36.5 mcg folic acid, 107 mg potassium, 150 mg sodium, 69 mg phosphorus, 30.7 mg calcium, and 17.8 mg magnesium.

Bringing It Home

Hummus is available in the refrigerator case in most supermarkets. Even better, make your own, and vary the spices to suit your own taste.

Keep track of the expiration date on the tubs. Store-bought hummus should keep in your refrigerator for about a week. Homemade hummus keeps in the refrigerator for three or four days.

A small tub of hummus, together with some pita bread, can be a good emergency lunch for busy days.

Livit Recipe

Homemade Hummus

         1 can (16 ounces) garbanzo beans, drained and rinsed (reserve liquids)
      1½ tablespoons tahini
         2 cloves garlic, minced
         1 tablespoon olive oil
        ½ teaspoon salt
1 or 2 fresh lemons, juice only

- In the container of a food processor or blender, combine the garbanzo beans, tahini, garlic, olive oil, and salt, together with ¼ cup of the liquid from the garbanzo beans. Add lemon juice to taste. Blend on low for 3 to 5 minutes or until smooth, adding more liquid from the garbanzo beans if needed.

YIELD 1½ cups

NUTRITION ANALYSIS PER SERVING 47.6 calories, 5.8 g carbohydrate, 1.4 g protein, 2.4 g fat, 1.1 g dietary fiber

164 Olives and Olive Oil

Benefits

Olives are high in monounsaturated fat and provide iron, vitamin E, and fiber, and they also contain anti-inflammatory flavonoids and phenols. Olives that are naturally purple or black contain anthocyanins as well.

Olive oil is a key component of the "Mediterranean diet," which appears to contribute to lower rates of heart disease and obesity.

> **NUTRITIONAL COMPOSITION (RIPE OLIVE)** One large pickled ripe olive provides 5 calories, 0.3 g carbohydrate, 0 g protein, 0.5 g fat, 0.1 g dietary fiber, 18 IU vitamin A, 38 mg sodium, and 4 mg calcium.

> **NUTRITIONAL COMPOSITION (OLIVE OIL)** One tablespoon of olive oil provides 124 calories, 0 g carbohydrate, 0 g protein, 14 g fat, and 0 g dietary fiber.

Bringing It Home

Olives are naturally quite bitter, so they are traditionally cured with lye, brine, or other substances. There are literally thousands of types of olives grown, and the olives may be prepared in many different ways—with or without pits, stuffed with nuts or pimientos, and marinated in liquids ranging from simple brine to sophisticated blends of liqueurs and spices. Armenian and Greek groceries sometimes include an olive bar, where you can select from more than a dozen varieties.

There are so many different descriptors for olive oil that it can be confusing. Expeller-pressed oil is extracted by crushing the olives. Olive oil that is "virgin" has not had chemicals or heat used to get more oil out of the olives. "Extra-virgin" goes through a subsequent battery of tests to assure that it has no defects of quality or taste. Olive oil that is safe for human consumption but does not meet the higher standards for virgin or extra-virgin is classified "fine."

For stir-frying, stay away from the extra-virgin and virgin grades. "Fine" olive oil goes through a more rigorous refining process than extra-virgin and virgin olive oils, which gives it a higher smoking point, meaning that it can take the high heat needed for stir-frying.

Livit Recipe

Livit Pantry Pasta Primavera

  12 ounces whole wheat pasta
   4 tablespoons olive oil
   3 cloves garlic, minced
  ⅓ cup pine nuts
   1 package (10 ounces) frozen broccoli
   1 package (10 ounces) frozen asparagus
   2 medium zucchini, sliced OR 1 zucchini and 1 yellow summer squash, sliced
   1 can (28 ounces) plum tomatoes, drained and coarsely chopped
   2 tablespoons dried basil
   1 tablespoon dried oregano
  ¼ teaspoon salt
  ¼ teaspoon black pepper
  ¼ cup grated Parmesan cheese

- Cook the pasta according to package directions. Set aside.
- In a large, deep pot, heat 2 tablespoons of the olive oil. Add the garlic and pine nuts, and sauté for 2 to 3 minutes, stirring constantly to make sure the pine nuts brown but do not burn. Add the broccoli and asparagus, and stir. Cover, and let steam for about 5 minutes. Add the squash, and cook, stirring, until the vegetables are brightly colored and crisp-tender. Add the tomatoes, basil, oregano, salt, and pepper, and heat through.
- When ready to serve, add the remaining 2 tablespoons of the olive oil and the Parmesan cheese to the vegetable mixture, and stir to combine. Serve over the pasta.
- NOTE You can make this recipe with items you have on hand, for a taste of springtime even in the winter. Add different fresh and frozen vegetables for variety.

YIELD 8 servings

NUTRITION ANALYSIS PER SERVING 309.7 calories, 35.9 g carbohydrate, 12 g protein, 12.6 g fat, 8.8 g dietary fiber

165 Pecans

Benefits

Pecans have the highest oxygen radical absorption capacity (ORAC) among nuts, and they are high in antioxidant properties in general. Pecans also play a role in lowering cholesterol, due not only to their fiber but also to plant sterols. Eating pecans may increase metabolic rate.

NUTRITIONAL COMPOSITION One ounce of raw pecans provides 190 calories, 5 g carbohydrate, 2 g protein, 19 g fat, and 2.7 g dietary fiber.

THE FDA POSITION ON HEART DISEASE AND NUTS

The U.S. Food and Drug Administration (FDA) has approved the following qualified health claim: "Scientific evidence suggests but does not prove that eating 1.5 ounces per day of most nuts [such as almonds, hazelnuts, peanuts, pecans, some pine nuts, pistachio nuts, walnuts] as part of a diet low in saturated fat and cholesterol may reduce the risk of heart disease. [See nutrition information for fat content.]" This applies to whole or chopped nuts (not nut-containing products) that are raw, blanched, roasted, salted, and/or lightly coated and/or flavored, and it is restricted to nuts that do not exceed 4 grams of saturated fat per 50 grams of nuts.

Although roasted nuts have several health benefits, for maximum health benefits consume raw nuts. Choose unsalted nuts if you have high blood pressure or are on a sodium-restricted diet. Nuts are considered low in sodium if they have less than 150 mg of sodium per serving. One ounce of nuts is considered to be a standard serving size.

Bringing It Home

When buying pecans, look for plump pecans that are uniform in color and size.

In-shell pecans can be stored in a cool, dry place for 6 to 12 months. When storing shelled pecans, airtight containers (such as jars with lids) are best for storage in the refrigerator, where they will keep for about nine months. Sealed plastic bags are best for storing shelled pecans in the freezer, where they will keep for up to two years. Pecans can be thawed and refrozen repeatedly during the two-year freezing period without loss of flavor or texture.

Livit Recipe

Ginger Pecan Muffins

1¼ cups unbleached all-purpose flour	1½ cups nonfat Greek-style yogurt
1 cup whole wheat flour	⅓ cup firmly packed brown sugar
2½ teaspoons baking powder	3 egg whites
½ teaspoon baking soda	2 tablespoons safflower oil
1¼ teaspoons ground ginger	1½ teaspoons vanilla extract
⅔ cup raisins	1 teaspoon orange extract
¼ cup coarsely chopped pecans	

- Preheat oven to 400°F.
- Line a muffin tin with 12 paper baking cups.
- In a large bowl, combine the flours, baking powder, baking soda, and ginger. Stir in the raisins and chopped pecans.

- In a medium bowl, whisk together the yogurt, brown sugar, egg whites, oil, vanilla, and orange extract until well blended.
- Add the yogurt mixture to the dry ingredients, stirring until the ingredients are just moistened.
- Spoon the batter into the muffin cups.
- Bake for 15 minutes, or until a tester in the center of a muffin comes out clean. Remove the muffins from the tin and cool on a wire rack. Serve.

YIELD 12 muffins

NUTRITION ANALYSIS PER SERVING 195 calories, 33 g carbohydrate, 6 g protein, 5 g fat, 2.2 g dietary fiber

166 Pine Nuts

Benefits

Pine nuts are the seeds of pine cones. China and Portugal are the largest exporters of pine nuts, and they are also grown in the United States. Most of the pine nuts grown in the United States are from one of three pinyon pines—the Colorado, Mexican, or Single-Leaf pinyons. There are more than 20 varieties of pine trees that produce an edible seed, and the nutritional value varies somewhat among them, but most pine nuts can be counted on to provide protein, fat, and the B vitamins thiamine, niacin, and riboflavin. They are also a source of magnesium, iron, and phosphorus. More than half of the carbohydrate in pine nuts is dietary fiber.

Pine nuts also contain pinolenic acid, which appears to stimulate the production of two hormones that suppress appetite.

NUTRITIONAL COMPOSITION One ounce of dried pinyon pine nuts provides 178 calories, 5.5 g carbohydrate, 3.3 g protein, 17.3 g fat, 3 g dietary fiber, 8 IU vitamin A, 1.2 mg niacin, 16 mcg folic acid, 178 mg potassium, 20 mg sodium, 10 mg phosphorus, 2 mg calcium, 66 mg magnesium, 1.21 mg zinc, and 1.23 mg manganese.

Bringing It Home

Shelled pine nuts are widely available. Pine nuts from China are often the least expensive, but having traveled the farthest may be less fresh. European pine nuts have the most traditional flavor and texture, as well as the highest protein content. United States–grown pine nuts remain a specialty item, since most are hand-harvested by Native Americans.

Because of the high oil content in pine nuts, they can go rancid within a few weeks if they are not kept cool and dry.

Livit Recipe

Turkey–Pine Nut Rice

2 cups brown basmati rice, rinsed and drained
4 cups water
1 cup pine nuts
1 tablespoon olive oil
½ pound ground turkey breast
1 onion, diced
2 teaspoons ground cinnamon
2 teaspoons ground cardamom
2 teaspoons ground coriander
2 teaspoons ground cumin
  Salt and pepper

- In a 2-quart saucepan, combine the rice and water, and bring to a boil. Reduce heat, cover, and let simmer for 45 minutes. Once the water is absorbed, remove from heat and set aside.
- In a large nonstick skillet, toast the pine nuts over medium heat until golden, shaking the pan constantly. Watch them carefully as they can burn very quickly. When the pine nuts are golden, transfer them to a small bowl.
- Lightly oil the skillet, using a paper towel to spread the oil evenly and absorb any excess. Add the ground turkey, onion, cinnamon, cardamom, coriander, and cumin. Cook the turkey mixture over medium heat until it is browned and cooked through.
- In a large bowl, combine the turkey, pine nuts, and rice. Add salt and pepper to taste. Fluff the ingredients with a fork. Serve.

YIELD 4 servings

NUTRITION ANALYSIS PER SERVING 365 calories, 29.7 g carbohydrate, 13.3 g protein, 22.3 g fat, 2.9 g dietary fiber

167 Pistachios

Benefits

Pistachios are rich in potassium, phosphorus, and magnesium, and they are also a good source of vitamin B_6 and thiamine. They are high in fiber, a good source of protein, and low in saturated fats. Pistachios are good for cardiovascular health, and they help maintain proper metabolism.

NUTRITIONAL COMPOSITION One ounce of dry roasted pistachios (47 nuts) provides 172 calories, 7.8 g carbohydrate, 4.2 g protein, 15 g fat, 3.1 g dietary fiber, 67 IU vitamin A, 17 mcg folic acid, 275 mg potassium, 135 mg phosphorus, 20 mg calcium, and 37 mg magnesium.

Bringing It Home

Pistachios in the shell do not keep as well as some nuts, because the shell splits open when the pistachio is ripe. Shelled or unshelled, store pistachios in an airtight container in the refrigerator. They will keep about 3 months.

Livit Recipe

Baked Pistachio Rice Pudding

Brown rice adds a chewy texture, more nutrition, and a lovely nutty taste to this rice pudding, but pistachios are the stars!

½ cup brown rice	½ teaspoon vanilla extract
1 cup water	¼ teaspoon ground cardamom
2 cups skim milk OR low-fat milk	¼ cup chopped pistachios
¼ cup sugar	

- In a medium saucepan, combine the rice and water, and bring to a boil. Reduce heat, cover, and let simmer for 45 minutes, or until all the liquid has been absorbed. Remove from heat.
- Preheat oven to 300°F.
- In a 1-quart baking dish, combine the cooked rice, milk, sugar, vanilla, and cardamom. Bake for 15 minutes. Stir the pudding gently, and return it to the oven for another 30 minutes of baking.
- Top with chopped pistachios. Serve either warm or chilled.
- NOTE Leftover rice can also be used in this dish. You need 1½ cups of prepared rice.

YIELD 4 servings

NUTRITION ANALYSIS PER SERVING 224.3 calories, 37.9 g carbohydrate, 7.4 g protein, 5.2 g fat, 2.1 g dietary fiber

168 Pumpkin Seeds

Benefits

Because they are high in zinc, pumpkin seeds are a natural protector against osteoporosis. They are also a great source of magnesium, which helps balance calcium metabolism and may contribute to bone health.

Pumpkin seeds are a natural anti-inflammatory and may help counteract the kidney stone–forming effects of oxalates found in many dark green, leafy foods that are otherwise good in nutritional value.

NUTRITIONAL COMPOSITION One-third cup of pumpkin seeds provides 110 calories, 14 g carbohydrate, 5 g protein, 5 g fat, 2 g dietary fiber, and 1000 mg sodium.

Bringing It Home

Prepared pumpkin seeds are available year-round. Because of the high oil content, it's especially important that the seeds be fresh. Don't buy pumpkin seeds that have sat on the shelf or in the bulk bins too long, or they may be rancid. Roasted pumpkin seeds should appear dry, not damp, but they should not look shriveled. Use your nose—pumpkin seeds should not smell rancid or musty.

Store pumpkin seeds in the refrigerator in an airtight container.

Pumpkin seeds add a new twist to hot or cold cereal, oatmeal cookies, and homemade granola—or even mixed into ground meat or vegetable patties. Add roasted pumpkin seeds to sautéed vegetables, and sprinkle them on salads.

Livit Recipe

Roasted Pumpkin Seeds

Part of the fun of cooking pumpkins is to roast your own pumpkin seeds.

1 pumpkin

- *A day ahead of roasting:* Scrape the seeds and strings from inside the pumpkin, and rinse the seeds gently to remove any pulp and strings. Spread them out evenly on a paper bag or double layer of paper towels and let them dry overnight.
- *The day of roasting:* Preheat oven to 170°F.
- Spread the pumpkin seeds in a single layer on a cookie sheet or jelly roll pan. Lightly roast them in the oven for 15 to 20 minutes.
- NOTE Using a low temperature and a short roasting time helps preserve the nutrient value of the pumpkin seeds.

YIELD Varies with the amount of seeds from the pumpkin

NUTRITION ANALYSIS PER SERVING 148 calories, 3.8 g carbohydrate, 9.3 g protein, 11.9 g fat, 1.1 g dietary fiber

169 Red Wine

Benefits

Red wine is listed here because in carbohydrate exchange programs, it is counted as a fat. It contains 7 calories of fat per gram, which is higher than both carbohydrates and proteins, though not quite as high as true fats.

Nonetheless, red wine has been shown to have significant benefits consistent with its origins in red grapes. It is a source of resveratrol, the substance found in the skins of red grapes and therefore in red wine that was originally thought to be among the reasons those who eat a so-called French or Mediterranean diet had a lower risk of obesity and heart disease. Resveratrol is produced by plants as an anti-microbial, to fight bacteria or fungus, and has been found in animal trials to lower blood sugar, reduce inflammation, and fight some cancers. It also appears to extend the lifespan of some insects and fish and, in a 2008 study, was shown to reduce the formation of plaques in the brains of animals, pointing toward a potential role in preventing Alzheimer's disease.

So far it has not lived up to its promise in human trials, in part because a human dose equivalent to those used on experimental mice would require between 761 and 5,000 glasses of wine per day. As a result, resveratrol is no longer regarded as the main factor in the "French paradox," but it is still the subject of study for its many and varied possible health-enhancing properties.

Red wine also provides polyphenols known as oligomeric procyanidins that may help reduce the risk of heart disease and diabetes.

NUTRITIONAL COMPOSITION Three and one-half ounces of red wine provides 74 calories, 1.8 g carbohydrate, 0.2 g protein, 0 g fat, 0 g dietary fiber, 2 mcg folic acid, 115 mg potassium, 5 mg sodium, 14 mg phosphorus, 8 mg calcium, and 13 mg magnesium.

Bringing It Home

Choose wines without added sulfites if possible. In the United States, a wine labeled as organic cannot contain added sulfites. However, this is not the case in all countries.

A glass or two of red wine a day can help improve your vital body functions. Red wine may help lower the risk of some dementias and heart disease. However, the benefits of red wine are limited after one or two glasses. Drinking more wine does not increase the health benefits, and more than one glass a day for women or two glasses a day for men is linked to increased risk of other health hazards.

Other food sources also provide the substances believed to account for the health benefits of wine, which is important for those who have concerns about addiction or alcoholism. Grapes and grape juice are good sources of resveratrol, and apples contain more procyandins than two glasses of wine.

Livit Recipe

Chicken in Red Wine

See Safe Handling of Poultry on page 211.

1 tablespoon olive oil	2 cups red wine
1½ pounds skinless, boneless chicken breasts	2 cups chicken broth
8 ounces fresh mushrooms, sliced	½ teaspoon dried thyme
3 cloves garlic, minced	Salt and pepper
2 tablespoons flour	

- Heat the olive oil over medium heat in a large, deep sauté pan. Add the chicken breasts. Cook for about 5 minutes on each side. Remove them from the pan, and set aside, keeping them warm.
- Cook the mushrooms and garlic in the pan for about 2 minutes, until they are soft. Add the flour. Cook, stirring constantly, for another 2 minutes. Stir in the red wine and chicken broth. Add the thyme. Season with salt and pepper to taste.
- Let the sauce come to a boil. Reduce heat, and return the chicken to the pan. Cover, and let the dish simmer for about 30 minutes. Serve over whole wheat pasta.

YIELD 4 servings

NUTRITION ANALYSIS PER SERVING 337.2 calories, 8.2 g carbohydrate, 42.3 g protein, 5.7 g fat, 0.9 g dietary fiber

170 Safflower Oil

Benefits

There are two types of safflower oil. The most common one is oleic safflower oil, which is largely monounsaturated and high in omega-9 fatty acids. The other type is linoleic safflower oil, which is largely polyunsaturated and high in omega-6 fatty acids. The oleic type may help increase memory and lower blood pressure, while the linoleic may help improve diabetes symptoms and has been shown to prevent some forms of cancer in mice.

> NUTRITIONAL COMPOSITION One tablespoon of safflower oil provides 124 calories, 0 g carbohydrate, 0 g protein, 14 g fat, and 0 g dietary fiber.

Bringing It Home

Choose safflower oil that is organic and cold-pressed to get maximum benefit, and look for light-resistant bottles (brown or amber glass). Safflower oil is good for relatively high-heat cooking as well as baking. Store it tightly sealed in a cool dark place. Oils keep longer if refrigerated, but most will solidify, making them inconvenient to use. Probably the best balance between convenience and freshness is to purchase your oils in quantities small enough to use before there is any danger of rancidity.

Livit Recipe

Safflower Oil with Fines Herbes

½ teaspoon dried parsley OR 2 sprigs fresh parsley, minced
½ teaspoon dried chives OR 1 teaspoon chopped fresh chives
½ teaspoon dried tarragon
½ teaspoon dried chervil
 1 cup safflower oil

- Place the parsley, chives, tarragon, and chervil in the bottom of a 10-ounce jar or other container with a tight-sealing lid.

- In a small saucepan over low heat, gently warm the oil. Pour it into the jar over the herbs, and cover tightly. Let the herbs infuse for about two weeks in a cool, dark place. Taste after the first week to see if the infused flavor is strong enough; if not, leave for another week.

- Strain the infused oil into a clean jar. Serve as a dipping oil, in salad dressings, or in marinades.

- NOTE The oil can also be drizzled over the top of low-fat soups just before serving, as a decorative, flavorful garnish.

- VARIATION Substitute other fresh or dried herbs, such as basil, marjoram, rosemary, or oregano.

YIELD 16 servings (1 tablespoon each), or about 1 cup

NUTRITION ANALYSIS PER SERVING 120.8 calories, 0.1 g carbohydrate, 0 g protein, 13.6 g fat, 0 g dietary fiber

171 Sesame Seeds

Benefits

Sesame seeds are high in iron, magnesium, manganese, and copper, and they also provide phosphorus, vitamin B_1, zinc, and dietary fiber. The hulls contain a significant amount of calcium, though seeds without hulls do not.

Sesame seeds also contain two unique substances: sesamin and sesamolin. Both of these substances belong to a group of special beneficial fibers called lignans, which have been shown to have a cholesterol-lowering effect in humans and to prevent high blood pressure and increase vitamin E supplies in animals. Sesamin has also been found to protect the liver from oxidative damage.

NUTRITIONAL COMPOSITION One ounce of toasted sesame seed kernels provides 161 calories, 7.4 g carbohydrate, 4.8 g protein, 13.6 g fat, 4.8 g dietary fiber, 19 IU vitamin A, 27 mcg folic acid, 115 mg potassium, 11 mg sodium, 219 mg phosphorus, 37 mg calcium, 98 mg magnesium, 2.21 mg iron, and 2.9 mg zinc.

OXALATE ALERT!

The hulls of sesame seeds contain oxalates, which can cause problems for those with kidney disease, gout, vulvar pain, rheumatoid arthritis, or other conditions that may require a low-oxalate diet. Some sesame products are available that are made without the hulls. For example, most tahini is made from seeds without hulls, and it is possible to buy hull-less sesame seeds.

Bringing It Home

Sesame seeds are available hulled and hull-less, though they are more commonly found sold in the hull. Other sesame products include tahini, halvah, and sesame oil. Keep sesame seeds in a cool, dry, dark place. If you store them in the refrigerator, keep them in an airtight container to protect them from moisture. Sesame oil keeps fairly well, not refrigerated, for several months, though it is important to be aware that toasted and spiced sesame oils are better as flavorings than as cooking oils.

Livit Recipe

Exotic Sesame Rice

1 cup brown rice	½ cup crushed pineapple, drained
2½ cups water	(reserve juice)
¼ cup orange juice	½ cup sliced water chestnuts, drained
1 teaspoon sesame oil	and quartered
2 tablespoons reduced-sodium soy sauce	½ red bell pepper, seeded and minced
1 teaspoon agave nectar OR honey	½ small onion, minced
1 teaspoon apple cider vinegar	2 medium stalks celery, minced
2 cloves garlic, minced	¼ cup raisins
2 to 3 drops bottled hot sauce, optional	1 tablespoon sesame seeds

- In a medium saucepan, combine the rice and water, and bring to a boil. Reduce heat, cover, and let simmer for 45 minutes, or until all the liquid has been absorbed. Remove from heat and transfer to a large bowl.

- In a small bowl, whisk together the orange juice, sesame oil, soy sauce, agave nectar, vinegar, and garlic. Add hot sauce, if using.

- Dress the rice with the orange juice mixture, and toss gently to flavor all the rice. Add the pineapple, water chestnuts, pepper, onion, celery, raisins, and sesame seeds. Stir everything together well, adding pineapple juice if necessary. Cover and chill for several hours or overnight.

- Just before serving, stir again to make sure the ingredients are well mixed. Serve chilled.

YIELD 4 servings

NUTRITION ANALYSIS PER SERVING 152 calories, 29 g carbohydrate, 3 g protein, 3 g fat, 2.9 g dietary fiber

172 Sunflower Seeds

Benefits

Can the stars of Major League Baseball be wrong? Sunflower seeds are increasingly their favorite snack, and with good reason. Sunflower seeds will satisfy your hunger and supply significant amounts of vitamin E, magnesium, and selenium, all of which are great for endurance and metabolism. Sunflower seeds are rich in phytosterols, plant chemicals that help reduce blood levels of cholesterol while supporting hormonal health.

Sunflower oil is high in vitamin E and linoleic acid. It also contains oleic acid, lecithin, tocopherols, and carotenoids. Sunflower oil also appears to contribute to lowering cholesterol.

> **NUTRITIONAL COMPOSITION (SUNFLOWER OIL)** One tablespoon of sunflower oil provides 124 calories, 0 g carbohydrate, 0 g protein, 14 g fat, and 0 g dietary fiber.

> **NUTRITIONAL COMPOSITION (SUNFLOWER SEEDS)** One ounce of unsalted dry roasted sunflower seed kernels provides 165 calories, 6.8 g carbohydrate, 5.5 g protein, 14.1 g fat, 3 g dietary fiber, 1.9 mg niacin, 2 mg pantothenic acid, 67 mcg folic acid, 241 mg potassium, 1 mg sodium, 327 mg phosphorus, 241 mg potassium, 20 mg calcium, 1.08 mg iron, and 37 mg magnesium.

Bringing It Home

Sunflower seeds are available both with and without the shells. If sold in the shell, the shells should seem clean and crisp. Seeds that have been shelled should be white or ivory in color, not yellowish. Because of their high fat content, sunflower seeds are at risk of turning rancid, especially those sold without shells. Store sunflower seeds in an airtight container in the refrigerator.

In addition to being a good snack, sunflower seeds can be added to all kinds of salads, or sprinkled on cereal.

Two forms of sunflower oil are available—linoleic and high oleic. Linoleic sunflower oil, the more common variety, is low in trans fats and is very good for cooking. There is also a hydrogenated version, which should be avoided. Store sunflower oil in a tightly sealed container away from light and heat. It can be kept in the refrigerator, but it will solidify when cold. The best compromise between health and convenience is probably to purchase sunflower oil in quantities small enough to use before there is a risk of rancidity.

Livit Recipe

Sunflower Seed and Kidney Bean Salad

Salad

2 cups mixed greens, washed and dried
1 can (15 ounces) red kidney beans, drained
½ cup roasted sunflower seeds
1 medium pear, quartered and thinly sliced

Dressing

2 tablespoons cider vinegar
2 tablespoons safflower oil
1 shallot, minced
   Salt and pepper

- *To prepare the salad:* In a serving bowl, combine the greens, kidney beans, sunflower seeds, and pear. Toss lightly to distribute.
- *To prepare the dressing:* In a small bowl, whisk together the vinegar and safflower oil. Add the minced shallot, and add salt and pepper to taste.
- Just before serving, pour the dressing over the salad, and toss gently. Serve.

YIELD 4 servings

NUTRITION ANALYSIS PER SERVING 321.6 calories, 35.6 g carbohydrate, 11.4 g protein, 16.1 g fat, 12.2 g dietary fiber

173 Walnuts

Benefits

One ounce of walnuts, or about 14 shelled walnut halves, provides the recommended daily value of omega-3 fatty acids, thereby contributing to cardiovascular protection, improved cognitive function, and anti-inflammatory benefits. Walnuts also provide ellagic acid, which is being investigated for its anticancer potential.

NUTRITIONAL COMPOSITION One ounce of walnut pieces provides 190 calories, 4 g carbohydrate, 4 g protein, 19 g fat, and 1 g dietary fiber.

Bringing It Home

Walnuts in their shells should feel heavy, and the shells should be intact. Still in their shells, walnuts will keep for up to six months, especially if kept away from light, heat, and moisture. If you are buying shelled walnuts from bulk bins, smell them to make sure they are not rancid—they should have a pleasant nutty smell. If they are pre-packaged, check the expiration date and try to choose nutmeats that appear to be plump and in good condition.

As with most nuts, walnuts' high fat content renders them susceptible to rancidity. Store shelled walnuts in a sealed container in the refrigerator. They will keep in the refrigerator for up to six months. In the freezer, they will keep for up to a year.

Livit Recipe

Mock Chopped Liver

4 eggs
1 cup walnuts
1 teaspoon olive oil
1 onion, minced
1 can (15 ounces) peas, drained
Salt and pepper

- Preheat oven to 300°F.
- In a small saucepan, arrange the eggs in a single layer and cover them by 1 inch with cold water. Bring to a boil over medium heat. Once the water has reached a full boil, remove pan from heat, cover, and let stand for about 17 minutes. Drain, and rinse the eggs in cold water.
- Meanwhile, spread the walnuts in a single layer on a cookie sheet or jelly roll pan. Toast the walnuts in the oven for 8 to 10 minutes, until they begin to brown. Remove from oven and allow them to cool.
- In a small nonstick skillet, heat the oil, and sauté two thirds of the onion, stirring often, until the onion is browned and caramelized.
- Put the walnuts in a blender jar, and process until they are finely chopped. Add the peas, the sautéed onion, and the remaining raw onion. Blend until smooth.
- Peel the eggs and cut them into quarters. Add the eggs to the walnut mixture, and process until smooth. Add salt and pepper to taste. Blend to combine.
- Refrigerate for several hours or overnight to give the flavors time to meld.
- NOTE This is delicious served with whole wheat crackers or matzo.

YIELD 2 cups

NUTRITION ANALYSIS PER SERVING 87 calories, 4.2 g carbohydrate, 3.7 g protein, 6.6 g fat, 1.4 g dietary fiber

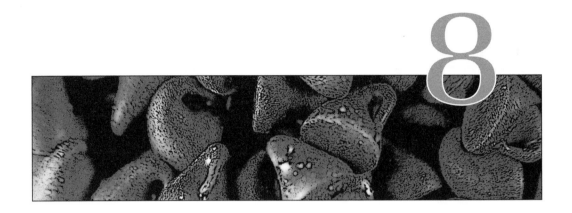

Sweeteners and Desserts

We all crave a little sweetness in life. Although fruits and dried fruits may satisfy the sweet tooth sometimes, it's amazing what a little honey or a few chocolate chips can do to brighten the palate. The sweeteners included as SuperFoods provide both more nutrients than refined white sugar and a less extreme spike to the blood sugar.

174 Agave Syrup

Benefits

Agave is a succulent plant, one species of which is used for making tequila. Although they are commonly referred to as cacti, agave plants are related to the lily family rather than the cactus.

The sap of some agave plants is sweet enough that native Mexicans called it "honey water," and it is now used commercially as the basis for a sweetener. The natural sap is a source of iron, calcium, potassium, and magnesium. However, the agave syrup or nectar currently marketed is heavily processed, and is therefore much more refined than the simple sap.

Agave syrup is 90 percent fructose and therefore tastes very sweet, so less of it can be used to provide the same sweetening effect as table sugar. Depending on

. . . . .
270

how heavily refined the agave syrup is, it may—or may not—have a better glycemic profile than refined cane sugar.

NUTRITIONAL COMPOSITION One teaspoon of agave syrup provides 15 calories, 4 g carbohydrate, 0 g protein, 0 g fat, 0 g dietary fiber, 4 g sugars.

Bringing It Home

Agave syrup is shelf-stable and does not need refrigeration. It can be used in place of sugar or other sweeteners in recipes, but a few adjustments are necessary: Because agave syrup is sweeter, use only about ¾ cup of agave syrup where you would use 1 cup of sugar, reduce liquids by one third, and lower oven temperatures for baking by 25°F.

Both light and dark agave syrups are available. The light syrup has a neutral sweetness, whereas the darker syrups have a more distinctive flavor.

Livit Recipe

Agave Teriyaki Sauce

1 cup agave syrup
1 cup reduced-sodium soy sauce
1 cup sake (rice wine)
1 clove garlic, minced
1 piece fresh ginger root (1 to 2 inches long), grated
1 teaspoon sesame oil

- In a small bowl, whisk together the agave syrup, soy sauce, sake, garlic, ginger, and sesame oil. Use immediately or store in a sealed container in the refrigerator.
- NOTE This teriyaki sauce is delicious on chicken, fish, or vegetables.

YIELD 48 servings (1 tablespoon each), or about 3 cups

NUTRITION ANALYSIS PER SERVING 22 calories, 1.2 g carbohydrates, 1.3 g protein, 0.2 g fat, 0.1 g dietary fiber

175 Honey (Raw)

Benefits

Honey's sweetness comes from fructose and glucose, as well as other complex sugars. It contains very slight amounts of vitamins and minerals, but given the amounts normally consumed, honey cannot be considered a significant source of any of them. For centuries, honey has been used topically for its antibacterial and antimicrobial properties.

One tablespoon of strained or extracted honey provides 64 calories, 17.3 g carbohydrate, 0.1 g protein, 0 g fat, 0.2 g dietary fiber, 11 mg potassium, and 1 mg sodium.

Bringing It Home

Honey is usually marketed according to the amount of processing it has received. Raw honey is removed from the comb without heating above 120°F and may contain some pollen and wax as a result. Pasteurized honey is heated to destroy yeast and other microbes; pasteurization also liquefies crystals and extends the honey's shelf life.

Honey is sometimes marketed according to the types of flowers from which it was made. Single-flower honeys often have unique flavors.

If honey absorbs moisture from the air, it may begin to ferment, so store it in a sealed container. Kept in a cool place away from light, it will keep for a very long time.

Although honey has antimicrobial properties, it sometimes also contains endospores of *Clostridium botulinum,* which can cause botulism poisoning in young children. Honey should never be given to children under one year of age.

Livit Recipe

Honey Cake

1 teaspoon vegetable oil
1 cup unbleached all-purpose flour plus enough flour to dust the oiled loaf pan
¾ cup whole wheat pastry flour
½ cup firmly packed dark brown sugar
1½ teaspoons baking powder
½ teaspoon baking soda
1 teaspoon cinnamon
¼ teaspoon ground allspice
¼ teaspoon nutmeg
¼ teaspoon ginger
¼ teaspoon salt
1 whole egg plus 2 egg whites OR 3 tablespoons pasteurized egg whites
⅞ cup honey
½ cup strong green tea
2 tablespoons unsweetened applesauce
½ cup coarsely chopped walnuts, rolled lightly in flour

- Preheat oven to 350°F.
- Lightly oil and flour a 9″ × 5″ loaf pan.
- In a large bowl, combine the all-purpose flour, whole wheat pastry flour, sugar, baking powder, baking soda, cinnamon, allspice, nutmeg, ginger, and salt.

- In a small bowl, whisk together the eggs, honey, tea, and applesauce.
- Add the egg mixture to the dry ingredients, and stir them together until the batter is smooth. Add the walnuts to the batter. Pour the batter into the loaf pan.
- Bake for 1 hour, or until a tester in the center of the cake comes out clean. Cool in the pan for 10 minutes, then turn out on a wire rack to cool completely.

YIELD 12 slices

NUTRITION ANALYSIS PER SERVING (WITH NUTS) 216 calories, 43.8 g carbohydrates, 4.3 g protein, 3.9 g fat, 1.6 g dietary fiber

176 Maple Syrup

Benefits

Maple syrup is an excellent source of manganese and a good source of zinc, though the amount of maple syrup that would be consumed as a sweetener would not provide a significant amount of either nutrient.

> **NUTRITIONAL COMPOSITION** One tablespoon of maple syrup provides 52 calories, 13.4 g carbohydrate, 0 g protein, 0 g fat, 0 g dietary fiber, 41 mg potassium, 2 mg sodium, 13 mg calcium, 3 mg magnesium, and 0.83 mg zinc.

Bringing It Home

Choose real maple syrup, not "maple flavored" or "pancake" syrups, which are mostly corn syrup. The U.S. Department of Agriculture (USDA) grading system for maple syrups dates from a time when maple was a cheap substitute for white sugar, so Grade A maple syrup has the most delicate taste and lightest color. At one time Grade B maple syrup was mainly reserved for cooking and commercial use because of its stronger maple taste and darker color—but these factors now make Grade B a popular choice among those who want every calorie packed with flavor.

To substitute maple syrup for sugar when cooking, use three quarters of a cup of syrup in place of one cup of sugar. In baking, also reduce the amount of liquid in the recipe by about three tablespoons for each cup of maple syrup.

Maple syrup is especially good on hot cereals and in yogurt. You can also use it in salad dressings, which may allow you to reduce or eliminate the oil.

Livit Recipe

Maple Syrup Vinaigrette

¼ cup apple cider vinegar
½ cup maple syrup
2 tablespoons lemon juice

¼ cup olive oil
1 clove garlic, minced
Salt and pepper

- In a small bowl, whisk together the vinegar, syrup, lemon juice, and olive oil until it is emulsified. Stir in the garlic, and add salt and pepper to taste. Serve over salad greens.
- NOTE This dressing is especially good on greens with a stronger taste, such as spinach or dandelions.

YIELD 16 servings (1 tablespoon each), or about 1 cup

NUTRITION ANALYSIS PER SERVING 56.7 calories, 7 g carbohydrate, 0 g protein, 3.4 g fat, 0 g dietary fiber

177 Blackstrap Molasses

Benefits

Blackstrap molasses is a product of sugar-making: It is the syrup that remains after the process has extracted all the sugar that it can. Although much of the sucrose has been crystallized out into sugar, most of the calories in blackstrap molasses still come from sugar. It is also a significant source of calcium, magnesium, potassium, and iron. This mineral content is good for building strong bones, maintaining hydration, and lowering blood pressure. The iron in molasses is vital to preventing anemia and producing red blood cells, especially important if one's diet is low in other sources of iron, such as red meat. This nutrient probably accounts for blackstrap molasses' early reputation as a health food.

NUTRITIONAL COMPOSITION One tablespoon of blackstrap molasses provides 47 calories, 12.2 g carbohydrate, 0 g protein, 0 g fat, 0 g dietary fiber, 498 mg potassium, 11 mg sodium, 172 mg calcium, 8 mg phosphorus, 3.5 mg iron, and 43 mg magnesium.

Bringing It Home

Sulfured blackstrap molasses is made from young sugar cane, processed with sulfur dioxide. Unsulfured molasses can be produced from mature sugar cane, because sulfur dioxide is not necessary for that production process. Since sulfur dioxide imparts a taste that some people find unpleasant and is toxic in large amounts, opt for unsulfured blackstrap molasses when possible.

Keep molasses away from light, heat, and moisture. It can be stored in the refrigerator. An unopened, factory-sealed bottle of molasses should keep for about a year. Once opened, it will keep for about six months.

Livit Recipe

Slow-as-Molasses Bread

1½ packages (4 teaspoons) active dry yeast
½ cup warm water (about 110°F)
1 teaspoon raw sugar
¼ teaspoon dried ginger
3½ cups water
3 cups quick-cooking rolled oats
¼ cup safflower oil plus enough to oil the bowl and pans
½ cup blackstrap molasses
1 teaspoon salt
1 cup 100% bran cereal
2 cups whole wheat flour
4 to 5 cups unbleached all-purpose flour

- In a small bowl, gently mix the yeast with the ½ cup of warm water. (The water should feel pleasantly warm, not too hot, or it will kill the yeast.) Add the sugar and ginger, and let the mixture sit in a warm place (80°F is ideal) to let the yeast begins its work.

- In a teakettle, bring the 3½ cups of water to a boil.

- Put the rolled oats into a very large bowl, and pour the boiling water over them. Add the oil, molasses, and salt, stirring until all is well combined. Mix in the bran cereal and whole wheat flour. Add the yeast mixture. Stir, combining everything thoroughly.

- Begin adding the all-purpose flour, ½ cup at a time, working it in until the dough is no longer sticky and becomes easy to handle.

- On a floured board or countertop, knead the dough for about 10 minutes, until it is smooth and elastic. It will still be soft.

- Lightly oil the inside of another large bowl, using a paper towel to spread the oil and absorb any excess. Put the dough into the oiled bowl, and roll it around to oil the entire outside of the dough ball. Cover the bowl with a clean dishtowel and set it in a warm place for about 90 minutes, or until the dough doubles in size.

- Lightly oil three 9″ × 5″ loaf pans.

- On a floured board or counter, punch down the dough. Divide it into three pieces, shape them into loaves, and put each loaf into an oiled pan. Cover the pans with a clean dishtowel, and set them in a warm place to rise until they are doubled, about 90 minutes.

- Near the end of the rising time, preheat oven to 350°F.

- When the loaves have doubled, put them in the oven to bake for about 40 minutes, or until they sound hollow when tapped on the bottom. Turn them out of the pans immediately onto wire racks to cool.

- NOTE After the bread has fully cooled, you may wish to freeze some of it. Wrap it tightly in plastic or put it in a plastic zipper bag to prevent it from drying out in the freezer.

YIELD 36 servings (1 slice each), or 3 loaves of 12 slices each

NUTRITION ANALYSIS PER SERVING 144 calories, 27.5 g carbohydrates, 4.2 g protein, 2.3 g fat, 2.8 g dietary fiber

178 Semi-Sweet Chocolate Chips

Benefits

Chocolate chips can satisfy your chocolate cravings without going overboard—you can eat just a few instead of giving in to a whole chocolate bar. It's a bonus that dark chocolate has been shown to provide some heart benefits—specifically, lowering blood pressure—thanks to its antioxidants and flavonoids. No wonder Valentine's chocolates come in heart-shaped boxes!

NUTRITIONAL COMPOSITION Twenty semi-sweet chocolate chips provide 50 calories, 5.5 g carbohydrate, 0 g protein, 3 g fat, 0 g dietary fiber, 20 mg calcium, and 1.08 mg iron.

Bringing It Home

Buy semi-sweet chocolate chips made with natural ingredients—organic is even better—and avoid vanillin, an artificial flavoring. Keep them in the freezer in a plastic zipper bag for a refreshing sweet-tooth satisfier.

Livit Recipe

Chocolate Chip Cookie Colossal

    1 cup non-hydrogenated margarine
    1 cup sugar OR evaporated cane juice
    ½ cup brown sugar
    1 egg
    3 tablespoons pasteurized 100% liquid egg white
    2 teaspoons vanilla extract
    1⅓ cups all-purpose flour
    1 cup whole wheat pastry flour
    1 teaspoon salt
    1 teaspoon baking soda
    1 package (12 ounces) semi-sweet chocolate chips (about 2 cups)
       Canola oil

- Preheat oven to 375°F.
- In the small bowl of a stand mixer or the container of a food processor, cream the margarine with the sugars, egg, egg white, and vanilla until fluffy.
- In a large bowl, combine the flours, salt, and baking soda. Stir the creamed butter and sugar into the dry ingredients. Add the chocolate chips, stirring to distribute them evenly.
- Grease cookie sheets lightly with canola oil, using a paper towel to spread the oil and absorb any excess. Drop the batter by teaspoonfuls onto the cookie sheets, about 2 inches apart. Bake for 10 minutes, or until golden brown. Transfer to a rack to cool.

YIELD 60 cookies

NUTRITION ANALYSIS PER SERVING 190 calories, 25 g carbohydrate, 2 g protein, 10 g fat, 0.3 g dietary fiber

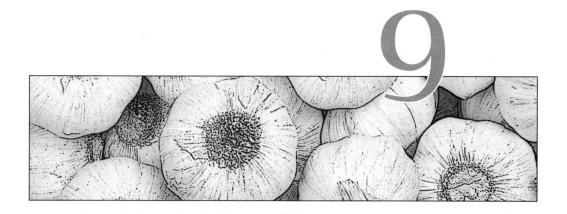

Dietary "Free" Foods: Herbs and Medicinals

These foods are used in such small quantities, or are so low in calories, that they don't "count" when used as part of a healthy diet—yet they add flavor and nutritive value! What's not to love?

179 Apple Cider Vinegar

Benefits

Vinegar is produced when alcohols converted from sugars undergo a process of fermentation. Apple cider vinegar is made from fresh apples. It contains vitamins, beta-carotene, pectin, and several minerals, including potassium, sodium, magnesium, calcium, phosphorus, and iron.

Vinegar appears to help lower blood glucose levels. It contains chromium, which can help regulate insulin levels and is important in glucose metabolism. Vinegar delays gastric emptying and helps lower blood glucose and insulin levels in people who are healthy.

Vinegar may contribute to lower cholesterol levels and lower blood pressure. Vinegar is also being investigated for its cancer-killing potential.

· · · · ·

As an ingredient in many types of traditional medicine for millennia, vinegar has been credited with the power to treat almost everything: constipation, arthritis, headaches, weak bones, indigestion, high cholesterol, diarrhea, eczema, sore eyes, chronic fatigue, mild food poisoning, hair loss, high blood pressure, and obesity.

Vinegar is a great fat-free component in recipes and salad dressings—though be sure to include some fat in your salad dressings to help your body digest and absorb all the good nutrients in the green vegetables.

NUTRITIONAL COMPOSITION One tablespoon of apple cider vinegar provides 2 calories, 0.9 g carbohydrate, 0 g protein, 0 g fat, 0 g dietary fiber, 15 mg potassium, 1 mg calcium, 1 mg phosphorus, and 0.1 mg iron.

ACIDITY ALERT!

Like all vinegars, apple cider vinegar is highly acidic—its primary component is acetic acid. Although commercially prepared vinegars are diluted to provide a consistent and safe level of acid, one should not drink vinegar straight. Pure vinegar can damage tooth enamel and the tissues in your throat and mouth. It has been known to cause contact burns.

If you drink a lot of vinegar, it can eventually deplete potassium levels and possibly lower bone density. It can interact with medicines including diuretics, laxatives, and some diabetes medicines. People with insulin-dependent diabetes should consult with their physicians before adding a lot of vinegar to their diets.

Bringing It Home

Choose organic apple cider vinegar whenever possible.

A tablespoon of raw apple cider vinegar mixed into four ounces of purified water can be a natural remedy for heartburn when taken after a meal.

Try mixing apple cider vinegar with honey to drink at night before going to bed—it's great for calming nerves, promoting relaxation, and relief of bone-related ailments. Adjust the amounts of vinegar and honey for comfort and taste, but the general proportions are eight ounces of warm water, one to two teaspoons of apple cider vinegar, and one to two teaspoons of honey.

Livit Recipe

Livit Vinaigrette Dressing

1 tablespoon extra-virgin olive oil
2 tablespoons apple cider vinegar
1 teaspoon agave nectar
½ lemon, juice only
1 teaspoon lemon pepper

- In a small bowl, whisk together the oil, vinegar, agave nectar, lemon juice, and lemon pepper.

- The dressing can be used immediately or stored in a sealed container in the refrigerator for future use.

- VARIATIONS For a creamier dressing, add 1 tablespoon of low-fat plain yogurt or plain soy yogurt. For honey-mustard dressing, add 1 teaspoon of organic Dijon mustard.

YIELD 4 servings (1 tablespoon each), or about ¼ cup

NUTRITION ANALYSIS PER SERVING 52 calories, 2 g carbohydrate, 0 g protein, 4 g fat, 0 g dietary fiber

180 Brewer's Yeast

Benefits

Brewer's yeast appears to help stabilize both serum triglycerides and glucose levels, due to its high levels of chromium. If you are interested in its sugar-regulating effects, seek out the type that has not been "debittered," because chromium is removed in the debittering process. Brewer's yeast also provides B vitamins, and it is one of the very few non-animal sources of vitamin B_{12}.

Sprinkle brewer's yeast on food to add extra B vitamins, protein, and minerals. Many folk remedies for poor skin include brewer's yeast, and some studies have suggested that consuming brewer's yeast can accelerate the healing time for cuts and similar injuries.

> NUTRITIONAL COMPOSITION One ounce of brewer's yeast provides 80 calories, 10.9 g carbohydrate, 11 g protein, 0.3 g fat, 1.1 g dietary fiber, 4.4 mg thiamine, 10.7 mg niacin, 1.2 mg riboflavin, 537 mg potassium, 34 mg sodium, 497 mg phosphorus, 60 mg calcium, and 4.9 mg iron.

Bringing It Home

When buying nutritional yeast, purchase an inactive form, because active yeast can grow in your intestines and crowd out the beneficial micro-organisms that belong there.

Brewer's Yeast Popcorn Topper

    4 tablespoons brewer's yeast
    ½ teaspoon salt
    ½ teaspoon garlic powder
    2 quarts air-popped popcorn

- Mix the brewer's yeast, salt, and garlic powder together. Sprinkle on top of warm popped corn. Serve.

- NOTE Brewer's yeast significantly raises the nutritional value of your popcorn snack.

- VARIATION Substitute other seasonings for the garlic powder. If using chili powder or curry powder that already contains salt, leave out the ½ teaspoon of salt in the basic recipe.

YIELD 4 servings

NUTRITION ANALYSIS PER SERVING 77.9 calories, 14.4 g carbohydrate, 4.6 g protein, 0 g fat, 3.8 g dietary fiber

181 Cardamom

Benefits

Cardamom is an exotic-tasting, sweet spice derived from the seeds of a ginger-like plant. Cardamom gives chai its spiciness and is a cuisine feature from India and the Middle East to Scandinavia. The Greeks and Romans used cardamom as a perfume.

Cardamom may help with cleansing the kidneys and the bladder, stimulating the digestive system, and reducing gas. It has been shown to be antispasmodic and can counteract excess acidity in the stomach, stimulate appetite, remedy infection, and cure halitosis (bad breath). It is also credited with improving circulation to the lungs, which benefits those with asthma and bronchitis.

> NUTRITIONAL COMPOSITION One teaspoon of ground cardamom provides 6 calories, 1.4 g carbohydrate, 0.2 g protein, 0.1 g fat, 0.6 g dietary fiber, 22 mg potassium, 4 mg phosphorus, 8 mg calcium, 0.28 mg iron, 5 mg magnesium, 0.01 mg copper, 0.15 mg zinc, and 0.56 mg manganese.

Bringing It Home

Cardamom is available in whole pods, as seeds, and as a ground spice. The flavors and nutrients last longest in the whole form, and they are most quickly released from the ground version. For best results, use whole cardamom pods and crack them right before cooking. If a recipe calls for ground cardamom, you can break open the whole pods and grind the tiny brown and black cardamom seeds yourself with either a spice grinder or a mortar and pestle.

Cardamom Spiced Chicken

See Safe Handling of Poultry on page 211.

Marinade

3 tablespoons honey
1 tablespoon sherry
1 teaspoon ground cardamom seeds
1 teaspoon freshly ground pepper

Chicken

6 chicken breast halves
3 tablespoons olive oil
1 lemon, thinly sliced
  Salt and pepper

- Preheat oven to 350°F.
- *To prepare the marinade:* In a small saucepan, warm the honey. Stir in the sherry, cardamom, and pepper.
- *To prepare the chicken:* Put the chicken pieces into a large bowl. Brush the chicken with marinade, using just enough marinade to coat it; reserve the rest of the marinade. Cover with plastic wrap and let sit at room temperature for 30 minutes.
- Heat the olive oil in a large frying pan over medium-high heat. Sear the chicken, skin side down, until golden.
- Line a roasting pan with lemon slices and lay the chicken on top. Brush with the marinade and season with salt and pepper. Place in the oven and bake until done, approximately 15 minutes. Let rest for 10 minutes. Serve.
- NOTE This dish is delicious served over brown rice or whole wheat couscous.

YIELD 6 servings

NUTRITION ANALYSIS PER SERVING 229.8 calories, 11.1 g carbohydrate, 27.5 g protein, 8.3 g fat, 1 g dietary fiber

182 Chamomile

Benefits

Chamomile is used primarily to treat stomach cramping and pain, including menstrual cramping and diarrhea. Aside from the treatment of aches and pains, doctors and researchers have found that chamomile can be used effectively to treat skin and eye problems, mood disorders, and even the flu.

For stomach problems, prepare a soothing chamomile tea using a mixture of one ounce of chamomile, two thirds of an ounce of peppermint, one ounce of caraway seeds, and two thirds of an ounce of angelica. For a cup of tea, add one teaspoon of this mixture to one cup of hot water. Steep for 10 minutes, strain, and drink.

For skin problems, prepare a healing chamomile tea using a mixture of one ounce of chamomile, one ounce of dandelion, and two thirds of an ounce of fennel. For a cup of tea, add one teaspoon of this mixture to one cup of hot water. Steep for 5 to 10 minutes, strain, and drink. This tea helps stimulate metabolic activity that aids in the healing of inflammatory skin conditions.

Chamomile is mild enough for everyday use, and almost everyone can enjoy it—unless you have a ragweed allergy, in which case it should be avoided.

NUTRITIONAL COMPOSITION One cup of brewed chamomile herbal tea provides 2 calories, 0.5 g carbohydrate, 0 g protein, 0 g fat, 0 g dietary fiber, and 2 mg sodium.

Bringing It Home

Choose organic chamomile tea, which is a perfect, all-natural sleep aid. Store chamomile tea in an airtight container away from heat, light, and moisture. Do not refrigerate or freeze.

Livit Recipe

Perk It Up Chamomile Tea

1 cup water	⅛ teaspoon cardamom
3 teaspoons freshly grated ginger root	⅛ teaspoon allspice
1 teaspoon coriander seeds	2 teaspoons chamomile
¼ teaspoon cinnamon	

- In a small saucepan, heat the water with the ginger, coriander seeds, cinnamon, cardamom, and allspice, stirring to combine. Simmer for 20 minutes. Remove from heat and add chamomile. Steep for another 10 minutes. Strain. Serve hot.
- NOTE The chamomile may be relaxing, but all that fresh ginger will perk you right back up.

YIELD 1 serving

NUTRITION ANALYSIS PER SERVING 3 calories, 0 g carbohydrate, 0 g protein, 0 g fat, 0 g dietary fiber

183 Chia Seeds

Benefits

Everybody has seen the silly "Chia Pet," a ceramic pot for growing chia greens. What you may not have known is that chia is a SuperFood! Chia seeds form a gel in the stomach that slows the conversion of carbohydrates to sugar, and the protein in the gel helps build muscle and other tissues. Chia also provides the trace mineral boron, which aids in the absorption of calcium. The seeds are high in omega-3 fatty acids and anti-inflammatories.

NUTRITIONAL COMPOSITION One tablespoon of chia seeds provides 40 calories, 5 g carbohydrate, 2 g protein, 4 g fat, 5 g dietary fiber, 6 mg vitamin C, 76 mg calcium, 1.8 mg iron, 150 mg phosphorus, 38 mg magnesium, 85 mg potassium, 2406 mg omega-3 fatty acids, 792 mg omega-6 fatty acids, 294 mg omega-9 fatty acids.

Bringing It Home

Chia seeds may be eaten raw or used in a number of dishes. Raw, they are an excellent source of dietary fiber and omega-3 fatty acids. They must be stored in a dry place.

Chia seeds may be ground into pinole, a coarse flour that can be used for porridge or baked goods. They may also be soaked in fruit juice or water to make a dish that is known as chia fresca in Mexico. Chia seeds' nutty flavor makes them a perfect addition to soups, sauces, smoothies, and baked goods. Enjoy them as a snack for a satiating boost, or sprinkle them on cereal, yogurt, or salads. An easy, balanced snack can be made by mixing one tablespoon of chia seeds with two tablespoons of peanut butter and spreading it on top of two organic apple halves.

Livit Recipe

Energizing Chia Muffins

1 tablespoon chia seeds, ground
1 cup whole wheat flour OR wheat-free whole grain flour
1 tablespoon cinnamon
¼ teaspoon nutmeg
2 teaspoons baking soda
½ teaspoon sea salt
1 can (16 ounces) organic 100% pumpkin
2 egg whites
⅓ cup sunflower oil OR safflower oil
½ cup agave nectar
1 tablespoon vanilla extract
1 cup chopped walnuts

- Preheat oven to 350°F.
- Line a muffin tin with paper baking cups.
- In a medium bowl, mix the chia seeds, flour, cinnamon, nutmeg, baking soda, and salt.
- In a separate bowl, mix the pumpkin, egg whites, oil, agave nectar, and vanilla.
- Fold the pumpkin mixture and walnuts into the flour mixture until the dry ingredients are just moistened. Be careful not to overmix.
- Spoon the mixture into muffin cups and bake for 25 to 30 minutes, or until a toothpick inserted into the center of a muffin comes out clean. Remove muffins from the tin and cool them on a wire rack.
- NOTE If you buy whole chia seeds, you can grind them yourself with a spice grinder or a mortar and pestle.

YIELD 12 muffins

NUTRITION ANALYSIS PER SERVING 226.9 calories, 24.8 g carbohydrate, 4.7 g protein, 13.3 g fat, 4.2 g dietary fiber

184 Cinnamon

Benefits

Cinnamon is one of the most popular herbs and spices. In one study, eating a gram of cinnamon per day appeared to reduce fasting blood glucose concentration and improve the blood lipid profile in patients with type 2 diabetes.

Cinnamon is also rich in anti-inflammatory compounds. In traditional medicine, it is recommended to treat indigestion, nausea, vomiting, upset stomach, diarrhea, and flatulence.

> **NUTRITIONAL COMPOSITION** One teaspoon of ground cinnamon provides 5 calories, 1.6 g carbohydrate, 0.1 g protein, 0.1 g fat, 1.1 g dietary fiber, 5 IU vitamin A, 1 mg vitamin C, 1 mcg folic acid, 10 mg potassium, 1 mg sodium, 1 mg phosphorus, 25 mg calcium, 0.76 mg iron, 1 mg magnesium, and 0.33 mg manganese.

CINNAMON ALERT!

Cinnamon—as well as cassia, which is also sold as cinnamon in the United States and is actually the more common form—has a mild anti-clotting effect in the blood, which could be beneficial. It is conceivable that too much cinnamon could cause bleeding problems, however, especially when combined with medications that "thin the blood," including aspirin. In traditional medicine, high doses are not given to pregnant women, due to possible stimulating effects on the uterus.

Bringing It Home

Most large grocery stores have a frequent turnover of cinnamon, so there's no need to worry about freshness. Once home, cinnamon is best stored in a dark, cool, dry place. Cinnamon sticks keep for two to three years, but powdered cinnamon will gradually lose its flavor and is best used within six months.

If you want to try a fun array of different cinnamons, visit a specialty spice shop.

Livit Recipe

Cinnamon Quinoa Comfort

- 1 cup organic unsweetened soy milk
- 1 cup water
- 1 cup organic red quinoa OR white quinoa, rinsed and strained
- ⅓ cup chopped pecans OR walnuts, toasted, as garnish
- 2 cups fresh organic blackberries
- ½ teaspoon ground cinnamon
- 4 teaspoons organic agave nectar

- Set toaster oven temperature to 350°F.
- In a medium saucepan, combine the milk, water, and quinoa. Bring to a boil over high heat. Reduce heat, cover, and simmer for 15 minutes, or until most of the liquid is absorbed. Remove from heat and let stand for 5 minutes.
- While the quinoa cooks, roast the pecans in the toaster oven for 5 to 6 minutes.
- Stir the blackberries and cinnamon into the quinoa. Transfer the quinoa to individual bowls. Top each serving with roasted pecans, and drizzle 1 teaspoon of agave nectar over each one. Serve.
- NOTE The nuts can also be toasted in a dry skillet over medium heat for about 3 minutes. Watch them carefully, and shake the skillet constantly so that the nuts don't burn or stick to the skillet. When browned, the nuts should be transferred to a small bowl to stop the cooking process.

YIELD 4 servings

NUTRITION ANALYSIS PER SERVING 316.8 calories, 68.7 g carbohydrate, 13.9 g protein, 13.5 g fat, 10.5 g dietary fiber

185 Cloves

Benefits

Cloves contain significant amounts of an active component called eugenol, which has been the subject of numerous health studies, including studies on the prevention of toxicity from environmental pollutants such as carbon tetrachloride, digestive tract cancers, and joint inflammation.

In the United States, eugenol extract from cloves has often been used in dentistry in conjunction with root canal therapy, temporary fillings, and general gum pain, because eugenol and other components such as beta-caryophyllene make cloves a mild anesthetic as well as an anti-bacterial agent. Because of these beneficial effects, clove oil is also found in some over-the-counter sore throat sprays and mouth washes.

The addition of clove extract to diets already high in anti-inflammatory components such as cod liver oil, with its high omega-3 fatty acid content, brings significant added benefits and, in some studies, further reduces inflammatory symptoms. Cloves contain a variety of flavonoids, including kaempferol and rhamnetin, which contribute to their anti-inflammatory and antioxidant properties.

NUTRITIONAL COMPOSITION One teaspoon of ground cloves provides 6 calories, 1.2 g carbohydrate, 0.1 g protein, 0.4 g fat, 0.7 g dietary fiber, 11 IU vitamin A, 2 mg vitamin C, 2 mcg folic acid, 22 mg potassium, 5 mg sodium, 2 mg phosphorus, 13 mg calcium, 5 mg magnesium, and 0.6 mg manganese.

Bringing It Home

Good quality whole cloves will release some of their oil when squeezed. Store cloves in a tightly sealed glass container in a cool, dark, dry place. Ground cloves will keep for about six months, while whole cloves will stay fresh for about a year. You can extend cloves' shelf life by storing them in the refrigerator.

Try piercing an onion with whole cloves and add it to soups, broths, or poaching liquids. Add ground cloves and curry powder to sautéed onions, garlic, and tofu for an Indian flair. Use ground cloves to spice up apple cider or fruit compote. Add ground cloves, walnuts, and raisins to your favorite stuffing recipe.

Livit Recipe

Aromatic Spicy Chai

¾ cup water
2 teaspoons sugar
1 whole cardamom pod
1 whole clove

2 black peppercorns
1 tablespoon black tea leaves
½ cup 1% low-fat milk, warmed

· Combine the water and sugar in a small saucepan, and bring to a boil.
· Add the cardamom pod, clove, peppercorns and tea leaves. Remove from heat and cover. Let the mixture steep for 2 to 3 minutes.
· Strain into a mug, and fill the mug with warm milk.

YIELD 1 serving

NUTRITION ANALYSIS PER SERVING 123 calories, 22 g carbohydrate, 5 g protein, 3 g fat, 4 g dietary fiber

186 Coriander and Cilantro

Benefits

Coriander is considered both an herb and a spice, since both its leaves and its seeds are used as a seasoning condiment. Fresh coriander leaves are more commonly known as cilantro; it bears a strong resemblance to Italian flat-leaf parsley. Coriander seeds have a health-supporting reputation that is high on the list of the healing spices. In parts of Europe, coriander has long been referred to as an "anti-diabetic" plant. In parts of India, it has traditionally been used for its anti-inflammatory properties. In the United States, coriander has recently been studied for its cholesterol-lowering effects.

In a study where coriander was added to the diet of diabetic mice, it helped stimulate their secretion of insulin and lowered their blood sugar. Another study demonstrated that when given to rats fed a high-fat, high-cholesterol diet, coriander lowered levels of total cholesterol and low-density lipoproteins (LDL), or "bad" cholesterol, while actually increasing levels of high-density lipoproteins (HDL), or "good" cholesterol. Research also suggests that the volatile oils found in the leaves of the coriander plant may have antimicrobial properties.

NUTRITIONAL COMPOSITION One-fourth cup of fresh coriander leaf (cilantro) provides 1 calorie, 0.1 g carbohydrate, 0.1 g protein, 0 g fat, 0.1 g dietary fiber, 111 IU vitamin A, 22 mg potassium, and 4 mg calcium.

Bringing It Home

Look for fresh whole coriander with leaves that are deep green in color, firm, crisp, and free of yellow or brown spots. Whenever possible, buy whole coriander seeds instead of ground coriander. Ground coriander loses its flavor more quickly, and coriander seeds can be easily ground with a mortar and pestle. Keep both coriander seeds and ground coriander in opaque, tightly sealed glass containers in a cool, dark, dry place. Ground coriander will keep for about four to six months, while the whole seeds will stay fresh for about one year.

Since it is highly perishable, always store fresh coriander in the refrigerator. If possible, store the coriander with its roots still attached by placing the roots in a glass of water and covering the leaves with a loosely fitting plastic bag. If the roots have been removed, wrap the coriander leaves in a damp cloth or paper towel and place them in a plastic bag. Whole coriander will last up to one week, while coriander leaves will last about three days.

Cilantro may be frozen, either whole or chopped, in airtight containers. Thaw the cilantro just before you are going to use it, since it will lose much of its crisp texture. You can put it in ice cube trays covered with either water or stock, then put the frozen cubes in a plastic zipper bag to keep in the freezer; add the "cilantro" cubes to soups or stews.

Livit Recipe

Cilantro Chicken Wraps

See Safe Handling of Poultry on page 211.

1 tablespoon safflower oil
1 small onion, chopped
2 skinless whole chicken legs (about 1 pound)
1 cup canned whole tomatoes, drained
½ cup water
½ teaspoon cayenne
1 teaspoon ground cumin
   Salt

1 English cucumber, seeded and cut lengthwise into very thin strips
3 tablespoons fresh lime juice
   Black pepper
1 firm ripe avocado, halved, peeled, pitted, and cut into ¼-inch slices
4 whole wheat flour tortillas
2 cups fresh cilantro sprigs

- Heat oil in a large, heavy saucepan over moderate heat. Add onion and chicken, and cook for 5 minutes.
- Add tomatoes, water, cayenne, and cumin to the chicken, stirring gently to combine. Simmer, covered, for 1 hour. Separate the meat from the bones, and return the chicken to the pan. Continue to simmer the chicken mixture, uncovered, for about 20 minutes, or until most of the liquid has evaporated. Add salt to taste. Cool the chicken mixture to room temperature.
- In a small bowl, toss the cucumber with 1 tablespoon of the lime juice. Season with salt and pepper.
- In a separate small bowl, toss the avocado with the remaining 2 tablespoons of lime juice. Season with salt and pepper.
- Cut one side of each tortilla to give it a straight edge and spread a bit of avocado along it (this will help hold the wrap together).
- Spread one fourth of the chicken mixture across the opposite edge of the tortilla, allowing 1 inch at the bottom to keep the wrap from breaking. Top with ½ cup cilantro sprigs, one fourth of the avocado slices, and one fourth of the cucumber strips. Roll the tortilla over the chicken and seal with the avocado edge. Make three more wraps with the remaining ingredients, and arrange wraps seam-side down. Cut the wraps on a slight diagonal. Serve chilled or at room temperature.

YIELD 4 servings

NUTRITION ANALYSIS PER SERVING 286.4 calories, 34.9 g carbohydrate, 10.5 g protein, 14 g fat, 8.1 g dietary fiber

187 Cumin

Benefits

Cumin seeds are a very good source of iron, a mineral that plays many vital roles in the body. Cumin has traditionally been thought to benefit the digestive system, and scientific research is beginning to bear out cumin's age-old reputation. Research has shown that cumin may stimulate the secretion of pancreatic enzymes, compounds necessary for proper digestion and nutrient assimilation. Cumin seeds may also have anti-carcinogenic properties. In one study, cumin was shown to protect laboratory animals from developing stomach or liver tumors. This cancer-protective effect may be due to cumin's potent free radical scavenging abilities as well as the ability it has shown to enhance the liver's detoxification enzymes.

NUTRITIONAL COMPOSITION One-fourth teaspoon of ground cumin provides 3 calories, 0.2 g carbohydrate, 0.1 g protein, 0.1 g fat, 0.2 g dietary fiber, 3 IU vitamin A, 11 mg potassium, 1 mg sodium, 5 mg calcium, and 0.2 mg iron.

Bringing It Home

Whenever possible, buy whole cumin seeds instead of ground cumin. Ground cumin loses its flavor more quickly, and the whole seeds can be easily ground with a mortar and pestle. Even though dried herbs and spices are widely available in supermarkets, explore the local spice stores or ethnic markets in your area. Often, these stores feature an expansive selection of dried herbs and spices that are of superior quality and freshness compared to those offered in regular markets. As with other dried spices, try to select organically grown dried cumin, since this will give you more assurance that it has not been irradiated.

Keep cumin seeds and cumin powder in tightly sealed glass containers in a cool, dark, dry place. Ground cumin will keep for about six months, while the whole seeds will stay fresh for about a year.

Livit Recipe

Israeli Cumin Lentil Stew

1 cup lentils, sorted and rinsed
3 cups water
3 tablespoons safflower oil
2 large onions, diced
3 cloves garlic, minced
1 teaspoon ground cumin
1 cup brown rice
Salt and freshly ground black pepper

· In a large saucepan, bring the lentils and water to a boil. Cook, covered, over medium heat for about 20 minutes, or until the lentils are tender. Drain the liquid into a 4-cup measuring cup and reserve. Set the pan with the lentils aside.

· In a heavy skillet, heat the oil over medium heat. Add the onions and sauté, stirring occasionally, for about 15 minutes, or until they are well browned. Add the garlic and cumin, and sauté for 30 seconds.

· Add enough water to the reserved liquid to make 3 cups total, and add it to the lentils in the pan. Bring to a boil. Add the rice, and return it to a boil.

· Add the onion mixture to the rice and lentils. Reduce heat. Cook over low heat, covered and without stirring, for about 35 minutes, or until the rice is done. Add salt and pepper to taste. Serve hot.

YIELD 6 servings

NUTRITION ANALYSIS PER SERVING 230 calories, 34.5 g carbohydrate, 6 g protein, 7.9 g fat, 5.3 g dietary fiber

188 Dandelion

Benefits

Dandelion is rich in calcium, which is essential for the growth and strength of bones. It is rich in antioxidants like vitamin C and luteolin, which protect bones from age-related oxidant damage. Dandelion juice is a diuretic and may stimulate insulin production. Dandelion is also used as a vegetable; it's a good source of fiber. Dandelion greens are rich in vitamin C and are among the best vegetable sources of beta-carotene. They provide potassium, iron, calcium, magnesium, phosphorus, and the B vitamins thiamine and riboflavin.

> **NUTRITIONAL COMPOSITION** One-half cup of raw dandelion greens provides 45 calories, 9 g carbohydrate, 2.7 g protein, 0.49 g fat, 3.5 g dietary fiber, 4931 IU vitamin A, 35 mg vitamin C, 4.8 mg vitamin E, 273.7 mcg vitamin K, 27 mcg folic acid, 187 mg calcium, 2959 mcg beta-carotene, 0.17 mg copper, 3.1 mg iron, 36 mg magnesium, 66 mg phosphorus, 397 mg potassium, and 76 mg sodium.

DANDELION CAVEATS

Though dandelion is generally safe and gentle, some people may have an allergic reaction to the milky latex in the stem and leaves. Dandelion root should not be taken with pharmaceutical diuretics or drugs that have a diuretic action. People who are taking medications for diabetes should use dandelion root with caution, as it may intensify the effect of those drugs in lowering blood sugar. Individuals with allergies to daisies may wish to stay away from dandelion. The greens are also a source of oxalates, which can cause problems for those with kidney disease, gout, vulvar pain, rheumatoid arthritis, or other conditions that may require a low-oxalate diet.

Bringing It Home

Dandelion greens are often available in open markets and health food stores. Choose brightly colored, tender-crisp leaves. If you want to gather your own, the best time is in early spring, before the flowers bloom.

Store dandelion leaves in the refrigerator, unwashed and wrapped in damp paper towels in a plastic bag. They can be kept fresh in the refrigerator for three to five days.

Young dandelion leaves make an excellent spring salad, and the young roots are delicious when cooked. Peel the roots and add them to boiling water with a pinch of baking soda. Pour off the water, cover with fresh water, and boil again. Drain, and season with salt, pepper, and butter.

Livit Recipe

Creamy Yet Lean Dandelion Soup

1 tablespoon olive oil
2 pounds dandelion greens, trimmed, washed, and chopped (about 6 cups)
1 carrot, peeled and diced
2 large leeks, white and light parts only, cleaned and sliced
4 cups low-sodium vegetable stock
2½ cups organic 1% milk
   Salt and pepper
   Dandelion buds and/or flower petals, as garnish

- Heat the oil in a large pot over medium-high heat. Add greens, carrot, and leeks. Cook, stirring often, for 15 minutes.
- Add stock and simmer for 15 minutes. Reduce heat to medium. Whisk in milk. Continue stirring until it thickens.
- Pour the mixture into a blender jar, and puree until smooth. (Be careful, it's hot!) Add salt and pepper to taste. Pour into individual bowls, and garnish with flowers or buds. Serve.
- NOTE If using mature or bitter greens, blanch them in a pot of boiling salted water and drain, squeezing out the excess water, before chopping.
- VARIATION For a tangier soup, add Dijon mustard to taste.

YIELD 4 servings

NUTRITION ANALYSIS PER SERVING 243.1 calories, 39.2 g carbohydrate, 12.3 g protein, 6.6 g fat, 10.2 g dietary fiber

189 Endive

Benefits

Endive, which is the second growth of the chicory plant, can be pale yellow or purple in color and has a pungent, bitter flavor. Endive is a good source of potassium, calcium, magnesium, iron, zinc, B vitamins, folic acid, vitamin C, and selenium. Endive is rich in compounds that help boost the immune system, detoxify the body, promote regularity, lower the risk of cataracts, and protect the heart.

This crisp, lettuce-like vegetable makes a unique addition to salads. It can also be served as a hot side dish if steamed or sautéed.

NUTRITIONAL COMPOSITION One-half cup of chopped, raw endive provides 4 calories, 0.8 g carbohydrate, 0.3 g protein, 0.1 g fat, 0.8 g dietary fiber, 513 IU vitamin A, 2 mg vitamin C, 36 mcg folic acid, 79 mg potassium, 6 mg sodium, 7 mg phosphorus, 13 mg calcium, and 4 mg magnesium.

Bringing It Home

When selecting endive at the market, choose crisp, firmly packed heads that are white or pale yellow in color. Endive that is decidedly green has been exposed to too much light and may taste more bitter than its paler counterparts. Look for flow-pack clear film packaging, which is made specifically to protect the endive from light and prolong its shelf life.

Store endive in the vegetable drawer of your refrigerator. If it is not in a flow-pack pouch, wrap the heads in a paper towel to protect them from excess light and place them in a plastic bag.

When you are ready to use the endive, remove any torn or damaged leaves, trim the bottom, and wash each leaf. If you are using the endive raw, you may want to remove the slightly more bitter core from the head. You can do this easily by cutting the endive in half lengthwise and then cutting away the core. If you are cooking the endive, it is not necessary to remove the core, as it will soften and sweeten with cooking.

Livit Recipe

Dive into Endive Salad

4 bunches fresh small beets, with stems removed	1 teaspoon crushed dried thyme
1 tablespoon olive oil	½ cup safflower oil
2 tablespoons lemon juice	Salt and pepper
2 tablespoons apple cider vinegar	1 pound spring lettuce mix
1 tablespoon honey OR agave nectar	2 medium heads endive
1½ tablespoons Dijon mustard	1 cup crumbled feta cheese

- Preheat oven to 450°F.
- Put beets and oil into a 9″ × 13″ baking dish. Turn the beets with a spoon to coat. Roast for about 45 minutes, or until tender. Allow beets to cool enough to be handled, then peel and dice them.
- To make the dressing, put the lemon juice, vinegar, honey, mustard, and thyme into a blender jar, and pulse to combine. Continue blending the ingredients, adding the oil gradually until the dressing is emulsified. Add salt and pepper to taste.
- Put lettuce mix into a salad bowl. Add dressing, and toss gently to coat.
- Rinse the endive, tear off whole leaves, and pat them dry. Arrange 3 leaves on each plate. Top the leaves with dressed salad greens, diced beets, and feta cheese. Serve.

YIELD 8 servings

NUTRITION ANALYSIS PER SERVING 297.2 calories, 24.7 g carbohydrate, 7.8 g protein, 20 g fat, 9.6 g dietary fiber

190 Fennel

Benefits

Fennel is a popular vegetable, spice, and flavoring, as well as an ingredient in traditional medicines. It is one of the key flavorings in absinthe. Fennel contains an anise-flavored compound called anethole, which is a potent antimicrobial against bacteria, yeast, and fungi. A lab study has shown anethole to be effective against some kinds of intestinal worms. Anethole may have some analgesic, or pain-reducing, effects and some anti-convulsant effects as well. Anethole also acts as a phytoestrogen.

> **NUTRITIONAL COMPOSITION** One cup of raw fennel bulb slices provides 27 calories, 6.3 g carbohydrate, 1.1 g protein, 0.1 g fat, 2.7 g dietary fiber, 117 IU vitamin A, 10 mg vitamin C, 23 mcg folic acid, 360 mg potassium, 45 mg sodium, 44 mg phosphorus, 43 mg calcium, and 15 mg magnesium.

FENNEL IN PREGNANCY

Because fennel's phytoestrogen effects have not been thoroughly studied, women who are pregnant should avoid over-consumption of fennel or using it as a supplement. Too much fennel may lead to breathing problems or irregular heartbeat.

Bringing It Home

Look for good quality fennel with bulbs that are clean, firm, and solid, and without signs of splitting, bruising, or spotting. Fennel bulbs should be whitish or pale green in color. Choose stalks that are relatively straight and closely packed around the bulb. Stalks and leaves should be green in color. Stay away from any flowering buds, because this indicates that the vegetable is past maturity. Fresh fennel has a fragrant aroma, smelling subtly of licorice or anise. It is usually available from autumn through early spring.

Store fresh fennel in the refrigerator crisper, where it will stay fresh for about four days. It is best to consume fennel soon after purchasing, since it tends to lose flavor as it ages. Although fresh fennel can be blanched and frozen, it seems to lose much of its flavor during this process. If dried fennel seeds are stored in an airtight container in a cool, dry location, they will keep for about six months. They will stay fresh somewhat longer if stored in the refrigerator.

Livit Recipe

Fennel Moist Salmon

1 fennel bulb (about 1 pound), trimmed and thinly sliced
2 carrots, peeled and julienned
4 skinless salmon fillets, 1½ inches thick (about 6 ounces each)
1 lemon, thinly sliced
1 tablespoon chopped fresh chives
½ cup white wine
2 tablespoons olive oil
  Sea salt
  Ground pepper

- Preheat oven to 400°F.
- Blanch fennel and carrot in boiling water for 4 minutes. Drain and rinse with cold water.
- Cut 4 pieces of parchment paper, approximately 12″ × 16″ each, and distribute the fennel and carrot evenly on each piece. Place a salmon fillet on each mound of the vegetable mixture. Top each fillet with lemon slices and chives. Drizzle each fillet with wine and olive oil, and sprinkle with salt and pepper to taste.
- Fold parchment to enclose salmon in a package, and twist ends to secure. Put the salmon packages on a baking sheet and bake for 14 to 16 minutes. Open a package to check doneness. Salmon is done when its center is slightly translucent.

YIELD 4 servings

NUTRITION ANALYSIS PER SERVING 242.6 calories, 10.3 g carbohydrate, 23.1 g protein, 10.8 g fat, 4 g dietary fiber

191 Fenugreek

Benefits

Fenugreek seeds are hard, yellowish brown, and angular. Both Indian Ayurvedic medicine and traditional Chinese medicine recommend it to treat arthritis, asthma, and bronchitis, and to improve digestion, maintain a healthy metabolism, increase libido and male potency, cure skin problems (such as wounds, rashes, and boils), treat sore throat, and cure acid reflux.

Fenugreek also has a long history of use for the treatment of reproductive disorders—to induce labor, to treat hormonal disorders, to help with breast enlargement, and to reduce menstrual pain.

Recent studies have shown that fenugreek helps lower blood glucose and cholesterol levels, and may have potential against diabetes and heart disease.

NUTRITIONAL COMPOSITION One teaspoon fenugreek seed provides 13 calories, 2.3 g carbohydrate, 0.9 g protein, 0.3 g fat, 1 g dietary fiber, 2 IU vitamin A, 2 mcg folic acid, 31 mg potassium, 3 mg sodium, 12 mg phosphorus, 7 mg calcium, 1.34 mg iron, and 8 mg magnesium.

Bringing It Home

Uncooked fenugreek seeds have an unpleasant, bitter taste, so the seeds are usually lightly roasted. Since they are extremely hard, fenugreek seeds are worth buying already ground—even in Indian curries, it is usually used ground.

Livit Recipe

Spiced-Up Dhal

A spicy and nutritious accompaniment to curries.

> 1½ cups lentils, sorted and rinsed
> 4 cups water
> 2 dried chilies, left whole
> ¼ teaspoon turmeric
>   Salt, optional
> 1 tablespoon safflower oil
> 1 teaspoon water
> ½ teaspoon cumin seeds
> 1 cup chopped onions
> 1 teaspoon freshly grated ginger root
> 1 cup finely chopped fenugreek leaves
> 4 cups chopped fresh spinach
> 1 lemon, juice only

· Put the lentils into a medium saucepan, and cover with the 4 cups of water. Add the dried chilies, turmeric, and salt, if using. Bring to a boil. Reduce heat and simmer, stirring often, until lentils are very tender, or about 35 minutes.

· About 10 minutes before the lentils are completely cooked, heat the oil in a small saucepan with the 1 teaspoon of water, and add the cumin seeds. Cook for 10 to 15 seconds. Stir in onions and ginger, and cook for an additional 7 minutes, or until the onions are softened and translucent. Add the fenugreek and spinach, and continue cooking for an additional 5 minutes.

· Once the lentils are cooked, discard the chilies. Add the onion-spinach mixture and lemon juice to the lentils. Add salt to taste. Serve.

· NOTE This dish is delicious served on top of brown or wild rice, or with a whole wheat roll.

YIELD 6 servings

NUTRITION ANALYSIS PER SERVING 111.4 calories, 15.1 g carbohydrate, 5.7 g protein, 3 g fat, 5.5 g dietary fiber

Benefits

Garlic is a member of the onion family, all of whose members are rich in a variety of powerful sulfur-containing compounds, including thiosulfinates, sulfoxides and dithiins—compounds responsible both for garlic's characteristically pungent odor and for its health-promoting effects.

Garlic is an excellent source of manganese, a very good source of vitamin B_6 and vitamin C, and a good source of selenium, though you probably won't eat enough of it for it to serve as a significant source of any of these nutrients.

The sulfur compounds in garlic and other alliums appear to stimulate the production of nitric oxide in the linings of blood vessels, which helps to relax them and may lower blood pressure. Garlic is also rich in antioxidants.

> **NUTRITIONAL COMPOSITION** Three cloves of raw garlic provide 13 calories, 3 g carbohydrate, 0.6 g protein, 0 g fat, 0.2 g dietary fiber, 3 mg vitamin C, 36 mg potassium, 2 mg sodium, 14 mg phosphorus, 16 mg calcium, and 2 mg magnesium.

Bringing It Home

For maximum flavor and nutritional benefits, always purchase fresh garlic. Although garlic in flake, powder, or paste form may be more convenient, you will derive less culinary and health benefits from these forms. Purchase garlic that is plump and has unbroken skin. Gently squeeze the garlic bulb between your fingers to make sure it feels firm and is not damp. Stay clear of garlic that is soft, shriveled, or moldy, or that has begun to sprout.

It is not necessary to refrigerate garlic. Some people freeze peeled garlic; however, this process reduces its flavor profile and changes its texture.

Livit Recipe

Garlicky Green Beans

   1 pound organic fresh green beans
   2 teaspoons safflower oil OR canola oil
   1 small onion, chopped (about ⅓ cup)
   2 cloves garlic, minced
   1 tablespoon all-purpose flour
   2 teaspoons paprika
   1 can (16 ounces) coarsely chopped tomatoes, drained (reserve liquid)

• In a steamer pot, steam the green beans for 5 minutes, then rinse with cold water to stop the cooling process. Set aside.

- Heat the oil in a medium saucepan. Add the onion and garlic, and sauté for about 3 minutes. Stir in the flour and paprika, and cook for 1 minute. Add the reserved liquid from the canned tomatoes, and stir until the mixture is slightly thickened. Add the tomatoes and green beans. Cook over medium heat, stirring well, for about 2 minutes, or until the beans are tender. Serve.
- VARIATION Frozen green beans can also be used.

YIELD 4 servings

NUTRITION ANALYSIS PER SERVING 94.6 calories, 15.3 g carbohydrate, 3.5 g protein, 2.4 g fat, 5.2 g dietary fiber

193 Ginger

Benefits

Historically, ginger has a long tradition of being very effective in alleviating symptoms of stomach discomfort. In herbal medicine, ginger is regarded as an excellent carminative (a substance that helps eliminate intestinal gas) and intestinal spasmolytic (a substance that relaxes and soothes the intestinal tract). Modern scientific research has revealed that ginger possesses numerous therapeutic properties, including antioxidant effects, an ability to inhibit the formation of inflammatory compounds, and direct anti-inflammatory effects. The possibility that gingerol, the main active component in ginger and the one responsible for its distinctive flavor, may inhibit the growth of human colorectal cancer cells was suggested in research presented at a major meeting of cancer experts in 2003.

> NUTRITIONAL COMPOSITION One-fourth cup of fresh ginger slices provides 17 calories, 3.6 g carbohydrate, 0.4 g protein, 0.2 g fat, 0.5 g dietary fiber, 3 mcg folic acid, 100 mg potassium, 3 mg sodium, 6 mg phosphorus, 4 mg calcium, and 10 mg magnesium.

Bringing It Home

Choose fresh ginger over the dried form of the spice whenever possible, since it is not only superior in flavor but also contains higher levels of gingerol and ginger's active protease (its anti-inflammatory compound). Fresh ginger root is sold in the produce section of markets. Choose firm ginger root that is smooth and free of mold. Ginger is generally available in two forms, either young or mature. Mature ginger, the more widely available type, has a tough skin that requires peeling. Young ginger, usually only available in Asian markets, does not need to be peeled. As with other dried spices, when purchasing dried ginger, try to select organically grown ginger that is less likely to have been irradiated.

Fresh ginger can be stored in the refrigerator for up to three weeks if it is left unpeeled. Store unpeeled ginger in the freezer for up to six months. Keep ground ginger in a tightly sealed glass container in a cool, dark, dry place. If stored in the refrigerator, it will last about a year.

Ginger is also available in several other forms, including crystallized, candied, and even pickled ginger.

Livit Recipe

Kim's Chilled Ginger-Peach Soup

6 medium peaches
3 cups water
2 teaspoons cinnamon
1 piece ginger, 3 inches long, cut into large slices
1 teaspoon ground cloves
¼ cup honey
   Pinch of salt
¼ cup fresh ginger juice

- Bring a large pot of water to a boil. Submerge peaches, whole, in the boiling water for 2 minutes, or until soft. Drain water. Allow the peaches to cool enough to be handled, then remove the skin and pit, and chop into ½-inch pieces.

- Put 3 cups of water into a medium saucepan. Add the chopped peaches, cinnamon, ginger, cloves, honey, and salt. Bring to a boil over high heat. Reduce heat. Simmer for 10 minutes, stirring occasionally. Turn off heat, cover, and let steep for 15 minutes. Remove the slices of ginger.

- Pour the rest of the peach mixture into a blender jar, adding ginger juice to taste. Process until smooth. Pour the mixture into a large container and refrigerate for at least 2 hours, until completely chilled. Serve cold.

YIELD 6 servings

NUTRITION ANALYSIS PER SERVING 97.6 calories, 24.1 g carbohydrate, 0.9 g protein, 0.2 g fat, 2.6 g dietary fiber

194 Green Tea and White Tea

Benefits

Green tea is light in color because of incomplete fermentation of the leaf. White tea is tea whose leaves are picked before they open fully, when the buds are still covered with fine, white hairs. That, of course, is why it's called "white" tea. Green tea and white tea come from the same plant, the tea plant *Camellia sinensis*. The main difference between the two types of tea is that the white tea leaves are harvested at a younger age than the green tea leaves. They both undergo very little processing, though white tea is the least processed of any tea. Green tea is only partly fermented, and white tea is not fermented at all. By contrast, black tea is fully fermented. Because they are so gently treated, green tea and white tea retain higher amounts of their beneficial antioxidants.

Studies have shown that white tea has a concentration of antioxidants that is three times higher than that of green tea. White tea contains less caffeine than green tea, about 15 milligrams per serving compared to 20 milligrams per serving for green tea. If caffeine tends to make you jittery, white tea may be the better choice. White tea has the highest antioxidant content of any tea, which for many is the main reason for drinking it. As a comparison, one cup of white tea contains approximately twelve times as many antioxidants as fresh orange juice. Active ingredients of green tea and white tea, including catechin, theanine, and saponin, work to scavenge active oxygen species in the blood, helping protect the body from harmful microorganisms.

NUTRITIONAL COMPOSITION One fusion green and white tea bag provides 0 calories, 0 g carbohydrate, 0 g protein, 0 g fat, and 0 g dietary fiber.

Bringing It Home

Fresh tea has a green luster and a tight shape, with a natural aroma like orchid or jasmine. Its tea liquor is emerald green or golden, with a hint of bitterness and a lasting sweet aftertaste.

Keep fresh tea in a cool, dry place.

Livit Recipe

White Tea Smoothie

1½ cups frozen fruit (raspberries, strawberries, blueberries, blackberries)
  1 banana, peeled, frozen, and cut into chunks
  ¾ cup nonfat milk OR soy milk OR plain yogurt
  ½ cup brewed white tea
  ½ cup pomegranate juice

• Put frozen fruit, banana, milk, tea, and pomegranate juice into a blender jar. Cover and blend until smooth. Serve immediately.

YIELD 2 servings

NUTRITION ANALYSIS PER SERVING 174.5 calories, 40 g carbohydrate, 4.7 g protein, 0.9 g fat, 5.1 g dietary fiber

195 Horseradish

Benefits

Horseradish is a member of the Brassica family, like broccoli and Brussels sprouts. Like other Brassica, horseradish contains significant amounts of glucosinolates—compounds that have been shown to increase the liver's ability to detoxify carcinogens and that may suppress the growth of cancerous tumors. But horseradish is especially rich in these compounds, providing ten times as many of them as broccoli does.

Horseradish is also said to aid digestion and contains compounds known to fight pathogens in food, such as Listeria, E. coli and Staphylococcus aureus.

> **NUTRITIONAL COMPOSITION** One tablespoon of prepared horseradish provides 6 calories, 1.4 g carbohydrate, 0.2 g protein, 0 g fat, 0.5 g dietary fiber, 44 mg potassium, 14 mg sodium, 5 mg phosphorus, and 9 mg calcium.

Bringing It Home

Fresh horseradish root is available year-round in most markets, but its prime season is in the spring. The roots are usually sold in two-inch long sections (although the whole root can be 20 inches long), measuring one to two inches in diameter. Choose firm roots that have no mold and no soft or green spots. Avoid older roots that look shriveled and dry—and those that may even have begun to sprout. The freshest horseradish is white inside, though you may have to brush the dirt off the end of a section to be able to tell!

To store horseradish root, wash it, pat dry, and put it in a plastic zipper bag in the refrigerator. It will keep for several months. Prepared horseradish also needs to be well-sealed and kept cold.

Bottled prepared horseradish is readily available in the refrigerated condiment section of grocery stores. Prepared horseradish is preserved in vinegar and salt. A red variety of horseradish gets its color from beet juice. Dried horseradish that must be reconstituted with water or other liquid before using is also available in many markets.

Livit Recipe

Popeye's Power Mashed Potatoes

4 large potatoes (Idaho or russet), peeled and halved
⅔ cup low-sodium vegetable broth
2 cups chopped, organic fresh spinach

2 tablespoons prepared horseradish
1 tablespoon Dijon mustard
Salt and freshly ground black pepper

- In a large pot of water, bring the potatoes to a boil over high heat. Reduce heat, and simmer until the potatoes are tender, about 30 minutes (depending on the size of the potatoes). Drain. Transfer the potatoes to a large bowl.
- In the same pot, bring the broth to a boil. Reduce heat, allowing it to simmer.
- Mash the potatoes with a fork. Slowly add broth to the potatoes until they reach the desired consistency.
- Steam the spinach for 2 minutes, then drain it well. Add the spinach to the mashed potatoes. Fold in the horseradish and mustard. Add salt and pepper to taste. Serve.

YIELD 4 servings

NUTRITION ANALYSIS PER SERVING 297.4 calories, 66.4 g carbohydrate, 8 g protein, 0.4 g fat, 8.9 g dietary fiber

196 Marjoram

Benefits

Marjoram is an herb with aromatic leaves. The flavonoids in marjoram have sedation qualities that help relieve insomnia, tension headaches, and migraines. They may promote a healthy heart and healthy arteries by preventing cholesterol buildup and improving blood circulation. It is also thought that they help individuals with Alzheimer's disease.

Marjoram has anti-inflammatory properties that can be beneficial for both internal and external use. It alleviates aches and pains and, when used externally, aids in the reduction of toothaches, muscular pain, bruises, arthritis, sprains, and stiff joints. Used internally, it eases severe stomach cramps, spasms, and painful menstruation.

> NUTRITIONAL COMPOSITION One teaspoon of dried marjoram provides 3 calories, 0.6 g carbohydrate, 0.1 g protein, 0.1 g fat, 0.4 g dietary fiber, 81 IU vitamin A, 1 mg vitamin C, 3 mcg folic acid, 15 mg potassium, 1 mg sodium, 3 mg phosphorus, 20 mg calcium, and 3 mg magnesium.

Bringing It Home

Marjoram is considered to be one of the rare herbs whose flavor intensifies when dried. When choosing a dried herb like marjoram, the best test is smell—the fragrance should be strong. If you're buying it in a sealed container where you can't get a whiff, the next best test is color—the herb should still be green, not gray or beige. Although herbs are usually sold in clear bags or bottles, it's important to keep them away from light, so consider transferring your marjoram to a dark, tightly sealed container.

Marjoram is excellent in stuffing for chicken and turkey or as an attractive garnish for bean and pea soups. It enhances the flavor of carrot and squash when cooked with them. It is also used in homemade sausages and meats that are to be cured or smoked. Its soothing herbal flavor can be enjoyed as a tea by pouring water over a few sprigs of marjoram.

Livit Recipe

Quick Chicken Marjoram

2 tablespoons olive oil
4 chicken thighs
1 teaspoon seasoned salt
1 large onion, halved and sliced
1 teaspoon marjoram leaves

- In a large nonstick skillet, heat the oil over medium-high heat. Sprinkle the chicken thighs with seasoned salt, and place them in the skillet, skin side down. Cover, and cook for 5 minutes.
- Turn the chicken pieces. Add the onion, and sprinkle marjoram over the top. Cover, and cook over medium heat for an additional 15 to 20 minutes, or until the onion is soft and the internal juices of the chicken run clear. Serve immediately.
- NOTE For a balanced meal, serve with steamed broccoli and roasted potatoes with the skin on.

YIELD 4 servings

NUTRITION ANALYSIS PER SERVING 156.4 calories, 3.3 g carbohydrate, 14 g protein, 9.5 g fat, 0.7 g dietary fiber

197 Mint

Benefits

Mint is a powerful antioxidant that contains many vitamins and minerals. This fresh herb is rich in vitamins A, C, and B_{12}, thiamine, folic acid, and riboflavin, as well as the minerals manganese, copper, potassium, iron, calcium, zinc, phosphorus, fluoride, and selenium.

Mint has been used for centuries to aid digestion and relieve indigestion. The chemical compound menthol, derived from peppermint oil, is well known for its therapeutic effect on the chest and respiratory system. It has also shown potential to inhibit the formation of cancerous cells and the growth of bacteria and fungus.

Peppermint oil is rich in monoterpene perillyl alcohol, which has shown potential against pancreatic, mammary, and liver tumors in animals.

NUTRITIONAL COMPOSITION Two tablespoons of fresh spearmint provides 4.9 calories, 0.9 g carbohydrate, 0.4 g protein, 0.1 g fat, 0.8 g dietary fiber, 456 IU vitamin A, 11.8 mcg folic acid, 7.1 mg magnesium, 6.8 mg phosphorus, 51.5 mg potassium, and 3.4 mg sodium.

COMPARING SPEARMINT AND PEPPERMINT

Peppermint's flavor comes from its menthol content. Spearmint's flavor is mostly due to carvone.

Spearmint's light, sweet taste is enjoyable, but it is peppermint with its menthol that has played a role in traditional medicines.

Peppermint's menthol is a mild anesthetic and it appears to aid digestion. Spearmint contains no menthol and therefore has neither of those properties.

Peppermint oil is thought to ease tension headaches, altitude sickness, and congestion. Spearmint oil is of some use in repelling mosquitoes.

Bringing It Home

Whenever possible, choose fresh mint over the dried form of the herb. The leaves of fresh mint should look vibrant and be a rich green color. They should be free of dark spots and yellowing.

To store fresh mint leaves, carefully wrap them in a damp paper towel and place them inside a loosely closed plastic bag for storing in the refrigerator, where they will stay fresh for several days. Dried mint should be kept in a tightly sealed glass container in a cool, dark, dry place, where it will stay fresh for 9 to 12 months.

Add chopped mint leaves to scrambled eggs and omelets. Be sure to add the mint toward the end of cooking eggs, because too much heat can make the mint turn bitter. Fresh mint leaves are a great addition to salads and as garnish for cool drinks and fruit desserts. For added flavor in vegetable dishes, try adding fresh mint leaves to the water when potatoes, peas, carrots, corn, or green beans are boiling.

Livit Recipe

Minted Rice

1 tablespoon safflower oil
2 whole cloves
2 slices fresh ginger root (1-inch diameter)
1 cinnamon stick
1 bay leaf

2½ cups water
1 cup brown rice
1 tablespoon finely chopped
    fresh mint leaves

- Heat the oil in a medium saucepan over medium heat. Add the cloves, ginger, cinnamon, and bay leaf. Cook, stirring constantly, for 2 minutes. Add the water, and bring to a boil. Stir in the rice, and return to a boil. Once the water is boiling, reduce heat. Cover, and simmer gently for about 40 minutes, or until the liquid has been absorbed. Remove from heat.
- Stir in the mint, cover, and let stand for 5 minutes. Fluff the rice with a fork, and remove the cloves, ginger root, cinnamon stick, and bay leaf. Serve.

YIELD 4 servings

NUTRITION ANALYSIS PER SERVING 177 calories, 36 g carbohydrate, 5 g protein, 3 g fat, 3 g dietary fiber

198 Rosemary

Benefits

Rosemary, a versatile and much-loved green herb, has recently shown potential against cancer and age-related skin damage. Caffeic acid and rosmarinic acid, which are potent antioxidant and anti-inflammatory agents, are believed to be the active elements.

These two natural acids appear to safeguard a protective protein called Hsp70, which itself reduces damage from stress and toxins. Rosemary extract may also inactivate toxins and help eliminate them from your liver before they can inflict any serious damage.

NUTRITIONAL COMPOSITION One tablespoon of dried rosemary provides 10.8 calories, 2.1 g carbohydrate, 0.2 g protein, 0.5 g fat, 1.4 g dietary fiber, 102 IU vitamin A, 2 mg vitamin C, 10 mcg folic acid, 41.6 mg calcium, 1 mg iron, 7.1 mg magnesium, 2.3 mg phosphorus, 31 mg potassium, and 1.6 mg sodium.

ROSEMARY WARNING!

Pregnant women should not take rosemary extract. In addition, you should not take rosemary supplements if you suffer from high blood pressure or epilepsy.

Otherwise, the recommended dosage is two 400 mg rosemary capsules up to three times a day.

Bringing It Home

Whenever possible, choose fresh rosemary over the dried form. The sprigs of fresh rosemary should look vibrantly fresh and should be a deep sage green in color, free of yellow or dark spots.

Fresh rosemary should be stored in the refrigerator either in its original packaging or wrapped in a slightly damp paper towel. To freeze rosemary, put it in ice cube trays covered with either water or stock, then put the frozen cubes in a plastic zipper bag to keep in the freezer; add the "rosemary" cubes to soups or stews. Dried rosemary should be kept in a tightly sealed container in a cool, dark, dry place, where it will keep fresh for about six months.

Livit Recipe

Rosemary Roasted Turkey

See Safe Handling of Poultry on page 211.

> 1 whole turkey (10 to 12 pounds)
> 6 to 8 garlic cloves, peeled
> 2 teaspoons dried rosemary, crumbled
> 1 teaspoon rubbed sage
> 2 large lemons, cut into quarters
> Vegetable oil spray

- Preheat oven to 325°F.
- Set the turkey in a **V**-shaped rack in a roasting pan.
- Mince half of the garlic cloves.
- In a small bowl, mix the dried rosemary, minced garlic, and rubbed sage.
- Working gently with your fingers, separate the skin from the breast meat, and spread the herb and garlic mixture between the skin and the meat. This allows the flavors to permeate the meat while it is cooking, carried by the fat in the skin. Rub the remainder of the mixture on the drumsticks and wings.
- Place the whole garlic cloves and the lemon pieces inside the cavity of the turkey.
- Spray the outside of the turkey with vegetable oil spray.
- Roast the turkey uncovered for the first hour, then cover with foil, making sure to cover the tips of the wings, which tend to burn. Roast for another 2½ to 3½ hours, until a meat thermometer inserted in the breast reaches 185°F. Remove the turkey from the oven. Take the lemons and garlic out of the turkey cavity and discard them.
- Let the turkey stand in a warm place for about 30 minutes before carving.
- NOTE Avoid 102 calories and 7.87 grams of fat per serving by not eating the skin.

YIELD 10 servings

NUTRITION ANALYSIS PER SERVING 394 calories, 0 g carbohydrate, 64.7 g protein, 13 g fat, 0 g dietary fiber

199 Saffron

Benefits

Saffron crocus is a flowering plant that is usually used as a spice. However, it is also used in herbal supplements. Some of the compounds in saffron may have anti-cancer activity; others may stimulate the secretion of stomach acids and can stimulate the contraction of smooth muscles (such as the uterus). Compounds in saffron may also have some effect on lowering cholesterol and triglyceride levels.

NUTRITIONAL COMPOSITION One teaspoon of saffron provides 3 calories, 0.7 g carbohydrate, 0.1 g protein, 0.1 g fat, 0 g dietary fiber, 5 IU vitamin A, 17 mg potassium, 3 mg phosphorus, and 3 mg magnesium.

Bringing It Home

Saffron is available in threads (whole stigmas) and ground. Your best bet is to go with saffron threads, because they retain their flavor longer and you can be more certain that you have purchased pure saffron.

If you cannot find saffron on your local market's spice shelves, try asking at the service desk. It is often hidden in the office to thwart would-be thieves.

Saffron threads should be crushed before using. Steep them in the cooking liquid before using. The longer you steep the saffron threads, the stronger the flavor and color. For ground saffron, lightly toast and grind the threads yourself. For maximum flavor, store saffron in an airtight container in a cool, dark place for up to six months. Saffron, like other herbs and spices, is sensitive to light, so wrap the packet in foil to protect it further. Saffron will not spoil, but it will gradually lose its flavor with age.

Livit Recipe

Saffron Rice

```
  1 clove garlic, minced
  2 leeks, both white and green parts, cleaned and thinly sliced (about 2 cups)
  2 cups water plus 1 tablespoon water
  1 teaspoon salt
1½ cups brown rice, rinsed and drained
  ½ pound button mushrooms, trimmed and cut into ½-inch slices
  1 carrot, diced
  1 teaspoon whole fennel seeds
  ¼ teaspoon saffron threads
  ½ teaspoon ground pepper
  2 tablespoons minced fresh parsley, as garnish
```

- In a pressure cooker, cook the garlic and leeks in the 1 tablespoon of water for 2 to 3 minutes, stirring often.
- Heat the 2 cups of water to the boiling point. Add salt.
- Pour the boiling water into the pressure cooker. Add the brown rice, mushrooms, carrot, fennel seeds, saffron, and pepper. Cover, lock, and immediately bring to high pressure for 25 minutes. Remove from heat and cool for 10 minutes.
- Open the cooker, stir, and transfer the rice mixture to a serving bowl. Garnish with fresh parsley. Serve.
- NOTE Older pressure cookers may require 2¼ cups of water instead of 2 cups for the cooking process.

YIELD 6 servings

NUTRITION ANALYSIS PER SERVING 211.4 calories, 44.9 g carbohydrate, 5.6 g protein, 1.6 g fat, 3.2 g dietary fiber

200 Sage

Benefits

Like rosemary, its sister herb in the mint (Labiatae) family, sage contains a variety of volatile oils; flavonoids, including apigenin, diosmetin, and luteolin; and phenolic acids, which act as anti-inflammatories. Sage has also shown potential to enhance memory.

NUTRITIONAL COMPOSITION One teaspoon of ground sage provides 3 calories, 0.6 g carbohydrate, 0.1 g protein, 0.1 g fat, 0.4 g dietary fiber, 59 IU vitamin A, 3 mcg folic acid, 11 mg potassium, 17 mg calcium, and 4 mg magnesium.

Bringing It Home

Whenever possible, choose fresh sage over the dried form. The leaves of fresh sage should look fresh and be green-gray in color. They should be free of dark spots and yellowing.

To store fresh sage leaves, carefully wrap them in a damp paper towel and place them inside a loosely closed plastic bag for storing in the refrigerator, where the sage should keep fresh for several days. Dried sage should be kept in a tightly sealed glass container in a cool, dark, dry place, where it will keep fresh for about six months.

Livit Recipe

Sage Potatoes

If you're growing fresh sage in your herb garden, this is a great way to use it.

> 4 medium potatoes, scrubbed
> 1 tablespoon olive oil
> 1 tablespoon ground sage
> 2 teaspoons paprika
> Salt and pepper

- Preheat oven to 400°F.
- Bake potatoes for 40 to 60 minutes. Allow to cool enough to be handled, then cut into small chunks, leaving the skin on.
- In a large skillet, heat the oil over medium-high heat. Add the potatoes, and sprinkle with sage and paprika. Add salt and pepper to taste. Fry, turning the potatoes occasionally, for about 20 minutes, or until the edges of the potatoes are crisp.
- NOTE Potatoes go particularly well with sage, because they both have an earthy flavor.

YIELD 6 servings

NUTRITION ANALYSIS PER SERVING 132.3 calories, 25.4 g carbohydrate, 3 g protein, 2.5 g fat, 3.5 g dietary fiber

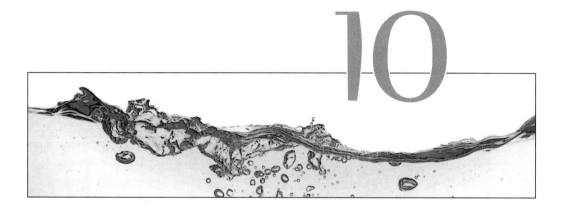

Beverages

Beverages are as important to your health as all of the SuperFoods taken together. Drink water throughout the day. Carry a water bottle with you wherever you go, and keep on sipping.

Make an effort to get your calories from food rather than drinks. To get some variety in your beverage selection without adding calories, add a wedge of lemon or lime to your water. Try sparkling waters with essence of flavor (and without artificial sweeteners) or unsweetened green, white, or herbal tea. Tea provides many more benefits than coffee in terms of antioxidants, increased immunity, and hydration—so drink tea instead of coffee as much as possible.

Add hot cocoa (made with non-alkaline cocoa) to your drink repertoire for an added immune boost from the antioxidant properties of the flavonoid catechin. It's a great way to lower your blood pressure.

If you are drinking more than one cup of coffee a day to keep yourself awake, change your strategy: Focus on getting more sleep, including daily exercise, and eating small Livit balanced meals or snacks every three to four waking hours for sustained energy.

Water

The human body is approximately 65 percent water, and it takes an average of 64 ounces of water or other liquids to replenish the water that our bodies lose each day. Not all of that water has to come from drinks, however. Many foods are also a good source of water—fruits and vegetables, for instance, are 80 to 95 percent water; meats are made up of 50 percent water; and grains, such as oats and rice, can have as much as 35 percent water.

By the time you feel thirsty, you're already dehydrated. If you make a point of drinking enough water, you may find yourself feeling more alert and energetic. Keeping well hydrated also helps keep you lean. Research shows that drinking water before meals can reduce the number of calories you consume by about 13 percent.

It's especially important to replenish the fluids that are lost due to exercise.

Before exercise: Drink about 16 ounces of cool water about 15 minutes before exercise—stay away from ice cold water.

During exercise: Drink 5 to 8 ounces of water every 15 minutes.

After exercise: Drink 16 ounces of water after exercise for every pound of body weight lost. Replace important electrolytes—sodium, potassium, chloride, and magnesium—by eating foods such as low-fat dairy products, oranges, grapefruit, and bananas.

If your exercise session lasts for more than an hour and a half, sports drinks are recommended during exercise to replenish your body fluids. Choose one that has 5 to 8 percent carbohydrate solution, or 50 to 80 calories per eight ounces. Sports drinks that contain fewer than 40 calories per eight ounces are not effective. Any beverage that contains more than 10 percent carbohydrate solution or over 100 calories per eight ounces is not recommended, because it will take longer to be absorbed and could cause abdominal cramping, nausea, bloating, and diarrhea if consumed during exercise.

You can make a sports drink that has all the benefits of those available commercially, but without the artificial colors, sweeteners, and flavors. Dissolve a tablespoon of sugar and a pinch of salt in one tablespoon of 100% orange juice (or two tablespoons of lemon juice), and then add seven and a half ounces of cold water.

Sample Livits
and Meal Plan Helper

Quick and Tasty Livits

To make meal planning easier and help you incorporate as many of the 200 Super-Foods into your diet as possible, we provide five sample daily Livit menus for each of four diets based on calorie intake: 1200, 1500, 1800, and 2000 calories per day. A **My Livit!** chart for your personal use follows page 332.

Sample 1200 Calorie Livits

The following five Livits are based on a diet of 1200 calories a day and follow the standard for nutrient sources as follows: 50 percent from carbohydrates, 20 percent from protein, and 30 percent from fat.

Sample 1200 Calorie Livit #1

TIME	MENU IDEAS
8:00 A.M. snack	1 medium (3″ in diameter) apple OR ¾ cup of fruit (CARBOHYDRATES) 1 piece of string cheese OR ¼ cup of low-fat cottage cheese OR 1 egg (PROTEIN AND FAT)
12:00 P.M. meal	1 cup of pasta OR fruit; 1 cup of steamed vegetables OR 3 cups of salad (CARBOHYDRATES) 2 ounces of grilled chicken; 1 tablespoon of salad dressing on salad (PROTEIN AND FAT)
3:00 P.M. snack	½ cup of fruit (CARBOHYDRATES) 1 ounce of nuts (peanuts and almonds, no oil added, OR soy nuts) (PROTEIN AND FAT)
7:00 P.M. meal	1 vegetarian burrito (½ cup of beans, 1 corn tortilla, 1 ounce part-skim cheese, 1 tablespoon guacamole) (CARBOHYDRATES, PROTEIN, AND FAT)
10:00 P.M. snack	5 whole wheat crackers (CARBOHYDRATES) 2 tablespoons of peanut butter (all-natural, no oils added, with most of the oil drained) OR soy nut butter (PROTEIN AND FAT)

Sample 1200 Calorie Livit #2

TIME	MENU IDEAS
7:00 A.M. snack	½ English muffin and 1 egg (CARBOHYDRATES, PROTEIN, AND FAT)
10:00 A.M. snack	Small (2″ in diameter) piece of fruit (CARBOHYDRATES) 10 almonds (PROTEIN AND FAT)
1:00 P.M. meal	2 slices of whole wheat bread; 1 cup of raw veggies (CARBOHYDRATES) 2 ounces of tuna combined with mustard and 1 teaspoon of mayonnaise (on bread) (PROTEIN AND FAT)
4:00–5:00 P.M. snack	5 whole wheat crackers (such as ak-mak crackers) (CARBOHYDRATES) 1 slice (1 ounce) of yogurt cheese (PROTEIN AND FAT)
7:30 P.M. meal	1 cup of fruit; 1 cup of steamed summer squash (zucchini, yellow squash) (CARBOHYDRATES) 2 ounces of chicken breast OR turkey breast, 1 teaspoon of extra-virgin olive oil (drizzle chicken with oil; add lemon, garlic, onion, or seasonings of choice) (PROTEIN AND FAT)
10:00 P.M. snack	¾ cup of high-fiber cereal (such as Puffins or Kashi Heart to Heart) (CARBOHYDRATES) ½ cup of organic 1% milk (PROTEIN AND FAT)

Sample 1200 Calorie Livit #3

TIME	MENU IDEAS
7:00 A.M. meal	1 slice of sprouted grain toast OR whole wheat toast and 1 teaspoon of buttery spread (such as Earth Balance); ½ cup of applesauce mixed with ½ cup of ricotta cheese, topped with cinnamon (CARBOHYDRATES, PROTEIN, AND FAT)
11:00 P.M. snack	1 apple (2″ in diameter) (CARBOHYDRATES) 2 tablespoons of all-natural peanut butter OR soy nut butter (PROTEIN AND FAT)
2:00 P.M. meal	1 cup of spinach and cheese ravioli with ½ cup of marinara sauce; 2 cups of mixed green salad with ¼ cup of garbanzo beans OR kidney beans on top and 1 tablespoon of vinaigrette dressing (CARBOHYDRATES, PROTEIN, AND FAT)
6:00 P.M. meal	Stir-fry (1 cup of sautéed vegetables [bok choy, onions, water chestnuts, mushrooms, bell peppers] and 2 ounces of lean chopped steak, mixed with ⅔ cup of brown rice and favorite sauce (sweet and sour, teriyaki, BBQ) (CARBOHYDRATES, PROTEIN, AND FAT)
9:30–10:00 P.M. snack	¾ cup of edamame (CARBOHYDRATES, PROTEIN, AND FAT)

Sample 1200 Calorie Livit #4

TIME	MENU IDEAS
7:00 A.M. snack	1 multi-grain waffle (such as Van's) with 1 teaspoon of maple syrup (CARBOHYDRATES) 1 egg OR 3 tablespoons of pre-packaged liquid egg whites (PROTEIN AND FAT)
10:00 A.M. snack	1 fruit (apple, orange, pear) (CARBOHYDRATES) ¼ cup of low-fat cottage cheese (PROTEIN AND FAT)
1:00 P.M. meal	1 large tossed salad (4 cups of baby romaine lettuce, 4 sliced strawberries, ½ cup of black beans, 1 ounce of fresh mozzarella cheese, 1 sliced avocado wedge, lemon, and seasonings of choice) (CARBOHYDRATES, PROTEIN, AND FAT)
4:00 P.M. snack	6 ounces of nonfat Greek-style yogurt (such as Fage's) with ¼ cup of granola (such as Back to Nature apple blueberry granola) (CARBOHYDRATES, PROTEIN, AND FAT)
7:00 P.M. meal	⅔ cup of brown rice; 1 cup of steamed asparagus (CARBOHYDRATES) 2 ounces of sliced grilled salmon on top of rice with soy sauce (such as Bragg's Liquid Aminos Soy Sauce) OR lemon and garlic (PROTEIN AND FAT)
10:00 A.M. snack	¾ cup of cereal (such as Puffins cereal) with ½ cup of unsweetened soy milk (CARBOHYDRATES, PROTEIN, AND FAT)

Sample 1200 Calorie Livit #5

TIME	MENU IDEAS
7:00 A.M. snack	½ cup of cooked oatmeal, ½ cup of organic 1% milk OR lactose-free milk, and 1 tablespoon of milled flaxseed (CARBOHYDRATES, PROTEIN, AND FAT)
10:00 A.M. snack	¼ cup of trail mix (2 tablespoons of dried fruit and 2 tablespoons of nuts) (CARBOHYDRATES, PROTEIN, AND FAT)
1:00 P.M. meal	1 vegetarian taco (1 corn tortilla OR whole wheat tortilla, ½ cup of black beans OR pinto beans, salsa, 1 tablespoon of guacamole, 1 ounce of shredded mozzarella cheese, ½ cup of vegetables [lettuce, fajita-style vegetables, cabbage]) (CARBOHYDRATES, PROTEIN, AND FAT)
4:00 P.M. snack	1 tangerine (CARBOHYDRATES) 1 piece of string cheese (PROTEIN AND FAT)
7:00 P.M. meal	1 whole wheat hamburger bun, ketchup, mustard, lettuce, and tomato (with turkey patty, below); side salad (CARBOHYDRATES) 1 ground turkey breast patty (2.5 ounces); vinaigrette dressing (on salad) (PROTEIN AND FAT)
10:00 P.M. snack	1 cup of warm vanilla soy milk (warmed with ¼ cup boiling water), mint herbal tea bag, and 1 teaspoon agave nectar (CARBOHYDRATES, PROTEIN, AND FAT)

Sample 1500 Calorie Livits

The following five Livits are based on a diet of 1500 calories a day and follow the standard for nutrient sources as follows: 50 percent from carbohydrates, 20 percent from protein, and 30 percent from fat.

Sample 1500 Calorie Livit #1

TIME	MENU IDEAS
9:30–10:00 A.M. meal	2 slices of whole wheat toast; ½ cup of fruit OR ½ cup 100% juice (not from concentrate) mixed with water (CARBOHYDRATES) ½ cup of ricotta cheese spread on the toast, with a sprinkle of cinnamon (PROTEIN AND FAT)
1:00 P.M. meal	⅔ cup of yams (1 small yam) OR 1 cup of baked winter squash (acorn, butternut); 3 cups of mixed green salad (CARBOHYDRATES) 3 ounces of grilled wild Alaskan salmon (PROTEIN AND FAT)
4:00 P.M. snack	1 sliced banana OR ½ cup of canned peaches in juice (not syrup) (CARBOHYDRATES) ½ cup of cottage cheese (PROTEIN AND FAT)
6:30–7:00 P.M. meal	⅔ cup of whole wheat couscous; 2 cups of steamed veggies (CARBOHYDRATES) 3 ounces of lamb tenderloin OR lean roast beef with garlic (PROTEIN AND FAT)
10:00 P.M. snack	Smoothie (1 cup of unsweetened soy milk, ¾ cup of blueberries, 1 teaspoon of honey OR agave nectar) (CARBOHYDRATES, PROTEIN, AND FAT)

Sample 1500 Calorie Livit #2

TIME	MENU IDEAS
8:00 A.M. meal	1 cup of oatmeal with 1 teaspoon of agave nectar OR honey (CARBOHYDRATES) 1 cup of soy milk, 2 tablespoons of nuts (24 almonds OR 14 walnut halves) (PROTEIN AND FAT)
11:00 A.M. snack	1 apple (CARBOHYDRATES) 1 hard-boiled egg (PROTEIN AND FAT)
2:00 P.M. meal	3 cups of salad (½ cup of black beans, ½ cup of corn, 5 crumbled organic tortilla chips, ⅛ of an avocado, and 1 tablespoon of vinaigrette dressing) (CARBOHYDRATES, PROTEIN, AND FAT)
5:00–6:00 P.M. meal	1 veggie burger (such as Dr. Praeger's Tex Mex) with 1 tablespoon of barbecue sauce (such as Robbie's) on 1 sprouted grain tortilla OR whole wheat tortilla with 1 ounce of fresh mozzarella, optional salsa; 2 cups of mixed green salad (CARBOHYDRATES, PROTEIN, AND FAT)
7:30 P.M. snack	5 whole wheat crackers (such as ak-mak) OR 18 all-bran multi-grain crackers (such as Kellogg's) (CARBOHYDRATES) ½ cup of edamame (PROTEIN AND FAT)

Sample 1500 Calorie Livit #3

TIME	MENU IDEAS
7:30 A.M. snack	1 whole wheat English muffin (CARBOHYDRATES) 1 ounce of mozzarella cheese and 1 poached egg OR 3 tablespoons of egg substitute, scrambled (on muffin) (PROTEIN AND FAT)
11:30 A.M. snack	1 cup of fruit OR 1 medium piece of fruit (CARBOHYDRATES) 6 ounces of nonfat Greek-style yogurt mixed with a drop of agave nectar and 1 tablespoon of ground flaxseed OR 6 almonds (PROTEIN AND FAT)
3:30 P.M. meal	Spaghetti Bolognese (1½ cups of whole wheat pasta, 1 cup of steamed spinach OR broccoli, ½ cup of marinara sauce) (CARBOHYDRATES) 3 ounces of ground turkey breast OR extra-lean ground beef (PROTEIN AND FAT)
7:30 P.M. snack	1 cup of high-fiber cereal (≥5 g dietary fiber per serving, such as Shredded Wheat or Clifford Crunch) with 1 cup of unsweetened soy milk OR organic 1% milk (CARBOHYDRATES, PROTEIN, AND FAT)

Sample 1500 Calorie Livit #4

TIME	MENU IDEAS
9:30–10:00 A.M. meal	1½ cups of fruit (CARBOHYDRATES) ¾ cup of cottage cheese (PROTEIN AND FAT)
1:00 P.M. meal	2 slices of whole grain bread; 3 cups of mixed green salad (CARBOHYDRATES) 3 ounces of tuna combined with 1 teaspoon of mayonnaise OR mustard; 1 teaspoon of oil-based dressing for salad (PROTEIN AND FAT)
4:00 P.M. snack	1 small piece of fruit (CARBOHYDRATES) ½ cup of edamame OR ¼ cup of soy nuts (PROTEIN AND FAT)
6:30–7:00 P.M. meal	⅔ cup of baked yams (1 small yam), 1 cup of steamed spinach OR chard OR broccoli (CARBOHYDRATES) 3 ounces of grilled chicken OR baked chicken with minced garlic, onion, lemon pepper, and seasonings of choice (PROTEIN AND FAT)
10:00 P.M. snack	1 cup of low-fat kefir (such as Lifeway Organic Lowfat Kefir Cultured Milk Smoothie) (CARBOHYDRATES, PROTEIN, AND FAT)

Sample 1500 Calorie Livit #5

TIME	MENU IDEAS
9:30–10:00 A.M. meal	1 cup of high-fiber cereal mixed with protein-based cereal (such as ½ cup of Cascadian Farm Clifford Crunch with ½ cup of Back to Nature Energy Start OR Kashi Go Lean), ½ cup of organic 1% milk, 1 tablespoon of ground flaxseed (CARBOHYDRATES, PROTEIN, AND FAT)
1:00 P.M. meal	½ cup of cooked brown rice, ½ cup of cooked black beans, 1 ounce of grated and melted white cheddar cheese, ½ cup of Mexican-style stewed tomatoes, ½ cup of steamed fajita-style vegetables (bell peppers, onions, zucchini), and ⅛ of an avocado OR 1 tablespoon of guacamole (CARBOHYDRATES, PROTEIN, AND FAT)
4:00 P.M. snack	1 small (2″ in diameter) piece of fruit (CARBOHYDRATES) 2 tablespoons of nuts (almonds, peanuts, walnuts) (PROTEIN AND FAT)
6:30–7:00 P.M. meal	1 whole wheat hamburger bun; 2 cups of raw vegetables (romaine lettuce, tomatoes, cucumbers); 1 tablespoon of barbecue sauce OR ketchup (on burger, below) (CARBOHYDRATES) 3 ounces of grilled turkey breast burger (on bun) (PROTEIN AND FAT)
10:00 P.M. snack	1 cup of Energizer Shake (see page 10) (CARBOHYDRATES, PROTEIN, AND FAT)

Sample 1800 Calorie Livits

The following five Livits are based on a diet of 1800 calories a day and follow the standard for nutrient sources as follows: 50 percent from carbohydrates, 20 percent from protein, and 30 percent from fat.

Sample 1800 Calorie Livit #1

TIME	MENU IDEAS
8:00 A.M. meal	1 whole wheat English muffin with 1 tablespoon of 100% fruit spread; ½ cup of freshly squeezed orange juice (CARBOHYDRATES) 1 egg plus ⅓ cup of egg substitute, scrambled; 1 teaspoon of organic buttery spread (such as Earth Balance) (on muffin) (PROTEIN AND FAT)
12:00 P.M. meal	1 medium apple, 1 large southwestern salad (romaine or mixed greens lettuce [4 cups], vegetables of choice [bell peppers, cucumbers, tomatoes], ½ cup of black beans, ½ cup of corn, 1 ounce of sliced fresh mozzarella, ⅛ of an avocado, 1 teaspoon of vinaigrette dressing (CARBOHYDRATES, PROTEIN, AND FAT)
4:00 P.M. snack	6 ounces of organic low-fat vanilla yogurt, 6 almonds; ½ cup of organic baby carrots (CARBOHYDRATES, PROTEIN, AND FAT)
7:30 P.M. meal	1 cup of steamed organic frozen green peas, 1½ cups of stir-fried vegetables (bok choy, mushrooms, onions, garlic, bell peppers) made with 1 teaspoon of cold-pressed high-heat safflower oil and a little water, ⅓ cup of cooked brown rice, 3 ounces of chicken breast strips stir-fried with 2 tablespoons of teriyaki sauce OR sweet and sour sauce OR low-sodium soy sauce (such as Bragg's Liquid Aminos) (CARBOHYDRATES, PROTEIN, AND FAT)

Sample 1800 Calorie Livit #2

TIME	MENU IDEAS
7:00 A.M. meal	2 corn tortillas; ½ cup of fruit on the side (CARBOHYDRATES) 1 scrambled egg, 1 ounce of melted cheese, optional salsa (on tortillas) (PROTEIN AND FAT)
10:00 A.M. snack	1 cup of fruit (CARBOHYDRATES) 2 tablespoons of nuts (walnuts, raw almonds, and peanuts combined provide complete protein and omega-3s) (PROTEIN AND FAT)
12:30 P.M. meal	⅔ cup of couscous; 3 cups of mixed green salad (CARBOHYDRATES) 3 ounces of grilled salmon OR baked salmon; 1 tablespoon of hummus (PROTEIN AND FAT)
3:00 P.M. snack	1 medium steamed artichoke, 1 teaspoon of Italian dressing OR mayonnaise for dipping (CARBOHYDRATES, PROTEIN, AND FAT)
6:30 P.M. meal	1½ cups of whole wheat pasta and ½ cup of marinara sauce mixed with 3 ounces of ground turkey breast stir-fried with 1 clove of minced garlic (CARBOHYDRATES, PROTEIN, AND FAT)

Sample 1800 Calorie Livit #3

TIME	MENU IDEAS
9:00 A.M. snack	1½ cups of Energizer Shake (see page 10) (CARBOHYDRATES, PROTEIN, AND FAT)
11:30 A.M. snack	½ bagel with 2 tablespoons of all-natural peanut butter OR soy nut butter (CARBOHYDRATES, PROTEIN, AND FAT)
2:00 P.M. meal	1½ cups of fruit; 4 cups of salad with 2 tablespoons of vinaigrette dressing and 3 ounces of grilled salmon (CARBOHYDRATES, PROTEIN, AND FAT)
6:00 P.M. meal	1 cup of pasta OR ⅔ cup of brown rice and 1½ cups of steamed veggies (broccoli, zucchini, collard greens) (CARBOHYDRATES)
	3 ounces of grilled chicken breast OR turkey breast (PROTEIN AND FAT)
9:00 P.M. snack	1 cup of fruit (CARBOHYDRATES)
	½ cup of cottage cheese (PROTEIN AND FAT)

Sample 1800 Calorie Livit #4

TIME	MENU IDEAS
9:00 A.M. snack	1 cup of cooked oatmeal made with 1 cup of unsweetened soy milk and 1 tablespoon of ground flaxseed (CARBOHYDRATES, PROTEIN, AND FAT)
11:30 A.M. snack	1 cup of raspberries OR blackberries mixed with ½ cup of ricotta cheese, sprinkled with cinnamon and 1 teaspoon of agave nectar (CARBOHYDRATES, PROTEIN, AND FAT)
2:00 P.M. meal	1 vegetarian burrito (1 whole wheat tortilla, 1 cup of black beans OR pinto beans, salsa, 1 tablespoon of guacamole, 1 ounce of shredded mozzarella cheese) (CARBOHYDRATES, PROTEIN, AND FAT)
6:00 P.M. meal	1 medium baked sweet potato; ½ cup of steamed green beans (CARBOHYDRATES) 3 ounces of seasoned grilled chicken breast (PROTEIN AND FAT)
9:00 P.M. snack	25 grapes (CARBOHYDRATES) ¼ cup of barbeque-flavored soy nuts (PROTEIN AND FAT)

Sample 1800 Calorie Livit #5

TIME	MENU IDEAS
9:00 A.M. snack	2 multi-grain waffles (such as Van's) and 1 teaspoon of pure maple syrup; scrambled eggs (1 egg and 3 tablespoons of prepackaged liquid egg whites) made with 1 teaspoon of buttery spread (such as Earth Balance) (CARBOHYDRATES, PROTEIN, AND FAT)
11:30 A.M. snack	1 large piece of fruit (apple, pear, peach, orange) (CARBOHYDRATES) 12 almonds (PROTEIN AND FAT)
2:00 P.M. meal	2 slices of whole wheat bread; 1 large piece of fruit; romaine lettuce with sliced tomatoes (CARBOHYDRATES) 4 ounces of oven-roasted turkey deli meat (without nitrites) with 1 teaspoon of mayonnaise and Dijon mustard (PROTEIN AND FAT)
6:00 P.M. meal	4 cups of mixed green salad tossed with 2 cups of sliced strawberries (about 12 berries), 4 ounces of grilled salmon, and 2 tablespoons of vinaigrette dressing (CARBOHYDRATES, PROTEIN, AND FAT)
9:00 P.M. snack	1 cup of high-fiber cereal (such as Kashi Go Lean) with ½ cup of organic 1% milk OR unsweetened soy milk (CARBOHYDRATES)

Sample 2000 Calorie Livits

The following five Livits are based on a diet of 2000 calories a day and follow the standard for nutrient sources as follows: 50 percent from carbohydrates, 20 percent from protein, and 30 percent from fat.

Sample 2000 Calorie Livit #1

TIME	MENU IDEAS
5:00 A.M. snack	1 banana (CARBOHYDRATES) ½ cup of low-fat cottage cheese (PROTEIN AND FAT)
7:30 A.M. snack	6 ounces of organic low-fat yogurt with fruit (such as Stonyfield Farms, Trader Joe's); 1 tablespoon of nuts (6 almonds) (CARBOHYDRATES, PROTEIN, AND FAT)
10:30 A.M. snack	1 small apple OR ¼ cup of unsulfured dried fruit (CARBOHYDRATES) ½ cup of edamame OR ¼ cup of soy nuts (CARBOHYDRATES, PROTEIN, AND FAT)
1:00 P.M. meal	Southwestern salad (4 cups of mixed greens OR romaine lettuce, ½ cup of corn, ½ cup of black beans, 1 ounce of sliced fresh mozzarella) (CARBOHYDRATES AND PROTEIN) ⅛ of an avocado with 1 tablespoon of vinaigrette dressing (FAT)
5:00 P.M. snack	20 spelt pretzels (4 g of fiber per serving, such as Paul Newman's) (CARBOHYDRATES) 2 tablespoons of peanut butter (peanuts and salt only, no oils or sugar added) for dipping (PROTEIN AND FAT)
8:00 P.M. snack	1 baked potato with skin and 1½ cups of steamed vegetables (broccoli, spinach, asparagus, zucchini, bok choy, chard) (CARBOHYDRATES) 3 ounces of wild fish (Alaskan halibut, salmon, orange roughy, cod), 1 teaspoon of buttery spread (such as Earth Balance) for potato, and salsa (PROTEIN AND FAT)

Sample 2000 Calorie Livit #2

TIME	MENU IDEAS
7:30 A.M. meal	2 slices of sprouted grain bread (such as Ezekiel sprouted grain) with 1 tablespoon of organic fruit spread; ½ cup of organic freshly squeezed orange juice OR pomegranate juice (not from concentrate) mixed with water (CARBOHYDRATES AND PROTEIN) 1 organic egg with omega-3s and 6 tablespoons of egg whites OR ⅓ cup of egg substitute (PROTEIN AND FAT)
10:30 A.M. snack	1 medium piece of fruit (apple, peach, pear, 1 cup of berries) (CARBOHYDRATES) 1 ounce of nuts without added oils (almonds, walnuts, peanuts) (about 2 tablespoons) (PROTEIN AND FAT)
12:30 P.M. meal	1 cup of cooked brown rice; 1 cup of steamed vegetables (CARBOHYDRATES) 3 ounces of grilled fish with fresh lemon and garlic (PROTEIN AND FAT)
3:00 P.M. snack	1 cup of fruit and 1 teaspoon of agave nectar OR honey (CARBOHYDRATES) 6 ounces of 2% fat Greek-style yogurt (such as Fage's) with optional cinnamon (PROTEIN AND FAT)
6:00 P.M. meal	1 cup of green peas; 4 cups of salad (mixed greens, cucumbers, carrots, bell peppers) (CARBOHYDRATES) 1 tablespoon of extra-virgin olive oil vinaigrette dressing (on salad); 3 ounces of baked chicken (PROTEIN AND FAT)
9:00 P.M. snack	¾ cup of high-fiber cereal (such as Puffins, Shredded Wheat, Kashi Heart to Heart) (CARBOHYDRATES) 1 cup of unsweetened soy milk OR organic 1% milk with 1 tablespoon of ground flaxseed (PROTEIN AND FAT)

Sample 2000 Calorie Livit #3

TIME	MENU IDEAS
5:30 A.M. snack	1½ cups of smoothie made with 1 scoop of protein powder (such as Trader Joe's Soybean Powder) OR powdered egg whites OR whey protein, 1 cup of berries, 1 cup of unsweetened soy milk OR 1% milk (CARBOHYDRATES, PROTEIN, AND FAT)
8:30 A.M. meal	1 whole wheat bagel OR multi-grain bagel (CARBOHYDRATES) 3 ounces of lox, 1 tablespoon of cream cheese (PROTEIN AND FAT)
12:30 P.M. meal	2 slices of whole wheat bread, romaine lettuce, tomato, other veggies of choice; ½ cup of fresh fruit OR 1 small piece of fruit (kiwi, plum, apricot) (CARBOHYDRATES) 3 ounces of albacore tuna combined with 1 teaspoon of mayonnaise and 1 tablespoon of Dijon mustard (on bread) (PROTEIN AND FAT)
4:00 P.M. snack	1 organic fruit of choice (CARBOHYDRATES) 1 ounce of nuts (raw almonds, roasted peanuts, soy nuts) (about 2 tablespoons) (PROTEIN AND FAT)
6:30 P.M. meal	1 large salad (mixed greens, cucumber, carrots, bell peppers, jicama); 1 ear of corn (CARBOHYDRATES) 3 ounces of turkey burger made with ground turkey breast (for added flavor, add sun-dried tomatoes, parsley, or garlic to the turkey before grilling); 1 teaspoon of extra-virgin olive oil with 1 tablespoon of apple cider vinegar OR balsamic vinegar, seasonings (lemon pepper, oregano) (on salad); barbeque sauce OR ketchup (on burger) (PROTEIN AND FAT)
9:30 P.M. snack	14 multi-grain crackers (such as Trader Joe's) (CARBOHYDRATES) 2 tablespoons of all-natural peanut butter (with oil drained) (PROTEIN AND FAT)

Sample 2000 Calorie Livit #4

TIME	MENU IDEAS
8:00 A.M. meal	2 pancakes (4" in diameter) (such as Maple Grove Farms Organics Buttermilk Pancake & Waffle Mix) made with unsweetened applesauce replacing the oil, 1 egg and ⅓ cup of egg substitute; 1 tablespoon of 100% organic pure maple syrup (CARBOHYDRATES, PROTEIN, AND FAT)
11:00 A.M. snack	1 piece of fruit (peach, pear, apple, orange) OR 1 cup of berries (CARBOHYDRATES) 2 pieces of organic part-skim string cheese (PROTEIN AND FAT)
2:00 P.M. meal	2 slices of whole wheat bread (3 g dietary fiber per slice), organic raw vegetables for sandwich (lettuce, tomatoes, shredded carrots); 15 spelt pretzels (such as Newman's Own Organics) (CARBOHYDRATES) 3 ounces of turkey breast (without nitrites) (on bread) (PROTEIN AND FAT)
5:00 P.M. snack	1 medium steamed artichoke dipped in 1 tablespoon of organic mayonnaise OR Italian dressing; sprinkle with some garlic powder for additional flavor (CARBOHYDRATES, PROTEIN, AND FAT)
8:00 P.M. meal	1 whole wheat or sprouted wheat tortilla (such as Ezekiel's) OR 2 corn tortillas, ½ cup of black beans OR pinto beans, 1 ounce of shredded mozzarella cheese, 1 tablespoon of guacamole and unlimited salsa; ½ cup of fajita-style veggies (bell peppers, mushrooms, onions) on the tortilla OR a tossed salad on the side (CARBOHYDRATES, PROTEIN, AND FAT)
11:00 P.M. snack	1 cup of high-fiber cereal (>5 g dietary fiber per serving) (such as Puffins, Nature's Path Organic Heritage Heirloom Whole Grains Multi-Grain Cereal), 1 cup of unsweetened soy milk (CARBOHYDRATES, PROTEIN, AND FAT)

Sample 2000 Calorie Livit #5

TIME	MENU IDEAS
7:30 A.M. meal	1 whole wheat English muffin, 1 tablespoon of organic fruit spread (such as Fiordifrutta or Dickinson's 100% Fruit Spreadable Fruit) (CARBOHYDRATES) 1 egg and ⅓ cup of egg substitute scrambled with 1 teaspoon of buttery spread (such as Earth Balance) (PROTEIN AND FAT)
10:30 A.M. snack	1 piece of fruit (apple, pear, orange) (CARBOHYDRATES) ½ cup of edamame (PROTEIN AND FAT)
12:30 P.M. meal	1 large Caesar salad (about 4 cups), 3 ounces of grilled chicken breast, ½ cup of mandarin oranges; 2 teaspoons of dressing on the side (CARBOHYDRATES, PROTEIN, AND FAT)
3:00 P.M. snack	7 whole wheat crackers (such as ak-mak) OR 2 brown rice cakes (such as Lundberg) (CARBOHYDRATES) 2 tablespoons of all-natural peanut butter sprinkled with 1 tablespoon of ground flaxseed (spread on the rice cakes) (PROTEIN AND FAT)
6:00 P.M. meal	1 cup of whole wheat macaroni OR quinoa macaroni, 1 ounce of organic mozzarella cheese, 3 ounces of canned wild Alaskan skinless boneless salmon; ½ cup of steamed broccoli on the side (CARBOHYDRATES, PROTEIN, AND FAT)
9:00 P.M. snack	1 cup of blueberries (CARBOHYDRATES) 6 ounces of 2% Greek-style yogurt (such as Fage's) (PROTEIN AND FAT)

And to help you plan your own meals, make copies of the **My Livit!** chart on the opposite page and keep track of your progress.

My Livit!

DATE _____

TIME	MENU IDEAS
_____	_____
_____	_____
_____	_____
_____	_____
_____	_____
_____	_____

DATE _____

TIME	MENU IDEAS
_____	_____
_____	_____
_____	_____
_____	_____
_____	_____
_____	_____

DATE _____

TIME	MENU IDEAS
_____	_____
_____	_____
_____	_____
_____	_____
_____	_____

From Deborah A. Klein, *The 200 SuperFoods That Will Save Your Life.* New York: McGraw-Hill, 2010.

12

Grocery Shopping

DECIPHER DIETARY DECEPTION

Before you go grocery shopping, be aware of the dietary deception on food labels. There are specific ingredients to look for and specific foods that cause concern. The key words to watch out for are *lite, free, diet,* and *sugar-free.* These words often translate into a packaged food that may contain carcinogenic chemicals, that is low in fiber and therefore has little satiety value, and that can actually increase your appetite.

If you see the words *diet* or *sugar-free* on a food product, leave it on the store shelf. Such foods often contain artificial colors or flavorings that may have links to attention deficit and hyperactivity disorder (ADHD) or cancer. Sugar-free foods get their sweetness from artificial sweeteners, at least one of which—aspartame—has been shown to make people even hungrier, due to its high level of sweetness.

Specific Food Labeling Tips

The most predominant packaging deceptions are with frozen foods, breads, crackers, cereals, and yogurts. For packaged foods in general, look at the ingredients list and then check the amounts of fat, sodium, and fiber. Pay special attention to the amount of dietary fiber in all starchy foods (for example, bread, crackers, cereal, rice, and pasta).

Choose High-Fiber Foods

Look for foods with three or more grams of dietary fiber per slice of bread or per snack—for example, crackers and sports bars—and five or more grams per serving of cereal or per frozen meal.

High-fiber starches or starchy vegetables are whole wheat couscous, sprouted grain bread, oatmeal, quinoa, amaranth, barley, bulgur, brown or wild rice, lima beans, peas, sweet potatoes, yams, and winter squash.

High-fiber fruits include "S or S" fruits—those fruits with either edible skin or edible seeds—for example, apples, peaches, pears, apricots, plums, strawberries, blackberries, cherries, blueberries, kiwi, and oranges.

High-fiber vegetables include the cruciferous vegetables—broccoli, Brussels sprouts, cabbage, cauliflower, chard, kale, mustard greens, rutabagas, and turnips. These have been shown to offer protection against certain cancers, and they are rich in fiber, vitamins, and minerals. Often a darker and richer color means that the vegetable is higher in fiber (for example, romaine lettuce and spinach have more fiber than iceberg lettuce). Focus on eating veggies twice a day, for example, with lunch and dinner, and aim for one cruciferous vegetable daily.

Choose a Variety of Fruits and Vegetables

When choosing fruits and vegetables, getting variety in their color will help ensure that they provide a variety of vitamins and minerals (for example, broccoli, spinach, tomatoes, chard, kale, collard greens, zucchini, red bell peppers, yellow bell peppers, apples, berries, pears, oranges, and limes).

Aim for five servings of fruits and vegetables every day: two fruits and three vegetables. You can get one serving of fruit in any of these ways: one small fresh fruit (two inches in diameter), one-quarter cup of dried fruit (try to buy it naturally dried and unsulfured), one-half cup of fruit canned in its own juice, one-half cup of fresh fruit, or one-half cup of unsweetened fruit juice (100% juice). Drink a maximum of one-half cup of juice a day mixed with water to keep the calories from adding up so quickly. It's better to eat your fruit rather than drink it, so that you get the fiber and the increased feeling of satisfaction that comes with it.

One serving of non-starchy vegetables is one-half cup of cooked vegetables, one-half cup of vegetable juice, or one cup of raw vegetables.

Choose Low-Fat Foods

Follow the Livitician's "3 Rule" to choose a low-fat food, defined as a food that provides less than 30 percent of its calories from fat. Look on a food label for the total grams of fat; multiply that number by 3, then add a 0 at the end or move the decimal one place to the right. Compare that number with the total calories. If the number is lower than the number of total calories, it provides less than 30 percent of its calories from fat and is therefore a *low-fat food*.

As an example, consider a food that has 5 grams of fat and provides 180 calories: $5 \times 3 = 15$, add a 0 = 150, 150 < 180 = *low-fat food*.

Choose Low-Sodium Foods

Eating low-sodium foods more often will help lower blood pressure and improve the health of blood vessels. Aim for less than 140 mg of sodium per serving for most products and less than 400 mg of sodium per serving for frozen foods. When eating a food that is high in sodium, drink a lot of water to flush the sodium from your system, and balance the high-sodium food with a lot of vegetables to provide more hydration and fiber.

If you have hypertension, aim for less than 1,500 mg (1.5 grams) of sodium per day. This is about the amount of sodium that is found in two-thirds of a teaspoon of salt. The American Heart Association and the federal Dietary Guidelines for Americans both recommend that healthy adults without any special risk factors have no more than 2,300 mg of sodium per day. For people who have already been diagnosed with heart disease, the American Heart Association suggests a maximum of 2,000 mg of sodium daily.

BECOME A GROCERY SHOPPING MASTER

Bringing healthy food home is an obvious key to living a healthy lifestyle, but shopping trips are often not well planned. Schedule grocery shopping in your calendar once a week. Choose the store that is most convenient for you to get to, and when you are there, shop the perimeter of the store first for fresh foods.

Broaden your palate rather than your waist with a banquet of foods. Eat a variety—the world is full of delicious foods, so partake of them. The Talmud says that one of the first questions that will be asked when one gets to heaven is "Did you taste all the different fruits?" Instead of buying the same fruits, vegetables, and grains week after week, try a food that you have never tried before or that you rarely have, for example, bok choy, chard, kale, pluots, cherimoya, or quinoa.

When selecting foods to purchase, check the labels for low-fat (<30 percent of calories from fat), high-fiber (≥3 grams of fiber per serving for snacks and ≥5 grams of fiber per meal) foods that are free of hydrogenated oils, artificial sweeteners, and artificial colors. Eat foods that are low in sodium (<140 mg of sodium per serving).

Always have staple Livit foods available in your house to help prevent noshing on "empty" calories—those that do not provide many nutrients with the calories—and to prevent overextending the time between meals.

Here's a staple inventory list to start with. Please modify it based on your dietary preferences, and add other food items from the grocery lists provided by the Livitician. Both the list of staple foods and the grocery shopping list that follows are alphabetized within food group sections.

Staple Livit Foods

Carbohydrate Foods

Bottled organic low-sodium pasta sauce

Brown rice

Corn tortillas

Fresh or frozen organic fruit

Fresh or frozen organic starchy vegetables (for example, yams, sweet potatoes, baked potato with skin, winter squash [butternut, spaghetti, acorn], green peas, corn, edamame, lima beans)

Fresh or frozen organic vegetables

High-fiber cereals (such as oatmeal, Puffins, Shredded Wheat)

Organic low-fat milk

Organic low-fat yogurt

Organic vegetable-based soups in shelf-stable boxes (such as Imagine Butternut Squash Soup, Pacific Natural Foods Cashew Carrot Ginger Soup)

Quinoa

Sprouted grain bread

Tomato paste

Whole wheat bread

Whole wheat couscous

Whole wheat crackers (such as ak-mak, Triscuit Reduced Fat)

Whole wheat pasta

Whole wheat tortillas

Protein Foods

Bean-based soups (for example, black bean, pinto bean, kidney bean, lentil, vegetarian chili)

Canned beans

Canned tuna packed in water

Cottage cheese

Edamame

Fresh or frozen lean beef

Fresh or frozen organic chicken

Fresh or frozen organic turkey

Fresh or frozen wild fish

Low-fat cheese

Low-fat kefir drink

Nuts and seeds (almonds, peanuts, walnuts, soy nuts, pistachios, sunflower seeds, pumpkin seeds), raw or roasted

Protein Foods (cont.)

Organic all-natural peanut butter
Organic eggs fortified with omega-3 fatty acids
Ricotta cheese

Fat Foods

Extra-virgin olive oil, expeller-pressed
Flaxseeds, ground or milled
Guacamole
Non-hydrogenated organic buttery spreads (such as Earth Balance)
Nuts
Organic avocado
Organic mayonnaise
Safflower oil, expeller-pressed

Seasonings and Condiments

Chili powder
Cinnamon
Dijon mustard
Fresh garlic
Garlic (fresh)
Garlic powder
Ginger
Lemon-pepper
Nutmeg
Onion powder
Onions
Paprika
Salsa
Turmeric

Keep these items as staples on your grocery list so that you always have them available. This will help you avoid getting trapped into eating high-fat, high-sugar, high-sodium foods or feeling starved because "there's nothing in the house to eat," setting yourself up for overeating at your next meal.

Bring your own snacks (BYOS) to work and when you travel so that you are not dependent on vending machines or whatever is provided.

An ounce of prevention is worth a pound of cure—be prepared!

RECOMMENDATIONS
FOR GROCERY SHOPPING

Whenever possible, buy products that are

- Organic
- Low-sodium
- High-fiber
- Low-fat

Livitician Grocery Shopping List

Natural Foods

Flaxseed, both milled and ground (such as Barlean's Forti-Flax Organic
    Cold-Milled Select Flaxseed)
Low-fat granola (such as Back to Nature)
Whole soybean powder (such as Trader Joe's Unflavored & Unsweetened)
Shredded wheat (such as Barbara's)
Soy crisps (such as Genisoy, Glenny's Naturals, Trader Joe's)
Soy nuts (such as Genisoy)
Wheat-free cereal (such as Barbara's Puffins)

Pretzels, Popcorn, Chips, Nuts, and Seeds

Air-popped organic popcorn (such as All Star Gourmet Popcorn Comets)
Almonds, raw
Baked tortilla chips, unsalted (such as Guiltless Gourmet)
Dry roasted almonds (such as Blue Diamond)
Dry roasted peanuts, unsalted or lightly salted (such as Planters)
Hemp seed nuts (such as Manitoba Harvest)
Microwave popcorn (such as Healthy Choice)
Nuts and seeds, raw (except Brazil nuts, cashews, and Macadamia, which are too
    high in saturated fat) (such as Health Best)
Pistachio nutmeats, raw
Pretzels (such as Snyder's of Hanover)
Pumpkin seeds, raw
Pumpkin seeds, roasted
Soy nuts (such as Dr. Soy)
Spelt pretzels (such as Newman's Own Organics)
Sunflower seeds, raw
Rounds pretzels (such as Newman's Own Organics)
Walnuts, raw

Frozen Foods

Blackberries

Blueberries (such as Naturally Preferred)

Broccoli florets

Corn (such as Naturally Preferred)

Dark sweet cherries

Edamame (such as Seapoint Farms)

Fat-free fruit bars (such as FrütStix Organic)

Fat-free sorbet (such as Haagen-Dazs)

Fruit (such as Cascadian Farms)

Green beans (such as Naturally Preferred)

Home-style potato pancakes (such as Dr. Praeger's)

Low-fat cheese ravioli (such as Rosetto)

Low-fat frozen yogurt (such as Ben & Jerry's, Haagen-Dazs, Stonyfield Farms)

Mixed veggies (such as Naturally Preferred)

Multi-grain waffles (such as Van's Gourmet)

Peaches

Peas (such as Naturally Preferred)

Petite whole beans (such as California & Washington)

Petite whole fancy mixed veggies (such as California & Washington)

Petite whole peas (such as California & Washington)

Raspberries

Sorbet (such as Natural Organic Choice)

Soybeans in pods (such as Seapoint Farms)

Spanakopita (filled with spinach, ricotta cheese, and feta cheese)

Spinach

Strawberries (such as Naturally Preferred)

Vegetables (such as Cascadian Farms)

Veggie burgers (such as Dr. Praeger's Tex Mex)

Waffles (such as Van's Organic)

Whole soy (such as Cultured Soy)

Refrigerated Foods

1% low-fat milk in paper cartons (such as Horizon)

100% juice, not from concentrate, and fortified with vitamins B_6, B_{12}, C, E, K, and folate

100% liquid egg whites (such as Papetti Foods)

All-natural fresh mozzarella (such as Ovoline, Ciliegine, D'Celli Mozzarella Fresca)

All-natural hummus, preservative-free (such as Tribe)
Cage-free eggs with omega-3s (such as Naturally Preferred)
Cultured soy non-dairy yogurt (such as Trader Joe's)
Extra-firm tofu (such as House, Nasoya)
Farmer cheese with no salt added (such as Friendship)
Fat-free fromage blanc (such as Vermont Butter & Cheese Company)
Fat-free milk (such as Horizon)
Firm tofu (such as Trader Joe's)
Kosher Muenster cheese (such as Naturally Good)
Kosher Pepper Jack (such as Naturally Good)
Kosher Swiss cheese (such as Naturally Good)
Lactose-free yogurt cheese
Low-fat cottage cheese (such as Horizon, Organic Valley)
Low-fat farmer cheese (such as Friendship All Natural)
Low-fat kefir (such as Lifeway Cultured Milk Smoothie, Helios Nutrition,
    Trader Joe's)
Low-fat ricotta cheese (such as Precious)
Multi-grain wraps (such as South Beach Diet Snack Size Wraps)
Nonfat plain Greek-style yogurt (such as Fage, Trader Joe's)
Organic 100% egg whites (such as Eggology)
Organic eggs fortified with omega-3 fatty acids (such as Chino Valley Ranchers)
Part-skim mozzarella, block and sliced (such as Horizon)
Part-skim ricotta cheese (such as Polly-O)
Part-skim string cheese (such as Horizon)
Plain fat-free yogurt (such as Stonyfield Farms, Horizon)
Plain low-fat yogurt (such as Stonyfield Farms, Horizon, Trader Joe's)
Puddings (such as Kozy Shack)
Reduced-fat Swiss cheese (such as Jarlsberg)
Refrigerated unsweetened soy milk
Refrigerated vanilla soy milk
Shirataki (tofu noodles) (such as House)
Silken or soft tofu (such as Whole Foods Brand, House)
Soy milk (such as 365, Silk)
Soy yogurt (such as Whole Soy)
Sprouted grain bread
Tofu steak, packed in water (such as House)
Whipped buttery spread (such as Earth Balance)
Whole wheat bread
Yogurt with fruit (such as Stonyfield Farms, Horizon, Whole Soy & Co.)

Produce

Apples
Avocados
Baby romaine lettuce
Bell peppers
Black seedless grapes
Broccoli cole slaw (such as Mann's, Foxy)
Carrots
Garlic
Ginger root
Lemons
Limes
Mixed greens
Onions
Oranges
Peaches
Pears
Peeled baby carrots
Red seedless grapes
Romaine lettuce
Sweet potatoes
Yams

Breads, Grains, and Cereals

100% whole wheat bread (such as Milton's, Whole Foods Organic)
Basmati brown rice (such as Della)
Cereal with fruit and nuts (such as Trader Joe's Triple Berry O's)
High-fiber cereal (such as Kashi Go Lean, Kashi Go Lean Crunch, Kashi Good
    Friends, Cascadian Farm Great Measure, Cascadian Farm Clifford Crunch)
High-protein cereal (such as Back to Nature Hi-Protein Crunch)
Kamut pasta (such as Eden)
Long grain brown rice (such as Lundberg)
Low-fat granola (such as Grandy Oats)
Multi-grain hot cereal (such as Country Choice)
Multi-grain pasta (such as Barilla Plus Enriched Pasta, Ronzoni Healthy Harvest)
Oat bran (such as Mother's 100% Natural)
Old-fashioned oatmeal (such as Quaker Oats)
Quick-cooking Irish oatmeal (such as McCann's)
Quinoa

Rice blends (such as Trader Joe's California Rice Trilogy, Brown Rice Medley)
Short grain brown rice (such as Lundberg)
Shredded wheat (such as Barbara's Original)
Sprouted 7-grain bread (such as Trader Joe's Organic Flourless)
Sprouted grain bread (such as Ezekiel 4:9)
Sprouted grain English muffins
Sprouted grain tortilla (such as Ezekiel 4:9, Food for Life)
Sprouted wheat pasta (such as Pappardelle)
Toasted oat cereal (such as Kashi Heart to Heart)
Tortillas (corn, sprouted grain, whole wheat) (such as La Tortilla Factory Sonoma Carb Cutting)
Wheat bran muffins (such as Trader Joe's Blueberry)
Wheat-free cereal (such as Barbara's Puffins)
Whole grain organic bulgur wheat
Whole grains cereal (such as Nature's Path Organic Heritage Heirloom)
Whole ground flaxseed meal (such as Bob's Red Mill)
Whole wheat bread
Whole wheat couscous
Whole wheat English muffins
Whole wheat pasta (such as De Cecco, DeBoles)
Whole wheat whole grain spaghetti (such as Ralph's)
Wild blend rice (such as Lundberg)

Crackers

100% Whole Wheat Crackers (such as ak-mak)
100% whole wheat matzos (such as Streit's)
Brown rice organic rice cakes (such as Lundberg)
Crispbread crackers (such as ak-mak, Wasa)
Low-sodium crackers (such as Nabisco Triscuit)
Multi-grain crackers (such as Kellogg's All Bran, Trader Joe's)
Reduced-fat crackers (such as Nabisco Triscuit)
Woven wheat wafers (such as Trader Joe's Reduced Guilt, 365)

Condiments, Sauces, Oils, and Spreads

100% fruit spread (such as Fiordifrutta, Dickinson's)
100% pure maple syrup (such as Camp, Shady Maple Farms)
Agave nectar (such as Sweet Cactus Farms)
All-natural unsweetened applesauce
Apple cider vinegar (such as Bragg, Solana Gold)

Condiments, Sauces, Oils, and Spreads (cont.)

BBQ sauce (such as Robbie's, Bone Suckin' Sauce)
Blue agave sweetener
Brown rice vinegar (such as Eden)
Canola mayonnaise (such as Hain Pure Foods)
Canola oil (such as Spectrum Naturals)
Canola oil spray
Chicken marinade and low-sodium stir-fry (such as Mikee)
Chocolate-flavored syrup (such as Trader Joe's Midnight Moo)
Chunky guacamole (such as Whole Foods)
Dijon mustard (such as Grey Poupon)
Extra-virgin olive oil (such as 365)
French onion dip mix
Garden veggie pasta sauce (such as Ragu)
Honey
Ketchup (such as Robbie's)
Low-fat vinaigrette salad dressing (such as Annie's Naturals raspberry vinaigrette)
Low-sodium salsa (such as Scotty's)
Low-sodium soy sauce (such as Bragg Liquid Aminos)
Marinara sauce with no salt added (such as Trader Giotto's)
Mild fresh salsa (such as Trader Joe's Fresh Packed)
Mustard (such as Natural Value)
Pasta sauce (such as 365)
Peanut butter (such as Laura Scudder's, Maranatha)
Raw almond butter
Roasted garlic hummus dip (such as Trader Joe's)
Sesame oil (such as Spectrum)
Sweet & sour sauce (such as Robbie's)
Teriyaki sauce (such as Mikee, Soy Vay Island)
Unfiltered apple cider vinegar
Unsalted peanut butter from unblanched peanuts (such as Trader Joe's)
Vegetable cooking stock (such as Kitchen Basics)
Whipped buttery spread (such as Earth Balance)
Whole cane sugar (such as Rapadura)

Spices

Black pepper (cracked)
Cayenne pepper
Chili powder

Cinnamon (ground or stick)
Curry powder
Dijon mustard
Garlic powder
Ginger (ground)
Lemon pepper
Low-sodium seasoning blend (such as Trader Joe's 21 Seasoning Salute)
Nutmeg
Onion powder
Organic seasoning blends (such as The Spice Hunter Seasonings, Simply Organic
    seasonings and extracts)
Paprika
Turmeric

Canned, Boxed, and Dried Products

Albacore tuna canned in water (such as Chicken of the Sea)
Amaranth
Applesauce (such as Solana Gold)
Black beans
Buckwheat
Bulgur wheat (such as Arrowhead Mills)
Canned wild Alaskan skinless, boneless pink salmon
Canned wild Alaskan sockeye smoked salmon (such as Echo Falls)
Cocoa powder (such as Scharffen Berger Natural)
Diced tomatoes (such as Del Monte, Muir Glen)
Dried beans (such as Health Best)
Dried blueberries sweetened with apple juice
Dried fruit cranberries
Dried fruits, unsulfured and with no sugar added (such as Health Best)
Dried Great Northern beans (such as Ralph's)
Goji berries (such as Navitas Naturals)
Hot chocolate (such as Ghirardelli)
Kidney beans
Light tuna canned in water (such as Chicken of the Sea)
Low-sodium vegetable broth (such as Imagine)
No salt added canned soups (such as Health Valley)
Pinto beans
Quinoa (such as Ancient Harvest)
Raisins (such as Pavich)

Canned, Boxed, and Dried Products (cont.)

Raw wheat germ (Arrowhead Mills)
Rice and beans (such as Eden)
Semi-sweet chocolate chips (such as 365)
Soups (such as Pacific Natural Foods, Imagine)
Vegetable medley bisque (such as Trader Joe's)
Vegetarian beans (such as Heinz)
White beans

Sweets and Desserts

All-natural jelly beans (such as Sun Ridge Farms Organic Jolly Beans)
All-purpose flour (such as Gold Medal Organic)
Brownie mix (such as Dr. Oetker Organic Chocolate, Trader Joe's No Pudge Fudge)
Buttermilk pancake/waffle mix (such as Maple Grove Farms Organics)
Chocolate chips (such as 365)
Cookie Mix (such as Dr. Oetker's Organics)
Dark chocolate (such as Scharffen Berger Extra Dark Fine Artisan with 82% cacao)
Flavored gelatin mix (such as Hain Pure Foods)
Lollipops (such as Yummy Earth)
Low-fat cookies (such as Chocolatey Eats Cookies for People)
Low-fat pudding mix (such as Mori-Nu Mates)
Low-fat rice pudding
Low-fat tapioca pudding
Muffin mix (such as Arrowhead Mills Perfect Harvest)
Multi-grain pancake/waffle mix (such as Up Country Organics)
Puddings (such as Hain Pure Foods)
Soy cocoa mix (such as Country Choice)
Stone-ground whole wheat flour (such as Arrowhead Mills)
Vanilla wafers (such as Country Choice Organic Snacking Cookies)
Whole wheat pastry flour (such as Bob's Red Mill)

Meats

Boneless, skinless chicken breast (such as Empire)
Ground turkey breast (such as Empire, Jennie O)
Kosher beef—Non-Glatt (such as David's)
Lean beef, such as shoulder steak, strip steak, brisket, shoulder pot roast

Seafood

Cod
Haddock
Halibut
Mahi-mahi
Orange roughy
Pollock
Salmon
Sole
Tilapia
Wild-caught fresh Alaskan halibut
Wild-caught fresh Alaskan king salmon

Beverages

100% fruit juices with no added sugar
100% pomegranate juice, not from concentrate
Apple juice plus 120% Vitamin C (such as Hansen's)
Caffeine-free herbal coffee (such as Teeccino Chocolate Mint or Hazelnut)
Chamomile tea
Echinacea elder tea
Ginger root tea
Golden green tea
Green tea (such as Kettle Brewed Unsweetened)
Juice (such as Wymans Wild Blueberry Juice)
Mineral water (such as Glacéau Smart Water)
Peppermint tea
Roasted grain instant beverage (such as Natural Touch Kaffree Roma)
Rose hips tea
Sparkling water (such as Arrowhead, Perrier, Pellegrino, Gerolsteiner, 365)
Sports drinks (such as Trader Joe's Traderade)
Unsweetened brewed white tea (such as Inko's Hint O'Mint 100% Natural White
     Iced Tea)
Unsweetened peppermint water (such as Metro Mint)
White tea (such as Kettle Brewed Unsweetened)

Wine

Red wine, made without sulfites (such as Larocca, Coates)

13

Livit Snacks

The following snacks are balanced with high-fiber carbohydrate and low-fat protein for either pre- or post-exercise or between meals. Each snack has about 150 calories in order to provide a metabolic benefit.

1 · Make your own trail mix with 1 tablespoon of roasted peanuts (check ingredients for peanuts with no oils added) + 1 tablespoon of raw almonds OR other nuts and seeds + 2 tablespoons of raisins OR dried blueberries OR dried cranberries (check ingredients for no sugar or additives).

2 · Make a shake with ¼ cup of nonfat dry milk powder OR whole soybean powder + ½ cup of a fruit of your choice + ¼ cup of plain yogurt + 2 cups of 1% milk or organic vanilla soy milk.

3 · Make mini-sandwiches with two tablespoons of all-natural peanut butter OR soy nut butter + ½ sprouted grain bagel OR whole wheat pita OR 5 small whole wheat crackers (such as ak-mak or Woven Wheats).

4 · Make a smoothie with ½ cup of plain yogurt OR nonfat Greek-style yogurt + 1 cup of vanilla soy milk + a small frozen banana + 6 frozen strawberries.

5 · Make a mini-pizza with ¼ cup of pizza sauce OR marinara sauce + 1 English muffin + 1 sliced tomato + 1 ounce of Jarlsberg light Swiss cheese on top; heat in a toaster oven until the cheese is melted.

6 · Make a layered waffle treat with 1 whole grain blueberry toaster waffle + ½ cup of plain low-fat yogurt + ½ cup of fresh berries OR defrosted frozen berries.

7 · Top ½ cup of low-fat cottage cheese with 1 cup of cantaloupe cubes OR honeydew melon cubes.

8 · Top 1 slice of sprouted grain cinnamon raisin bread with ¼ cup of low-fat ricotta cheese; sprinkle 1 teaspoon of cinnamon on top.

9 · Combine ¼ cup of low-fat ricotta cheese OR cottage cheese with ½ cup of applesauce and 1 teaspoon of cinnamon. Sprinkle 1 tablespoon of low-fat granola on top.

10 · Make a wrap with 1 whole wheat tortilla + 1 whole egg and 2 egg whites, scrambled + salsa as topping.

11 · Make a stuffed pita with ½ whole wheat pita + ½ cup of low-fat cottage cheese + ½ cup of sliced peaches OR pears (canned in juice or water, and drained).

12 · Make a stuffed pita with 1 whole wheat pita + 1 ounce of sliced turkey breast OR 1 ounce of sliced part-skim cheese OR soy cheese + tomato + a squirt of mustard.

13 · Make mini-sandwiches with 2 ounces of chicken salad OR tuna salad + 5 whole wheat crackers.

14 · Mix ½ cup of low-fat cottage cheese with ¼ cup of strawberry yogurt; sprinkle with muesli cereal.

15 · Combine ¼ cup of cereal (≥ 5 g dietary fiber) with 1 cup of plain low-fat yogurt.

16 · Make apple treats with 2 tablespoons of soy nut butter + 2 apple halves.

17 · Make PBJ treats with 2 tablespoons of all-natural peanut butter + 1 tablespoon of all-fruit jam + 5 small whole wheat crackers (such as ak-mak).

18 · Top a mini-bagel with 1 ounce of turkey breast OR chicken breast.

19 · Combine 1 tablespoon of slivered almonds with 1 cup of vanilla yogurt.

20 · Combine ¼ cup of raisins with ¼ cup of soy nuts (such as Dr. Soy or Genisoy).

21 · Have ½ cup of edamame and a small piece of fruit (2″ in diameter) for a complete balanced snack.

22 · Combine 1 cup of coffee-flavored soy milk with ¼ cup of nonfat dry milk powder, 1 teaspoon of cocoa powder, and ice for a high-protein ice mocha.

23 · Make mini-pizzas with 1 ounce of fresh mozzarella cheese + fresh organic tomatoes + basil + 5 small whole wheat crackers (such as Woven Wheat).

24 · Have 1 piece of low-fat string cheese (such as Horizon) and a medium (4″ in diameter) apple OR pear.

25 · Make a mini-pizza with 1 ounce of part-skim mozzarella cheese + 1 whole wheat tortilla OR toasted wheat pita + veggies (tomatoes, bell peppers, broccoli); heat in a toaster oven until the cheese is melted.

26 · Make a peanut butter treat with 1 tablespoon of all-natural peanut butter spread on celery sticks + slices from 1 apple; sprinkle with 1 tablespoon of sunflower seeds.

27 · Make a frozen banana by dipping 1 peeled banana into a mixture of cocoa and a dash of honey OR pure maple syrup; roll the banana in 2 tablespoons of ground nuts (ground peanuts and walnuts OR soy nuts); freeze individually in plastic wrap.

28 · Have 1 cup of flavored low-fat organic kefir (such as Lifeway or Helios).

29 · When ordering at coffee houses, have 2 tea bags of your favorite tea with foamed nonfat milk OR soy milk, and 1 reduced-fat muffin OR 1 slice of banana bread OR pumpkin bread OR ½ cup of the "house" granola.

Incorporate these snacks as part of your meal plan. If you still feel hungry beyond your individualized snack or meal times, nosh on vegetables—the "free foods" (for example, bell peppers, celery, carrots, cucumbers, and cherry tomatoes). Drink a lot of water and unsweetened tea (or try drizzling a few drops of agave nectar into tea) between snacks or meals.

Invest time in yourself and in your health. The healthier you are, the more productive you'll be, the more you can contribute, and the more fulfilling your life will be.

Actions That Will Save Your Life

Keep yourself on a healthy path by scheduling time for self-care, sleeping seven to eight hours per night, and focusing on the following tips to help you eat for physical fuel rather than emotional fuel.

TAKE ACTION

1 · Before you eat, take a few seconds to do a mind-body check. Ask yourself, "Am I hungry or am I stressed/anxious/depressed?" If you are not hungry, move on to something else, perhaps call a friend. Address the emotion you are feeling. What does your mind really want?

2 · Sit down while eating. This promotes enjoyment and aids digestion. Standing up while eating encourages mindless eating—calories that we may forget we ate.

3 · Eat slowly. Try to give yourself 20 minutes to eat a meal; put your fork down between mouthfuls. It takes about 20 minutes for your brain to send the message that you're full.

4 · Pre-portion your plate with food, rather than having serving plates or bowls on the table.

5 · Have one designated location for eating your meals and snacks.

6 · Cut up your three- to four-ounce portion of meat or fish in small cubes or strips mixed with whole grains and a lot of vegetables so that you have visual cues to help you feel more satisfied.

7 · Use a smaller plate (about 8 inches in diameter) for your meal so that it looks fuller, even with less food; fill it with a lot of non-starchy vegetables.

8 · If you still feel hungry after your meal, drink more water and distract yourself by moving away from the table and doing a non–food-related activity (for example, take a bath, paint, exercise, or shop). If distraction doesn't work,

enjoy your "free foods" (bell pepper sticks, carrots, celery, cherry tomatoes, and hot unsweetened cocoa with cinnamon and agave nectar).

9 · Have one indulgence a day to prevent feeling deprived and to promote mental satisfaction. Fit it in as part of your meal by reducing the carbohydrates and fat in that meal.

10 · Eat before you leave the house. If you're on the go all day, pack some balanced snacks in an insulated lunch bag with an igloo ice pack.

11 · After you eat your pre-portioned snack or meal, brush your teeth, which will help affirm the completion of that eating time.

12 · Get up off your seat and *move*! For every hour you work, move for five to ten minutes—for example, use a portable phone and walk around, do leg lifts at your desk, go up and down a flight of stairs, or dance.

13 · If you have some extra body fat to work off, increase your awareness of what is really going on with your eating habits: Write down what you eat and when you eat it for three days (two work days and one non-work day). You may discover that you are waiting too long between eating, overloading on food, or perhaps not eating any protein until noon.

14 · Increase your physical activity by parking farther away from your destination and walking the distance or by taking the stairs instead of the elevator.

15 · Before you take another cookie, ask yourself, "Is this food really that important? No, spending time with my family, talking, playing, reading, and spiritual growth are the priorities."

16 · Write down three action-oriented and doable goals every two weeks. Choose positive wording for the goals.

17 · Watch how your clothes fit rather than what the scale says. Focus on decreasing body fat and increasing muscle mass.

18 · Be a trendsetter for others. Realize that the choices you make and your actions have a lasting impact on the people you interact with.

19 · Erase "good" food and "bad" food talk. Wipe away feelings of guilt.

20 · To nourish a healthy relationship with food, picture yourself living the "blue lagoon" lifestyle: Imagine that you grew up on an island and never heard of a fad diet, never heard all the societal verbiage about fattening foods, never heard about foods that are too high in carbs—all you know is which foods you like to eat. Write down what those foods are for you. What do you truly like to eat? Erase the voices that you have heard in the past telling you, "Don't touch that food—it will go right to your belly." Just think of foods that you like.

ENGAGE IN MENTAL HEALING

Realize that food does not have a heart or mind or soul. It is simply your fuel and physical nourishment.

To have mental healing, focus on doing a recreational activity—RE-CREATION. Spend time with your hobbies, talk to an inspiring friend, meditate, write your thoughts down in a journal, and *move*—emotion is the state of motion.

Enjoy Liviting!

1 · Fit *moving* into your day (schedule it on your calendar).

2 · Take time to *meditate* (even if only for 30 seconds when you are feeling stressed), visualize yourself at the ocean, take three deep breaths.

3 · *Sip water* throughout the day.

4 · Ask yourself, before you eat, *"Am I hungry or stressed?"*

FITNESS FUEL

You need fuel to burn fuel. Eat a meal no more than three hours before exercising, or have a snack an hour or less before. After exercise, eat within an hour and a half.

The American College of Sports Medicine (ACSM) has demonstrated that if you wait more than three hours after exercise to eat, you do not get full replenishment of your glycogen stores—you get only 75 percent replenishment—so your muscles do not have what they need for optimal repair.

If you are going to be exercising in the morning—whether a morning run or walk or an exercise session—try to have at least a carbohydrate source prior to moving. If you will be moving for longer than an hour, try to have a carbohydrate and a protein source so that you have more sustained energy. Because liquid foods are easier to digest, which helps prevent cramping during exercise, have something like a single serving of yogurt or a cup of the Livit Energizer Shake (see page 10).

Nutrients That Benefit Moving

Overall, the main components to focus on for optimal performance and for getting the most benefit from moving are the following.

Carbohydrates

Choose complex carbohydrates from whole grains, breads, cereals, beans, pasta, and starchy vegetables. They are the most efficient body fuel, the main source of energy for muscle function, and the best way to prevent using protein to maintain your muscle.

Protein

Choose lean protein sources (skinless poultry, fish, 1% or nonfat milk, low-fat cheese, egg whites, vegetarian combinations of proteins) so that your protein sources will maintain muscle mass rather than contribute to excess fat. Get your protein from foods. The supplements for proteins or amino acids can cause dehydration and electrolyte imbalance.

Calcium

Adequate calcium is important for bone density, nerve conduction, and muscle function. Aim for 1,000 to 1,500 milligrams a day. Calcium foods include 1% or nonfat milk, low-fat or nonfat yogurt, low-fat cheese (<5 g fat per ounce), salmon or sardines with bones (water-packed), tofu, broccoli, and kale.

Iron

Iron is needed to carry oxygen in the blood to the various tissues, including muscles. Not having enough iron in the body can cause decreased endurance and chronic fatigue. Foods high in iron include lean, fat-trimmed red meat and fortified cereals and grains. Eat a vitamin C source like oranges, grapefruit, or strawberries with your cereals and grains to increase iron absorption. Limit drinking tea with your iron foods, since the tannic acid in tea may interfere with iron absorption.

Omega-3 Fatty Acids

Support your heart health by including dietary sources of omega-3 fatty acids, which have anti-inflammatory benefits. The American Heart Association has recommended eating fish two to four times a week for protection from heart disease.

Omega-3 dietary sources include wild cold-water fish (salmon, mackerel, herring, and fresh bluefin tuna), fish oil capsules, ground flaxseed, shelled hemp seed, beans (soybeans, navy beans, mung beans, pinto beans, lima beans, peas, split peas, and kidney beans), winter squash, chia (a little-known omega-3–rich super-grain that can be found in tortilla chips and may appear in other products), walnuts, green leafy vegetables (lettuce, broccoli, kale, purslane, and spinach), citrus, melons, cherries, omega-3 rich eggs, extra-virgin olive oil, soybean oil, walnut oil, canola oil, wild venison, and buffalo.

Subject Index

- For individual SuperFoods, see the **Contents** listings on pages v–ix.
- For information about nutrients (vitamins [e.g., vitamin A, vitamin B$_6$, and folate] and minerals [e.g., calcium, iron, and potassium]), see the **Benefits** section and the **Nutritional Composition** paragraph for each SuperFood.
- For information about nutrient sources (carbohydrate, protein, and fat), calories, and dietary fiber, see the **Benefits** section for each SuperFood, as well as the **Nutrition Analysis** section for each recipe.
- For information about the relationship between medical conditions, disorders, and diseases and individual foods, see the **Benefits** section for each SuperFood.

356

Recipe Index

ABOUT THE AUTHOR

Deborah Klein is the world's first Livitician, a term she coined as an alternative to Dietician to emphasize eating without deprivation. Her mission is to educate others about achieving optimal wellness through individualized nutrition counseling, balanced eating, intrinsic coaching, and exercise and movement. She has been a top local dietitian, nutritionist, and media nutrition consultant in Los Angeles for 14 years.

At the University of California, Davis, Deborah received a Bachelor of Science in Dietetics and a minor in Exercise Physiology. She received her Registered Dietitian license in Georgia and completed a Master of Science in Foods and Nutrition with an emphasis in Sports Nutrition at California State Polytechnic University in Pomona.

Her career experiences include hosting a television show in Georgia on Midday News Live, teaching "5 A Day—For Better Health," and working for CNN and for Food & Health News. She was honored as "Registered Dietitian of the Year" by the Spectrum Health Club in Los Angeles. Recently, she was named "Young Dietitian of the Year" by the American Dietetics Association and served as President of the Los Angeles Dietetics Association.

Currently, Deborah has a private practice conducting individualized nutrition counseling, nutrition education, corporate seminars, class lectures, and health fairs. She focuses on medical nutrition therapy, weight loss/management/control, optimal nutrition, meal planning, diabetes, cardiovascular disease (hypertension, hyperlipidemia, high cholesterol, high triglycerides), disease prevention, compulsive overeating, gastrointestinal disorders (irritable bowel syndrome, celiac disease [gluten intolerance], Crohn's disease, diverticulitis, diverticulosis, fibromyalgia, pre- and post-pregnancy, children and adolescents who are selective ["finicky"] eaters), family nutrition, food allergies and intolerances, healthy dining, grocery shopping tips, supermarket tours, quick and easy recipes, vegetarian (vegan, lacto-ovo, pesco) eating, "baby boomer" health, geriatric and senior nutrition, and long-term wellness.

She is writing a nutrition and health book, *Good-bye Diet, Hello Livit,* that details her Livit philosophy for achieving your wellness goals and fitting these goals into your lifestyle while maintaining the enjoyment of eating. Through nutrition education and discovering each individual's full potential, Deborah offers her clients "A Plan to *Live* For!"

Deborah is one of the most sought-after speakers and spokespersons in the area of nutrition, wellness, and optimal lifestyle. She is a frequent guest on television and radio shows promoting a healthy diet. Her website (www.Livitician.com) provides detailed information about her services.

Throughout Deborah's 15 years as a Registered Dietitian, she has expressed her passion for nutrition and health by walking the talk, inspiring her patients daily to stay motivated, respect their bodies, and do what is best to save their lives!